CG 101:

A COMPUTER GRAPHICS INDUSTRY

REFERENCE

Terrence Masson

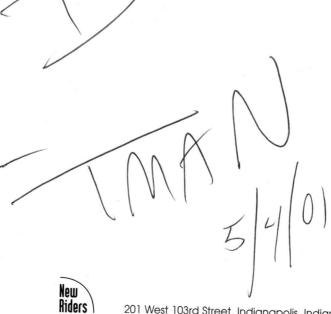

To Dan

—TMAN 5/4/01

New Riders

201 West 103rd Street, Indianapolis, Indiana 46290

CG 101: A COMPUTER GRAPHICS INDUSTRY REFERENCE

International Standard Book Number: 0-7357-0046-X

Library of Congress Catalog Card Number: 99-63016

Printed in the United States of America

First Printing: August, 1999

03 02 01 00 99   7 6 5 4 3 2 1

Interpretation of the printing code: The rightmost double-digit number is the year of the book's printing; the rightmost single-digit number is the number of the book's printing. For example, the printing code 99-1 shows that the first printing of the book occurred in 1999.

TRADEMARKS

All terms mentioned in this book that are known to be trademarks or service marks have been appropriately capitalized. New Riders Publishing cannot attest to the accuracy of this information. Use of a term in this book should not be regarded as affecting the validity of any trademark or service mark.

WARNING AND DISCLAIMER

Every effort has been made to make this book as complete and as accurate as possible, but no warranty or fitness is implied. The information provided is on an "as is" basis. The author and the publisher shall have neither liability nor responsibility to any person or entity with respect to any loss or damages arising from the information contained in this book.

Executive Editor
Steve Weiss

Acquisitions Editor
Laura Frey

Development Editor
Audrey Doyle

Managing Editor
Sarah Kearns

Project Editor
Caroline Wise

Copy Editor
Amy Lepore

Indexer
Lisa Stumpf

Technical Editors
Christophe Hery
Steve Upstill

Author Assistant
Michael B. Shahan

Interior Designer
Louisa Klucznik

Cover Designer
Aren Howell

Layout Technician
Amy Parker

Graphic Conversion Technicians
Benjamin Hart
Tammy Graham
Oliver Jackson

CONTENTS AT A GLANCE

TABLE OF CONTENTS

ABOUT THE AUTHOR

Terrence Masson is a Visual Effects Director living in the San Francisco Bay area. He is the founder of the consulting company Digital Fauxtography, and is co-founder of The Visual Effects Resource Center online at `http://visualfx.com`.

After receiving his B.F.A in Graphic Design with a minor in Art History and a Masters in Computer Animation, he worked for several years as a freelance graphic designer, 3D animator, and design consultant. After working at Industrial Light & Magic in 1991 on the movie *Hook*, he went on to serve as Image Engineering Supervisor for Douglas Trumbull on the Luxor trilogy of ride films.

In 1993, Terrence moved to Los Angeles to join the company Digital Domain, where he was a Technical Director. Next, he was a CG Supervisor at the new Warner Brothers Imaging Technology, working closely with John Dykstra in preparation for *Batman Forever*. In 1994, he founded Digital Fauxtography, a visual effects company specializing in commercial, theatrical, and large-format film projects. Some of his feature film work included the opening credit sequence to *Batman Forever,* and effects animation for *Judge Dredd, Under Siege II*, and *Cutthroat Island*. Other interesting projects were creating the CG tongues in the original Budweiser frogs broadcast commercial (for client Digital Domain), and developing the original CG production methodology for the *South Park* television series with producer David White.

Terrence returned to ILM in 1996 to work on the *Star Wars Trilogy Special Editions, Spawn,* and *Small Soldiers*. While at ILM, he also designed and directed a personal project, the short animated film *Bunkie & Booboo*. The short has won numerous awards including a first place at the World Animation Celebration 1998, and it has screened worldwide including SIGGRAPH 98 and NICOGRAPH 98. Most recently at ILM, Terrence served as a CG Sequence Supervisor on *Star Wars Episode 1: The Phantom Menace*.

In addition to writing this book, Terrence is a much-sought-after lecturer on the history and techniques of computer-generated visual effects. He can be contacted through his Web site at `http://visualfx.com/tman.htm` or by email at `tman@visualfx.com`.

DEDICATION

This book is dedicated to Laura, my wife, who is my best friend and my daily inspiration.

And for Chelsea and Elise.

Daddy loves you.

ACKNOWLEDGMENTS

It was a great pleasure to interview so many wonderful people for this book, and I want to thank them all for their generous contribution of time and kind support.

To single out just one example, I must especially thank Ed Catmull. His many hours of recollections during many days of interviews spanned the breadth of this book's history. From the early days of Utah to the start of NYIT, the Lucasfilm Computer Division, and Pixar, Ed's stories always remained humble and engaging.

Thank you to the hundreds of contributors who opened their homes and memories to me, for sharing their history and recollections and also for just helping me get the facts straight.

Thank you to Alicia Buckley for having faith in me, and to everyone else at New Riders, especially Laura Frey and Audrey Doyle, for making this a completely wonderful experience. My eternal gratitude also goes to Steve Upstill for his inspiration and to Christophe Hery for his expertise.

Thank you to my many coworkers over the years who have put up with me, especially those at ILM who have constantly challenged, amazed, and humbled me.

Thank you to my true friends for all the great times, for all the laughs, and especially for reminding me how much I value honesty.

Most of all, thank you to my family for supporting me through school, showing me the world, and teaching me that there is nothing you cannot do if you set your mind to it. I love you Mom and Dad, you're the greatest.

Terrence Masson

Tell Us What You Think!

As the reader of this book, *you* are our most important critic and commentator. We value your opinion and want to know what we're doing right, what we could do better, what areas you'd like to see us publish in, and any other words of wisdom you're willing to pass our way.

As the Executive Editor for the Professional Graphics and Design team at New Riders Publishing, I welcome your comments. You can fax, email, or write me directly to let me know what you did or didn't like about this book—as well as what we can do to make our books stronger.

Please note that I cannot help you with technical problems related to the topic of this book and that, due to the high volume of mail I receive, I might not be able to reply to every message.

When you write, please be sure to include this book's title and author as well as your name and phone or fax number. I will carefully review your comments and share them with the author and editors who worked on the book.

Fax: 317-581-4663

Email: graphics@mcp.com

Mail: Steve Weiss
           Executive Editor
           Graphics
           New Riders Publishing
           201 West 103rd Street
           Indianapolis, IN 46290 USA

achromatic

additive color model

ambient color

ambient light

angle of incidence

ASA

backlight

banding

barn doors

bounce light

brightness

calibration

Cartesian coordinate system

chroma

chrominance

chromatic aberration

CIE

CLUT

CMY/CMYK color model

color banding

color calibration

color chart

color correction

color cycling

color depth

colorimetry

Colorific

color management

color model

ColorReady

ColorSense

color separation

color space

ColorSuites

ColorSync 2.5.1

color temperature

ColorTune

ColorWeb Pro

CGATS

complementary colors

contouring

contrast

cookie

cool colors

Cromalin

cucaloris

cutter

cyan

da Vinci 2K

decay

DIC

diffuse reflection

direct color

directional light

distant light

dither

DMax

DMin

dynamic range

falloff

fill light

flag

flaps

footcandle

fresnel

full color

gamma

gamma correction

gamut

Grey Color Replacement

hexachrome

hexadecimal

high color

histogram

HSB

HLS

HSV

hue

H V/C

HWB

Color and Light

ICC

incident light

indexed color

intensity

International Color Consortium

key light

kicker

L*A*B

lens flare

lightness

luminance

lux

Macbeth Chart

monochrome

Munsell

ND

OptiCal 2.5

palette

Pantone Inc.

Photo YCC

PMS

point light

primary colors

radiosity

reflective color

rim light

RGB

saturation

scrim

shade

snoot

spectrum

specular

spotlight

subtractive color model

target

tint

tone

true color

UCA

UCR

value

warm colors

wash

white

YcbCr

YIQ

YUV

COLOR

Broken down to its simplest component (the pixel), computer graphics simply consist of many millions of little colored dots (actually, they're rectangles, to be completely accurate). Despite the importance of these red, green, and blue dots, many people making images with these pixels do not know basic color theory. Whether you have formal art-school training or not, the more you know about color, the better prepared you will be to improve your imagery. There is much more to color than meets the eye!

It seems appropriate to start with the concept of "primary." The very name suggests importance, but what is special about red, green, and blue (RGB)? In art school, red, blue, and yellow are called primaries. Primary colors are those that cannot be created by mixing any other two. Green is a secondary color, and most kindergarten children know it can be made by mixing yellow and blue. Unfortunately, what is primary in one system might be secondary in another.

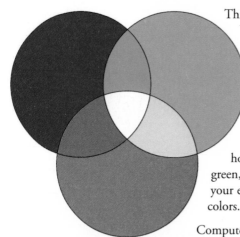

The RGB color wheel diagram.

This is all well and good, but why RGB in CG? Well, a little biology review is in order to provide the proper background. The human eye contains two types of neurons that capture and interpret light: rods and cones. Rods are not color–sensitive. Although they happen to be very useful in low-light situations, they are not important to this discussion. Cones are important, however, and come in just three types: red, green, and blue. All the colors you perceive with your eyes are a combination of these three primary colors.

Computer graphics color is created on a monitor and is viewed by your eyes. These monitors contain three phosphor types (RGB) that produce the combination of wavelengths you perceive as color. These three colored-light components, when combined, form all the other hues of the spectrum up to and including white. The RGB color model, therefore, is referred to as additive transmitted color—the color transmitted as light directly to your eyes.

The opposite of transmitted color is reflected color. This is when you see colors only because of the resultant wavelengths remaining of white light reflecting off an object. In print work, the color model CMYK (Cyan, Magenta, Yellow, and blacK) is specifically designed to represent colors by these reflective color properties. (See the following CMYK definition for more details.)

In print, the primary colors blue, red, and yellow are more accurately described as cyan, magenta, and yellow. This CMY is called the subtractive color model because you subtract (or filter out) some color component from the white light to achieve other colors. This compares, as previously stated, to the RGB additive color model in which all RGB light components combine (add up) to form white.

How these two very different systems describe color is very important when transferring image data between them, as in the many hard-copy printing processes.

One very important thing about color in general—and computer-generated color in particular—is that it is not an absolute. Rather, it is a subjective interpretation. An object's final color values are influenced in several different ways before you actually view it. Two major influences are as follows:

1. **The object's environment and surroundings.** If a red ball is lit with a blue light in a white foggy room, for example, chances are the ball is going to look light purple instead of red. Similarly, if an object is illuminated by a light with a complimentary color, the overall apparent saturation and intensity of that color will be decreased, making it appear more dull.

The CMYK color wheel diagram.

2. **The viewing medium.** By its very nature, computer graphics are viewed on monitors. Each monitor almost certainly is just a little bit—or perhaps quite a bit—different from the next. In addition, the final output for your imagery might not be video at all but print or

motion-picture film. Each of these output formats is going to have its own way of describing, calibrating, and judging color.

With this in mind, it is never advisable to take color for granted. Whenever you are in a position to judge color, always be mindful of just how you are viewing it—with respect to find your final output medium.

LIGHT

You can see that color and light are inseparable partners... one cannot exist without the other. Any modern discussion about color and light can be traced back to the mid-seventeenth century and Sir Isaac Newton's experiments passing sunlight through glass prisms. He observed that pure white light separates itself into the many hues you now most associate with the colors of the rainbow. Because of this fact, it is useful to keep in mind that most light sources, both natural and artificial, rarely transmit pure white light. In addition, knowing the differences between natural and artificial light sources and how they behave differently can help you achieve the look you want faster and more effectively.

Exterior settings that use natural light generally have a softer, more balanced feel than interior scenes lit with local, artificial light. This is partially because natural sunlight is full-spectrum, illuminates very evenly, and naturally absorbs and interacts with the colors in the surroundings of your subject. To emulate a typical daylight exterior, the sun as our *key light* usually wants to have a yellowish tint and be complimented with bluish *fill lights* as if from the sky. *Bounce lights* contain some color component of whatever surrounding environment is closest to your subject. Low green or brown bounce light as if reflected from grass and foliage is common.

Interior lighting by nature is more localized and directional. A typical room's lighting setup might not have many more key, fill, and bounce lights than a daytime exterior scene, but the color direction and coverage must be more closely adjusted. For more discussion about the nature of lighting effects and how it can help you integrate CG with live-action photography, see Chapter 6, "Compositing."

TERMS

achromatic

This means "without color," just shades of gray.

additive color model

This is the process by which adding amounts of primary colors (red, green, and blue) produces white. Additive color models are used with hardware light-emitting devices such as CRT monitors. The familiar computer graphics RGB colors are additive primaries.

— see also reflective color, subtractive color model, RGB

ambient color ▶ see ambient light

ambient light

This is light that has no specific source or direction. To simulate the real-world effect of multiple surfaces scattering light uniformly in the world, computer graphics uses this ambient-light model as a cheat, as a mathematical simplification. It often is used in very low intensities to fill in small areas of a scene that otherwise would not receive any direct light. Dense fog also creates the appearance of a nondirectional or ambient light by scattering all direct sources randomly. In most average lighting situations, the same effect often is created by judicious placement of several bounce lights or by a more global illumination process such as radiosity.

As a rule, avoid using an ambient-light model whenever possible. It tends to flatten out forms and give away its use as unrealistic.

angle of incidence

This is the angle at which a light ray intersects with a surface, in which 0 degrees is parallel with the surface and 90 degrees is perpendicular to the surface aiming directly at the light source. This is a basic function used in calculating the effect of a light source on a surface shader to calculate the nature of its specular highlights (the appearance of which also depends on the viewing angle). The greater the angle of incidence (from 0 to 90 degrees), the stronger the specular component.

— see also specular, shader

ASA

This represents film-speed ratings that gauge sensitivity to light. They originally were set down by the American Standards Association, and are now called EI (Exposure Index).

backlight

This is light whose source is positioned on the far side of an object with respect to the camera, aiming at the subject. This source can generate very dramatic effects, such as silhouetting and halos. When aimed at, and when visible to the camera, lens-flares result from reflections off the individual camera lens elements. This also is called a kicker or a rim light.

A diagram of different types of light on an object.

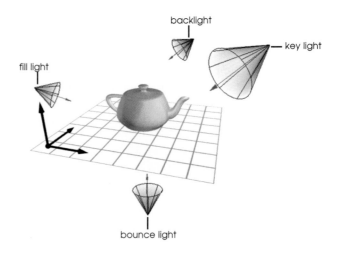

banding ▶ see contouring

barn doors

Physical shutters are attached to stage lights to restrict the coverage of that light. They also are called flaps.

bounce light

This is a light source that simulates the reflected light that occurs naturally but must be faked in CG. Radiosity rendering calculates this reflected diffuse light properly (albeit at great expense), often yielding very realistic images.

brightness

This is a general and subjective term for the intensity or amount of light from a luminous body such as a stage lamp or a candle. This also is referred to as "black level" in video terminology. Brightness formally is defined by the CIE (Commission Internationale de L'Éclairage) as "the attribute of a visual sensation according to which an area appears to emit more or less light."

calibration

This refers to adjusting a computer or video monitor to more properly display the color values with respect to their final output format such as for motion-picture film. Color calibration is essential to have continuity among viewing workstations and to have as close an approximation as possible to the final viewing medium (such as motion picture film.)

Cartesian coordinate system

This is the basis of the RGB and CMY color models. The three linear axes of X, Y, and Z describe the 3D location of any point in (color) space.

chroma

This is a video term for the purity of a color. It refers to the saturation or intensity of a color relative to the amount of its black or white component. A pure red, for example, has a higher chroma than pink, which has been desaturated or tinted with white.

— *see also* chrominance

A chroma scale.

chrominance

This is a video term describing the color (hue) component irrespective of its luminance. All electronically simulated colors are a combination of chrominance and luminance.

chromatic aberration

This is an optical shifting of color components most often found in wide-angle anamorphic lenses. The more imperfect a lens and the wider its angle of view, the more the lens shifts the light unevenly across its curvature. This appears as subtle color fringing at the sharp edges of objects characterized by a separation of the film's RGB color components. Reproducing this effect in CG elements during a composite can add subtle realism to the final image.

— *see also*   anamorphic

The chromatic diagram.

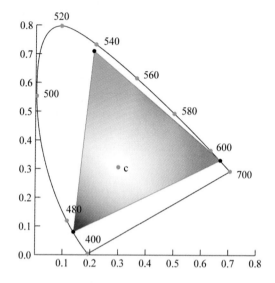

CIE

The Commission Internationale de L' Éclairage (International Commission on Illumination) is an international standards committee formed in 1934. It developed the angled, heel-shaped chromaticity diagram of color as well as the refined L*A*B color model. The CIE can be found online at: www.hike.te.chiba-u.ac.jp/ikeda/CIE/home.html.

— *see also*   L*A*B, chromatic diagram

CLUT

This stands for Color Look-Up Table. It contains gamma correction and other conversion information that automatically is applied to the CG image data between the framebuffer and the display device. Because equal steps in linear RGB values do not correspond to equal steps in nonlinear monitor brightness, a CLUT is used to correct and compensate between the two. The calculation to produce a particular intensity value is called gamma correction.

— *see also*   indexed color

CMY/CMYK color model

This stands for Cyan, Magenta, Yellow, and blacK. This is a Cartesian coordinate system–based subtractive (reflective) color model used in printing processes. CMYK is used for calculating the percentage of colored inks as opposed to digital color value components. The black is used as a practical and cost-saving consideration because black ink is cheaper to add for making darker colors rather than a heavy mixture of the more expensive CMY. Mixed equally, blue and green make cyan, red and green make yellow, and blue and red make magenta.

— *see also*   RGB

color banding   ▶ see contouring

color calibration

This refers to matching the colors of a video monitor or software program to a standard reference such as a color temperature (6,500k), a film stock, or print standards (Pantone, for example). This calibration is essential to be able to make qualitative judgments about CG images relative to their final output media. It also is essential to remember that no monitor can be perfectly calibrated to display exactly what an image will look like on film or in print. Film wedges and test prints always should be integral to the final approval process.

— *see also*   wedge

color chart

This is a reference card of various standard hues, intensities, and gray values used to calibrate CG lighting and color levels to those in live-action photography. A color chart (such as the Macbeth), along with an 18% gray card, is photographed at the head of each take and is scanned in along with the running footage to be used as a known reference of that environment.

— *see also*   Macbeth chart

color correction

This refers to any modification to a pixel's RGB values. This is used both to match elements within a shot to background plates and to match whole shots together in a sequence. The term is abbreviated as CC.

— *see also*   Chapter 6, "Compositing"

color cycling

This is an old trick that is rarely, if ever, used today. To simulate movement in low-color bit depth software systems, the colors of a palette are continuously changed in sequence and repeated. This might be seen in Las Vegas neon light signs and used in such systems as DeluxePaint II on Amiga home computers.

color depth

This is the number of individual colors a file format can express for each pixel. The greater the color depth, the greater the number of colors and the more flexibility to create realistic CG images. (Stay with me—this confuses even the best of them.) Options vary between the 8-bit (2^8 or 256 colors), 16-bit (2^16 or 65,536 colors), and 24-bit (2^24 or 16,777,216 colors) systems. In film work, the 24-bit systems are most common and, in most cases, are sufficient to reproduce enough colors in a given scene to look realistic. These 24-bit systems are more commonly referred to as 8-bit because they use 8-bits per RGB channel. 10-bit systems (such as Kodak Cineon format: 10-bits each for RGB or 30-bits total) are used to come much closer to replicating the number of total color differences the human eye can perceive. Because most software only deals with 8-bit color data, higher bit depth only benefits the image as an original format to gain a better final 8-bit color choice— and then mostly in the dark shadow detail.

colorimetry

This is the area of physics that describes color in precise detail by wavelength and electromagnetic energy.

Colorific

This is simple and user-friendly color-matching and calibration software for Windows and Mac. It costs $50 from

Sonnetech, which can be reached at 415-957-9940 or www.colorific.com.

color management

Producing consistent, correct color is a surprisingly challenging task. Color management software is required to deal accurately with the conversion, correction, and adjustments between hardware, software, and display devices. Transformations between color systems and calibration control also can be found. Advanced color-management systems currently available include ColorReady and ColorWeb-Pro from Pantone, ColorShop 2.5 from X-Rite, ColorSync from Apple, and FotoFlow from Agfa.

color model

This is sometimes also called color space. This is the type of additive or subtractive representation used to describe the colors in a software system. Examples include RGB (red, green, blue) used in CG and display monitors, CMYK (cyan, magenta, yellow, and black) used in printing, and YIQ for NTSC video-broadcast signals. HLS (hue, lightness, and saturation) and HSV (hue, saturation, and value) are alternative ways to represent and modify color in software program interfaces.

A good Web page for converting between several color models can be found at: www.cs.rit.edu/~yxv4997/ t_convert.html.

ColorReady

This is color-space conversion software for Adobe Illustrator, QuarkXpress, and Macromedia Freehand from Pantone.
— *see also* Pantone

ColorSense

This is Kodak's color-management system. It uses WYSIWYG GUI control for cross-platform and application-independent consistency. Call Kodak at 800-242-2424 or contact the company online at: www.kodak.com/productInfo/ productInfo.shtml.

color separation

For color printing processes, the final color representation needs to be defined as a percentage mixture of individual colored inks. Color separation breaks down the additive primaries (RGB) into their subtractive counterparts (CMY). These separate CMY colors (combined with black) are then used to dictate the amount of ink used in the printing process. Careful attention needs to be paid when converting between any two different color models, especially between the additive color space of RGB and the subtractive color space of CMYK. Colors can easily become muddy and dull when printed compared to their displayed intensities on a monitor.

color space ▶ see color model

ColorSuites

There are specially packaged color-management software tools from Pantone for business, Internet, graphics, or hexachrome.

— *see also* Pantone

ColorSync 2.5.1

Apple's popular color-management software is now available as a Photoshop plug-in or a native AppleScript utility. It supports 16-bit-per-channel images, comes with a Monitor Calibration Assistant, and is a system extension that "synchronizes" input and output devices. You can find more information at www.apple.com/colorsync.

color temperature

This term is used to describe the appearance of a light source, measured in degrees Kelvin (0 Kelvin is equal to –273 Celsius and –459.4 Fahrenheit). Color temperature is used to balance the look and effect of the many different light source types used in live-action cinematography. The choice of lights with a particular color temperature depends on how those lights will react with the particular film stock being used, and the artistic look desired by the cinematographer. The standard reference used for calculating a color temperature is (strangely enough) the color emitted by a theoretical "neutral black-body" heated to a specific temperature.

Monitors used in CG production also must be color-temperature calibrated to more closely approximate the look of the film stock used in the production. Higher color temperatures tend to look blue; lower temperatures appear somewhat yellow. For example:

(Cool/Blue)

Blue sky above 8000

Overcast daylight 6500 to 8000

Xenon arc 6000 ***

Daylight about 5500 *

Carbon arc about 5000 ***

"White light" about 3500

Tungsten/halogen** about 3300

Florescent cool white 4300

Florescent warm white 3000

Standard household/incandescent 2800

Candle light about 1500

(Warm/Yellow)

* Direct sunlight varies between about 4900 and about 6500 depending on the time of day and the time of year.

** Tungsten lamps' color temperature varies with voltage between 2900 and 3400.

*** Xenon and carbon arc lamps are typical light sources used in motion-picture stage lighting. They're very bright!

ColorTune

This is standalone professional color-management software from Agfa. You can find more information at:
www.agfahome.com/products/dtp/software/colortune.html.

ColorWeb Pro

This is color-management software for Mac and Windows from Pantone Inc.

— *see also* Pantone

Committee for Graphic Arts Technologies Standards (CGATS)

The following statement is from www.npes.org/standards/cgats.htm: "The Committee for Graphic Arts Technologies Standards (CGATS) was formed in 1987 following a year-long assessment of the need for an umbrella standards committee by the Image Technology Standards Board (ITSB) of ANSI, and it received ANSI accreditation in 1989. The goal for CGATS is to have the entire scope of printing and publishing technologies represented in one national standardization and coordination effort, while respecting the established activities of existing accredited standards committees and industry standards developers."

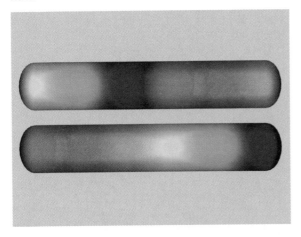

An example of complementary colors.

complementary colors

Complementary colors are two colors that, when added in equal amounts, produce white. Colors positioned opposite each other on a color wheel. When used together in a composition, these colors tend to stand out against one another very strongly. Complementary pairs include red and cyan, green and magenta, and blue and yellow.

FACTOID

In full sunlight, your eyes can distinguish a contrast range of about 250:1. Film has a contrast ratio of about 80:1, and television has an effective range of only about 30:1. The failure of TV to correctly reproduce the full range of subtle contrast originating on film explains the "flying box" artifacts found, for example, around spaceships in some sci-fi movies. (The next time you watch *Star Wars* at home on video, watch for the random box-like shapes that surround the X-Wings and Tie-Fighters flying in space!)

contouring

This refers to large areas of CG images in which continuous, gradual color change is represented with insufficient color depth (usually 8-bit) to reproduce smooth, indistinguishable transitions. This is visible as abrupt changes in value. It sometimes also is referred to as color banding. (This is a bad thing.) Because using a higher bit depth usually is not an option on a per-shot basis, other more practical solutions are necessary. You can try to increase the range of colors across the area as much as possible, creating brighter highs (DMax or maximum density) and darker lows (DMin or minimum density). Introducing noise also helps break up the apparent steps in color.

24-bit

8-bit

24-bit produces smooth transitions while 8-bit shows visible color changes.

contrast

This refers to the difference between the lightest lights and the darkest darks of a scene, usually expressed as a ratio such as 4 to 1 or 4:1. To raise or increase the contrast is to increase this difference; decreasing the contrast "flattens" these extremes toward a common middle tone. High contrast usually is a good thing, depending on the mood of the shot, but the important consideration is to match the contrast of the corresponding live-action plate, if any. A good technique is to check separately— both by eye and by pixel value— the darks, mid-tones, and highlights of all your elements.

High contrast.

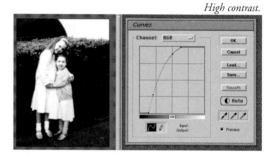

Low contrast.

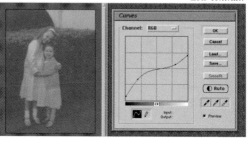

Do this both in color and in monochrome (grayscale) if possible. Refer to Chapter 6, "Compositing," for more on the topic of matching contrast.

— *see also*   value

cookie

This is also called "kook," short for cucaloris. An irregularly perforated card or screen placed in front of a light source to create the impression of foliage or other obstructing patterns. This often is used for a more natural look in stage lighting when shooting outdoor scenes and in CG for the same reason.

— *see also*   flag

cool colors

These are hues that appear to recede away when placed next to warm colors. Most green and blue hues are considered cool.

Cromalin

This is a color-proofing system from DuPont. You can find more information at `www.dupont.com/proofing/links.html`.

cucaloris   ▶ see cookie, flag

cutter   ▶ see flag

cyan

This is the complementary color to red, between blue and green. Cyan, along with magenta and yellow, are the primary subtractive colors in print media, processed with black.

— *see also*   CMYK

da Vinci 2K

This is a new real-time, high-resolution (and HDTV-compatible) color-enhancement system. You can find more information at `www.davsys.com/2k.htm`.

decay

This is how a light's intensity decreases with distance from its source. Natural light decays at a rate of 1 divided by the square of the distance. A CG light with 0 decay affects objects equally at all distances from its source. Sometimes this term is used interchangeably with falloff.

DIC

This stands for Device Independent Color. This is an ideal color model that can be transported between platforms with no alteration to the color information. The L*A*B model is excellent for containing both the RGB and CMY color spaces simultaneously, thereby easing portability of a broad range of color information.

diffuse reflection

This is the predominant light reflected by most surfaces. It is scattered equally in all directions, independent of the viewing direction. This also is called Lambertian reflection. See Chapter 5, "Rendering" for more information.

— *see also*   specular

direct color   ▶ see true color

directional light

This is a light source with color, intensity, and a single direction only. In CG, the sun is often represented as a directional light source. The light effect remains parallel to the direction of the light no matter the distance, therefore simulating a very distant light source. Directional lights generally do not have any decay, falloff, spread, or other attributes. This sometimes is referred to as a distant light model because very distant sources (such as the sun) do not have any falloff or divergence in small-scale practical use.

— *see also*   light

distant light   ▶ see directional light

dither

This is an attempt to approximate a higher number of colors in a lower bit-depth color system. This is done by assigning two similar colors that are able to be reproduced to adjacent pixels, hopefully creating the illusion of a third. This is one possible solution to banding or contouring caused by insufficient color depth.

DMax

This stands for maximum density.

— *see also*   contouring

DMin

This stands for minimum density.

— *see also*   contouring

dynamic range

This is the ratio between minimum and maximum values of a raster image. In more general use, dynamic range defines the upper and lower limits of any system.

— *see also*   contrast

falloff

In a spotlight, falloff is the rate at which the apparent brightness decreases from the center to the edge of the light cone. A falloff of zero means the intensity is equal across the entire spread. A falloff of one decreases intensity linearly from full at the center to nothing at the edge.

— *see also*   decay

fill light

Secondary light sources are used to "fill in" wherever the main key light is not illuminating the object. In CG, these secondary lights also might be called bounce lights if the imagined source is a reflective surface. In most practical cinematography, a bounce light is directed not at the subject but at some other area, such as the ceiling of an interior or off a bounce card, to produce nondirectional illumination.

flag

Any of several types of forms can be placed in front of light sources to block light or cast shadows. This also might be called a card, cutter, dot, finger, gobo, scrim, target, or teaser.

flaps   ▶ see barn doors

footcandle

This is a standard measurement of a light's intensity as it illuminates an object's surface.

— *see also*   lux

fresnel

This is an enclosed lighting element designed for maximum light control; it is a universal studio standard, either in floor-standing or suspended versions. Its soft edge beam makes it ideal to use in overlapping coverage of larger areas.

full color   ▶ see true color

gamma

Gamma can mean different things to different people, and it often is the subject of many heated debates about its usage, definition, and nature. Strictly speaking, gamma can be described as "the nonlinear relationship of intensity reproduction." The intensity of light and your visual perception of its brightness are both nonlinear in nature. The mathematical curves used to describe this intensity, therefore, are described as a value raised to an exponent. That exponent value is referred to as gamma, and a useful range usually falls between 1.5 to 3.0. Increasing the gamma value makes the response curve steeper, thus making the image darker and giving it more contrast. One representation can be shown as:

Gamma (inputVal, gamVal) = pow (inputVal, 1.0 / gamVal)

— *see also*   gamma correction

FACTOID

Poynton gamma factoid: Why does video use a gamma 2.2? It is assumed that television is viewed in dim surroundings and, therefore, has the appearance of a lower contrast than intended. Because a television monitor's CRT is thought of as using a 2.5-power exponent, the signal is undercorrected at the camera by using an exponent of about 1/2.2 instead of 1/2.5.

Further reading on gamma: An acknowledged authority on gamma-related topics of digital video, computer graphics, and film is Charles Poynton. Refer to his book *A Technical Introduction to Digital Video*. New York: Wiley, 1996. Chapter 6, "Gamma," is available online at www.inforamp.net/~poynton/PDFs/TIDV/Gamma.pdf.

gamma correction

The calculation to produce a particular intensity value is called gamma correction. Gamma-correction values are applied at the color lookup table (CLUT), altering the image data in the framebuffer before it is viewed on a monitor. The NTSC signal standard gamma-correction value is 2.2.

gamut

This is a color range—the total number of colors reproducible in a given format such as (NTSC or film).

Grey Color Replacement (GCR) ▶ see UCR

hexachrome

This is a relatively new six-color printing process (developed by Pantone) that provides a much greater range of colors than the traditional four-color (CMYK) process printing. Green and orange are added to cyan, magenta, yellow, and black. With the usual color-printing order, you could call it CGMYOK!

hexadecimal

This is a method of notation used in various computer schemes, such as color notation for the HTML code used in Web browsers. Hexa (six) decimal (ten) is a naturally convenient way for computers to keep track of information for several reasons. Binary, the most basic form of information notation in computers, is used in conjunction with the fact that each byte of computer data is made up of 8 bits, usually grouped together in pairs. Hexadecimal begins counting with 00 through 09, continues with 0A through 0F, and then 10 through 19, 1A through 1F, 20 through 29, and so on. Hexadecimal color, therefore, is notated as three pairs such as "#00 00 00" for black and "#FF FF FF" for white. If you need to convert between a CG/RGB decimal and a WWW hexadecimal notation, you need to remember that you are going between your familiar base 10 system and one with base 16. Normally, the leftmost digit of the pair is used to multiply by 10. In hexadecimal, however, you must multiply that left number by 16 and then add the right number. To find the hexadecimal equivalent of a decimal number, first divide the decimal number by 16. That whole number becomes the left digit; the remainder is the right digit. Therefore, the decimal number 16 would be equal to the hexadecimal 10. (16/16 = 1 remainder 0 =1 0). Reversing the process makes the hexadecimal color code for white ("FFFFFF") break down in this way... "F" in hexadecimal is 15, so each pair of three "F"s (15×16=250 + 15 = 255) is 255,255,255. It can be a little confusing until you get used to it. Thankfully, some Web sites can convert colors for you so you don't have to worry about doing it by hand. Here are a few:

www.cyberbits.com/Backgrnd/hexcolr2.htm ,
http://utopia.knoware.nl/users/lieuwe/kleur.htm,
www.insyncimaging.com/converter.

high color

This is a video and PC term sometimes used to describe 16-bit color depth. High color only has two bytes of information to store the values of all three colors. This is divided into 5 bits for blue, 5 bits for red, and 6 bits for green (32 different values for blue, 32 for red, and 64 for green).

— *see also*   full color

histogram

This is a map of an image's grayscale luminance values. What is it good for? A histogram gives you a good representation of how an image's tonal range is distributed at a glance. Some color-correction tools use a histogram as an adjustable input for remapping these values.

An image and its histogram.

HSB

This stands for Hue Saturation Brightness. This is an interchangeable term for HSV.

— *see also*   HSV

HLS

This stands for Hue Lightness Saturation. This often is used as an interchangeable term for HSV. The actual color model differs slightly as double-inverted cones, with the peak of the top being white and the peak of the inverted bottom cone being black. Munsell color space is essentially the same.

— *see also*   HSV

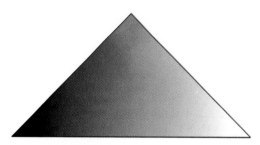

The HSV color model.

HSV

This is the Hue Saturation Value color model defined by A.R. Smith in 1978. It is a more intuitive way to describe color by affecting the overall color directly, not by three discrete subcolors as in RGB or CMY color models. The HSV color model is described as a hexcone derived from viewing the RGB color cube diagonally from its white corner to its black corner.

hue

This is the apparent color irrespective of brightness or saturation. Red, green, purple, and yellow are all hues. This is defined by the dominant wavelength of the light.

H V/C

This is the notation of the Munsell color system: Hue, Value, and Chroma. This is the same idea as the HSV color model.

HWB

This stands for Hue Whiteness Blackness. This color model is closely related to both HSV and HSL, but it is meant to avoid the known flaws in other color models including RGB. It is slightly faster to compute than these other color models, and it also very intuitive to understand. You simply choose a hue, lighten it with white, and darken it with black. This was presented as "HWB—A More Intuitive Hue-Based Color Model" by Alvy Ray Smith with Eric Ray Lyons in *The Journal of Graphics Tools* Vol. 1, No 1: 3-17, 1996. For more information, see Alvy Ray Smith's Web page at www.research.microsoft.com/~alvy.

ICC

This stands for International Color Consortium.

incident light

This is any light that comes directly from a light source when falling on an object without first being reflected off some other object.

indexed color

This is a subset of RGB. Although there are only 256 indexed colors, they can be selected to be any of the 16.7 million of a full 24-bit pallet. This selective color palette is the basis for the GIF image format (used widely in Web graphics) to provide the best possible representation of a higher-color-depth image. This sometimes is erroneously called "pseudo color." By some definitions, this is similar in concept to a CLUT.

intensity

This is a linear measure of light power. This sometimes is used synonymously with luminance, saturation, and chroma. It generally is used to describe the purity of the color. To lower the intensity of a color in a subtractive system, a neutral gray or complimentary color usually is added. In an additive color system such as RGB, adding more of the two least-dominant colors decreases the intensity of the whole. This should not be confused with value or brightness.

— *see also* brightness, value

International Color Consortium

Here is a statement from npes.org/icc/index.htm: "The International Color Consortium was established in 1993 by eight industry vendors for the purpose of creating, promoting, and encouraging the standardization and evolution of an open, vendor-neutral, cross-platform color-management system architecture and components. The ICC has made significant progress in gaining acceptance for color-management profiles, which enable color to be transportable without degradation. NPES serves as administrative secretariat for the ICC. For more information about the ICC, please contact William K. Smythe at NPES at 703-264-7200 or by fax at 703-620-0994."

key light

This is the primary source of illumination in a scene. It is complemented with fill and bounce lights. For exterior daylight scenes, the sun is often the key light.

kicker ▸ see backlight

L*A*B (lab)

This is a 3D color model that combines both the RGB and CMYK color spaces. It was developed by the French CIE (Commission Internationale de L'Éclairage) in 1976. Each of the three axes in the model represents green-to-red, blue-to-yellow, and luminance (0 to 100). The intent of this color model is to translate colors accurately between RGB and CMYK while retaining their original components.

lens flare

This is an optical effect caused by a bright light shining into the camera lens and reflecting off the individual lens elements therein. In early motion-picture cinematography, any light contamination or effect such as lens flare was strictly frowned upon by camera operators. Later, more recent films learned to treat this kind of "imperfection" as a natural artistic effect to be used deliberately. In computer graphics, the effect was almost unknown until the 1990s when sophisticated plug-ins such as Lens Effects by Knoll Software became commonplace. Recently, the effect has become a bit of an overused cliché like the chrome logos and morphing in the past.

An example of lens flare.

lightness

This is the apparent achromatic value of a reflecting surface.

luminance

This is the intensity of a light source. Luminance is the graytone value computed from RGB using the formula: RGB luminance value = 0.3 R + 0.59 G + 0.11 B. These numerical ratios derive from how your eyes perceive color brightness differently for each of the three hues. An RGB color of (120, 180, 100), for example, would compute its luminance as (120 x 0.3) + (180 x 0.59) + (100 x 0.11) = 153. Luminance commonly is denoted with the letter Y in formula and notation such as the YIQ color space.

lux

This is a metricstandard measurement of a light's intensity (10.76 lux is equal to 1 footcandle).

Macbeth Colorchecker chart

The Macbeth chart is an industry-standard reference for color and gray values commonly used in film calibration. The Colorchecker is a checkerboard array of 24 scientifically prepared colored squares representing common objects such as human skin, foliage, and blue sky. These squares not only are the same color as their counterparts, they also reflect light the same way in all parts of the visible spectrum. Because of this unique feature, the squares match the colors of natural objects under any illumination and with any color reproduction process.

The ColorChecker chart is produced in the Munsell Color Lab at GretagMacbeth. You can find more information at www.gretagmacbeth.com.

— *see also*   color chart

monochrome (monochromatic)

This is a color palette that varies in shade and tint but not in hue. This literally means "of one chromanance."

Munsell

This is a color-order system using hue, value, and chroma. It is denoted as H V/C, which is called the Munsell notation. This is from GretagMacbeth. You can find more information at www.gretagmacbeth.com and munsell.com.

ND

This means to darken a scene or an image overall with a Neutral Density filter. These are colorless filters of varying densities used to decrease the amount of light entering a lens.

OptiCal 2.5

This is a standalone calibration package for the Mac OS, SGI, and Windows. It is an accurate, easy-to-use, and relatively affordable tool. You can obtain more information by calling 800-554-8688 or by visiting www.colorpartnership.com.

palette

Traditional artists' palettes consist of a hard surface for holding and mixing paints, and they usually are hand-held for convenience. The CG palette is the selection of colors available in a graphics application or format whose variety depends on the color depth of the image format in use. Options vary between the most common 8-bit (256 colors) systems, 16-bit (64,000) systems, and 24-bit (16.7 million colors) systems.

Pantone Inc.

This is the maker of the standard printed color-reference system for the graphics design and desktop publishing industries. (PMS colors number over 3,000.) Some examples of Pantone's color-management software programs are ColorReady, ColorSuites, and ColorWeb Pro. Pantone Inc. is located in Carlstad, New Jersey, and can be reached at 888-726-8663 or www.pantone.com.

Photo YCC

This is Kodak's own color-model specification used in Photo CDs. It also is compatible with the CIE model. You can find more information at www.kodak.com/productInfo/productInfo.shtml.

PMS

This stands for Pantone Matching System. This is an industry standard color-identification system for print work. You can find more information at www.pantone.com.

point light

This is a light source that illuminates equally in all directions, such as a candle or a light bulb.

— *see also*   spot light, directional light, and area light.

primary colors

Red, green, and blue are used in additive color models of light. Cyan, magenta, and yellow (along with black) are used similarly in subtractive printing applications.

radiosity   ▶ see radiosity in Chapter 5, "Rendering"

reflective color

This is the color you perceive from the light reflected off a surface, such as with the CMYK color model.

rim light   ▶ see back light

RGB

This stands for the three additive primary colors of computer graphics. (They are additive because red added to green added to blue make white.) When mixed equally, blue and green make cyan, red and green make yellow, and blue and red make magenta. The RGB color model is based on the Cartesian coordinate system.

— *see also*   CMY color model

saturation

This is the level of purity in a single color's hue. This also is known in video graphics terms as chroma.

scrim

This is a cloth-like material placed in front of a light to decrease its intensity.

shade

To shade is to add an amount of black to a color. This is the opposite of tint.

snoot

This is a cone-like version of barn doors used to focus light beams.

spectrum

This is the range of color in a given palette. The spectrum of visible light found in a natural rainbow are red, orange, yellow, green, blue, indigo, and violet.

specular

These are the highlights or localized bright-white spots on a surface. The more shiny a surface, the more pronounced its specular highlight. See Chapter 5, "Rendering" for more information about Phong shading.

spotlight

This is a light source directed outward from a point in a cone whose spread is less than 180 degrees. Other common parameters might include penumbra, falloff, and decay.

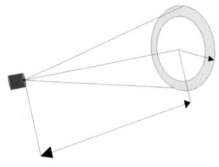

Spotlight illustration showing the light source, spread, and falloff information.

subtractive color model

Color is achieved by subtracting (or filtering) white light. The three subtractive primary colors—cyan, magenta and yellow (CMY)—are the compliment of red, green, and blue (RGB). Combined with black as CMYK, this color model is used in four-color separation printing processes. Black, a single and less expensive ink, is substituted for equal amounts of CMY as a practical and cost-saving method. Mixed equally, yellow and magenta make red, magenta and cyan make blue, and cyan and yellow make green. Conversion between the two color spaces can be accomplished with the following formula: RGB = 1 - CMY.

target ▶ see flag

tint

To tint is to add an amount of white to a color. This is the opposite of shade.

tone

This is a hue with some amount of black and white added. This decreases its saturation.

true color

This is the common name sometimes used for 24-bit color depth. It provides 8 separate bits for each of the three RGB color components. It also sometimes is called full-color or direct-color.

UnderColor Addition (UCA)

This is the process of adding amounts of CMY color to neutral areas in place of black. This also is called Grey Color Replacement (GCR) and is the opposite of UCR.

UnderColor Removal (UCR)

This is the process of replacing amounts of CMY color in neutral area with black. This is the opposite of UCA.

value

This is the relative lightness or darkness of a color. A high value range in an image is said to have high contrast and generally gives a subjectively richer and more detailed look than one with a low value range.

— *see also*   shade, tint, contrast

warm colors

These are red and yellow hues that tend to predominate when used next to cool colors such as blues and greens.

wash

To wash is to modify a color by affecting its hue and saturation. This also is known (incorrectly) as tint. The term originates in the use of watercolor painting.

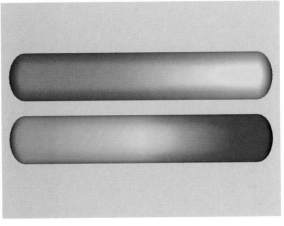

An example of warm colors.

white

What is white, you say? It is a black body radiating at precisely 6,447 degrees Kelvin.

YcbCr

The YcbCr model is a scaled and shifted YUV color space used in the MPEG and JPEG compression schemes.

YIQ

This is a remapped RGB color model used in NTSC color-television broadcast signals. Y is luminance, I is the orange-blue axis, and Q is the purple-green axis. Black and white televisions only display the Y component of the signal, which accounts for approximately 60 percent of the total signal strength.

YUV

This is the signal format of digital video. Y stands for luminance, and U and V are the color difference or chromanance components.

REFERENCES

Poynton, Charles. *A Technical Introduction to Digital Video.* New York: Wiley, 1996. Chapter 6, "Gamma," is available online at `inforamp.net/~poynton/PDFs/TIDV/Gamma.pdf`.

Adobe Systems Inc.
Acrobat
After Effects
Agfa
Alladin Pro
Alien Skin Software
Altamira Composer
Amazon
Animo
Art Dabbler
Aura
Aurora
Autodesk® Inc.
AVA
banding
Barco
BigPaint
BigPaint3
bitmap
canvas
CGATS
Claris Corporation Inc.
ClarisDRAW
clone
Commotion
contouring
CorelDRAW
Corel Corporation
Corel Photo-Paint 8
Crayon
Create 5.0
Creator 7.1
Creator2
Chyron Corp.
Cubicomp
DeBabelizer

DALiM
Deluxe Paint
Designer
Digital Morph
Director 7
Discreet Logic
dither
DPIA
dpi
Dreamweaver
DVExtreme
Dynamic Media Studio
Eclipse
effect*
embossing
Epson
Equilibrium
Expression
Extensis
feathering
FileMaker Inc.
flame*
FlashPix
font
Fractal Design Corp.
Freehand
FXDeko
GENESISvfx
GIMP
GoLive CyberStudio
Graphic Communications Association
Graphic Paintbox
Graphics Suite
grayscale

greeking
halftone
Harry
histogram
iGrafx
Illustrator
Illuminare
Image Composer
image processing
ImageReady and ImageStyler
Imaginator
Imapro
inferno*
Integrated Computing Engines Inc.
IntelliDraw
Intellihance Pro
Interactive Effects
Kai's Power Tools 5
kerning
Layerpaint
LIBERTY® 64
Live Picture Inc.
lookup table
lpi
Lumena
MacDraw
MacPaint
Macromedia
mach banding
Magic Inkwell Photomagic
marquee
Matador
MetaCard Corp.
MetaCreations Corp.

Painting and Graphic Design

MetaTools Inc.
Micrografx Inc.
Nowhouse
nTitle
Opaque
Pagemaker
PageMill
Paint
Paint3
Paintbox
Painter
Painter 3D
Paint Shop Pro
Pandemonium
Pantone Inc.
PDF
PhotoDeluxe
PhotoDraw 2000
PhotoEnhancer Plus
PhotoFinish
PhotoGraphics
PhotoLine 32
PhotoPaint
Photoshop
Photo Soap
PhotoSuite
PhotoTools
Picture It!
PictureMaker
Picture Publisher
Pinnacle Systems Inc.
Piranha Animator
PixelPaint Pro
pixmap
posterization
Positron

PostScript
Premiere
presentation graphics
Print House Magic 3
Propeller Paint Engine
QFX
Quantel
Quark Inc.
RasterOps
RasterTech
RIO
rotoscope
SatoriPaint
Shima-Seiki
SoftCel
S-Paint
Studiopaint 3D
SuperPaint
3D paint software
3Space Publisher
TIPS
Trinity
Truevision Inc.
TrU-V
Ulead Systems
USM
Valis Group
VideoPaint
Vignette
Visualizer Paint
wire removal
Xaos Tools
Zaxwerks 3D Invigorator

Since the very first days of computer graphics, artists creating and manipulating 2D canvases of pixels have demanded more and more sophisticated tools. True to the laws of supply and demand, computer scientists have risen to the challenge over the past 25 years, and have provided a tremendous variety of software from which to choose.

This chapter discusses the software tools used in 2D computer graphics. In particular, it covers many of the early ground-breaking software tools that paved the way to today's state-of-the-art tools.

Including these important historic milestones will put in perspective current tools that might otherwise be taken for granted.

An important distinction always should be made between the three very different kinds of tool sets discussed here:

- Painting
- Illustration
- Image processing/photo editing

Although some packages might include some aspects of all three of these techniques, most specialize in just one.

PAINTING

Perhaps the most difficult technical challenge for computer graphics tools is to emulate the real tools to which artists are accustomed, tools such as charcoal, water colors, oils, and pencils. The best painting programs (such as MetaCreations Painter) do a remarkable job of reproducing the look and feel of traditional nondigital media.

ILLUSTRATION

Spline-based graphic design and illustration have been dominated by tools such as CorelDRAW, Adobe Illustrator, and Freehand. The vector graphics files from these programs usually are stored in PICT or EPS formats. Precise control, text manipulation, and overall speed and flexibility make the best illustration programs stand out.

IMAGE PROCESSING AND PHOTO EDITING

Image processing and photo editing for a long time has been dominated by Adobe Photoshop (now in v5.0).

In recent years, a wide range of affordable products that focus on this specialty market have successfully found a following: Adobe PhotoDeluxe 2.0, Corel Photo-Paint 8.0, Jasc Paint Shop Pro 5.0, Metacreations Kai's Photo Soap, Micrografx Picture Publisher 8.0, and others.

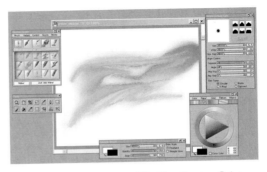

The MetaCreations Painter interface.

TERMS

Adobe Systems Inc.

This pioneering desktop-publishing company was founded in 1982 by John Warnock (Ph.D. University of Utah 1969) and Charles M. Geschke (Xerox PARC's Computer Sciences Lab/Imaging Sciences Laboratory 1980). Adobe is the maker of such programs as After Effects, Pagemaker, PhotoDeluxe, Photoshop, Premiere, Illustrator, Image Ready, and ImageStyler. The newly marketed Graphics Studio bundles Illustrator, Pagemaker, and Photoshop at a more affordable price than purchasing the programs separately.

Adobe also is the developer of Acrobat and the licensee of PostScript. The San Jose, California, company, which merged with Aldus in 1994, can be reached at 800-822-8856 or www.adobe.com.

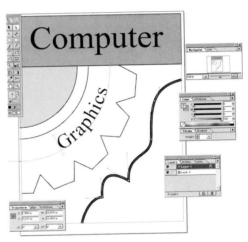

The Adobe Illustrator interface.

Acrobat

This is a platform-independent document-viewing system based on an extension to PostScript. It contains text and images and was developed by Adobe.

The Adobe Photoshop interface.

After Effects (v4.0)

This is a compositing, 2D effects, and animation program for PowerMac and Windows platforms. The standard edition contains all the core tool sets and costs about $995. The Professional Bundle adds advanced keying and other features and costs $2,195. Real-time RAM playback is a great new feature, as is a new interface design that combines the look, feel, and tight integration with Photoshop, Illustrator and Premiere, all of which are from Adobe.

Many plug-ins for After Effects are available from companies such as Alien Skin, DigiEffects, and Ultimatte.

Agfa

The Agfa-Gevaert Group manufactures and markets electronic and photographic desktop-publishing and presentation-graphics systems for graphic arts and publishing companies. It is headquartered in Mortsel, Belgium, and is part of the Bayer Group of companies. It can be reached at 00-32-3-444-2111 or www.agfa.com.

Alladin Pro

This is high-end digital video effect (DVE) software with keying, color correction, and visual effects. It costs about $25,000 from Pinnacle Systems, which can be reached at www.pinnaclesys.com.

Alien Skin Software

Alien Skin is the maker of special effects and image-processing plug-ins, including Eye Candy and Xenoflex for the Mac, and Windows products such as Adobe Photoshop and Corel Photo-Paint. The company is located in Raleigh, North Carolina, and can be reached at 888-921-7546 or www.alienskin.com.

Altamira Composer

This product is based on the IceMan image-editing software created by Alvy Ray Smith while he was at Pixar prior to 1991. With funding from Autodesk, Smith then founded Altamira Software Corporation in 1991. The software evolved into Microsoft Image Composer when Smith joined Microsoft as its first graphics fellow in 1994. It is designed mainly for sprite-based Web graphics creation with editable text objects, a Button Wizard tool, interactive warps, and more. You can find more information at www.microsoft.com/imagecomposer/default.htm.

Amazon

This paint system by Interactive Effects Inc. is a multi-layered paint and image-processing system for Silicon Graphics workstations. Open architecture makes for easy plug-in and custom-brush creation. Amazon is used heavily at Pixar.

Ampex Video Art (AVA)

Ampex Corp. bought Alvy Ray Smith's Paint program in 1976 and incorporated it with a hardware/software system created in 1979–80 by Larry Evans, Tom Porter, Junaid Sheikh, Rodney Stock, and Ken Turkowski.

This new system, called AVA, ran on a DEC PDP 11/34 minicomputer and had a 768×512 resolution with 8-bit color plus 1-bit overlay for the color display. A separate 768×1024 terminal display was used for menus. It was never further developed for newer hardware platforms.

— *see also* Paint

Animo

Released in 1990 by Cambridge Animation (in Cambridge, England), Animo is the world's most widely used 2D cel animation system. It is available for SGI and NT platforms. Cambridge Animation has offices worldwide including in Los Angeles, California. The company can be reached at 818-551-4500 or www.animo.com.

Art Dabbler

Such a deal! This is a great beginners' paint and effects software for all ages. It is available for only $49 for Macintosh and Windows 95 from MetaCreations. Its features include flip-book animation, recordable macros, paint scanned-in photos, Kai's Power Tools plug-ins, and an easy-to-use, icon-based interface. It's perfect even for the youngest of users. You can learn more about Art Dabbler at `www.metacreations.com/products/dabbler/dabbler.html`.

Aura

Aura is a professional video painting, effects, and compositing software package from NewTek. Its features include 2D animation, rotoscoping, recordable actions, and character generation—all on unlimited layers. It costs about $700. You can learn more about Aura at `www.newtek.com`.

— *see also* NewTek in Chapter 4, "Animation"

Aurora

Originally made by Aurora Systems (founded by Richard "SuperPaint" Shoup and Damon Rarey in 1980), the Aurora/100 paint system was released in 1981 as a video-resolution tool for television applications. The Aurora ran on a PDP 11/23 minicomputer and used three 8-bit DeAnza color frame buffers with a 512×512 resolution.

With Shoup, Tom Hahn was a key engineer of the Aurora system. Hahn later moved on to Pixar, aiding in the design of the CAPS system for Disney.

The Aurora 125 system was really the first widely used commercial paint system with a very friendly GUI. Aurora introduced subpixel accuracy and full 24-bit color in 1983. At the time, Aurora competed mainly with Quantel's Paintbox system.

Aurora is now available as the Liberty paint system from Chyron Corp.

Autodesk® Inc.

Founded by John Walker and Dan Drake, Autodesk is the fourth-largest PC software company in the world with three million customers in 150 countries. Autodesk released

AutoCAD version 1 in 1982. In 1989, it unveiled an animation package for the PC called Autodesk Animator, a full-featured 2D animation and painting package. It released the 3D computer animation product 3D Studio in 1990. It now is the parent company of Kinetix and Discreet Logic and is based in San Rafael, California, with more than 60 offices worldwide. Autodesk can be reached at 415-507-5000 or www.autodesk.com.

AVA ▶ see Ampex Video Art

banding ▶ see contouring in Chapter 1, "Color and Light"

Barco

Barco is the manufacturer of professional photo-retouching workstations and graphics software for Silicon Graphics workstations. Barco, founded in 1934, has offices worldwide. You can find more information at www.barco.com.

BigPaint

BigPaint was written as a university research tool at the New York Institute of Technology Computer Graphics Lab and as an increased-resolution version of Alvy Ray Smith's Paint in 1976. BigPaint enabled a user to work on a 512×512 section of a larger image stored on disk, swapping sections of framebuffer memory with sections of a stored file on disk. You also could zoom in and out of lower-resolution versions of the full image.

— *see also* Paint, Paint3, and BigPaint3

BigPaint3

Developed in 1978 and 1979, BigPaint3 combined the 24-bit painting capabilities of Paint3 with the high-resolution capabilities of BigPaint.

bitmap

This describes images made with just one bit of color information (black or white) per pixel.

canvas

A colloquial name for a pixmap, it is usually used in graphics program interfaces to represent the working area.

CGATS

This stands for the Committee on Graphic Arts Technologies Standards for printing and publishing technologies. Formed in 1987, you can find more information about this committee at www.npes.org/standards/cgats.htm.

Claris Corporation Inc.

Claris Corporation Inc. is the maker of Claris Draw and the original MacPaint and MacDraw programs. The company was reorganized into FileMaker Inc. by Apple Computer in 1998. You can find more information at www.filemaker.com.

ClarisDRAW

One of the first vector-drawing applications for the Macintosh personal computer, ClarisDRAW basically was just an upgrade and renaming of the original MacDRAW application. The name change helped with marketing to other non-Mac platforms, mainly Windows.

— *see also* Claris Corporation Inc.

clone (cloning)

To clone is to copy, offset, and paint with a portion of an image canvas. This is sometimes used to "repair" artifacts when doing dirt-and-scratch removal or plate restoration. Some automated wire-removal programs clone image-pixel values from either side of the plotted wire to fill in over the wire's pixels, essentially erasing the offending portion of the image.

Commotion (v2.0)

This provides real-time rotoscoping, painting, and motion tracking for Mac and Windows NT. Commotion is optimized for multiple-frame sequence touch-up work such as wire removal. It contains animatable parameters and brushes as well as support for TrueType and PostScript text.

Commotion is available with the accelerated ICEd Motion Tracker from Integrated Computing Engines Inc. Third-party plug-ins are now available, including those designed for Adobe After Effects. Created by Scott Squires, Commotion is about $2,500 and is distributed by Puffin Designs Inc. based in Sausalito, California. Puffin

Designs can be reached at 415-331-4560, 800-401-0009, or www.puffindesigns.com.

contouring ▶ see contouring in Chapter 1, "Color and Light"

CorelDRAW ▶ see Corel Corporation

Corel Corporation

Corel is the maker of the CorelDRAW graphics suite, including Photo-Paint 8 and CorelTrace 8. These often are compared to Adobe Illustrator and Macromedia Freehand. Corel Corp., based in Ottawa, Canada, can be reached at 800-722-6735 or www.corel.com.

Corel Photo-Paint 8

Long a standard on the Windows platform, it recently was released for the Mac as a standalone application or as part of the CorelDRAW suite. It is compared to products such as Adobe Photoshop and MetaCreations Painter and is from Corel Corporation.

Crayon

Crayon is a limited 8-bit paint system designed by James Blinn at the University of Utah in 1974 that ran on the Evans and Sutherland frame buffer.

Create 5.0

This is illustration and layout software based on Display PostScript for real-time text manipulation. Versions are available for NeXT OpenStep OS, Windows, and Mac from Stone Design, which is based in Albuquerque, New Mexico. Stone design can be reached at 505-345-4800 or www.stone.com.

Creator 7.1

Creator 7.1 is Barco's latest image-manipulation software product. It performs continuous tone manipulations on files as large as 300MB in either RGB or CMYK. It contains powerful color correction, masking, and warping tools with a WYSIWYG interface. It is based on the SGI O2 and Octane platforms. You can find more information at www.barco.com/graphics/data/creator.htm.

Creator2 (v1.5)

This is professional publishing, illustration, and layout software for the Mac from Multi-Ad Services Inc. Multi-Ad is based in Peoria, Illinois and can be reached at 800-245-9278 or www.creator2.com.

Chyron Corp.

Chyron Corp. is the maker of character-generation, graphics, editing, compositing, and PC products for video and broadcast production. iNFiNiT! is the industry standard in high-end graphics, character generator, and animation turnkey workstations. Liberty is a film resolution professional digital paint and compositing software package for the SGI. Chyron is based in Melville, New York and can be reached at 516-845-2000 or www.chyron.com.

Cubicomp ▶ see Cubicomp in Chapter 4, "Animation"

DeBabelizer

A powerful image format-handling software by Equilibrium, it converts and optimizes in batch-processing mode still images, digital video, and movie formats for both Windows and Mac platforms. DeBabelizer-Lite for the Mac is a perfect basic-image translator. You can find more information at www.debabelizer.com.

DALiM

This is a manufacturer of digital content and management products including LiTHO image retouching, GALERiE asset management, and TWiST for prepress and publishing. Its headquarters are in Neu-Isenburg-Zeppelinheim, Germany, and Bedford, New Hampshire. The company can be reached at 603-624-5994 or www.dalim.de.

Deluxe Paint

Deluxe Paint and Deluxe Paint II were color painting software programs available for Amiga home computers. Deluxe Paint had a color cycling feature with a glorious 32 colors.

Designer ▶ see iGrafx

Digital Morph 2.0

This is morphing, warping, and dissolving software from Pacific Coast Software Inc. It was originally sold by HSC Software, which is now part of MetaCreations. This software is no longer available. You can find more information at

www.pacificcoastsoftware.com/DigitalMorph.htm.

Director 7

This standard in multimedia authoring software works with Flash, PowerPoint, QuickTime 3.0, and QuickTime VR. Iti is available for Windows, NT, and Mac. Currently, it is only available as part of the Director Multimedia Studio suite from Macromedia. You can find more information at www.macromedia.com.

Discreet Logic

Discreet Logic is the maker of SGI-based digital effects software including effect* (Mac/Windows/SGI-O2), flame* (for Octane), and inferno* (for Onyx 2). The product, originally known as flint*, was remarketed as "effect* option 3" for the O2 platform. Flint then was reintroduced in February 1999 as an entry-level flame* feature-based product. Discreet Logic is based in Montreal, Quebec, and can be reached at 800-869-3504 or www.discreet.com.

dither

Dithering is an attempt to approximate a higher number of colors in a lower bit-depth color system. This is done by assigning two similar colors that are able to be reproduced to adjacent pixels, hopefully creating the illusion of a third color. This is one possible solution to banding or contouring caused by insufficient color depth.

— *see also* quantizing

An example of dithering.

DPIA

DPIA stands for Digital Printing and Imaging Association, a membership organization for the exchange of ideas, new technology, and industry-related conferences. You can find more information at www.dpia.org.

dpi

Dpi stands for dots per inch, the number of individual points reproduced horizontally or vertically in any inch of input or output. The typical resolution of scanners or laser printers is 300dpi (300×600), often interpolated to 600dpi (600×600). Ppi (pixels per inch) and lpi (lines per inch) sometimes are used incorrectly as analogous terms.

— *see also*   resolution

Dreamweaver

This is professional Web-authoring software that supports DHTML standards from Macromedia.

DVExtreme

This is a video effects system from Pinnacle Systems that features ParticleFX and PainterlyFX tools such as lava melt, sand, bubbles, and stained glass. Warping tools create everything from page turns to explosions, and lighting tools cast shadows. This system costs about $35,000 for NT platforms. You can find more information at www.pinnaclesys.com.

Dynamic Media Studio

This is the bundled package of products just released by Adobe Inc. It includes After Effects 4.0, Illustrator 8.0, Photoshop 5.0, and Premier 5.1. It offers totally integrated functionality and menu systems all for $3,495.

Eclipse

Eclipse is object-based image-editing RGB and CMYK software from Alias for the SGI. It is no longer available.

effect*

This is the Mac-, Windows-, and SGI O2-based compositing and 2D visual effects software product from Discreet Logic. Three options exist based on the products previously known as Flint and Illuminare Composition. Features include resolution independence, unlimited layers, displacement, warping, 3D-model integration, a particle system with depth of field, lights and shadows, color correction, advanced keying, tracking and stabilizing, and more.

— *see also* flame* and inferno* in Chapter 6, "Compositing"

embossing

Embossing is an image-processing effect to "raise up" text or images in relief using false shadows and highlights based on luminance values of an image.

Epson

Epson is the maker of professional color printing and proofing hardware including the EPSON Stylus Pro 5000. This company (located in Torrance, California) can be reached at 800-463-7766 or www.epson.com.

The emboss filter applied to an image in Photoshop.

Equilibrium

This is the maker of Debabelizer image-conversion software. Located in Sausalito, California, Equilibrium can be reached at 800-524-8651 or www.equilibrium.com.

Expression

Expression is a vector-based illustration program that incorporates more natural-looking brush and drawing techniques. It uses unique "skeletal stroke" technology to create complex and natural-looking illustrations. Transparency even allows for watercolor-like effects. Designed to complement other existing programs such as Illustrator, FreeHand, and CorelDRAW, it is a great bargain at only $149 from MetaCreations for Mac or Windows.

Extensis

This is the maker of many great plug-in products for Adobe Photoshop and QuarkXpress including Mask Pro and PhotoGraphics. Based in Portland, Oregon, Extensis can be reached at 800-796-9798 or www.extensis.com/.

feathering

To feather is to softly merge the borders of color areas, blending one edge into another.

FileMaker Inc.

Formerly Claris Corporation, this company is now a subsidiary of Apple Computer. Located in Santa Clara, California, FileMaker can be reached at 800-325-2747 or www.filemaker.com.

— *see also*   Claris Corporation

flame*   ▶ see flame* in Chapter 6, "Compositing"

FlashPix

FlashPix is an image file format recently developed by Kodak, Hewlett-Packard, Microsoft, and Live Picture. It is intended as an all-purpose, cross-platform standard for scalable digital-image storage. FlashPix attempts to solve problems inherent in formats such as JPEG and GIF, which must compromise between image size and image quality. FlashPix provides a scaleable file format that can adapt to the needs of different applications (from low-resolution monitor display and Web use to higher-resolution printing). FlashPix uses the original image data to make a series of lower-resolution versions known as levels. Each successive level has half the resolution of the preceding one (up to a minimum of 64dpi).

Applications that can use FlashPix include Adobe's PhotoDeluxe and Kai's Photo Soap. You can download a free FlashPix viewer from www.kodak.com/daihome/flashpix.

font

This term describes the style and type of lettering of ASCII characters. This usually defines such parameters as the name, size, weight, and style (Example: Helvetica 10 Bold Italic). Other type characteristics include kerning, leading, and serifs.

The most widely used font-editing software is probably Macromedia Fontagrapher for Mac and Windows. For Windows, there also is FontLab and Composer for Windows from Pyrus North America Ltd. (located in

Millersville, Maryland). You can find more information at www.pyrus.com.

Fractal Design Corp. ▶ see MetaCreations

Freehand (v8.0)

Freehand is a powerful vector-based illustration and desk-top-drawing program. Originally developed on the Macintosh platform from Aldus, it now is available from Macromedia.

FXDeko

This is a professional real-time character-generation and effects system for Windows NT from Pinnacle Systems Inc. Pinnacle can be reached at 888-484-3366 or www.pinnaclesys.com.

GCA ▶ see Graphic Communications Association

GENESISvfx

A relatively new effects plug-in package available for Adobe Photoshop (Windows 95/NT and Mac) and 3D Studio MAX, it is especially optimized for LightWave 3D running on the DEC Alpha. It provides more than 300 effects including all sorts of particles, flames, gases, lightning, and smoke, all of which are fully animatable, adjustable in 3D space, and previewed in real-time. The package is available from Positron Publishing, which can be found at www.3dgraphics.com.

GIMP

Such a deal! GIMP stands for GNU Image Manipulation Program. It is freeware used for such tasks as photo retouching, image composition, and image authoring. It comes with a full suite of painting tools, tile-based memory management so image size is limited only by available disk space, subpixel sampling for all paint tools for high-quality anti-aliasing, layers and channels, advanced-scripting capabilities, multiple undo/redo, and the capability to open a virtually unlimited number of images at one time. More than 100 plug-ins are available. GIMP is written and developed under X11 on UNIX platforms. You can find more information at www.gimp.org.

GoLive CyberStudio

This company that offers original, professional Web design and publishing software was recently purchased by Adobe. You can find more information at www.golive.com/three/cyberstudio/index.html.

Graphic Communications Association

A volunteer nonprofit membership association, the Graphic Communications Association (GCA) was formed in 1966 to apply computer technology to printing, publishing, and related industries. You can find more information at www.gca.org.

Graphic Paintbox   ▶ see Harry

Graphics Suite   ▶ see iGrafx

grayscale

A grayscale image is an image with a single 8-bit channel producing 256 (0–255) levels of gray.

greeking

Greeking is a standard typography term for simulating text in page layouts with pseudo-Latin gibberish or simple squiggly lines.

halftone

This creates the illusion of shades and colors by introducing dot pattern variations. The size and spacing of the individual dots determine the implied intermediate tones. The dots themselves do not vary in color.

Typically, in low bit depth images, a greater number of values is implied by printing the same solid tones at varying sizes relative to an original image's intensities. Dark values are represented by large dots close together; light values are implied by smaller dots farther apart. Our eyes perform "spacial integration" to blend larger areas of these varied dot patterns into an overall average value. Newspaper printing is a common use of this technique.

— *see also   Digital Halftoning* by Robert Ulichney, MIT Press 1987, ISBN 0-262-21009-6

Harry

Harry, released in 1985, was the successor to Paintbox from Quantel. Compositing and rotoscoping with disc-based image storage made this fast and interactive video paint system a huge market success. The system was beefed up to a 14,000-line-resolution-capable 35mm film version called Graphic Paintbox, which was released in 1987. It is used exclusively in the print and desktop publishing industries. You can find more information at www.quantel.com.

— *see also*   Domino, Shima-Seiki

histogram

A histogram is a graphic representation of an image's color information. This often is useful as an interactive tool for remapping an image's color ranges and values.

iGrafx

The iGrafx line includes a whole family of business graphics products from Micrografx. The Graphics Suite bundles three major products. Designer is a vector-based illustration program that is both fast and precise. Simply 3D is an easy-to-use 3D modeling, animation, and rendering package that enables quick logo design by even the novice user. Picture Publisher is a powerful image-editing tool set that now includes a full set of Web-design features. You can find more information at www.micrografx.com.

Illustrator (8.0)

One of the most established and popular vector-based illustration and design program from Adobe Systems Inc.,

An example of halftones.

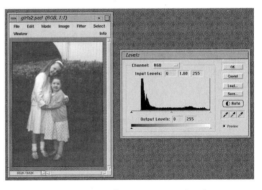

A picture and its histogram.

Version 8.0 is a major upgrade that includes unrivaled text-manipulation tools. It is available for Mac OS and Windows 95/NT. You can find more information at www.adobe.com.

— *see also* Freehand, CorelDRAW

Illuminare

Illuminare was purchased by Discreet Logic, and its software, both Composition and Paint, is now part of the effect* paint package. Both are available on Mac, Windows, and SGI O2 platforms.

Image Composer ▶ see Altamira Composer

image processing

This general term is used when a raster image's pixel values are modified in some way (such as through color correction and manipulation, sharpening, blurring, special effects filters, and so on). Image processing is the main functionality of programs such as Adobe Photoshop.

ImageReady and ImageStyler

These are Web graphics packages for the Mac available from Adobe.

Imaginator

Introduced in the early 1990s, Imaginator is Dicomed's PC-based personal workstation designed for professional photographers. It provides smooth real-time interaction with files up to 500MB! The SPORT and ULTRA models offer different capabilities at different price-points. You can find more information at www.dicomed.com/index.html.

Imapro

The maker of Windows-based image-retouching and manipulation workstations since 1976, this company was acquired by the Agfa Division of Bayer Corporation in February 1986. It is headquartered in Ottawa, Ontario, and can be reached at 613-738-3000 or www.imapro.com.

inferno*

This is the top product from Discreet Logic's family of SGI-based compositing and effects products. Its capabilities include all those of flame*, plus up to 4k (4000 lines) resolution in 8- or 12-bit-per-channel color depth. It costs about $500,000.

— *see also*   inferno* in Chapter 6, "Compositing"

Integrated Computing Engines Inc.

This is the maker of dedicated hardware and optimized software including desktop video effects accelerators such as BlueICE and ICE Finish Pack. These work with many IBM, Windows, and Mac software products such as Commotion, After Effects, and Media 100 NLE system. The company is based in Waltham, Massachusetts, and can be reached at 888-423-8447 or www.iced.com.

IntelliDraw

This is a spline-based illustration software program with unique shape blending and automatic warping and perspective features. Originally from Aldus for Mac and Windows, it was discontinued in May 1996 by Adobe, which had by then acquired Aldus. Adobe now recommends its Illustrator product instead.

Intellihance Pro 4.0

This is image-enhancement software for the Mac and Windows platforms. It is designed to provide a range of automated color-correction features to Photoshop and Corel Photo-Paint for less than $200. It is made by Extensis, which can be found at www.extensis.com.

Interactive Effects

This is the maker of Silicon Graphics-based software products such as Amazon Paint, Amazon 3D paint, Sweet 16 Paint, and Piranha Animator. The company is based in Irvine, California, and can be reached at 714-551-1448 or www.ifx.com.

Kai's Power Tools 5

A collection of surreal graphics plug-ins for Adobe Photoshop, this includes 3D lighting tools and FraxPlorer, the new update to Fractal Explorer. It has a unique and funky (if somewhat confusing) interface design by Kai Krause. It costs about $200 for both Windows and Mac platforms.

— *see also* MetaCreations

kerning ▶ see font

Layerpaint

Designed by hardware engineer Mark Leather in 1985–86 to test and demonstrate the Pixar Image Computer system, it was the first paint program to introduce the concept of layers. Three independent layers could be painted on and rearranged in any order, enabling users to paint through from one layer to another. It also had air brushing, user-definable brushes, and blur and smear tools within film-resolution images. Image size and the number of layers were only limited to what would fit in an off-screen framebuffer.

In 1988–89, Doug Smythe added a sequencing module, enabling users to very quickly jump around from one frame in a sequence to another. This also enabled users to load a previous or subsequent frame in another layer behind the frame being worked on in lock-step as users moved between frames. These features made Layerpaint ideal for many image-retouching operations.

Originally run on a Sun workstation connected to a Pixar Image Computer, Layerpaint was one of the first interactive applications written for the Pixar. Leather later ported Layerpaint to run on Silicon Graphics workstations.

A later version of Layerpaint was an important part of ILM's Digital Retouching System, which received a Science and Engineering Award in 1994.

LIBERTY® 64

This is a full 64-bit, 2.5D digital paint, animation, and compositing tool. Features include motion tracking, image stabilization, corner warping, resolution independence, and an interface to Ultimatte's Cinefusion blue screen software package. Liberty also supports the MetaCreations Final

FACTOID

The first ever digital wire removal for a feature film (*Howard The Duck*) was done at ILM using Layerpaint in 1986.

Effects plug-ins. It is resolution independent up to 8,000 lines and is available for both NT and SGI hardware platforms. Liberty HDTV is the only existing high-definition product of its kind for the SGI. Liberty costs about $5,500 from Chyron, which can be found at www.chyron.com.

Live Picture Inc.

Live Picture Inc. is the inventor of zoomable images for the Internet and the developer of a wide variety of software products for image retouching and manipulation. High-resolution images are composited in layers in almost real-time. Located in Campbell, California, Live Pictures can be reached at 800-724-7900 or www.livepicture.com.

lookup table (LUT) ▶ see lookup table in Chapter 5, "Rendering"

lpi

This stands for lines per inch. This is an infrequently used term to measure print resolution. The higher the lpi, the sharper the possible detail in an image.

— *see also*   dpi and ppi

Lumena

Time Arts' professional paint and color image-editing software for the PC was developed in partnership with John Dunn in 1983. Lumena/16 was developed in 1984 to take advantage of the AT&T TrueVision graphics board.

MacDraw

Originally available from Claris Corp. (now FileMaker Inc., a division of Apple) for the Mac, MacDraw was the first vector-based drawing software available on that platform. MacDraw Pro now features a full set of illustration and CAD tools and is available as ClarisDRAW.

— *see also*   ClarisDRAW

MacPaint

Originally available from Claris Corp. (now FileMaker Inc., a division of Apple) for the Mac, MacPaint was the first bitmap image-painting software available on that platform. It was discontinued on January 1, 1998.

Macromedia

This is the maker of Freehand 8 (the standard for illustration applications), Director 7 multimedia authoring studio, Dreamweaver for Web authoring, Flash 3 Web 2D vector graphics and animation, and Fireworks for Web graphic design. Based in San Francisco, California, Macromedia can be reached at 800-457-1774 or www.macromedia.com.

mach banding

This is an optical illusion visible at the boundary of two different surface colors. The area immediately adjacent to the boundary appears to be darker than the actual surface colors themselves. This illusion was named for Ernst Mach, an Austrian philosopher/physicist who developed many new principles in the areas of optics, mechanics, and wave dynamics.

Magic Inkwell Photomagic (4.3)

This is a Sun Solaris–based graphics software package. It works in 8- or 12-bit mode, and offers super-fast image composition, color correction, and mask generation. It is made by Magic Software Company, an ISTR Inc. business in San Mateo, California. The company can be reached at 800-455-9273 or www.qualixdirect.com/html/magiclink.html.

marquee

In software programs, the marquee is the rectangular area formed by a crawling dotted line denoting a selected part of an image.

Matador

This is digital paint and rotoscoping software available from Avid. The latest Version 7.5 includes all the resolution-independent tools for spline-based keyframable rotoscoping, painting, tracking, and multilayered animation. It was originally created and marketed by Parallax Software.

— *see also* Avid in Chapter 6, "Compositing"

MetaCard Corp.

MetaCard is the maker of graphics application development and multimedia authoring tools for UNIX, Windows, NT, and Mac. This company (located in Boulder, Colorado) can be reached at 303-447-3936 or www.metacard.com.

MetaCreations Corp.

This company was formed with the merger of Fractal Design Corp. and MetaTools Inc. in 1997. MetaCreations is the maker of Painter (5.5 Web Edition), a powerful art and design package with many new Web-creation tools for Mac OS and Windows. Other products include Painter 3D, Bryce 3D, Infini-D 4.5, RayDream Studio, and Kai's Power Tools.

MetaCreations Corp. recently teamed with Eastman Kodak and Intel to develop MetaFlash, a new 3D Web content technology. The idea is to avoid modeling an object at all. Rather, the user just takes a digital picture, and a 3D geometry mesh is created, covered with a texture map of the object from the original photo. As a boost to this effort, MetaCreations recently acquired Canoma Inc., a software company developing 2D-to-3D tools for Internet use. MetaCreations Corp. is located in Carpinteria, California, and can be reached at 888-707-6382 or www.metacreations.com.

MetaTools Inc. ▶ see MetaCreations

Micrografx Inc.

This is the maker of the iGrafx line of business graphics software products, including the Graphics Suite bundle. Since 1982, Micrografx's headquarters have been in Richardson, Texas. The company can be reached at 972-994-6525 or www.micrografx.com.

— *see also* iGrafx

Nowhouse

This is the maker of the very cool Photoshop painting and compositing plug-in tool Propeller Paint Engine. This tool uses a unique, dynamic, and patterned-based technique that is both fun to use and intuitive to learn. It costs just $59.95 for PowerMac and Windows platforms and is downloadable at www.nowhouse.com. Nowhouse is located in Santa Cruz, California.

nTitle

This is cool titling-effects software from Xaos Tools. It provides a full suite of text creation, animation, and manipulation at film-resolution quality. This product is for the SGI platform. You can find more information at www.xaostools.com.

Opaque

This is an 8-bit paint program developed as part of a multiplane animation system at Cornell University by Marc Levoy in 1976–77. It had simple anti-alias controls that worked even better when Levoy later modified the paint program to work in 24-bit depth in 1978–79. Opaque was later used for a time at Hanna Barbera for digital ink-and-paint work on their television cartoons. It was not further developed or distributed.

— *see also*   SoftCel

Pagemaker (v.6.5)

This is professional page layout and desktop publishing software for Mac and Windows from Adobe.

PageMill (3.0)

PageMill is presently the most popular Web-authoring software for the Mac. It also is available for Windows, and its WISIWYG interface is used mostly in the consumer and small business market. This Adobe product often is compared to Freeway from SoftPress Systems or the simpler ImageStyler also from Adobe.

Paint (Alvy Ray Smith)

Paint was developed as an extension of SuperPaint at the New York Institute of Technology Computer Graphics Lab from 1975–76 by Alvy Ray Smith, who had worked with Richard Shoup at Xerox PARC. Colors were available from a palette of 256 out of 68 billion (12-bit per RGB). Paint had a simple anti-aliasing capability and included tint and brightness painting as well as a new "rubber stamp" function.

Paint was expanded upon as BigPaint in 1976. It was sold to Ampex Corporation in late 1976, where it was modified to become the Ampex Video Art (AVA) system.

— *see also*   SuperPaint, BigPaint, Paint3

Paint (Tom Porter: 1981–82)

This is the first full 24-bit paint system designed specifically for feature film use with an additional 8-bit alpha channel used for compositing. It had excellent anti-aliasing and was the first paint system with sub-pixel accuracy and the capability to handle film-resolution images. Paint stored full-resolution images on disk without compression.

Paint ran on a DEC Vax 750 with an Ikonas 512×512 resolution frame buffer. It is no longer available.

Paint3

This was developed at NYIT in 1977 as a full 24-bit extension of Alvy Ray Smith's Paint and BigPaint. It relied on a trio of 8-bit Evans & Sutherland frame buffers with 512×512 resolution.

— *see also*   Paint, BigPaint and BigPaint3

Paintbox

First introduced as the "Telegraphic" system in 1981, it featured the first ever pressure-sensitive stylus and full-color selection palette instead of individual color selection areas. It was designed by Paul Kellar, Tony Searby, Richard Taylor, and Ian Walker at Quantel.

The video paint system was released commercially in 1982 as Paintbox and was based on the YIQ color space. Quantel's successor to Paintbox was Harry, which was released in 1985. Other related products include the Graphic Paintbox (the high-end, real-time workstation), the Mac-based Desktop Paintbox, and the Repro Paintbox, a real-time page-layout system. You can find more information at `www.quantel.com`.

— *see also*   Harry

Painter

This is not an image-processing program like Photoshop or an illustration program like CorelDraw. It's a superior all-around painting program dedicated to providing the very natural look and feel of brush and paint. This product is the standard by which all other digital painting programs are judged. (It even comes shipped in a real paint can!) It is

MILESTONE FACTOID

Tom Porter's Paint system was used by matte painter Chris Evans to create the clouds and terrain detail for the Genesis sequence of Star Trek II: The Wrath of Khan in 1982. This was the first use of a digital paint system for motion picture film work.

available for Mac OS, Windows, and NT. Painter 5.5 Web edition is $299, Painter Classic is only $99 (for Mac and Windows), and Painter 3D is about $300. Originally by Fractal Design Corp., it now is a product of MetaCreations Inc. You can find more information at www.metacreations.com.

Painter 3D

You can paint directly on 3D models with this affordable paint program from MetaCreations.

— *see also*   Painter

Paint Shop Pro

This is full-featured painting software available for Windows. It is available on CD for about $70 or as down-loadable shareware from Jasc Software Inc. in Eden Prairie, Minnesota. Jasc Software can be reached at 612-930-9800 or www.paintshoppro.com.

Pandemonium

This is special effects software for the SGI from Xaos Tools. It contains more than 50 different integrated effects tools for really creative compositing alternatives. You can find more information at www.xaostools.com.

Pantone Inc.

The maker of the standard, printed color-reference system for the graphics design and desktop publishing industries, Pantone also offers several color-management software programs such as ColorReady and ColorWeb Pro. This company (located in Carlstad, New Jersey) can be reached at 888-726-8663 or www.pantone.com.

PDF

Adobe's portable document format completely describes the content of a document including fonts, text layout, graphics, and illustrations. PDF might replace PostScript as the new standard, digital, prepress file-exchange format. It is full-color compatible.

PhotoDeluxe

This consumer image-editing and photo-retouching software features a wide range of special effects filters and other tools based on its professional cousin Photoshop. It is available from Adobe Inc.

PhotoDraw 2000

This is image-editing and illustration software from Microsoft. It combines painting (raster) and drawing (vector) tool sets. You can find more information at `www.microsoft.com/office/photodraw`.

PhotoEnhancer Plus

This product is primarily bundled with digital cameras that have basic image-editing features. It costs $99 from Picture Works for Mac and Windows. Located in Danville, California, Picture Works can be reached at 800-303-5400 or `www.pictureworks.com`.

PhotoFinish

This is affordable (only $40) image-editing software for the Mac and PC from the Learning Co. Paint tools, filter effects, and thousands of photos and fonts are included, as is complete digital camera and scanner support. The Learning Co. has its headquarters in Cambridge, Massachusetts, and can be reached at 617-494-1219 or `www.learningco.com`.

PhotoGraphics

Version 1.0 of the vector-illustration plug-in for Adobe Photoshop is from Extensis. It is available for Mac and Windows for about $150. You can find more information at `www.extensis.com`.

PhotoLine 32

This is a powerful, 32-bit image-editing application with both raster-painting and vector-shape tools and vector-painting software. Its many input and output formats, combined with batch capabilities, make a good file format converter. Macro recording also makes lengthy and repetitive tasks much easier.

This product is available for Windows 95/98 and NT from Computerinsel of Germany. Computerinsel can be reached at 09445 953140 +49 or www.pl132.com/.

PhotoPaint

This product from Corel Corp. features an unparalleled collection of tools for image retouching, painting, vector graphics, and text manipulation. A fully customizable menu selection also is very helpful.

— *see also*   Adobe Photoshop

Photoshop

This is the worldwide de facto standard in image processing and enhancement from Adobe. Features include layers, automated functions, color-correction and painting tools, and precise CMYK and color-separation controls. It is available for Mac, Windows, and UNIX workstations, and was originally developed by John Knoll. www.adobe.com

Photo Soap

This is photo-retouching software from Kai's (MetaCreations) for Mac and Windows. This is a really nice interface and basic tool set for only $50.

PhotoSuite

This is image-editing software from MGI Software Corporation in Richmond Hill, Ontario. This company can be reached at 888-644-7638 or www.mgisoft.com.

PhotoTools 3.0

This is a Photoshop plug-in from Extensis Corp. for cool texturing, animating, special effects, and beveling. Extensis can be reached at 800-796-9798 or www.extensis.com.

Picture It!

This is the newest Picture It! 99 photo image-editing software from Microsoft. A special effects touchup and Paint effects grouped as tools sets make for good menu organization. You can find more information at www.microsoft.com/pictureit.

PictureMaker   ▶ see Cubicomp in Chapter 4, "Animation"

Picture Publisher

Part of the Graphics Suite from Micrografx, it offers macros, special effects, and other simple tools for creating great Web graphics quickly.

— *see also*   iGrafx

Pinnacle Systems Inc.

Founded in 1986, Pinnacle makes professional DVE, effects, and compositing software including AlladinPro, FXDeko, and GeniePlus. This Mountain View, California, company can be reached at 888-484-3366, 650-526-1600, or www.pinnaclesys.com.

Piranha Animator

This is a complete 2D painting and animation system from Interactive Effects.

PixelPaint Pro

This is one of the first color painting programs for the Mac. A little bit of painting and a little bit of image processing provides editable spline paths for raster paint functions. This was available from Pixel Resources (at least until about 1995) for about $350.

pixmap

This is a raster image file with more than 8 bits per pixel.

— *see also*   bitmap

posterization

This is the result of greatly reducing the grayscale levels of an image. Severe contouring results in sudden changes between large areas of solid colors.

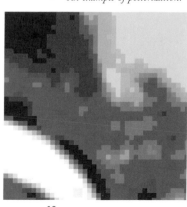

An example of posterization.

Positron

Positron is the maker of several innovative 2D and 3D texturing programs meant to compliment 3D Studio MAX and LightWave. TrU-V is a new standalone application that makes it very easy to paint and adjust 2D maps to complex 3D surfaces. TrU-Viewer is a 3D object viewer, and MeshPaint is a 3D paint program. These programs are available online at www.3dgraphics.com. Positron is located in Omaha, Nebraska, and can be reached at 402-330-7011.

PostScript

This is a file-exchange format developed in 1985 by Adobe.

Premiere

This is digital video editing software from Adobe.

presentation graphics

This is a term used to refer to corporate business presentation graphics. What used to be accomplished with overhead projectors, pie charts, and bar graphs is now a very large multimedia market. Macromedia Director is perhaps the most widely used of this type of software application.

Print House Magic 3

This is a robust but easy-to-use image-manipulation program that includes thousands of clip art pieces and photos to create dozens of projects such as greeting cards and stationery. It costs just $59 from Corel Corp.

Propeller Paint Engine   ▶ see Nowhouse

QFX

This is a high-level image-editing, painting, and photo-retouching program for DEC Alpha and Windows platforms. Written by professional photographer Ron Scott, QFX is both a raster paint and object-based drawing program, has a full batch mode, and is both multithreaded and multiprocessor capable. It is a serious alternative to Adobe Photoshop and the like. The full CD version is only $495 ($399 if you down load it online), and a free shareware version (QFX/LE) also is available online at www.qfx.com from Ron Scott Inc.

Quantel

This is the leading manufacturer of digital equipment for real-time television graphics. The name is derived from "Quantised Television." A brief history of its product line includes:

- 1982 Paintbox®: A breakthrough production of real-time electronic television graphics.

- 1983 Mirage: The world's first true, live 3D picture manipulator introduces many real-time video effects that are now standard fare in this area of graphics.

- 1985 Harry: Digital multilayering and true random-access features are introduced.

- 1986 Graphic Paintbox® : The features of Paintbox® are made available for the graphics prepress industry.

- 1989 V-Series Paintbox® : This is a major update to the popular video-industry Paintbox technology.

- 1990 Harriet: This is integrated V Series Paintbox with live video, animation, graphics, and effects.

- 1992 Hal: This is a totally self-contained digital compositing and video design environment.

- 1993 Domino: This is the all-in-one, real-time, film resolution effects and compositing system.

Henry-v8 and Henry Infinity complete video post effects editing workstations (see the Chapter 6, "Compositing" for more information on Henry and Domino systems). Quantel has headquarters in Berkshire, England, with offices worldwide. The company can be reached at www.quantel.com.

QuarkXpress
A professional page-layout program for Windows 95/98/NT and Mac from Quark Inc., it is the principal competitor to PageMaker. www.quark.com

Quark Inc.
Named after the subatomic particle, Quark was founded in 1981 by Tim Gill, who previously had written the first word processing program for the Apple III. Quark can be reached at its Denver, Colorado headquarters at 800-676-4575 or www.quark.com.

RasterOps

A developer of color video technology for graphic arts applications, it is the original parent company of Truevision.

RasterTech

This is the maker of the first "affordable" ($30,000 in 1981) full-color, 24-bit framebuffer.

RIO

Resolution Independent Objects (RIO) was desktop PC design, illustration, and presentation graphics software developed in 1986 by AT&T. RIO was the first object-based drawing application designed to work on the Truevision graphics card. It included advanced features such as 8,000×8,000 pixel resolution, anti-aliased objects, and a 32-bit image format with full alpha support. Version 7.0 was still available as late as 1996, but this software no longer is available.

rotoscope

To rotoscope is to trace the form and outline of a shape in a live-action image to isolate it in some way. Typical roto work is used for matting purposes to composite CG images behind objects in the live action or to apply some image processing to the roto'd area itself. Long a tedious frame-by-frame task, many new software packages have animatable spline-based tools for automating much of the tasks.

SatoriPaint 3.0

This is object-oriented drawing, painting, 2D graphics, and image-editing software for Windows and Alpha NT. It is one of the very few easy-to-handle bitmap and vector graphics packages available. It has a very cool workflow and feature set with several product options for all types of budgets and projects. Spaceward Graphics Ltd., the maker of this product, is located in Cambridge, England. It can be reached at 01954 261333 or www.satoripaint.com.

Shima-Seiki

This company developed the SDS-1000 Shimatronic Design System in 1981 followed by the Shima-Seiki SDS-

---

FACTOID

Shima Seiki Mfg. Ltd. was first established in 1962 to develop a fully automated glove-knitting machine.

---

380 graphics system in 1985 to compete with the Quantel Graphic Paintbox. It focused exclusively on the Japanese textile industry and cost more than $1 million. It was similar in many respects to today's Quantel Domino system with a large Hi-Def monitor and 35mm film input and output at 8k resolution. Its very fast custom hardware and 3D features also were similar to the Discrete Logic Flame systems developed 10 years later. Other CAD/CAM and design graphics systems were developed over the years, and they are still available in several configurations as the ATD-DE apparel design system. You can find more information at www.shima-seiki.com/homee.html.

SoftCel

Written at the University of Utah, Garland Stern later brought this 8-bit system with him to NYIT. Bruce Doll continued work on it there in 1979. It used a unique "press once to start painting, press again to stop" interaction paradigm and was designed more like modern digital ink-and-paint systems than a paint program.

S-Paint

S-Paint was a LISP-based 32-bit paint system designed by Craig Reynolds, Tom McMahon, Bob Coyne, and Eric Weaver at the Symbolics Graphics Division in 1983. When Symbolics hit hard times in 1992, it sold S-Paint to Triple-I, who renamed it ArkImage. Nichimen Graphics later acquired the rights and is presently marketing the paint system as N-Paint. You can find more information at www.nichimen.com.

Studiopaint 3D 4.0

This program was developed by Alias|Wavefront to be a high-resolution, highly responsive airbrush paint system for top-of-the-line SGI graphic servers. Initial high-cost markets included automotive design and industrial design applications. Later versions were designed to run on less expensive SGI workstations, although the recommended optimum platform is still the Infinite Reality Graphics of the Onyx2. You can find more information at www.aw.sgi.com.

SuperPaint

The original granddaddy paint system of them all, SuperPaint was developed by Richard Shoup from 1973 to 1975 at Xerox Palo Alto Research Center. Part of a larger system called the Color Video System, SuperPaint ran on a Data General Nova 800 graphics minicomputer using a graphics tablet for input.

The interface consisted of three display screens: two 4-bit color displays, each with a fixed resolution of 640×480 pixels,one display was used for the working area, one was for the menus. The third terminal screen was used for command-line input.

The 16 total colors were modified with hue, saturation, and brightness controls by input from newly developed stylus and tablet technology. You could erase, draw lines, create custom brushes, and use a boundary-fill function.

Although primarily a research tool, Superpaint was used in some broadcast television and government illustration projects into the late 1970s. Shoup went on to cofound Aurora Systems in 1980.

— *see also*   Paint

3D paint software

This allows traditional 2D digital painting directly on 3D geometry for more accurate placement. Popular products include Interactive Effects' Amazon 3D Paint and Alias|Wavefront's StudioPaint-3D.

3Space Publisher

This is an affordable Web graphics and animation suite for Windows from Template Graphics Software Inc. This company is located in San Diego, California and can be reached at 800-544-4847 or www.tgs.com.

TIPS

Truevision Image Processing Software was a paint program used in conjunction with Truevision's PC-based TARGA or AT-Vista boards. TIPS last release was 2.1, and it was not further developed. Truevision does still bundle copies of TIPS with old or used AT-Vista boards.

Trinity

From Play Inc., Trinity is a real-time video 2D/3D expandable effects system. You can warp, texture, and manipulate multiple real-time video sources with variable transparency, soft shadows, and reflections. It costs about $5,000 for Windows and NT. Play Inc. is located in Rancho Cordova, California and can be reached at 916-851-0800 or www.play.com.

Truevision Inc.

Pioneering makers of video graphics cards, Truevision Inc. introduced the TARGA® video graphics card for IBM PC compatibles in 1984. TARGA 2000 is a digital video-editing solution for the Windows® NT and Macintosh® operating systems. The Santa Clara, California, company was acquired by Pinnacle Systems in early 1999 in a deal worth more than $14 million. It can be reached at 800-522-8783 or www.truevision.com.

TrU-V ▶ see Positron

Ulead Systems

This is the maker of the Windows-based Cool 3D software for generating 3D text, objects, and special effects and PhotoImpact for image manipulation. This company (located in Torrance, California) can be reached at 800-858-5323 or www.ulead.com.

unsharp mask (USM)

This is a "cheat" to make it look like there is more detail in an otherwise soft image or scan.

Valis Group

The Valis Group is a publisher of award-winning 2D and 3D graphics and animation software products for Windows and Mac platforms. Flo', Metaflo', and Movieflo' enable radical manipulation of images without destroying the original image quality. This Clinton, Washington, company can be reached at 800-825-4704 or www.valisgroup.com.

VideoPaint

This is a paint and image-processing software program for the Mac that included some 3D modeling capabilities. It no longer is available. It was originally from Olduvai Corporation in Miami, Florida. The company can be reached at 305-670-1112 or www.olduvai.com.

Vignette　▶ see vignette in Chapter 6, "Compositing"

Visualizer Paint

Currently released by Alias|Wavefront with their Power Animator 3D animation system, Visualizer Paint originally was a Wavefront product based on the Barco Paint system from 1987.

wire removal　▶ see the sidebar article by Gary Jackemuk

Xaos Tools

Founded in 1990, Xaos Tools (pronounced "ka-os") develops desktop digital effects plug-ins for Windows, Macintosh, and Silicon Graphics workstation users at affordable prices (based on technology developed at the production company XAOS, Inc. in San Fransisco). Photoshop plug-ins include Total Xaos, Paint Alchemy, Terrazzo, and TypeCaster. For the SGI, Pandemonium and n/Title are in a class by themselves. The recently introduced FlashBox is a fun, easy imaging program that enables users to create their own photo reality. Xaos Tools can be reached at 415-477-9300 or www.xaostools.com/.

Zaxwerks 3D Invigorator

This is a Freehand, Illustrator, Photoshop, AfterEffects, and Alias|Wavefront Maya plug-in for generating 3D models from 2D vector artwork and illustrator files, complete with surfaces and lighting effects. Zaxwerks can be reached at 800-549-0250 or www.zaxwerks.com.

3D Construction Company

adaptive subdivision

Amapi 3D

Amorphium

Ashlar Inc.

Artisan

auto-des-sys.Inc.

axis (XYZ)

back-face culling

back face

bendy box

Bezier curve

blobby modeling

Boolean

BSP Trees

b-rep

Bryce 4

B-spline

CAD/CAM/CAE

Canoma v1.0

CATIA

centroid

child

constructive solid geometry

concave

control vertices

convex

coordinate system

coordinate space

Crystal 3D Designer

curve

cut

CV

DAG node

DaVinci 3D

deformation

double-sided

DXF

e-on

ElectricImage Inc.

ElectricImage Modeler

extrude

face

form-Z 3.0

Free form deformation

Fusion

Geometique

grid

H-splines

Hermite

hierarchy

hidden surface

IGES

IMBR

implicit surfaces

instancing

isosurface

knot

maquette

Mirai

metaballs

Nendo

NURBS

N-World

octree modeling

Modeling

In the past few years, there have been several new advancements in modeling technology. Methods such as subdivision surfaces are not new; they simply have been reinvigorated and applied to modern production methods. Other areas of modeling are truly new, coming as most new technology does[md]from university research. A good example of this is the photogrammetry software that creates 3D geometry from analyzing multiple 2D photographs by interpolating corresponding points in the different images.

Still other technologies seek to combine multiple techniques, such as UberNURBS from ElectricImage or Artisan from Alias|Wavefront, both of which make complex organic modeling simpler.

The most important thing I can say from experience is to be mindful of your data. There is a tendency to want to use all the highly detailed capability one has available now. In a real world production example, it is all too common to over-model your object. Two major considerations should be analyzed before committing to your model resolution. First consider how good your shader and painting capabilities are. Most people would be surprised at how little actual geometry you need with beautifully detailed textures and sophisticated bump and displaced shaders. The other important aspect of your modeling is how the model will be used in production. This might seem obvious, but consider the spaceship model that is only going to be used in the background, flying around smeared with motion blur. You wouldn't want the model in this case to have individual nuts and bolts built. Simple shapes and texture maps will are fine in this case.

Fortunately, new options are available (as with RenderMan v3.8) that allow multiple-resolution models to be swapped out and replaced on the fly depending on their screen size in the scene. The bigger (closer) the object is in camera, the higher the resolution model that will be used. Even the need for building multiple-resolution models is becoming less necessary, at least in polygonal-based game production. New decimation tools can take a single high-resolution model and reduce its polygon count to any level, depending on the desired scene complexity, playback speed, or detail. Of course, I do still think there is something quite pleasing about just looking at a wireframe of a well-made, highly detailed model.

TERMS

3D Construction Company

3D Construction Company makes 3D Builder, a Windows-based software tool for creating 3D objects from 2D photographs, complete with texture maps. The technique employed is generally known as photogrammetry. You can find more information at www.3dconstruction.com/.

adaptive subdivision

Adaptive subdivision is a flexible technique for tessellating spline surfaces into triangles for rendering. It is more complex than simple surface evaluation, but it reduces overall triangle/polygon count by conforming to varied surface curvature and size. The technique changes the intervals or shading rate of a surface (number of polygons) based on the patch's curvature.

Amapi 3D

This is the powerful and fast NURBS and polygon modeler formerly known as Amapi Studio and Ashlar's Design Reality. Amapi is OpenGL compatible and is a popular modeler for use with Kinetix 3D Studio MAX, ElectricImage, Strata Studio Pro, and Softimage. It is available from Template Graphics Software, which was acquired from Yonowat (www.yonowat.com/Amapi/index.html) in 1997, for Mac and Windows 95/98/NT. Template Graphics can be reached at 800-544-4847. You can find more information at www.tgs.com.

Amorphium

This 3D painting and modeling software package is available for Windows and Mac from Play Inc. It supports the Wacom Intuos graphics devices.

Artisan

Artisan is a new feature within the Alias|Wavefront Maya 3D environment that enables a modeler to paint cluster weights and deform geometry with 3D brush strokes directly on a 3D CG model. It is a very fast and intuitive way to create organic shapes. You can find more information at www.aw.sgi.com/.

Ashlar Inc.

Ashlar Inc. makes professional 2D and 3D CAD/CAM modeling, surfacing, and rendering software for industrial design applications. The company was founded in 1988 by Martin Newell (Ph.D., University of Utah, 1975), the creator of the famous "Utah Teapot." Its products include Vellum Draft, Vellum 3D, and Vellum Solids, which are available for both Windows and Power Mac platforms. Ashlar Inc. is located in Santa Clara, California, and can be reached at 800-877-2745. You can find more information at www.ashlar.com.

Artisan

This unique interactive modeling technology is offered by Alias|Wavefront for the Maya interface. It is ideally suited for sculpting detailed organic models in a very short amount of time. You also can use Artisan to select goal weights for defining rigidity on surfaces such as cloth or for creating and defining texture maps on polygon objects. You can find more information at www.aw.sgi.com.

auto-des-sys.Inc.

This company makes form-Z modeling software and can be reached at 614-488-8838. You can find more information at www.autodessys.com.

axis (XYZ)

An axis is the orientation reference of an object or a space. The way to describe "which way is which" usually is with the notations X, Y, or Z.

— *see also*   coordinate system

back-face culling ▶ see back face

back face

A polygon's back face is the surface normal that faces away from the camera and is completely occluded by other polygons. It can be removed from a scene to speed up further calculation by a process called back-face culling.

bendy box

This term is slang for free-form deformation matrix tool.

Bézier curve

This type of cubic polynomial curve was first described by Pierre Bézier in 1970. It is defined by four total points, two end points along with two additional points that control the end vectors.

— *see also* curve, Hermite

blobby modeling (blobbies)

Unlike geometry based on some basic primitive shape or polygon form, mathematically described implicit surfaces (or isosurfaces) are the basis for what generally is called potential function modeling. First described by Jim Blinn for Carl Sagan's *Cosmos* television series, Blinn's blobby molecules were based on simulating electron density fields. Specifically, Blinn used the superposition of Gaussian potentials (representing individual atoms) to define a surface. Blobby modeling also has been further developed into variations of this technique, most famously as metaballs at Toyo Links in Japan.

— *see also* metaballs, potential function modeling

Boolean

Named for English mathematician George Boole (1815–1864), these rules govern the functions of logical (true/false) operations. The OR operator is the union, AND is the intersection, NOT is minus, and XOR is exclusive.

— *see also* constructive solid geometry

BSP Trees

Binary Space Subdivision Trees are a preprocessing technique for polygon scenes used to speed up raytracing, solid modeling, and other visible surface calculations. The BSP technique was first introduced in 1980 by Henry Fuchs, Zvi M. Kedem, and Bruce F. Naylor in their paper "On Visible Surface Generation by a Priori Tree Structures." BSP is a generalization of octree spatial-partitioning.

b-rep

This stands for boundary representation, meaning to describe an object by its edges, faces, and vertices as with patches or polygons (as opposed to solid modeling, which describes an object by its volume).

Bryce 4

This 3D landscape and terrain design and rendering software is available for Windows or Mac from MetaCreations. You can find more information at www5.metacreations.com/products/bryce4/B4nav.cfm.

B-spline

Short for "basis-spline," this concept was first described by Rich Riesenfeld at Syracuse in 1973. B-splines have local control and are faster to computer than cubic polynomial curves such as Hermite and Bezier. Uniform B-splines have equally spaced knots. They can be rational and nonrational.

CAD/CAM/CAE

These acronyms stand for Computer Aided Design, Computer Aided Manufacturing, and Computer Aided Engineering. An example of an inexpensive PC-level CAD/CAM program is Claris CAD for the Mac. Other, higher-end CAD/CAM packages include Parametric Technology's Pro/Engineer, SDRC's I-DEAS, and Dassault Systemes' CATIA.

— *see also* AutoCAD, CATIA

CAID

CAID stand for Computer Aided Industrial Design. The term is used synonymously with CAD.

— *see also* CAD/CAM/CAE

Canoma v1.0

This new software product enables users to quickly create realistic 3D models from photographs. Its applications include Web content, game development, interior design, and graphics design. It is newly available this year from MetaCreations for Power Mac (OS8) and Windows. You can find more information at www5.metacreations.com/products/canoma/.

CATIA

The Computer Aided Three-dimensional Interactive Application is a powerful and widely used CAD (computer aided design) package. CATIA was created by Dassault Systemes of France and is marketed in the United States by IBM. CATIA is available on the UNIX and Windows NT platforms. You can find more information at www.dsweb.com/ and www.catia.ibm.com/catmain.html.

centroid

The center of mass in an object of uniform density is called the centroid.

child

An object or node grouped below or under another object or node is called the child. The higher node is called the parent.

constructive solid geometry (CSG)

CSG is the modeling of whole objects, not just surfaces. It sometimes is referred to as Boolean modeling because objects are created by the application of Boolean operations on simple primitive solids. It also is called solid modeling. This technique was used uniquely in production by Magi/Synthavision, particularly in their work on the movie *TRON*. This same code was then taken and used at Blue Sky when the company was founded by Magi employees. Otherwise, CSG is only used in some industrial CAD/CAM applications.

concave

A concave surface is curved inward like a dent in a surface. This is the opposite of convex.

control vertices

Control vertices are the points by which one describes and modifies a spline or patch.

convex

A convex surface is curved outward like the exterior of a sphere's surface. This is the opposite of concave.

coordinate system

A local coordinate system (also called a modeling or object coordinate system) is restricted to an individual entity within a scene (a node, an object, a light, and so on).

- The worldspace coordinate system defines the entire 3D scene.

- The camera-coordinate system (also called the eye-coordinate or view-reference coordinate system) is sometimes left-handed. This means the Z-axis increments are increasingly positive when going away from us.

- The screen-coordinate system (also called the raster-coordinate or device-coordinate system) is the final 2D projection of the 3D world that we see displayed on our screen.

coordinate space

Coordinate space is another name for coordinate system.
— *see also*   right hand rule, Cartesian

Crystal 3D Designer

You can model and render realistic images easily with this Windows product from Crystal Graphics. It essentially is Crystal TOPAS without the animation capability. You can find more information at www.crystalgraphics.com.

curve

A curve is a line defined by two or more points. It is used to define the edges of patches, to form surfaces of models, or to guide the direction of an object's translation. Types of curves include:

1. Hermite: These curves are defined by two end points and their tangents.

2. Bézier: These curves are simpler to calculate than a B-spline. End-point tangents are modified by the use of two additional control points that do not lie on the spline itself.

3. B-spline: These curves come in uniform and nonuniform types and include NURBS (nonuniform rational B-splines).

cut

To cut is to break one patch into two patches along a span. This differs from a trim, which can define a cut across any arbitrary line on a surface. When trimmed, a patch does not actually become two halves of the whole; rather, it becomes two duplicates of the entire original surface. Each of the duplicates is then represented by the new bounded area defined by the trim curve, all the while retaining the representation of the original whole. This way, all the separate pieces of a trimmed patch can always be "untrimmed" back to the original shape.

CV ▶ see control vertex

DAG node

This stands for Directed Acyclic Graph node, which is a fancy term for a parent and child-grouped hierarchy.

DaVinci 3D

This new, advanced modeling plug-in for 3D Studio MAX introduces a new technique called TEMS, which combines features of NURBS and polygonal tools. It is available from

New Technologies Inc. You can find more information at www.davinci3d.com.

deformation

To deform is to change a model's shape through means other than basic modeling. Deformations can be applied by forces such as gravity or through controlling forms such as a bendy box or curve lattice.

double-sided

Double-sided geometry usually means the surfaces will be split in two groups of rendering primitives: one with normals attached to the direction of the surface normal, and one with normals facing the other way (back facing). Both sides of the polygon or patch will render. Ordinarily, only the side with the surface normals facing toward the camera will render. This most often is needed when both sides of the same patch are seen simultaneously, as in rendering an open sphere.

DXF

The Drawing Exchange Format is a polygonal geometric file format developed by Autodesk, Inc.

e-on

This company makes the low-cost but powerful Vue d'Esprit 2 3D landscape software including the Mover 2 plug-in. This software creates realistic vegetation and natural effects. The company is located in Paris, France, and can be reached at 33-14-314-2815. You can find ore information at www.e-onsoftware.com.

ElectricImage Inc.

Originally founded by Jay Roth, Mark Granger, and Markus Houy, the ElectricImage 3D animation software led a revolution in low-cost, high-speed, high-quality 3D animation and rendering. In fact, the first ever PC-based visual effects for a major motion picture were done for *Terminator 2: Judgment Day* (a scene of Los Angeles being destroyed by a nuclear explosion). Play Incorporated merged with EI in April of 1998. Electric Image is located in Pasadena, California, and can be reached at 714-556-0333. You can find more information at www.electricimage.com.

ElectricImage Modeler

This is part of the ElectricImage Animation system 2.9 for the Mac. It includes an interactive hybrid solids and surface modeler called UberNURBS, which makes molding organic surfaces very fast and easy. It also has a full complement of Boolean, trim-like "Knife" tools and subdivision surfaces.

extrude

To extrude is to create a surface by defining a cross section and a path length. It is a simple form of sweep.

face

A face is a flat, usually polygonal primitive that might be one component of a larger surface.

form-Z 3.0

This is a professional modeling package for the DEC Alpha, Windows 95/NT, and Mac platforms from auto-des-sys, Inc. The newest version 3.0 includes a fully customizable interface and new animation controls. For the most advanced rendering images possible, upgrade to form-Z RenderZone (raytracing) or form-Z RadioZity (radiosity). This package is compatible with both OpenGL and Apples's QuickDraw 3D hardware acceleration. Located in Columbus, Ohio, auto-des-sys, Inc. can be reached at 614-488-8838. You can find more information at www.formz.com.

Free form deformation (FFD)

This is a technique where complex objects are created by deforming simpler primitives.

Fusion

This is a 3D surface blending technology for the PiXELS 3D software package by Pixels.

— *see also*   PiXELS 3D

Geometique

This brand-new, standalone 3D subdivision surface modeler for Windows NT is OpenGL-compatible and is available online at www.geometique.com. You can email inquiries to hinderman@we.mediaone.net.

grid

A grid is a visual reference comprising a right-angle series of lines. Grid-snap restricts movement to only the intersections of these lines.

— *see also*   snap

H-splines

This new type of curve technology is used by Radical Entertainment of Vancouver, British Columbia. It is supposed to allow for increased local detail and overall scalable detail. Commercial application comes by way of Radical's Ronin software product for 3D Studio MAX. You can find more information at www.hspline.com or www.radical.ca.

Hermite

This simple, parametric cubic curve representation was named for the mathematician Charles Hermite (1822–1901).

— *see also*   curve

hierarchy

A hierarchy is the nested grouping of objects in a scene that defines dependencies of translation, rotation, and scale. An object node grouped above another is called the parent; the node below is called the child.

hidden surface

The hidden surface is the portion of an object not seen by the camera's current view. Hidden surfaces usually are instructed by the renderer not to be calculated in the final raster picture.

IGES

IGES stands for Initial Graphics Exchange Specification, a standard spline-based geometric file format.

IMBR

IMBR stands for Image-Based Modeling and Rendering.

implicit surfaces

This type of modeling description is more commonly known as blobby or metaball. It is distinguished by the type of field function.

instancing

Instancing means making a virtual copy of an object. The new object basically is a "mirrored ghost" that cannot be modified directly; rather, it is updated with changes made to the original. Instanced copies typically can only be translated and rotated (and sometimes scaled), and they also typically must retain all the original's shader and material values.

isosurface

An isosurface is a surface of constant value in a 3D scalar field. As in isoparametric and isoparm, iso- means at a constant value. Scientific visualization usage of isosurfaces techniques is a way to visualize data results of the same value in a larger sample. A point cloud of topographical elevation data, for example, might have an isosurface displayed to correspond to a given height. Varying the function that defines the data (point cloud) likewise changes the isosurface.

knot

A knot is the join point between segments (and endpoints) of a B-spline curve.

maquette

Pronounced "mak-ette," this small-scale model is used as an artist's reference. Having a real object to hold in your hands and to see from any angle is a real advantage when modeling, animating, and painting a CG object.

Mirai ▶ see Nichimen Graphics

metaballs

Metaballs is the more recent and popular term for blobby or implicit surface modeling advanced by the Japanese company Links, Osaka University, and the artist Yoichiro

Kawaguchi. Current PC software examples include Clay Studio Pro by Digimation, a plug-in for 3D Studio MAX, and Blubble for Ray Dream Studio from RAYflect. You can find more information at www.rayflect.com.

Nendo

Such a deal! This amazing polygonal modeling and 3D painting package is available for only $99 from Nichimen. For beginners and professional alike, this package is available for Windows and Sun Solaris platforms. For more information, you can email sales@nichimen.com or go to the Web site www.nichimen.com.

NURBS

NURBS stands for nonuniform rational B-spline. A special class of B-splines were first made commercially available in Alias and many CAD/CAM software systems. NURBS give very complex control to the user, resulting in more accurate and complex surfaces than with other representations.

N-World

This is Nichimen's game-production software, which the company recently replaced with its new Mirai product.

octree modeling

This type of modeling technique is used to store 3D volumetric data.

— *see also* BSP, quadtrees

origin

The origin is the default place where an object is first created with no transforms applied. It has a coordinate of "zero-zero-zero" (0,0,0) in an X,Y,Z worldspace system.

patch

A patch is a four-sided 3D geometric surface formed by splines to which materials are assigned.

Patchdance

Such a deal! This shareware modeling software by Paul Sexton is available for the Power Mac platform. It is a powerful spline-based modeler that exports numerous formats, including for the POV-Raytracer. You can download the full version for only $75 from www.patchdance.com.

photogrammetry

This is the process by which a textured 3D CG object is created by analyzing 2D photographs. Commercial products include 3D Builder from the 3D Construction Company and PhotoModeler from Eos Systems Inc.

PhotoModeler

PhotoModeler is a Windows-based software tool for measuring real objects and scenes from 2D photographs and automatically creating 3D CG textured objects. The technique employed generally is known as photogrammetry. It was developed by Eos Systems Inc., which can be reached at 604-732-6658. You can find more information at www.photomodeler.com/.

pivot point

The pivot point is the point at which an object will rotate about in three dimensions. Translations and scales applied to an object also center about this point.

point

This is a discrete point in space defined in 2D by two numbers (X,Y) and in 3D by three numbers (X,Y,Z). A minimum of two points makes a line.

polyhedra

A polyhedra is a multi-sided polygon.

polyline

End-to-end vector primitives connected at their endpoints make a polyline.

polygon

A polygon is a closed-loop polyline composed of at least three vertices and three edges. A four-point polygon is called a quad.

polygon mesh

A polygon mesh is a surface described with numerous connecting polygons. Accurate representation of curved surfaces requires a very high number of polygons. Even then, they achieve only an approximation of the desired curve.

potential function modeling

This is commonly referred to as blobbies.

primitive

These basic modeling forms often come as part of a library of shapes with standard 3D software packages. Examples of primitives are cubes, cylinders, and spheres.

procedural

Generated by program or mathematical function, procedures can be used in modeling, texture mapping, animation, and of course, rendering.

quad ▶ see polygon

Rhino

Rhino is a superb and cost-effective NURBS modeler from Robert McNeel & Associates. The software offers a huge set of tools including Booleans and trims. It also offers a large array of export settings that allow for easy use with just about any file format including the venerable IGES and DXF as well as Softimage and Alias|Wavefront formats. This is available as Rhino Beta freeware on the Web. The full commercial version is only $795 ($195 for students). You can find more information at www.rhino3d.com.

scaling

To scale is to change an object's size about some defined center. An equal scaling in all three axes is called proportional scaling. A nonequal scaling is called nonproportional scaling.

skinning

To skin is to create a patch by interpolating between two or more splines.

solid modeling

Solid modeling means representing an object by a volume as opposed to a surface. This commonly is combined and created with Boolean set operations.

— *see also*   Magi/Synthavision

solidThinking

This is a NURBS-based 3D modeling and rendering software for Sun SPARC and Windows platforms. It is marketed for a wide variety of applications including industrial design, architecture, and multimedia. It has an excellent standalone renderer or can be imported to packages such as Lightwave and Alias|Wavefront's Maya. It is available from Gestel Corp., which is located in Vicenza, Italy, and can be reached at 39 0444 99 11 00. You can find more information at www.gestel.com.

spatial-occupancy enumeration

This type of spatial-partitioning/cell decomposition uses the voxel as its most fundamental unit. It commonly is used in medical applications to represent 3D volumes of scanned data.

— *see also*   octrees

spatial subdivision ▶ see voxels

spline

A spline is a curve defined by a mathematical function (as opposed to a polyline, which is defined by two endpoints). Many different kinds of splines have been developed over the years in the hopes of having better representation of form and easier manipulation. Some examples of splines include Bézier, B-spline, Hermite, and nonuniform rational B-splines (NURBS).

subdivision surfaces

The first subdivision surfaces were created by Ed Catmull and Jim Clark while they were students at the University of Utah in 1978. Tony DeRose (now a senior scientist at Pixar and previously a professor of computer science at the University of Washington) joined Catmull and developed subdivision surfaces for the short film *Geri's Game* in 1997.

A type of subdivided surface (called a MetaForm) was actually implemented in NewTek's LightWave a few years ago.

— *see also*   Geometique

Note

For more details about subdivision surfaces, see:

"Recursively Generated B-spline Surfaces on Arbitrary Topological Meshes." *Computer Aided Design*, 10(6), 1978.

The technical paper from the SIG-GRAPH/93 conference proceedings: "Efficient, Fair Interpolation Using Catmull-Clark Surfaces," by Mark Halstead, Michael Kass, and Tony DeRose.

surface modeling

Surface modeling is a step up from wireframes, but it is not as accurate as solid models. Surface models are composed of polygons, curved patches, or spline patches. Explicit surfaces list all patches composing that surface. Implicit surfaces are described by mathematical functions. Some types of patches are quadradic, biquadratic, or bicubic.

— *see also*   isosurface, modeling, NURBS, B-spline

sweep

This is an extension of the simpler extrude function. A surface is defined by passing one curve along one or more guide curves.

teapot ▶ see Utah teapot

tessellation (also called splitting/dicing/subdividing)

To tessellate is to transform a spline-based patch into a polygonal mesh (or triangles or micro-polygons and so on) to perform shading calculation to the surface.

— *see also*   adaptive subdivision

transformations

To transform is to apply a translation, scaling, or rotation to an object. It is "transformed" to another state different from its present one.

trim ▶ see cut

Utah teapot

The Utal teapot was designed by Martin Newall at the University of Utah in 1976. The original geometrical data can be found at www.cs.utah.edu/projects/alpha1/local/man/html/model_repo/model_teapot/model_teapot.html. In 1992, Hank Driskill got the idea to make a modern trimmed-NURBS solid model of the Utah teapot.

This was featured (with the addition of *Star Trek*-like warp nacelles) on his SIGGRAPH T-shirt contest winning "Utah, the Next Generation" T-shirts. The original teapot is now in the Computer Museum in Boston.

— *see also* Chapter 11, "Computer Graphics Time Line," under 1976 for more details

U & V coordinates

These two surface directional descriptors are used, among other things, to place texture maps.

Vellum Draft

This mechanical design detailing software from Ashlar Inc. uses the classic Vellum interface for powerful 2D wireframe modeling. You can find more information at `www.ashlar.com/Products/Draft/draft.html`.

Vellum Solids

Vellum Solids is a unique and powerful industrial design hybrid surface and solid modeling software from Ashlar Inc. It is available for Windows and Power Mac platforms. You can find more information at `www.ashlar.com/Products/Solids/solids.html`.

VersaCAD

This fully programmable CAD software package is available for both Mac and PC. Versacad Corp. was purchased by Prime Computer in 1987. Prime then purchased two additional CAD companies, Computervision and Calma. VersaCAD, the product, later became part of Computervision when it was spun off as an independent company. In early 1998, Computervision was purchased by Parametric Technology Corp. At this moment, VersaCAD is owned by PTC. You can find more information at `www.archwaysystems.com/Versacad.htm`.

vector primitive

Vector primitive is another name for a line segment. This should not be confused with a vector.

Viewpoint Datalabs

Viewpoint Datalabs is a provider of prebuilt and custom-built 3D CG models and textures for commercial use. It is now known as Viewpoint Digital after being acquired by Computer Associates International, Inc. in October 1998. Located in Salt Lake City, Utah, Viewpoint Digital can be reached at 801-229-3000. You can find more information at www.viewpoint.com.

voxel

A voxel is a 3D discrete, indivisible "volume element" used to approximate and encode an object. It's like a 3D pixel in spatial-occupancy enumeration.

wireframe

A wireframe model shows only the polygon edges or spline patch hulls of objects with no surfaces at all. This is the usual display mode of an interactive modeling system. It is like seeing a ball made out of chicken wire.

World Construction Set

This plug-in from Questar lets users create, animate, and render 3D terrain and trees for use with such packages as LightWave 3D and 3D Studio MAX. You can find more information at www.questarproductions.com.

xform

This is shorthand for transforming an object in some way.

— *see also* transformations

Nichimen Graphics

nodal point

nodal point offset

particle system

path animation

performance anima-
tion

PiXELS 3D

Play Inc.

previsualization

Prisms

RayDream Studio 5

rigid body dynamics/
simulation/animation

right-hand rule

Shade
Professional/Personal

shape deformation

skeleton

slope

slow-in/slow-out

Softimage|3D 3.8

sprite

squash and stretch

stop motion

Strata Inc.

strobing

StudioPro 2.5

Sumatra

Symbolics

tangent

TDI

temporal aliasing

TGS Corp.

Thomson Digital
Image

TicTacToon

timeline

Toon Boom
Technologies Inc.

Topas

trueSpace 4.0

USAnimation

Vertigo

Video Toaster

Virtus Corp.

Vision3d 5.0

Waldo

Xara 3D

ZapIt!

Animation

A purist definition of animation is "to give life to." In a simpler sense, it means changing something over time, whether a character's posing or a color value in a shader.

In computer graphics, animation often is accomplished with one of two main techniques: procedural or keyframe. Procedural animation is generating motion through mathematical or rule-based languages. Recent feature-film examples include the tornadoes in the movie *Twister*, the water in *Deep Impact*, and the sand in *The Mummy*, for which Technical Directors defined complex rules to control the behavior of thousands of particles. These rules can be based on accurate physical principles, or they can be "faked" to skew towards a particular desired effect. After these rules are started, the simulation runs its course, creating on its own the effects desired by the artists. This "fire and forget" technique often results in a very different outcome than what was intended. This necessitates changing the rules and rerunning the simulation. When done well, procedural animation adds a sense of complex realism that is all but impossible with any other means.

In traditional keyframe animation, you set values for a given attribute you want to animate and then let the computer create curves that join successive keyframes. At any arbitrary point along that curve between these keys, the computer evaluates the curve to resolve a value. Most often, the whole-number frames are used to generate the beauty pass of the image; the intermediate frames (0.5, 1.5, and so on) are used to calculate motion blur.

These two methods differ fundamentally from most other traditional forms of animation such as stop-motion or cel, which requires the animator to pose or draw every single successive frame one at a time from start to finish.

TRADITIONAL ANIMATION TIPS AND TRICKS

Many excellent books have been written about bringing drawings (or CG) to life through animation. There is still no substitute for the classic text *Disney's Illusion of Life* for a thorough discussion about traditional principles of animation.

Memorize this book and keep it close for reference. You'll be many steps closer to creating better-looking animation. More recently, George Maestri's *Digital Character Animation* is a great introduction to translating the same basic principles to 3D CG character animation.

It is important to remember that just setting two keyframes does not make a person an animator. It takes years of experience, loads of raw talent, and knowledge of past masters' works to begin to understand the complexities of character animation.

More than any one single thing, many subtleties must act together to truly bring a character to life. Here are a few things to keep in mind.

WEIGHT, MASS, AND INERTIA

- Does a character really seem to have the weight it is suppose to? Realistic walk cycles must have footsteps that are solid and firm, not light and floaty.

- Keep in mind the intended bulk of the object when changing its speed and direction. Watch how a butterfly flits about in quick, sudden movements. Compare this to a running elephant changing direction or to a car driving around a corner too fast. All motion is greatly dependent on the mass of the object being moved. (A fully loaded supertanker takes several miles to come to a complete stop!)

- If the rate of change for any given object is too great relative to its perceived mass, the illusion of reality is broken. This holds true for both a character waving its arm or a jet in an aerial dogfight.

- Mass and inertia are just as important when flying spaceships as they are in making a person walk. In general, the quicker something moves and changes direction, the lighter it tends to appear. (Pixar created a short animation called "Light & Heavy" for the *Sesame Street* PBS television show that perfectly illustrates this concept with little Luxo Jr. pushing balls around.)

■ When using squash and stretch to exaggerate action, always remember to conserve mass. The amount of squashing usually should equal the amount of stretching to keep a realistic feel to the action.

ANTICIPATION, OVERLAPPING ACTION, AND FOLLOW-THROUGH

■ Real objects do not instantly start or stop their actions. Rather, they do a wind up before the pitch and then settle into place. Just getting out of a chair is a great example—try it yourself. No one just stands right up. First, you put your hands on the chair arms. Then you lower your head, arch your back, and press your feet to the floor. The speed with which all this takes place also implies the age and weight of your character at the same time.

■ Any loose or dangling extremities of an object naturally continue to move after the main object has settled. A large character coming to a sudden stop has its hair, clothing, and fat belly continue to oscillate for a bit.

Cartoons can get away with breaking or exaggerating these rules for dramatic slapstick impact, but don't try this if your intent is anything other than Looney Toons!

This discussion so far is an extreme simplification of most cases. Character animation gets extremely complex as soon as any realistic motion is desired. Some techniques have been developed over the past decade or so to provide an alternative to the very time-consuming task of keyframe animating a character by hand.

Motion capture is one technique that literally captures a performer's body motions and stores them in a software package so they can be applied to the skeleton of a CG creature. Very realistic motion can be captured in this way, often in real time. This enables a performer to experiment and be directed with the knowledge that the exact actions being performed will be copied onto the CG replacement. Actual use of the final data most often requires some data filtering or cleanup to fit most precisely to a given character. Magnetic or optical

sensors most often are used to track the performer's movements, and each system has advantages and disadvantages.
(See the motion capture entry in this chapter for more
details.)

Performance animation takes the notions of motion capture
and direct input to their ultimate conclusion. Operating in
real time, a puppeteer performs as usual but with recording
devices driving a CG creature that is textured, lit, and often
even broadcast live. It simply replaces a traditional puppet
with its digital twin, allowing for all sorts of additional digital manipulations that otherwise would not be possible.

The origin of real-time characters dates back to 1986, when
Jim Henson first contracted Digital Productions to digitize
Kermit the Frog and puppet him with computers. Though
just a wireframe test, it inspired Brad deGraf and Michael
Wahrman to create the first real-time character performance,
"Mike the Talking Head", at SIGGRAPH 1988. Brad's company, Protozoa, and its founders have been leaders in the
medium ever since. A true pioneering company in the field,
Protozoa created Moxy, the first-ever live 3D character for
television. Other Protozoa projects have included the development of its ALIVE software, the creation of its Emmy
award-winning *Dev Null* show, and *Floops*, the first live 3D
episodic cartoon for the Web.

ALGORITHMIC ART VERSUS COMPUTER ANIMATION

All of the animation techniques discussed so far have
assumed conscious human control of the process. An animator or performer has a certain goal in mind, and he achieves
that goal with directions and modifications of his choosing.
Some of the very first uses of computer graphics were by
artists who took an entirely different approach. The goal for
abstract artists such as Larry Cuba and John Whitney Sr. is to
present a pure "algorithmic art form" by allowing the computer itself to directly generate the final images with little or
no additional interpretation by the human artist. The creative results come from a computer program written with
certain parameters that the artist hopes will develop interesting imagery on their own. Typically, many hours of imagery

generated this way are created, viewed, and discarded for every second of final animation. The result can be a beautiful and unique art form that constantly drifts to and from conscious design in form and motion.

TERMS

3D Studio MAX

3D Studio MAX was originally created for Autodesk by Gary Yost and was introduced by Autodesk in 1990. When Autodesk formed the Kinetix division in 1996, the product was renamed 3D Studio MAX. It has since become the world's best selling 3D animation software for the PC, with over 53,000 licenses installed by 1998.

3D Studio MAX R2 has available a powerful scripting language called MAXScript. With MAXScript, users can customize features and automate complex tasks easily. The Character Studio R2 extension combines Biped, a motion-capture and keyframe hybrid animation tool set, with Physique, a skinning and deformation system.

Extensive plug-in libraries are available from many third-party developers, including Digimation's LenZFX (www.digimation.com), PyroCluster from Cebas (www.cebas.com), procedural textures from Darkling Simulation (www.darksim.com), and SmoothMoves Panoramas from Infinite Pictures (www.smoothmove.com).

Available for Windows NT and Windows 95 from the Discreet entertainment division (formerly Kinetix) of Autodesk (San Rafael, CA). 800-879-4233. Retail cost of 3D Studio MAX R2 is $3495 US. Retail cost of Character Studio R2 is $1495 US.

3D Studio MAX R3, just announced at NAB in April of 1999, has a new customizable interface, new rebuilt renderer, and many new upgrades and features. www.3dstudio.com

3D Studio VIZ

For architects and interior designers, 3D Studio VIZ dynamically links AutoCAD .DWG files to a real-time creative visualization environment. Previously available from

Kinetix of San Francisco, California, this product is available from the Discreet entertainment division of Autodesk (San Rafael, California). Its retail cost is $1,995. You can find more information at www.3dstudio.com/3dvizr2.

Amapi Studio 3D ▶ see Amapi in Chapter 3, "Modeling"

angle of view

When setting up your CG camera, the angle of view defines how much of the 3D environment you can see. In a real camera, the angle of view is defined by a lens with a given focal length and film gauge. A wide-angle (12mm) lens has a much greater angle of view than a 200mm telephoto lens. This often is incorrectly referred to as field of view.

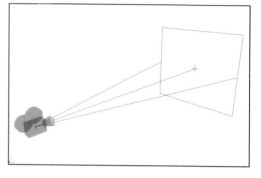

The camera's angle of view.

animatic

In its simplest form, an animatic need not be any more than a sequence of storyboard frames videotaped and edited for playback. The purpose is to give the director an idea of the overall pacing of the scene and to make judgments as to individual shot lengths and cut sequences. It is common, however, to take the concept of an animatic much further by including fully rendered 3D models and environments. It is at this stage that the simple animatic begins to take on a larger role in the area known as previsualization.

—*see also* previsualization

Animation Master (v6.1)

Such a deal! Animation Master is a 3D animation software for Windows NT from Hash Inc. It includes spline modeling, inverse kinematics (IK) animation, unique decal texture mapping, and a whole lot more for only $199, making this one of the best deals around. Animation Master 99 has added new features and increased speed to further sweeten the deal. For more information, you can contact Hash Inc. at 360-750-0042 or www.hash.com.

Animation Stand

This is an advanced cel-based digital animation system available for the Mac, SGI, and Windows NT platforms from Linker Systems in Irvine, California. For more information, you can contact Linker Systems at 949-552-1904 or www.linker.com.

ANIMATOR

Developed in 1971 at the University of Pennsylvania, ANIMATOR was used strictly as an in-house research tool.

anime

This is the term used to describe Japanese animation style. Some characteristics include highly detailed backgrounds, a live-action cinematic style, and adult themes. The best examples include *AKIRA* and *Ghost in the Machine*.

Animo

This is professional 2D cel animation, digital ink and paint, and compositing software from Cambridge Animation Systems. It is used by both Dreamworks SKG and Warner Brothers Feature Animation departments and is now available for the new SGI NT 320 and 540 workstations. You can find more information at www.animo.com.

—*see also*   AXA Animation

Ashlar's Design Reality

This is the previous name for Amapi Studio 3D animation software now available from Yonowat, which is part of the TGS company. (Confusing, isn't it?)

—*see also*   TGS

AXA

This is full-featured, professional 2D cel animation software for Windows platforms. It is available in a great basic pencil test package, a personal edition, or a full pro suite. It exports perfectly to Adobe After Effects from AXA Corp. in Yorba Linda, California. You can contact AXA Corp. at 714-974-2500 or www.axacorp.com.

ball joint

A ball joint is capable of three axes of rotational movement. When used in an inverse kinematic (IK) skeleton, a ball joint should have limits placed on its rotations to better approximate a realistic range of motion, such as when attaching an upper arm to a shoulder.

bank (camera)

To bank is to roll and translate the camera in the same direction simultaneously, as in banking a plane into a turn. This gives a more natural transition of direction to a virtual camera than rotations or translations alone.

—*see also*   camera

BBOP

This is an interactive keyframe vector animation system developed by Garland Stern at the NYIT Computer Graphics Lab in the early 1980s.

bendy box

This is a colloquial term for the 3D shape-deformation controllers found in most animation packages. This term is used because the controllers often resemble a bounding box shape used to contort or bend an object. Also called lattices or free form deformations (FFD).

BEFLIX

This is a contraction of "Bell Flicks." The BEFLIX computer-animation language was designed and used extensively at Bell Telephone Laboratories throughout the 1960s by artist Kenneth Knowlton. Others at Bell Labs created films with BEFLIX, including Stan Vanderbeek and Lillian Schwartz. The mosaic-like patterns were created with lines, dots, arcs, and curves filled with shades of gray. Resolution was a humble 252×184 pixels.

Blender

Such a deal! Blender originally was developed as an in-house tool for the animation studio NeoGeo. Not a Number (NaN) is the company founded to maintain the current Blender releases. (It also is responsible for all future development.) Blender 1.6 is available for SGI, Sun Solaris, and Linux. This amazing animation production software has many features, but here are the highlights: polygon and NURBS modeling, IK animation and shape interpolation, particle system, volumetric light effects, and up to 4K resolution output—all in an application that is only 1.5 megs! You can download it for free (yes, free) at www.neogeo.nl. A commercial version, distributed on CD-ROM, is available as of spring 1999. NaN is based in the Netherlands and can be reached at `blender@blender.nl`.

bones

Bones are individual components of a skeleton animation system using forward or inverse kinematics (IK). The bones define the rotation and translations of a character's limbs. Often, the bones themselves are controlled with constraint information derived from other handles directly manipulated by the animator.

   —*see also*   forward kinematics, inverse kinematics (IK)

Bryce 3D

Such a deal! This is a very affordable 3D animation system from MetaCreations Corp. It is hardware accelerated, has real-time previewing, and specializes in natural-phenomenon atmosphere and lighting effects, procedural landscapes, and terrain modeling with 3D volumetric textures. All this costs only $199. It is available for Windows and Mac . You can find more information at `www.metacre-ations.com/ products/bryce3d`.

Caligari Corporation

This company originally was called Octree Software Inc. when it first formed in 1986, and it offered 3D animation programs for both the Amiga and PC computer platforms. Caligari is now the maker of trueSpace, which includes an advanced modeler for polygon and NURBS as well as a high-quality rendering software. Its relatively low cost, full feature set, and flexibility make trueSpace popular with games production companies. Located in Mountain View, California, Caligari Corporation can be reached at 800-351-7620 or `www.caligari.com`.

Cambridge Animation Systems

This is the maker of Animo (2.0) for Windows NT, a professional 2D digital ink and paint animation system used in feature film and broadcast television production. The company, whose worldwide offices include Cambridge, England, can be reached at 44-1223-578-1000 or www.cam-ani.co.uk.

camera

How you see a 3D computer graphics scene is defined most simply by where your eyepoint is and where your viewpoint makes you look. The digital camera itself typically has many other parameters such as an up-vector that orients your view around the vector between the eyepoint and the viewpoint, an aspect ratio that defines the shape of your window to the scene, and an angle of view that tells how many degrees left and right you can see through that window. The camera is manipulated in one of two basic ways. The most intuitive method involves changing the position of the eyepoint or the viewpoint. Especially when working in a film environment, however, it pays to treat the virtual camera as a real camera by manipulating the entire camera model as a single group about a fixed point. By translating and rotating about this nodal point, it is much more intuitive to get realistic-looking motion. Translating toward or away from the scene is called trucking or dollying. Translating side to side or at an angle is called crabbing, and translating up or down is called craning or booming. In a Y-up world space, rotating about the Z-axis is to roll, about the X-axis is to tilt, and about the Y-axis is to pan.

The many ways you can move your camera about a scene.

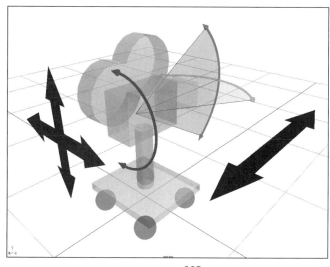

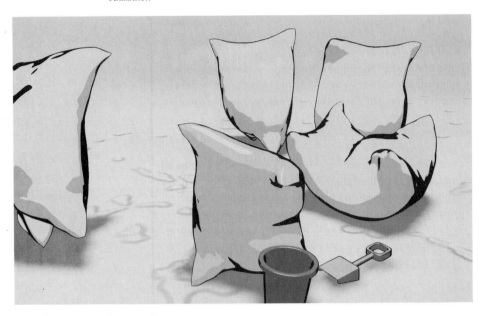

A still from Bunkie and Booboo, a short film that uses flour sacks as characters.

character animation

This general term is used to describe the realistic motion of a human, creature, or object when it is meant to appear alive. The term is used to differentiate between rigid body animation (such as flying a space ship) and procedural animation (such as a particle system). The *Luxo Jr.* lamp character in the Pixar short film and the author's flour-sacks in *Bunkie & Booboo* are just as much character animation as the dinosaurs in *Jurassic Park*.

Character Studio

This is a 3D inverse kinematics (IK) animation plug-in package from Kinetix (now the Discreet entertainment division of Autodesk, San Rafael, California). that includes Physique and Biped modules for 3D Studio MAX software.

—*see also* 3D Studio MAX

Cinema 4D

This is a full-featured, low-cost 3D modeling, animating, and rendering software originally written in 1991 for the Amiga. Since September 1996, Cinema 4D Go (entry level) and SE (standard edition) have run on Mac OS and Windows platforms. The XL (high-end) product also runs on Dec Alpha and includes a particle system and NURBS modeling. As of the end of 1998, Cinema 4D v4.0 is still made available for the Amiga. All products are known for creating beautiful, high-quality ray trace renderings at a relatively quick speed. You can get more information from Maxon (Friedrichsdorf, Germany) at www.cinema4d.com or www.maxon.de.

collision detection

This is an automatic function that detects when points of two different surfaces occupy the same space. The resulting action usually is governed with dynamic simulation to affect the surfaces in some way, such as causing two pool balls to bounce off one another.

constraints

This is to govern the motion of an object by referencing it in some way to a factor (such as the direction, position, or orientation) of another object. An example might be constraining an inverse kinematic (IK) driven arm to a tennis racket held in the hand. Moving the racket automatically affects the translation of the chain up to the shoulder joint point.

Crystal Graphics

This is a 3D graphics product line for PC and Mac. Crystal3D Impact is for 3D animation Web content. It includes TOPAS, a 3D modeling, animation, and rendering package for professional broadcast animators, and FlyingFonts Pro. Located in Santa Clara, California, the company can be reached at 800-394-0700 or www.crystalgraphics.com.

Crystal 3D ▶ see Crystal Graphics

Cubicomp

Initially called Cubic Systems, Cubicomp was founded in March of 1982 by Edwin P. Berlin Jr., and Pradeep Mohan. Later in 1982 they were joined by Stephen Crane.

They created a 3D rendering and animation system consisting of a special frame buffer and software running on a PC, one of the first, fastest and cheapest available in the early 80s. They also sold the PictureMaker line of products, which had extended features for doing video animation. In the late 80s they acquired Vertigo Corp. in Vancouver, Canada. Cubicomp went out of business in 1991.

Edwin P. Berlin Jr. has a new company that is developing a next generation gaming engine. Check it out at www.secretsoftware.com.

Cubicomp PictureMaker

The Cubicomp PictureMaker was a PC-based 3D video graphics workstation used in the 1980s. Manufactured by Cubicomp/Vertigo based in Vancouver, Canada.

CyberMotion 3D-Designer

Such a deal! CyberMotion is a professional and easy-to-use 3D designing program for modeling and animating 3D objects. It features an integrated 3D modeler, an animation module, a ray tracer, and special effects such as lens flares, motion blur, depth-queuing, particle systems, volumetric lightning, and much more. It is available in a free shareware version or for $69 as the full professional product. Reinhard Epp Software is located in Bielefeld, Germany. You can find more information at www.3d-designer.com.

cycle

This refers to an animation sequence that repeats seamlessly when the last frame is followed again by the first.

deformation

To deform is to change an object's shape using some controlling force such as a bendy box, curve, worldspace axis, or skeleton chain. Deformations actually perturb the control vertices of the patches as opposed to displacement mapping, which only perturbs surface normals in the shading pass of the rendering.

Digimation

This is the preferred third-party publisher of Discreet 3D Studio MAX plug-ins. A comprehensive listing and description of plug-ins can be found online. Located in St. Rose, Louisiana, you can contact Digimation at 800-854-4496 or www.digimation.com.

Digital Input Device (DID) ▶ see Stop Motion

double buffering ▶ see double buffering in Chapter 5, "Rendering"

Dynamation

Distributed by Alias|Wavefront, this particle system software is based on original code written by Jim Hourihan, et al. It is widely used today in motion picture visual effects and animation production. Originally called "Willy" in its early development phase in 1992, it defines particle behavior by complex procedural rules rather than by keyframing. Dynamation is being fazed out of production use in favor of the integrated dynamic environment of Maya. You can find more information at www.aw.sgi.com.

dynamics or dynamic simulation

This is the definition of mathematical procedures for the description and control of complex natural behaviors. Typical particle system examples include water, smoke, and fire. It is too time consuming and costly to try to duplicate these in a realistic manner with keyframe techniques. Drawbacks to dynamic simulation include a lack of precise control over selected aspects of the simulation and computationally expensive (slow) render calculations. Dynamation, Houdini, and Maya are typical high-end animation systems capable of dynamic simulation. In soft-body dynamics, at least one of the colliding entities can deform (as in cloth simulation). Rigid-body dynamics are like pool table balls or bowling pins bouncing around. (They move and interact, but they do not deform when they collide.)

ease-in/ease-out

This refers to one of several standard or default settings for curves defining animation parameters. Also called slow-in/slow-out, the rate of change begins very slowly, speeds up, and then halfway into the range slows down again to zero out at the other keyframe.

The different ease-in/ease-out curves.

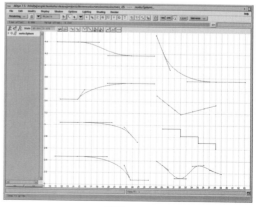

effector

An effector is the endpoint of an inverse kinematic (IK) chain that is directly translated to pose the rest of the chain. This also is called an end effector.

Electric Image 2.9

This version is less than half the price of v2.8 with many improvements and speed increases. This one product combines the previous Electric Image Animation System and Electric Image Broadcast products.

The Electric Image Modeler includes hybrid surface uses with NURBS, Boolean operations, solid/surface modeling, and the unique UberNURBS for simulated sculpting in clay.

Rendering includes many realistic lighting effects such as glows and volumetric lights, lens flares, projection maps, motion blur, and depth of field. It also is one of the fastest renderers available, even with such high quality.

Animation features include inverse kinematics (IK), function curve editing, object morphing, particle generation, and Mr. Nitro, which allows dynamic control over exploding models. Many third-party plug-ins also are available, including those from Endless Corporation (www.endlesscorp.com). LightWave project files also can easily be imported to take advantage of EI's rendering.

EI is available now on Mac platforms, and it is coming soon for Windows, SGI, and Sun Solaris. You can find more information at www.electricimage.com. It costs about $2,295 from Play Incorporated (www.play.com).

emitter

An emitter is a geometric entity that creates particles. It can be most anything including a surface, a point, or a light source.

evolutionary art

This is animation based upon simulated living systems and AI principles. Notable artists of this genre include Karl

Simms (Genetic Arts Inc.), William Latham (Computer Artworks Limited at www.artworks.co.uk and Steven Rooke.

exposure sheet

Used in traditional animation for charting timing and frame-count relationships this can also be found in some animation packages (such as Softimage and early versions of Alias). It sometimes also is called a dope sheet.

Explore

Explore was originally sold by TDI (France) until TDI software was purchased by Wavefront in 1993. Explore is now part of the Alias|Wavefront product line.

　　—*see also*　TDI

Famous

This is facial animation software. Famous Animator 1.0 works as a standalone product for NT and also has interface options for use directly within Maya, Softimage and 3DS Studio MAX. Famous supports input from all major motion capture vendors, including Motion Analysis, Vicon and X-ist. San Francisco, CA. www.famoustech.com/features.html

FiLMBOX

This is a set of powerful character-animation tool sets available from Kaydara. As a standalone product, it includes such advanced features as inverse kinematic skeletons, constraints, and expressions. Translating to and from other animation packages (such as Alias|Wavefront, LightWave, Softimage, and 3D Studio MAX) is clean, fast, and easy.

It is marketed as a base product with additional upgrade options: Capture Reality (a motion-capture suite), Cartoon Reality (real-time performance animation), Video Reality, and Voice Reality (real-time lip-synch control). This is not for the tight budget, as it costs about $30,000 for the complete package. Located in Montreal, Quebec, Canada, Kaydara can be reached at 514-842-8446 or www.kaydara.com.

flying logo

Ah, the flying logo! This is an affectionate term for the general class of broadcast 3D graphics. The majority of flying logos comprise station IDs, sports-event openers, movies of the week, and other beveled/extruded/reflecting chrome and gold letters and numbers. Until the early 1990s, this type of work comprised the vast bulk of the 3D animation market.

forward kinematics

This refers to an animation technique that requires direct rotation of each joint in a hierarchy (as opposed to inverse kinematics, which automatically drives a skeleton's chain by manipulating just one end effector). To have a human's arm reach out, rotate the elbow up first and then the wrist and finger joints with IK. Then simply grab the finger joint and position it, and the rest of the arm chain will rotate automatically.

frame rate

How many individual frames are contained in one second of animation? NTSC video has a frame rate of 30 (actually 60 fields per second), motion picture film has 24, PAL&SECAM video has 25. This usually is denoted as frames per second (fps).

frames per second (fps) ▶ see frame rate

free form deformations ▶ see deformations

function curve

This is the graph-based representation of a parameter over time; a mathematical description of some function represented in a graphical user interface (GUI) as a curve. Good software animation editing tools have extensive function curve editing tools for modifying the many underlying channels of data comprising an animation.

—see also in-betweening, keyframes

GIG Inc.

This stands for Global Information Group USA, Inc., the maker of GIG3DGO and GIGVIZ modeling, animation, and rendering software. Offices are located in New York and Amsterdam. The company can be reached at 212-246-9842, www.gig.nl/contact/index.html or by email at `info@gig.nl`.

GIG3DGO

This is 3D animation software from GIG Inc. that has many advanced modeling features such as Boolean operations, Constructive Solid Geometry (CSG) modeling, and NURBS. It also includes a particle system and a raytracing renderer. It is available for Silicon Graphics, Sun Microsystems, and Hewlett-Packard UNIX workstations as well as for Linux on Intel x86. You can find more information at `www.gig.nl/products/gig3dgo/gig3dgo.html`.

GIGVIZ

This is a 3D CAD/CAM software package from GIG Inc.

go-motion

This is not a computer graphics technique, but it's important history nonetheless. This computer-controlled playback of stop-motion animation creates the realistic motion blur not found in traditional stop-motion techniques.

handles

This term has two meanings. First, it refers to the small GUI devices that allow for interactive manipulation of a curve's tangents about a given point. Second, it refers to the extra frames at the head and tail of a motion picture shot. These frames are delivered for editing purposes, but they're seldom used. Typical handle lengths are between 4 and 9 frames.

Hash Inc.  see Animation Master

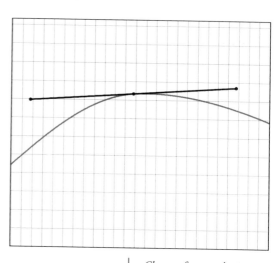

Closeup of a control point on a curve

Houdini

This is a professional 3D animation package available for both SGI and Windows NT platforms. It is based on the previous generation software Prisms from Side Effects Software. Its interface and architecture is based on the idea of "operators"—surface operators(SOPs), procedural particle operators (POPs), and channel operators (CHOPs). You can find more information at www.sidefx.com.

—see also Side Effects in Chapter 8," Historically Significant Companies"

inbetweening

This refers to the interpolation of values between two keyframes.

Infini-D (4.5)

MetaCreations developed this 3D modeling and animation software for Windows and Mac. Its advanced features include particle systems, volumetric lighting, video footage input, modeling deformation tools, and film resolution output. It costs about $600. You can find more information at www.metacreations.com.

Inspire 3D

This is a great 3D modeling, rendering, and animation program designed for graphic designers, multimedia artists, and Web designers. This is an inexpensive alternative (about $400) to LightWave 5.5 (about $1,800), both of which are from NewTek. You can find more information at www.newtek.com.

Intelligent Light

This 3D animation system ran on Apollo hardware, and had a small market in post houses and military/industrial animation. The code was originally based on that founded by a military flight simulator software company in New Jersey. The most notable company that used the software that I know of was Filigree Films in New York City.

inverse kinematics (IK)

Inverse kinematics is a method of controlling a skeleton hierarchy by means of end effectors that define goal positions for bones. This means that, to move an arm, simply have the finger or elbow move to a desired position, and the rest of the arm skeleton automatically will follow. IK contrasts traditional forward kinematics, which necessitates that individual joint rotations be applied to all levels of a hierarchy to achieve a given pose. IK not only saves time, it is much more intuitive for an animator to use.

—*see also*   forward kinematics, skeleton

joint

This is the point at which two or more bones are joined in a skeleton's hierarchy.

keyframe

This refers to setting the value of an animatable parameter at a given point (frame) in time. Setting two or more keyframes creates a curve between the two that describes the value of all the in-between frames. This in-betweening can in turn be controlled by modifying the slope of this curve through the use of tangent handles on the keyframes themselves.

Kinetix

The Discreet entertainment division of Autodesk (San Rafael, California) has its headquarters in San Francisco, California, and more than 60 other offices worldwide. (Kinetix gains about half its revenues from outside North America.) Autodesk spun off its Multimedia Markets Group as Kinetix in 1996 as an independent business unit focused on PC-based 3D graphics. In 1996, Kinetix announced the release of 3D Studio MAX, a new version of 3D Studio completely restructured for Windows NT. You can contact Kinetix at 800-225-7904 or www.ktx.com.

Lambsoft

A spin-off company of the digital production studio Lamb & Company, Lambsoft provides custom software products and plug-ins for animation systems such as LightWave 3D

115

and 3D Studio MAX. SMIRK is for facial animation, MoveTools is for translating geometry and motion data between different 3D animation software packages, and Swurve is for curve editing. Located in Minneapolis, Minnesota, Lambsoft can be reached at 800-791-0290, 800-535-5117, or www.lambsoft.com.

lattices

Lattices are simply a means to control freeform deformations. They might take the form of bounding box-like 3D meshes that surround the object to be deformed.

Life Forms 3

This is a character animation walk editor to complement Infini-D, Extreme 3D, 3D Studio Release 4, Pixel Putty, or any package that supports VRML 1.0. It has many ready-to-use models and data, including the "PowerMoves" motion capture library. Life Forms eXtension for trueSpace 4.0 enables you to import and export Life Forms data. It costs only $299 from Credo Interactive Inc., located in Greater Vancouver, BC, Canada. Credo can be reached at 604-291-6717 or www.credo-interactive.com.

—see also   Life Forms Studio 3

Life Forms Studio 3

This package combines all the basic features of Life Forms 3 with a full suite of extended options including the "PowerMoves" character-movement library. It is compatible with ElectricImage, LightWave 3D, Cinema 4DXL, Alias|Wavefront, Infini-D, Extreme 3D, 3D Studio Release 4, Pixel Putty, and any package that supports BioVision or Acclaim motion capture data or any package that supports VRML 1.0 or VRML 97. It is a real bargain at only $500 from Credo Interactive Inc.

LightWave 3D (v5.6)

This was introduced by NewTek Inc. in 1995 as a low-cost, high-quality 3D animation software included with the NewTek Video Toaster. "Skeleton Maker" is an IK-based skeletal character animation system option. An advanced character animation and motion capture plug-in is Life

Forms Studio by Credo Interactive. It also features ScreamerNet distributed rendering, which often is run on the DEC Alpha workstation. The HyperVoxels volumetric rendering plug-in runs on Windows, Mac, and UNIX. Popularized by Flat Earth Productions' work on the *Hercules* and *Xena* television shows, LightWave is available for SGI UNIX, DEC Alpha, Windows, Mac, and Sun SPARC workstations.

The next-generation version code is named "Project Purple" and is due out in April 1999. It promises even faster user interaction. You can contact NewTek Inc. at 800-847-6111 or www.newtek.com.

Martin Hash Animation Master ▶ see Animation Master

matchmoving

This refers to creating a 3D CG environment and camera to precisely match live action and CG components in a scene. The purpose most often is to match 3D objects "into" the scanned 2D background or "plate" footage. Specialized software products include "Maya Live" from Alias|Wavefront, 3D Equalizer from 4D Vision www.4dvision.com/products/3dequlzr), and the SynaFlex package from SynaPix (978-970-5300).

Maya

This is the next generation of integrated modeling, animation, and rendering software packages from Alias|Wavefront. Tool sets include inverse kinematics character animation, open architecture with high-level MEL (Maya Embedded Language) script-based controls, and plug-in capability. Advanced features include dynamics, hard- and soft-body simulation, and integrated particle systems. The "Artisan" module provides a unique brushstroke-like interface for innovative user control of many basic functions.

"Maya Complete" is the latest competitively priced package from Alias|Wavefront. It includes F/X, Artisan, Modeling, Rendering, Animating, and MEL—all for only $7,500. It is available for SGI or NT platforms. You can find more information at www.aw.sgi.com.

MetaCreations ▶ see MetaCreations in Chapter 2, "Painting and Graphic Design"

morphing

Morphing is a 2D effect that smoothly transitions between corresponding points of two different images. Some form of curve mesh is placed on arbitrary points of the two images. It then transitions the position of these points while cross-fading to the other image. This originally was described by Tom Brigham at N.Y.I.T in 1982 and was presented at SIGGRAPH that same year. The first morphing code written for use in a motion picture production was written by Doug Smythe at Industrial Light & Magic for the feature film *Willow* (1988). More recently, this term also has been used to describe 3D shape interpolation, demonstrated graphically in the feature film *Spawn*.

motion capture

This refers to precisely recording the position and movement of an actor so you can later apply that motion to a digital figure's skeleton. There are two basic types of motion capture systems: optical and magnetic. A magnetic system records both position and rotational information; an optical system only directly records positional information. (The rotational information is then interpreted from that data.) Optical systems enable complete freedom of movement, but they typically do not offer real-time performance feedback. Although earlier optical systems suffered from loss of data due to occlusion of tracking points, modern software has alleviated this concern for the most part. Conversely, magnetic systems do offer real-time data feedback but at the expense of being physically tethered to the system.

motion path

This is a spline curve used to guide an object's translation over time. The object is attached to the curve at its pivot point, which follows the curve's length over a given frame range. A railroad track is an example of a motion path for a train. To modify the path that the object travels, you simply change the shape of the curve in space without direct manipulation of the object.

> ### QUOTE
>
> "One of the most amazing pieces Triple-I produced with the Fooley F1 was the famous scene of 'Adam' or 'The Juggler.' A very primitive form of motion capture was done painstakingly, frame by frame to capture live-action footage of an actual juggler, which was then digitized and applied to Adam. In the sequence, he juggles a three-dimensional cube, cone, and sphere, and in the end, dives into his hat. For its day (1983), this was a truly amazing piece of work!"
>
> —Dave Sieg (former chief engineer of Triple-I)

NewTek Inc.

Founded in Topeka, Kansas, by Tim Jenison in 1985, NewTek introduced DigiView, a video digitizer for the Amiga, in 1986 and DigiPaint in 1987. The Video Toaster was introduced in 1990 as a production card for the Amiga PC. The two sold together for about $5,000 and offered 3D animation, 24-bit paint software, and other digital video effects. This was very popular in the early 1990s for broadcast television effects on shows such as *SeaQuest* and *Babylon 5*. Video Toaster Flyer was introduced in 1994 as an affordable, online-quality, nonlinear editing alternative. The Flyer was configured as an add-on board that worked with the Video Toaster. Other current products include Frame Factory for 2D animation and video effects on an Amiga computer. Located in San Antonio, Texas, NewTek can be contacted at 800-862-7837 or www.newtek.com.

—*see also* LightWave 3D

Nichimen Graphics

This is the maker of the popular N-World modeling and animation software and the super-cheap modeling spin-off product Nendo. Fast Track SGI is a content-creation tool for modeling, texturing, and exporting polygonal characters and scenes for consoles, PCs, VRML, or the Web.

New in 1999 is Mirai (previously codenamed Dune), an integrated 3D animation system that includes modeling, 2D and 3D painting, IK tools, and a ray tracing renderer. It mostly is marketed for the game development arena. Mirai incorporates motion-capture data software technology from Testarossa. Nichimen Graphics also are the makers of the game-development software Game Exchange 2.0, distributed with Alias|Wavefront Maya software. Early employees of Nichimen included Bob Coyne and Larry Malone from Symbolics Graphics Division. Located in Los Angeles, California, Nichimen can be reached at 310-577-0500 or www.nichimen.com.

nodal point

This is the point in a real camera that is located precisely where the focal point of the lens meets the film plane.

Ideally, it also is the point about which the camera rotates. When this isn't the case, a nodal point offset is calculated between these two points.

—*see also* camera

nodal point offset

This is the distance between a camera's nodal point and the actual point of rotation.

particle system

This is software that creates and animates particles using realistic dynamic simulation and behavior rules. Sets of terms and conditions are described for the particle to follow and react to without having the animator explicitly keyframe each particle. Dynamation is a powerful stand-alone particle system that is rapidly being replaced by the new Maya tools from Alias|Wavefront. The benefit is to be able to realistically describe the behavior of very complex systems with millions of elements such as smoke or tornadoes. Other brands do exist, however. Softimage has a particle system made by Animation Science, and many more entry-level systems are now beginning to include at least rudimentary particle system options.

path animation ▶ see motion path

performance animation

This is character animation based on real data input from motion-capture or real-time puppet devices. This was pioneered by companies such as Windlight (just closed in the spring of 1999), Protozoa, Medialab Modern Cartoons, and SimGraphics

PiXELS 3D

This is a modeling, animation, and rendering package for the Mac that is sold on a monthly subscription basis. It is offered from Pixels in San Diego, California. You can find more information at 619-220-4902 or www.pixels3d.com.

Play Inc.

Formed in 1994, its first software products included the Snappy Video Snapshot, Trinity, Gizmos98, and

SpaceCam. Play Inc. is the maker of Electric Image 2.9 and the new Amorphium. It is located in Rancho Cordova, California, and can be reached at 916-851-0900 or www.play.com.

previsualization

This refers to preplanning an animation project or a visual effects shot in a complete and accurate way, thus foreseeing problems and avoiding costly mistakes and delays. This is preferable to discovering problems later in a much more expensive production environment. If created with the correct planning and foresight (using the right software tools and utilities), the information from previsualization also can be fed directly into the production pipeline.

Sharing Information

The most common form of shared information often is camera control data used to drive motion-control cameras or miniature rigs. Robert Abel's company used computer graphics techniques to preplan and then transfer animation data to motion-control cameras for use in traditional effects work in the early 1980s. Another early example of completely integrated computer graphics previsualization was implemented in 1992 by the author for Douglas Trumbull's Luxor project in Lenox, Massachusetts. Software programs were written to transfer motion-control camera data between the motion-control PCs and the main SGI graphics workstations running Alias software. To further integrate the elements of the project, the camera and scene data was additionally converted for matchmoving use by the Kleiser Walczak Construction Company, which was providing the final 3D CG elements for the films. One member of Trumbull's Image Engineering team, Colin Green, went on to form his own company, The Pixel Liberation Front, which has specialized in providing full-service previsualization and scene planning for films such as *Judge Dredd* and *Starship Troopers*.

Prisms

This professional 3D animation system from SideFX Inc. is now marketed as Houdini.

—*see also* Houdini

RayDream Studio 5

Such a deal! This very affordable, full-featured 3D animation software is from MetaCreations. The unique "Mesh Forms" modeler enables you to manipulate geometry as if by pushing and pulling clay. You also can make photo-real, fine art, and cartoon-like rendering with the "Natural-Media" renderer that is multiprocessor-capable and really fast. Animation includes both IK and dynamics, all for about $300. The true entry-level artist or 3D novice should try RayDream 3D for only $99. Both are available for Windows and Mac.

rigid body dynamics/simulation/animation

An example of this is Reelmotion from Motion Realms. You can find more information at `www.reelmotion.com`.

—*see also*   dynamics

right-hand rule

This is the standard 3D animation and mathematical coordinate system convention of orientation. Relative to screen space, the Y-axis is "up," the X-axis is "left to right," and the Z-axis is "toward and away." Positive rotational transformations are counterclockwise when viewed along any positive axis toward the worldspace origin.

Shade Professional/Personal

This is an affordable 3D modeling, animation, and rendering software package distributed mainly for the Japanese domestic market. It features B-Spline modeling tools, ray tracing, film resolution output, and multiprocessor rendering capability. It is available for Mac and Windows from Expression Tools Inc. You can find more information at `shade.ex-tools.co.jp`.

shape deformation   ▶ see deformation

skeleton

This refers to the controlling structure an animator uses to pose a character. Named for the literal analogy when used with humanoid characters, the individual bones that make up the skeleton are repositioned in translation and rotation at different frames that in turn translate, rotate, or deform the character's surface model itself.

—*see also*   inverse kinematics (IK)

slope

This is the rate of change described by a curve over time, with the curve representing some animated parameter in a software program. A shallow or gradual slope describes a slowly changing value for that curve; a steep slope shows a more rapidly changing value. A slope of zero describes a flat line representing no change for that curve's values at that point.

—see also   tangent

slow-in/slow-out ▶ see ease-in/ease-out

Softimage|3D 3.8

This is the latest version of the popular film industry animation software from Avid. Softimage was formed in Montreal by Daniel Langlois in 1986. It was acquired first by Microsoft in 1997 and then by Avid in 1998. It contains many advanced features such as fast, inverse kinematics (IK) character animation and deformation tools, Meta-Clay modeling, dynamic and expression control, a built-in 3D paint program, camera rotoscoping, and an open plug-in architecture. A separate standalone particle system also is available. It is available for both Windows NT and SGI. Avid is located in Montreal, Quebec, Canada, and can be contacted at 800-576-3846. You can find more information at www.softimage.com.

—see also   Twister, Sumatra

sprite

This is a low-resolution raster image sequence used in multimedia games for fast refresh times and better local control over complex scenes. The images typically contain alpha or matte channel information that enables them to be composited over the background scenes.

squash and stretch

This is one of the basic key principles of animation. It describes how an object's shape should distort to create a more interesting and dynamic character. The classic bouncing ball example has the sphere striking the floor, scaling down (squashing) in Y and scaling out (stretching) in X and

Z to preserve the apparent mass. When rebounding from the surface, the sphere's scale reverses, stretching in Y and squashing in X and Z.

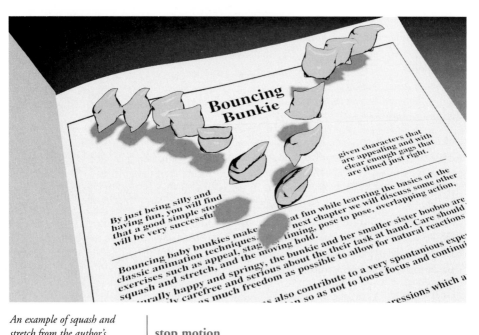

An example of squash and stretch from the author's Bunkie and Booboo *animation.*

stop motion

This is a traditional animation technique that manually positions an object slightly differently at each successive frame of exposure on film or video. When Willis O'Brian's portrayal of *King Kong* premiered March 2, 1933, stop motion began a renaissance that was carried on by his apprentice Ray Harryhausen. Harryhausen's dozens of films included *Mighty Joe Young* (the original version), *Jason And The Argonauts*, *The Seventh Voyage Of Sinbad*, and *Clash of the Titans*. More modern examples include Will Vinton's claymation California Raisins and the various productions by Skellington such as *The Nightmare before Christmas* and *James And The Giant Peach*.

Traditional stop motion techniques have transitioned the CG in the modern production environment with so-called Digital Input Devices (DIDs). First designed by Phil Tippet and Industrial Light & Magic for *Jurassic Park* in

1992, more recent commercial incarnations also have been made available by other companies. These devices are wired armatures that record the poses to computer memory where they then can be applied to a CG creature of the same proportions.

Strata Inc.

Strata Inc. is the maker of StudioPro, MediaPaint, VideoShop, and Vision3D. Sometime in 1999, Strata hopes to have all products available for Windows as well as the current Mac platforms. Formed in 1989 with headquarters in St. George, Utah, Strata Inc. can be reached at 435-628-5218 or http://strata.com.

strobing

Strobing is the jerky movement of objects in a scene due for most part to a lack of sufficient motion blur. In nature, a still frame of an object in motion appears blurred or streaked along the axis of motion. If this effect is not re-created in CG animation, each frame stands out sharply in sequence and appears to jump from position to position unnaturally. This effect is not really a jump as much as a pause in the flow of action caused by the 24 frames per second playback speed of motion picture film displaying each frame twice.

—*see also*   temporal aliasing

StudioPro 2.5

This 3D modeling, animation, and rendering software from Strata replaces the old Strata Vision3D product. It doesn't have NURBS for modeling, but it supports OpenGL and has a beautiful and quick ray tracer and radiosity renderer as well as inverse kinematics (IK) animation, volumetric shaders, and global environment effects such as gravity wind and air. A new 3D particle effects system also is included. One of the cool plug-ins is Jiggle, which can make any object wiggle like Jell-O. It costs about $1,000 and is available for Windows 98/NT and Mac . Strata was acquired by C3D Digital Inc. in early 1999. You can find more information at http://strata.com/html/studiopro.html.

Sumatra

This is the next-generation modeling and animation application from Softimage. It is intended to be a fully integrated production package including features for modeling, animating, rendering, and compositing. Currently highly anticipated vaporware.

Symbolics ▶ see Symbolics in Chapter 8, "Historically Significant Companies"

tangent

The tangent of a point on a curve describes the slope of that curve at that point. A tangent of 0.0 means no slope (or a flat curve). A practical range increasing to 1.0 describes steeper slopes for the curve. Tangents usually are controlled interactively with handles or numerical input. InTangent and OutTangent numbers must be identical for a smooth transition of the curve through the point in question. Different In and Out numbers produce a sudden jump in value for the curve at that point, as in a step curve.

TDI ▶ see Thompson Digital Images (TDI) in Chapter 8, "Historically Significant Companies"

temporal aliasing

This refers to aliasing over time. This usually is the result of too few images or samples per second. It also commonly is called strobing. The classic example is a wagon wheel that appears to turn slower or even run backwards because the number of revolutions per second is greater than the frame rate of the film.

TGS Corp.

This is the maker of a wide variety of 3D development tools and visualization software products. 3D-MasterSuite is the de facto standard interactive 3D visualization tool kit for C++ and Java developers on UNIX and PCs. 3Space Publisher is the easiest way to create stunning 2D/3D graphics for the Web and more. Amapi 3D is a low-cost, full-featured NURBS modeling software package used in conjunction with many 3D animation packages.

TGS teamed with SGI in 1995 to establish the Internet 3D standard VRML. TGS also acquired Portable Graphics, Inc. (a subsidiary of Evans & Sutherland) and Yonowat S.A. (makers of the Amapi family of desktop 3D modeling applications). TGS is a privately held company located in San Diego, California. It can be reached at 619-457-5359, www.tgs.com, or www.yonowat.com.

Thomson Digital Image ▶ see TDI

TicTacToon

This is 2D vector-based, resolution-independent animation software. It is the only paperless vector-based 2D animation system available. Animators draw directly into the system with pen and tablet control. Real-time playback, 3D perspective and multiplane controls, "lip assignment" dialog control, and digital ink and paint are just a few of its major features. It is available for the SGI platform from Toon Boom Technologies. You can find more information at www.toonboom.com/Products/TicTacTo/TicTacTo.htm.

timeline

A timeline is a graphical representation of a sequence of frames. It also usually shows some other information such as the current frame being viewed or where keyframes are placed for a given parameter in the scene.

Toon Boom Technologies Inc.

This is the maker of TicTacToon and USAnimation 2D animation software products. The company's headquarters are in Montreal, Quebec, Canada (514-278-8666), with offices in Los Angeles, California (818-954-8666). You can find more information at www.toonboom.com.

TOPAS

TOPAS is very successful early 3D animation software for the PC developed by Crystal Graphics Inc. in 1986. It still is a great product for broadcast quality, ease of use, and fast 3D animation creation. (TOPAS Professional is the full suite of tools.) Standard TOPAS v5.11 costs $399; TOPAS Professional costs $699. It is available for Windows PC

(DOS) platforms. You can find more information at www.crystalgraphics.com/products.topaspro.html.

trueSpace 4.0

Such a deal! This very affordable 3D animation software is from Caligari. It includes many advanced features such as IK character animation tools, collision detection, Metaballs, Boolean and NURBS modeling tools, hybrid radiosity rendering, film resolution output, and python scripting. trueSpace1 is $199, trueSpace2 is $395, and trueSpace4 is $595. You can find more information at www.caligari.com/products/index.html.

USAnimation

This is a vector-based, resolution-independent 2D animation system for large-scale, high-quality production volume. It is available for the SGI workstation from Toon Boom Technologies Inc. (For a fascinating history of the USAnimation company, see the Whitney/Demos Productions entry in Chapter 8, "Historically Significant Companies.") You can find more information at www.toonboom.com/Products/Usanim/Usanim.htm.

Vertigo

The 1986 Vertigo animation system was the first complete 3D animation system on the market. Vertigo was designed from the ground up to be a complete and easy-to-use animation environment for graphic artists.

In 1988, the Vertigo system was ported to run on the Silicon Graphics 4D workstations (e.g., Personal Iris), lowering the base price and increasing the number of sales. The VideoPak frame buffer was the first digital video out (D1 and D2) frame buffer for the SGI workstation, and was eventually sold to SGI (and renamed "VideoFramer").

Vertigo 9.0 as developed under the Cubicomp ownership was designed with Picturemaker in mind.

Vertigo still exists and functions on the SGI, although the Mac port was never fully completed. The company is currently redeveloping and rebuilding.

Vertigo 3D can be reached at 604-684-2113 or
www.vertigo3d.com.

—*see also* Cubicomp, as well as the Vertigo entry in the
Companies Chapter for more details.

Video Toaster

A hardware and software package available for the Amiga
PC platform, it was first released in 1990 from NewTek
Inc. This is a very affordable broadcast-quality digital
effects and animation platform used on many breakthrough
programs such as *Babylon 5* and *Space Above and Beyond*.

Virtus Corp.

This is the maker of real-time 3D environment software
such as OpenSpace 3D for the Windows versions of
Macromedia Director. Virtus Corp. can be reached at 800-
847-8871 or www.virtus.com.

Vision3d 5.0

This is a modeling, rendering, and animation package for
QuickTime VR and VRML World Wide Web content
creation from Strata. Very advanced features set in all its
operations make for an extremely cost effective and realistic
production package. It is available for Power Mac only. You can
find more information at strata.com/html/vision3d.html.

Waldo

This is a remote-control animation device first connected
to computer graphics in about 1983 when Jim Henson
contracted Brad deGraf and a team at Digital Productions
to produce a test for a 3D Kermit the Frog.

Xara 3D

This is a product used to build spinning and zooming animated text, logos, buttons, and dividers. You also can
import 2D line drawings and can build custom 3D logos
with .wmf files. Xara Webstyle is a collection of thousands
of flexible graphics templates. You can download a freeware
version or purchase the registered version for only $39 at
www.xara.com/xara3d. Xara Ltd. Is located in Hemel
Hempstead, England, and can be reached at +44 1442
350000.

FACTOID

The name "Waldo" was
applied by NASA engineers
years earlier. It refers to a
fictional scientist in a book
by Robert Heinlein from the
1940s called "Waldo &
Magic, Inc."

ZapIt!

This is a real-time animation graphics engine designed primarily for gaming use. It offers 24 or 30 fps playback on any SGI O2 platform and is available from Alias|Wavefront. You can find more information at www.sw.sgi.com.

ART
Afterburn 1.0
aliasing
alpha channel
anamorphic
Animal Logic
animated texture
anti-aliasing
aperture
articulated matte
aspect ratio
beauty pass
bit depth
bitmap
Blinn shading
blobbies
BMRT
bucket
bump mapping
camera
CAPS
cast shadow
CG
CGI
channel
clipping plane
cloth simulation

cubic environment map
depth cueing
depth of field
displacement mapping
double buffering
eccentricity
environment map
faceted shading
field
field of view
film grain
focal length
flat shading
frame
framebuffer
global illumination
Gouraud shading
hidden-line removal
hidden-surface removal
highlight
Hypervoxels 2.0
image-safe
index of refraction
interlace
interpolated shading

jaggies
Lambert
lens flare
light*
local illumination
lossless/lossy
LumeTools
mach-banding
mapping
material
mental ray
motion blur
moire pattern
multi-pass rendering
noise
normal
normal vector
natural phenomena
orthogonal
opacity
Panavision
parallel projection
POV-Ray
perspective projection
phong
photorealism
pipeline

Rendering

pixel

pixel aspect ratio

pixmap

procedural texture

projection map

Radiance

radiosity

raster

ray casting

ray tracing

reflection mapping

refraction

reflectivity

RenderGL

rendering

RenderMan

res

resolution

REYES

RGB

scan lines

shader/shading

ShadeTree

shadow

shininess

smooth shading

specular

surface attribute(s)

surface normal

teapot

temporal aliasing

tessellate

texture mapping

tiling

title-safe area

translucent

transparent

Twister

vector graphics

view-point

viewport

visible surface determination

voxel

wedge

widescreen

Xfpovray

yon

Z-buffer

zoom

Rendering is the cinematography of computer graphics, turning geometric designs, simulated lighting, and mathematical motion paths into alternate realities. With a charter like that, a little selectivity is necessary within the space of a single chapter.

This chapter does not attempt to delve into writing shader code or try to explain the mathematics behind stochastic sampling. (It makes my eyes glaze over just thinking about those things anyway.)

What it does talk about is a general history of rendering solutions, where they came from, and what their differences are. Along the way, you'll learn the key terms and concepts involved in making CG images.

The bias here will be pointing out ways to make CG images more realistic—that is, more like reality. This is the focus primarily because it is a very difficult thing to do. It helps not to think about how difficult it is to create CG images that look realistic. Rather, you should focus on how straightforward it should be, given all the reference for reality around you. (We'll sidestep the philosophical arguments here and assume that what you see around you actually *is* reality.)

Also, you should know upfront that most of what you learn from this chapter goes hand in hand with Chapter 6, "Compositing," where everything finally comes together.

Perhaps it is best to start with a list of what you do *not* see in reality and, therefore, what to avoid in CG if the end result should be realism.

- **There are no straight lines in nature**: Even if you think you see a straight line, it is better represented instead by something that is not quite so. Art school teaches you not to use a straightedge (ruler) in most cases. By drawing freehand as close to a linear edge as you can, the final result always has a much more natural look and feel. The same rule applies in 3D CG modeling or spline-based illustration. Instead of using a two-point linear polyline to define, for example, the edge of a desk, use a complex spline you draw by hand without grid-snap on. Not only does the form itself immediately begin to look less perfectly digital, the subtle perturbations continue to work for you by breaking up highlights and shadow lines.

- **There are no perfectly smooth surfaces in nature**: Go ahead, put your nose up to a window or down on the table top. Watch how light reflects off shiny surfaces, how it's affected by all the subtle imperfections, warping, and pitting. What this means for your rendering is lots of extra maps to break up those mathematically perfect planes. Bump, displacement, and specular maps all can give surfaces a more realistic character.

- **Shadows are not all created equal**: Look at any table-top collection of items with multiple light sources illuminating them. Default CG shadows all are equally dense and hard-edged. Real shadows fall off in density and sharpness as they are cast farther from an object. Like most things worth doing, soft and natural-looking shadows are expensive to calculate. Most productions cannot afford to raytrace to get them, and most productions likewise should not need to. If your object does not move relative to the light that casts the shadow, paint it as a faked texture on the surface. More often than not, scenes are not completely static, so plan B is to fake it in the comp. Use articulate mattes to isolate ramps and to soften cast-shadow elements in the composite. Look at the color of the shadow itself; it is almost never black. Rather, it simply is a darkening of whatever surface color it falls upon.

- **The real world is dirty**: George Lucas knew this when he designed the *Star Wars* world with dirty, smeared X-Wing fighters and banged-up droids. They looked battered and used, not like they just popped out of a model-shop mold. In CG, you can break up scanned textures with procedural noise functions and can paint on oil, dirt, rust, and dust maps to break up surface colors and highlights.

- **We do not live in a vacuum**: There's lots of stuff between our eyes and what we see (especially if you live in LA). The air itself, even on the clearest day, affects the color of distant objects more than those close to us. Airborne particulate interacts with light and shadow to create all sorts of subtle effects. Subtle glow effects around highlights (not just neon signs) help soften the hard-edge look of most CG rendering. Notice how black levels will change in value the greater the distance they are from the camera, gradually raising to midrange values. Sit in a large space and stare with your eyes unfocused for a quiet minute. Notice the particulate in the air and the subtle shafts of light from windows that illuminate it.

Hopefully, none of the changes you add will be very obvious by themselves. Rather, they should contribute to a subtle, almost subliminal sense of realism. The viewer should look at an image and should simply take for granted that it is real and not simulated. Of course, it helps to start with something like a tabletop still-life and not a dinosaur or a spaceship!

There are several identifiable major milestones in the refinement of creating computer-generated renderings. These can most simply be broken down into the following:

- **Wireframe**: The simple, vector graphic representation of polylines or surface patch geometry. No solid surface is visible at all.

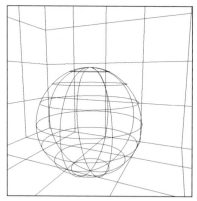

A wireframe representation of a sphere.

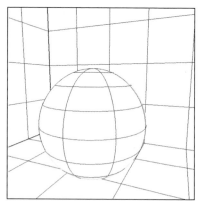

Notice now that only the front-facing surfaces are visible on the sphere.

A flat-shaded sphere with no pixel interpolation applied.

A Gouraud-shaded shpere.

Notice the highlights in this Phong-shaded sphere.

With ray tracing applied, you get reflections of the sphere's environment.

- **Hidden line**: Visible-line determination shows only the portions of an object that face you directly.

- **Surface shading**: Flat shading of one color calculation per polygon. No interpolation at all.

- **Gouraud**: Interpolates individual pixel values from each vertex illumination value.

- **Phong**: Interpolates individual pixel values from the polygon surface's normal vectors. Creates realistic specular highlights.

137

Notice how the surrounding environment affects the reflected light on the sphere.

- **Ray tracing**: Great for calculating reflections, refractions, and specular lighting.

- **Radiosity**: Great for rendering diffuse global illumination but not so good for specular light. A good compliment to ray tracing.

TERMS

A-buffer

This is A. Carpenter's further development of the Z-buffer concept in 1984 as an "anti-aliased hidden surface method." The A-buffer technique was intended to overcome the main disadvantage of Catmull's earlier Z-buffer method, which had the tendency to produce aliasing artifacts.

Advanced Rendering Technology (ART)

ART was founded in 1995 and developed the ART AR250 ray tracing chip technology that automatically calculates reflections, refractions, and soft shadows with Pixar's RenderMan shader library. ART can be reached in Mountain View, California, at 650-254-7610; in Cambridge, England, at 44-1223-563-854; and on the Web at www.art.co.uk/

Afterburn 1.0

Like Hypervoxels 2.0 for LightWave users, Afterburn works with 3D Studio MAX to render realistic volumetric effects such as smoke and fire. It is particle-based with tons of fully animatable parameters, glow effects, and dynamic forces. It is from ID8Media, which is located in San Francisco, California, and can be reached at 415-495-3930 or www.id8media.com.

aliasing

Generally not a desired effect, aliasing is a sharp difference in value along boundaries that appear as stair-stepping or blocky-looking edge artifacts. It also is called "stair-stepping" or "the jaggies." Animation with crawling edges and other aliasing artifacts screams out "bad computer graphics!" to even an inexperienced eye.

—*see also*   anti-aliasing, dithering, temporal aliasing

The X on the left is aliased and the X on the right is anti-aliased.

alpha channel ▶ see compositing, alpha channel

anamorphic

This is a theatrical film format that is optically squeezed 2:1 sideways with an anamorphic lens so that the images captured on the negative are "tall and skinny." The complimentary lens is fitted to the projector to expand the image out to create a widescreen 2.35 aspect ratio format. The process was first used in Hollywood on the 20th Century Fox film "The Robe" in 1953. The anamorphic lenses and processes would be marketed by Fox as CinemaScope and by other studios under various other "scope" names. Panavision is the trade name later used for today's most popular widescreen process developed by Panavision Inc. The term "anamorphic" is of Greek origin and means "to form anew."

Animal Logic

Animal Logic is a developer of several useful shader and plug-in software products. SoftMan is a Softimage-to-RenderMan plug-in that enables both Prman and BMRT use from within Softimage. The Shader Pack is a collection of mental ray shaders, and ALMB (Animal Logic Motion Blur) is an optional Eddie plug-in that offers an extremely rapid alternative to normal m-ray motion blur. Animal Logic is located in Sydney, Australia, and can be reached at 61-2-9906-1232 or www.animalogic.com.

animated texture

This is any texture map replaced sequentially frame by frame to convey change or movement.

anti-aliasing

This refers to any steps taken to reduce aliasing artifacts in CG imagery. The first anti-aliasing methods were developed by Frank Crow (Ph.D., University of Utah, 1975). These methods are a cure for "the jaggies." The most basic technique introduces varying shades of color between the foreground and background elements to better smooth their apparent edges.

— *see also*   aliasing, dithering

aperture

This is the opening in a camera mechanism that allows light through the lens and onto the film. The aperture setting (size) is described in f-stops (also called t-stops). The smaller the f (or t) number, the larger the opening in the aperture. The amount of light allowed to pass through increases with the size of the opening.

articulated matte   ▶   see rotoscope

aspect ratio

This is the ratio between width and height of a rectangular area, specifically a film frame or raster image. Classic motion pictures and NTSC television most often are composed and projected at an aspect ratio of 1.33:1 (also called Academy aperture). Other common present-day film aspect ratios include the 1.85:1 and 1.66:1 "flat" formats and the 2.35 anamorphic widescreen format.

— *see also*   pixel aspect ratio, anamorphic

beauty pass

1. This is a filmed element that contains the primary image information or a model lit with all the main set illumination. This is distinguished from a light pass or a reflection pass. These passes are then composited together for individual control over the final look of the shot.

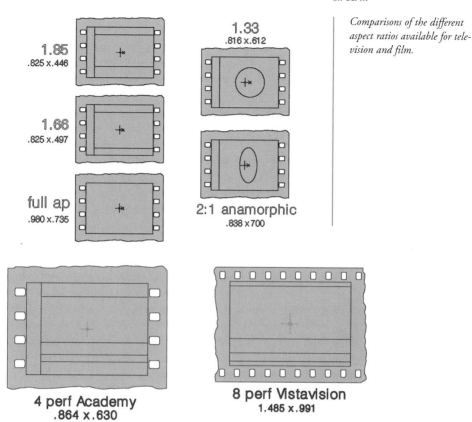

2. This is a CG element that contains the main color information of a rendering. This is distinguished when part of a multi-pass rendering method.

3. This is not to be confused with a Clean Plate.

bit depth

Also referred to as color depth, this is a logarithmic scale defining the number of colors capable of being stored in a single pixel. 1 bit = 2^1 = 2 colors (black or white), 4 bits = 2^4 = 16 colors, 8 bits = 2^8 = 256, 16 bits = 2^{16} = 65,536 colors, 24 bits = 2^{24} = 16,777,216 colors. (Notice that the number of colors is derived from calculating the number 2 raised to the number of bits.)

bitmap

This is a two-dimensional array of pixels used to store an image. This is referred to as raster graphics as opposed to vector graphics. It also is referred to as bit plane. Strictly speaking, a bitmap only has a single bit of color information per pixel, therefore it is black or white. When more than 1 bit is used per pixel, the image information is referred to as a pixmap.

Blinn shading

This is a shading method developed by James Blinn in 1977 that uses diffuse, specular, eccentricity, and refractive index attributes. Increased control over the specular component makes for good representation of metallic surfaces. The Blinn shading model was initially inspired by Phong's work at the University of Utah, and Blinn's desire to represent a more accurate specular lighting model. Blinn then spent many weeks researching extensively at the University library, discovering many papers dating back to the 1920s by an "optical illumination society". More recent work was done by Torrance and Sparrow at the University of Minnesota, but all these theories were fairly cumbersome to describe and not directly related to CG. What Blinn did was to codify the theory into a practical light reflection model that was both physically based and accurate.

The Blinn shading model was later expanded upon by Ken Torrance and Rob Cook at the University of Cornell.

blobbies

This term is a colloquial name for potential function modeling. First proposed by Jim Blinn in the ACM Transactions periodical on Graphics in July 1982. Also known as "meta-balls," the implicit surfaces are not described directly with geometric surfaces but as mathematical volumes.

BMRT

This stands for Blue Moon Rendering Tools, a shareware toolkit for rendering 3D images under the RenderMan standard. Written by Larry Gritz, BMRT is based on his work at George Washington University. (Larry currently works full-time at Pixar.)

BUMP MAP FACTOID

Jim Blinn could not initially test his new bump map code at Utah because the prototype E&S frame buffer was broken (in the fall of 1976). Because he had made some friends while at NYIT the previous summer, he flew out there on his own, during Christmas vacation, and tested a simple algorithm on one of their frame buffers. The Utah frame buffer was again working in early '77, and Jim was then able to finish and refine his technique.

BMRT supports such advanced features as ray tracing, radiosity, and area light sources as well as more standard features such as texture and environment mapping. BMRT is available for SGI, Sun SPARC, Linux, NextStep, and Windows. You can find more information at www.bmrt.org.

bucket

This is a subportion of a final rendered image's framebuffer devoted to rendering as one unit. It often is useful to subdivide an image for calculation this way. Multiprocessor rendering assigns a separate bucket to each processor, for example.

bump mapping

This is a technique for creating surface detail through surface normal perturbation. The shader function is defined by 8-bit (grayscale) data. It only perturbs surface normals and does not directly affect underlying geometry as displacement mapping does. James Blinn developed bump mapping as a graduate student at the University of Utah in the fall of 1976, publishing the technique in 1978. Blinn wanted to visualize a stylized atom as a tightly wound ball of yarn; the threads symbolizing the electron paths. As a painted texture, the threads surface still appeared smooth. The idea of perturbing surface normals came to him while looking at the rough surface of his shoes, and how the slight variation in tilted surface areas relate to the incident light angles.

A bump map applied to the sphere.

—*see also* displacement mapping

camera

The camera defines what you see of the 3D CG worldspace. What you really need to define a CG camera are four parameters: where you are looking from (the eye point), where you are looking to (the view point), the angle of view, and the aspect ratio. A definition of an up-vector also helps control how the camera is oriented about its viewing vector. (The up-vector simply defines the neutral orientation of the camera as which way is up.)

CAPS

CAPS is the Computer Animation Production System that computerizes traditional ink and paint methods and adds many multiplane animation camera techniques and effects. The digital ink and paint system was awarded a Scientific and Technical Achievement Academy Award in 1992. Seven individuals shared the award between Pixar Animation Studios and Disney. Tom Hahn, Peter Nye and Michael Shantzis of Pixar developed the scan and paint part of the system. Randy Cartwright, Lem Davis, David Coons, Mark Kimball, Jim Houston, and David Wolf of Disney developed the Disney Logistics System (DALS) component.

CAPS was first used on a single scene at the end of *The Little Mermaid* in 1989. *The Rescuers Down Under* (1990) was the first film to be produced with no traditional cells at all (making it the first all digital feature film in one respect).
— *see also* the "Computer Graphics Time Line" chapter for more details

cast shadow

Any portion of a surface occluded by another object with respect to a light source is said to have a shadow cast upon it by that occluding object. Ray tracing is the most direct way of calculating this state. More advanced methods soften a cast shadow depending on its distance relative to the occluding object for a more realistic appearance.

CG

This stands for computer graphics.

CGI

This stands for Computer Graphic Imagery.

channel

1. This is part of the information available at each pixel: Red/green/blue channel, alpha channel, and so on.

2. This is a sequence of information usually evaluated every frame and used to control some attribute of a process.

clipping plane

A clipping plane is a plane in front of the camera that defines the area evaluated for viewing and rendering operations. Parallel to the viewport, the near (hither) and far (yon) planes define the bounds of the view volume, beyond which geometry is discarded.

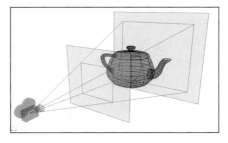

A clipping plane as shown in Maya.

cloth simulation

One of the new frontiers of realistic CG, cloth simulation was first introduced at SIGGRAPH in 1986 by Jerry Weil. The late 1990s saw some great advances in this area, particularly with subdivision surface technology from Pixar used in *Geri's Game* (the 1998 Academy Award–winning short film) and from Alias|Wavefront in their Maya commercial software. ILM also made wide use of digital cloth simulation in *Star Wars Episode I: The Phantom Menace* (May 1999).

The textures are laid out on a virtual cube, one on each side. The teapot image is placed in the middle, and the result is an environment map that conforms itself to the teapot shape.

cubic environment map

This is mapping space comprised of six textures applied to the various faces of a virtual cube. The object to receive the reflection is placed in the center of the cubic volume.

—*see also* environment map, reflection map

depth cueing

This refers to affecting the appearance of distant objects by implying the existence of an intervening atmosphere. This aids in our perceptual clues of distance and scale.

—*see also* flashing in Chapter 6, "Compositing"

depth of field

This is a traditional camera term denoting the area in front of and beyond the subject that falls within focus. To achieve a greater depth of field with a given f-stop, a smaller aperture can be used with proportionally more light added and/or a longer exposure time to compensate for less light entering the lens. Shorter focal-length (wider angle) lenses also provide greater depth of field, which is measured linearly away from the camera lens in world units such as feet.

displacement mapping

This is a technique for actually distorting surface geometry during rendering by using 8-bit grayscale map values. In displacement, mapping the profile of an object is affected as opposed to bump mapping, which only affects the appearance of the surface shader normals. This technique was developed by R. Cook in 1984.

double buffering

This is done to avoid showing a resolving image onscreen by using two display buffers. Double buffering creates a "backbuffer" or an "offscreen buffer," which holds the accumulating pixels. The display swaps the pixmap all at once only after it is complete. This way, the two alternating buffers are shown one at a time in their entirety.

Greater depth of field is realized in the image on the bottom. Notice how the smaller sphere is clear and focused in this image compared to the image on the top.

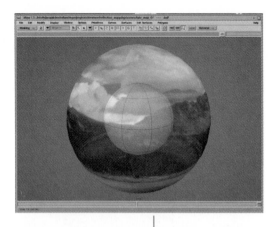

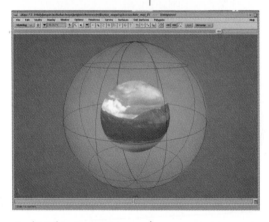

A spherical environment map is used to place a texture map onto the sphere.

eccentricity

This is an attribute of the Blinn shading model that controls specular highlight size.

—*see also*   Blinn shading

environment map

An environmental map, also known as a reflection map, can be thought of as an image surrounding an object that is used in shader calculations to simulate reflections. (The actual math basically simulates this situation.) A cubic environment map uses six different images arranged like the faces of a cube around the object; a spherical environment uses a single texture mapped onto (you guessed it!) a sphere. Environment mapping was first introduced by Jim Blinn in 1976 while a graduate student at the University of Utah. The implementation was based on an idea by his professor at that time, Martin Newell with whom he was a teaching assistant.

faceted shading

This is when the individual polygon surface components are shaded with a single color value each. The result looks something like a geodesic dome. This also is called flat shading.

—*see also*   Gouraud shading

field

1. This is a set of odd or even scan lines that comprise half a video frame. NTSC video runs at 30 frames or 60 fields per second.

2. This is a reference to a standard 12-field chart used in animation artwork and backdrops. It is used to denote a linear distance in a given frame.

—*see also*   frame

field of view

This is the area defined by the camera's angle of view at a given linear distance from the lens. Field of view very often is confused with the angle of view itself. Many commercial software packages incorrectly label angle of view parameters as field of view.

—*see also* angle of view

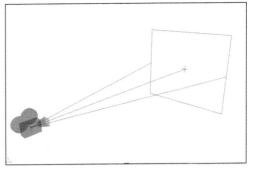

Field of view as represented in Maya.

film grain

The emulsion pattern of silver halide crystals that make up photographic film creates a distinctive-colored noise pattern under most conditions. This subtle-colored pattern must be matched in the CGI element to blend naturally with the live-action plate. The amount of apparent film grain varies with the type and speed of film used. The faster the film, the greater the size of the grain.

A close-up of a photograph, showing the film grain. Notice how the film grain is separated into its RGB channels.

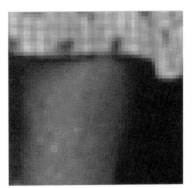
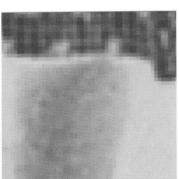

focal length

The distance between the film and the center of the main lens of a camera is measured in millimeters. The larger the focal length number, the longer the lens. A telephoto lens might be 200mm, while a fish-eye/wide-angle lens might have a 12mm focal length. The shorter focal lengths of wide-angle lenses provide a greater depth of field for a given aperture.

flat shading

This is the most basic shading method that uses only one single color per polygon. It therefore is very quick but very limited in its representation. This also is called faceted shading. A sphere rendered this way will not look smooth but rather like a geodesic dome.

frame

This refers to one raster image. One second of motion-picture imagery consists of 24 frames. One second of NTSC video signal consists of 30 frames (actually 60 fields).

—*see also*   field

framebuffer

This is the digital memory required to store and display one single frame. The first (3-bit) framebuffer was designed and built at Bell Labs in 1969. It was further developed by a team that included Jim Kajiya (Ph.D. University of Utah 1979) while at Evans & Sutherland, and it was made available as the first commercial frame buffer in 1973. The first 8-bit framebuffer was developed by Dick Shoup at Xerox PARC in 1972. This was followed in 1978 by the Ikonas framebuffer (England/Whitton). The first low-cost, color-graphics framebuffer commercially available for the PC was the TARGA board in introduced by AT&T in 1985.

The amount of memory needed for a framebuffer is the product of pixel width, pixel height, and bits per pixel plus some slight additional overhead.

global illumination

This is a significant amount of light in the real world does not come directly from a light source. Rather, it is the result of reflected and transmitted light and color from the many surfaces around us. Global illumination is a general term for specific rendering techniques, such as radiosity, that account for this natural-lighting phenomenon. Techniques such as radiosity are view independent because all the lighting calculations are computed based on the entire scene's multiple surfaces interacting as one.

These lighting models are not good at representing specular surface attributes, so they are a good compliment to local illumination models that do this well (such as ray tracing).

—*see also*   radiosity, local illumination

Gouraud shading

This interpolated shader method was developed by Henri Gouraud (Ph.D., University of Utah, 1971) to add a smooth alternative to flat shading. Although it does not affect the polygonal profile of the object, it does approximate a single continuous surface for rendering purposes.

—*see also*   interpolated shading, shader

hidden-line removal

A vector rendering technique, this only displays the portions of a wireframe model that directly face the camera. This also is called visible-line determination.

hidden-surface removal

This is the process of determining which surfaces are visible and which are occluded, or hidden, by others closer to the camera. This also is called visible-surface determination. The self-named "warnock recursive subdivision algorithms for hidden surface elimination" were developed by John Warnock (Ph.D., University of Utah, 1969).

highlight

This refers to the focused specular light component of a surface. It is dependent upon the viewing angle as well as the angle of incidence between the light and the surface.

Hypervoxels 2.0

This is a recent upgrade to an already unique volume-rendering combination of realistic natural phenomenon effects. Beautiful clouds, smoke, steam, fire, and explosions compliment blobby, viscous, liquid effects and naturalistic terrain features. Hypervoxels is available from NewTek for LightWave. This San Antonio, Texas, company can be reached at 210-370-8000 or www.newtek.com.

image-safe ▶ see title safe

index of refraction

This is the parameter in ray tracing calculations used to represent the bending of light at the boundary between two transparent media. All materials have an index of refraction greater than the 1.0 of a perfect vacuum.

interlace

To interlace is to alternately draw odd and even scan lines on a video monitor. Television monitors are interlaced; some professional CG monitors are not.

interpolated shading

Instead of assigning just a single color to each polygon, illumination values are calculated at the polygon vertices and are used to interpolate the pixel values in between. This is generalized in the Gouraud shading model.

jaggies

This is slang for aliasing or stair-stepping. This is the stepped-edge artifact that results when values are not smoothly gradated between two regions.

—*see also*   anti-aliasing

Lambert

This is a diffuse reflection component found in matte or dull surfaces. It reflects and scatters light equally in every direction.

—*see also*   shader

lens flare

This is the (usually) unintentional reflection of light off camera lens elements that results in the flashing of an image resembling the shape of the individual camera lens elements. In the early days of cinematography, a camera operator that allowed a lens flare to contaminate a shot was severely frowned upon by the DP in charge. The early 1990s saw a surge in overuse of digital lens flares as a gag to make a scene look more realistic.

light*

This is radiosity and ray tracing software now available from Discreet Logic (originally from Lightscape).

local illumination

This refers to the way light is emitted, reflected, and transmitted by a specific individual surface or light. Ray tracing is an example of a local illumination model.

—*see also* global illumination

lossless/lossy ▶ see compression

LumeTools

Originally developed in 1996 in conjunction with Cyan, Inc. for use in Riven (the sequel to the CD game Myst), LumeTools is a collection of plug-ins originally developed for Mental Ray that is now available for 3D Studio MAX, LightWave 3D, and Alias|Wavefront versions. The collection consists of five individual sets: LumeLandscape, LumeWater, LumeLight, LumeMatter, and LumeWorkbench. The company is based in San Francisco, California and can be reached at 800-650-8679 or www.lume.com.

mach-banding

This is an optical illusion in which two edges of different values are adjacent, and the border area appears darker than the surface color it actually is.

mapping

This is the application of any 2D raster or procedurally generated image to a 3D geometric surface, usually for the purpose of adding detail and realism. Most commonly applied as color information, texture mapping also can be applied to modify an object's surface normals as a bump map or to actually modify the surface itself as a displacement map. Environment maps or reflection maps do not directly affect the object; rather, they affect its surface shader qualities.

—*see also*   texture mapping

material

This is the set of surface attributes that describes how an object looks and behaves when lit. Simple materials might only contain the most basic specular and diffuse characteristics, while more complex materials have multiple shaders describing several texture maps, procedural functions for noise, transparency, and relectivity.

mental ray

This rendering software was developed by mental images GmbH & Co. KG. It is used mainly as an SGI-based alternative renderer to SoftImage's own output. This company is located in Berlin, Germany, and can be reached at +49 30 882 1088.

An example of a Moire pattern.

motion blur

Motion blur is directional blurring of objects along their path of motion to minimize undesirable strobing effects.

Moire pattern

This is a naturally occurring optical phenomenon in which overlapping or finely spaced parallel lines appear to form flowing arching patterns. This generally is not a desirable effect.

multi-pass rendering

This is a technique for separating many different surface shader characteristics into separately rendered elements. This enables very flexible (and fast) changes and effects to be completed in the compositing instead of rerendering an entire scene. Typically surface colors, specular highlights, shadow passes, and glow elements benefit from being separately rendered and composited.

noise

This refers to random procedural functions applied to break or irregularly perturb otherwise regular CG imagery. Noise can be applied to almost everything including surface shaders, particle systems, lights, and even positional attributes of modeling or animation.

normal ▶ see normal vector

normal vector

A normal vector is at a right angle (perpendicular) to a surface that defines which way the surface faces for rendering calculations.

natural phenomena

This refers to effects with some basis in nature such as clouds, water, rocks, or smoke. These effects sometimes are set up as preset render libraries in rendering software such as Alias PowerAnimator or as specialized plug-ins such as Hypervoxels from NewTek or Afterburn from Id8Media.

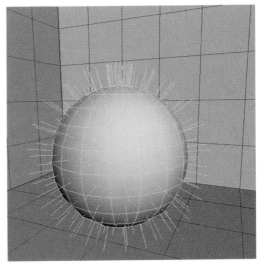

The sphere with normal vectors protruding from its surface. Notice how they are all positioned directly perpendicular from the surface.

orthogonal (orthographic projection)

The most common type of parallel projection, this also is called flat projection. It is used in top, front, and side views of 3D GUI programs. The scale is constant for the entire area, and parallel lines never converge to a vanishing point as in true perspective. This display method contrasts with perspective projection.

155

opacity

Usually, opacity is the compliment of transparency. An object with 20 percent opacity value would be 80 percent transparent.

Panavision ▶ see anamorphic

parallel projection ▶ see orthogonal projection

Persistence Of Vision Ray Tracer (POV-Ray)

Such a deal! The Persistence of Vision Raytracer is a high-quality and free ray tracer available in official versions for Microsoft Windows 3.1/Win32s, Windows 95/NT, DOS, Mac, i86, Linux, SunOS, and Amiga. The source code is available for people wanting to do their own ports. Use with xfpovray for a GUI. You can find more information at www.povray.org.

—*see also* PatchDance modeler

perspective projection

This is the optically correct foreshortening of an object with distance. All parallel lines eventually converge at a vanishing point. This projection method contrasts with orthogonal projection.

phong

This is a shader method developed by Bui Tuong-Phong (Ph.D., University of Utah, 1975). It introduces the specular reflection component of surfaces giving shiny highlights. It interpolates the vertex normal as opposed to the vertex intensity as in Gouraud shading. It is best for representing plastic surfaces.

—*see also* shading

photorealism

This is an arbitrary and misused term for a CG image that is indistinguishable from reality. CG easily creates images that look like clean plastic, but making the necessary enhancements to make it look "real" is very time consuming and difficult. Essential "realistic" additions include dirt and scratches, subtle bump and specular maps, film grain and motion blur, and imperfect lines curves and angles.

pipeline

This term is usually seen in the following form: graphics pipeline. The step-by-step process by which computer-generated images are created. There is a distinction between the image-generation pipeline of a single animation software package and the production pipeline of a facility and how it ties its many different elements together.

pixel

This stands for picture element. The tiny (usually rectangular) colored dots that make up a computer graphic image. TV images have about 720×486 or 349,920 pixels. High-quality film images might require more than 6 million pixels in every frame.

—*see also*   pixel aspect ratio

pixel aspect ratio

This is the shape of the individual pixels in a raster image. Although they're usually square in CG applications, some video formats use rectangular pixels (0.9 percent tall) and must be compensated for when rendering.

pixmap   ▶ see bitmap

procedural texture

A procedural texture is one that is not an applied image but rather a pattern created by a programming procedure such as fractal or noise functions. This can be used on top of otherwise plain surfaces to break up evenly colored areas and to add a more realistic look.

projection map

This is an image that is literally projected (as if with a slide projector) onto objects in a scene. The image is not dependent upon surface mapping structure such as UV coordinates and is, therefore, an easy way to apply label maps and such.

Radiance

Radiance is UNIX freeware used for lighting design and rendering. It was developed by the U.S. Department of Energy and the Swiss federal government, and it is copyrighted by the Regents of the University of California.

radiosity

This is a rendering principle that calculates diffuse reflections of light and color among all surfaces in a scene. In 1946 at MIT, Parry Moon and Domina Eberle Spencer devised a technique they called "interflection reflection" to calculate mathematically the lighting design for architectural purposes.

—*see also*   the "Computer Graphics Time Line" chapter for complete details

Our modern form of this popular global illumination method was developed in 1984 by a team including Cindy Goral and Don Greenberg at Cornell University. It was published in a paper called "Modeling the Interaction of Light Between Diffuse Surfaces." The paper described a new rendering method called radiosity, a new type of diffuse (global) illumination light simulation. Radiosity is the rate at which light energy leaves a surface. Unlike ray tracing, which only uses specular reflection and is view dependent, radiosity calculates the combined diffuse illumination of an entire scene once and is thereafter view independent. Commercial packages include Lightscape 3.0 (now available from Discreet Logic) or share/freeware such as RAD (contact Bernard Kwok at `http://hometown.aol.com/radiv/index.htm`) and Radiance (contact Greg Ward at `http://radsite.lbl.gov/radiance/HOME.html`).

raster (graphics)

This is an image made up of rows of dots or pixels as opposed to vector line representations. The first color raster graphics displays were developed simultaneously at several universities and early production companies in the mid-1970s.

—*see also*   vector graphics, bitmap

ray casting

Although technically synonymous with ray tracing, ray casting is most commonly used to describe the simpler visible-surface rendering techniques.

ray tracing

This is a rendering technique for determining visible surfaces and for producing realistic shadows, reflections, and refractions. Basic ray tracing calculates one or more rays from the eye-point through each pixel in the 2D image plane to determine object intersections and, therefore, visible surfaces in the 3D environment. If an object is found to be intersecting that ray, you can generate several secondary rays. A shadow ray is traced toward each light source from that point. If another object is encountered before a given light, the original point is known to be in the shadow of that light. If an object is reflective, a reflection ray is calculated to each other object in the scene. If the object is transparent, a transmitted ray is traced to every other object in the scene also. The propagated secondary rays are calculated until they intersect other objects or until a preset limit is reached.

When calculating for multiple secondary rays, recursive ray tracing quickly becomes more computationally expensive than the more common ray-casting methods.

Ray tracing was first developed in the late 1960s by Bob Goldstein.(The key paper was published in "Simulation" in 1968.) Other developers at this stage included A. Appel, Herb Steinberg, Marty Cohen, and Eugene Troubetskoy (Magi/Synthavision).

Papers presented at SIGGRAPH by Alan Kay and Turner Whitted in 1979 and 1980 expanded its utilization with specular reflection and refraction.

—*see also*   ray casting

> ### FACTOID
> Because this method traces backwards from your eye (camera) into the scene, it originally was called backwards ray tracing.

reflection mapping

—*see also*   environment mapping

refraction

This is the bending of light when passing from one medium to another is calculated only in true ray-tracing. The angle of light deflection depends on the refractive indices of the two media.

—*see also*   ray tracing and index of refraction

reflectivity

This is the capability of a surface to reflect the world around it. This is described by a shading parameter that determines the level of influence of environment maps. It is a natural occurrence found in ray tracing calculations.

RenderGL

RenderGL works with 3D Studio MAX as a fast ray tracing preview renderer. It works very fast for tweaking complicated scenes before using the final full software raytracer in MAX. This product is available from Intergraph, which is located in Huntsville, Alabama, and can be reached at 800-763-0242 or www.intergraph.com.

rendering

This is the generic term for "creating the picture" from a scene's models, surfaces, lighting, and camera angle. Basic aspects of any rendering algorithm include:

Visible surface determination: Exactly what does the camera see of objects in a scene?

Shading: Assigning surface qualities to objects.

Scanline conversion: Projecting a 3D scene's world coordinates into the 2D raster image while determining their resulting color values based on the scene's lighting and many other factors.

The pixels resulting from scanline conversion can be written to a framebuffer or memory buffer before being saved to disk. Different renderers yield very different "looks," depending on how they deal with simulating light. There always is a major tradeoff between speed and quality. Ray tracing and radiosity renderers, for example, can very accurately depict a scene but at a very high cost in calculations.

RenderMan

RenderMan is a standardized interface specification for sending modeling and animation data to a rendering system. It is not a renderer itself, as is often believed. RenderMan was developed by Pat Hanrahan (now at Princeton University) while at Pixar in 1986, was patented in 1988, and was publicly introduced in 1989.

Photorealistic RenderMan is the renderer used at Pixar. BMRT is a shareware rendering tool set that is fully RenderMan-compliant and that includes ray tracing and radiosity.

The developers of RenderMan received a Scientific and Technical Achievement Award from the Academy of Motion Picture Arts and Sciences in 1993.

—*see also* REYES

How did RenderMan get its name?

"Well, the short version of the story is that back in '86 or '87, the hardware people were building VME boards with 16 transputers to run the renderer. Just for grins, one of them (Jeff Mock) built a postcard-size, 4-TP board. Pat was in his office, and they were admiring the coolness of it, thinking how you could put it in a box and render while you're walking around. Presto—RenderMan!"

—*Steve Upstill*

res
Pronounced "rez," this is a popular abbreviation for resolution.

resolution
The resolution of a raster image most typically refers to simply the horizontal and vertical number of pixels—720×480 video output or a 1024×1024 texture map. Because resolution describes an area, doubling these dimensions necessarily quadruples the number of pixels as well as the file size. Resolution also can refer to bit depth.

—*see also* frame buffer

REYES
"Render Everything You Ever Saw." This render code was written by Loren Carpenter and Rob Cook for Lucasfilm in 1981. Much of this code found its way into Pixar's RenderMan renderer, Photorealistic RenderMan (PRMAN).

—*see also* RenderMan

RGB

This stands for red, green, and blue. These are the three primary colors used to describe almost all digital images. They also are the colors produced by CRT displays.

—*see also*   RGB in Chapter 1, "Color and Light"

scan lines

These are the horizontal rows of pixels that make up a raster image. NTSC broadcast signals provide 486 scanlines. Digitally created imagery with enough resolution for a motion picture requires about 2,000 lines (which often is doubled to 4,000 lines during film out).

shader/shading

This is a generic term used to describe the optical qualities of a surface such as color and shininess. The four most commonly used shading algorithms, in order of complexity, are: Lambert, Gouraud, Phong, and Blinn.

The Torrance-Cook surface model (1966–67) used the concept of planar "microfacets" to very accurately represent specular reflection. Originally developed for applied physics considerations, Jim Blinn adapted the model for computer graphics at SIGGRAPH in 1977.

The Gouraud shading model was developed by Henri Gouraud in 1971. It also is called linear shading because the rate of color change for all pixels per polygon is constant, or linear. Lambert shading is limited to the diffuse component of a surface and, as such, is best suited for objects with a matte finish. The Phong shading algorithm was developed by Phong Bui Tuong in 1975. It uses separate color computation for each pixel across a polygon and, therefore, is more complex and expensive to calculate than Lambert and Gouraud but is less so than Blinn. It often is used to describe plastic-like surfaces. The Blinn shading model, named by its author James Blinn in 1977, is commonly used to describe metallic surfaces and has additional controls for specular roll-off and eccentricity. It has more accurate calculations for specular roll-off and eccentricity than does Phong.

All shading calculations are a product of the surface descriptions and the lighting environment with respect to the location of the viewer.

—*see also*   interpolated shading

ShadeTree

This is an interactive tool for developing RenderMan 3.8 shaders for Mental Ray. This product is sold by Cinema Graphics, which is located in Chatsworth, California, and can be reached at 818-718-6320 or `www.cinegrfx.com`.

shadow   ▶ see cast shadow

shininess

This is an indirect surface attribute related to the size and sharpness of the specular component. The "shinier" the object, the smaller and more distinct its specular component highlight.

smooth shading

This is a shading method that interpolates pixel values across polygon boundaries for creating a continuous and smooth surface appearance.

specular

This is a shading component that describes the amount of highlight on an object. It was first developed in the Phong shading model. The relationship between specular intensity and the angle of incidence is defined by the Fresnel Law of Reflection. (The angle of reflected light is equal to that of the incident light.)

surface attribute(s)

This refers to the parameters described that define how a surface's appearance is calculated with a renderer. Surface attributes generally are contained in a material description.

surface normal   ▶ see normal vector

teapot

This was first modeled by Martin Newell in 1975 at the University of Utah to demonstrate shading techniques. The teapot developed over many years into an oft-used subject of both parody and respect as the first true icon of computer imagery.

temporal aliasing   ▶ see temporal aliasing in Chapter 4, "Animation"

tessellate

To tessellate is to break down a smooth, curved surface into discreet polygons for rendering purposes. 'To tesselate a sphere into triangles.' This often is accomplished using recursive subdivision.

texture mapping

This is the process by which raster image information is applied to CG geometry, like applying wallpaper or giftwrap paper on a box. The intent is to add a great amount of retail to enhance realism and/or avoid the need for massive amounts of geometric detail. Color texture mapping was developed by Edwin Catmull at the University of Utah in 1974 and later was refined by Jim Blinn and Martin Newell in 1976 at NYIT. The idea is to take an image and "wrap" it onto 3D CG geometry like a sticker or wallpaper. This adds a tremendous amount of realistic detail without having to resort to massive amounts of geometrical data or complex procedural shader methods.

—*see also*   bump mapping, displacement mapping

tiling

This is to procedurally repeat an image more than once, as with a brick wall rendered by repeating a single brick. Although this is very handy for covering large surfaces, it generally is not a desirable effect to see unless you are attempting to duplicate naturally repeating patterns.

title-safe area

This is the subarea of broadcast television resolution used for placing overlaid text that is (mostly) guaranteed to be visible upon viewing. This falls within the larger area of image-safe.

The inner-most box indicates the area safe for including titles. Notice that it is smaller than the area safe for including images.

translucent

This is the partially transparent quality of materials that modify the light passing through in a more complicated way than simple color filtering. This is one of the more expensive attributes to simulate in rendering, and it is not readily available in most rendering software.

transparent

A transparent material lets light pass through it with little effect on the object or the light itself. An object with no transparency is said to be opaque.

Twister

Twister is the successor to the mental ray rendering application from Softimage. It is intended to allow rapid, near real-time adjustment to shader and lighting parameters. You can find more information at www.softimage.com.

vector graphics

A vector is the simplest form of computer-generated object, formed by two points (a line). Three points form a polygon. The earliest graphics displays simply drew lines on a screen, in contrast to the pixels of today's raster graphics. The vector-graphics standard PHIGS was developed in 1986.

Vector graphics have persisted into modern times in the form of object-based graphics, in which each graphic entity (object) remains distinct and editable among the whole. Object-based graphics today are popular in software such as Adobe Illustrator and Aldus Freehand.

—*see also* PHIGS in Chapter 9, "Programming and Mathematics"

view-point

This is the point at which the camera is looking, in contrast to its eye-point or origin. The vector between eye-point and view-point, in conjunction with the angle of view, defines what the camera sees.

viewport

This is the virtual window by which you see inside the 3D world. This is the rectangular area defined by screen coordinates. It is the result of the viewing system imposed upon the 3D world space.

visible surface determination ▶ see hidden surface removal

voxel

This stands for Volume Elements. A volume rendering of 3D regions of data (the equivalent of pixels) used in space subdivision modeling. This was developed by the CG Group at Lucasfilm for use in medical imagery around 1984.

wedge

Traditional film wedging is a series of sequential exposure steps filmed out to judge their relative differences for calibration purposes.

In CG, "wedging" something generally means to pick one parameter (such as the intensity of a light or the saturation of a color) and do several different renderings with all other factors in the scene fixed. This way, you can quickly do a comparison and see that you usually want to split the difference between two of the tested values.

widescreen ▶ see anamorphic

Xfpovray

This is a graphical user interface (GUI) to the freeware ray tracing program POV-Ray developed by Robert S. Mallozzi. It is written with the XForms library and supports most of the numerous options of POV-Ray. According to his Web site, the interface was developed with POV-Ray version 3.0, but it should work fine for earlier versions as well. You can find more information at `cspar.uah.edu/~mallozzir/software/xforms/xfpovray.html`.

yon (clipping plane)

This is the distance limit from the camera beyond which objects cannot be seen or rendered.

—*see also* clipping planes

Z-buffer

This is a visible-surface determination method in which each pixel records (in addition to color) its distance from the camera. As each surface is scan converted, overlapping pixels are sorted so that only the ones closest to the camera ultimately get rendered. Although this is great for optimizing reasons, it also prone is to aliasing artifacts. It was developed by Ed Catmull in 1974 at the University of Utah.

—*see also* A-buffer

zoom

This is a camera term for varying the focal length of the camera lens, thereby making the subject larger or smaller in the view. The camera itself does not physically move as with a dolly or truck.

After Effects

alpha channel

Altamira Composer

articulated matte

Avid Technology Inc.

bg

black levels

BlueICE

blue screen

blue spill

Boris AE

box filter

CBB

center matte

Chalice

chatter

chroma keying

Chyron Corporation

CineLook

Cineon FX

clip

color spill

comp

Composer

composite

component video

composite video

Concerto

contrast

corner pinning

crop

cut

data-flow diagram interface

Digital Fusion

Discreet Logic

dissolve

Domino

double expose

DVE

DX

edge blending

edge matte

EDL

effect*

Effetto Pronto

Elastic Reality

fettle

fill matte

film grain

flame*

flash

Flint

fringing

garbage matte

generation loss

glow

grain

green screen

Henry

holdout matte

ICE

Illuminaire

inferno*

inverted matte

key/keying

KnockOut

Liberty

light*

mask

Mask Pro

matte

Media Illusion

paint*

Panoptica

plate

Primatte

Quantel

roto-mattes

Shake 2.0

Silicon Grail

sobel filter

soft/softness

super/superimpose

tracking

Ultimatte

Zbig Chromakey

Compositing

Even if you are realizing a fully digital scene, it rarely makes sense to do an entire shot all in one pass. By analyzing your scene carefully (with creative control in mind), you will see that having individual control over multiple elements in a composite is a far superior approach to creating a great-looking shot. Having separate control over many elements in a scene enables you to optimize not only creative considerations, but also time and cost considerations.

- **Break it down by distance:** If you have objects at varying distances from the camera, rendering them as separate elements enables you to add selective amounts of blur to imply focal distance. Objects also tend to get more desaturated and cooler in hue with increased distance. Having the control to instantly dial these parameters into the separate comp elements (as opposed to re-rendering an entire scene) both allows for many more supervisor tweaks and makes you the friend of every producer.

- **Light passes:** As with traditional model shoots, it pays to have a separate pass of any illuminating elements in a scene. This includes windows and lights on a spaceship, lamps on a city street, or headlights on a car. Not only does this give you control over the obvious color and intensity of the element, it also provides great flexibility in adding softening glow elements when appropriate. (Safety disclaimer: You don't have to stare at a bare light bulb. Just look at the moon on a hazy night or at a street lamp in the rain.)

- **Changes:** Believe it or not, people will want to change your shot. If your scene has dozens or hundreds of components and you only need to slightly change the color of one spaceship in a fleet, you don't want to have to re-render the whole scene, do you?

Insider's Information

When an artist speaks of a shot in the possessive case, it does not immediately imply sole ownership. "My shot is coming along nicely" or "My shot got finaled today" should be seen as a positive sign of pride in accomplishment and not as selfish intent. At the same time, always remember to fully acknowledge your partners. It is a rare shot indeed that does not have many hands involved in its creation.

- **Rendering resources**: Trying to render every element in one pass can be very expensive in terms of memory and CPU usage. This is the job of a CG Supervisor. He or she makes sure that the technique employed for a given shot is not only adequate but optimal. Smaller components of a scene can be distributed to smaller workstations, with larger components sent to more capable servers.

In the more common case of integrating CG elements with live-action footage, compositing is not a luxury but a necessity.

When your model is textured, animated, lit, and rendered, it is time to put it into the shot. Let's walk step by step through a typical composite for a feature film, bringing the many elements from many different artists together into one picture good enough for the big screen.

Even the simplest composite, one involving just a background (or "bg") plate and a single CG element, requires careful attention to detail to work effectively. This example assumes the CG element is meant to appear as though it is part of the original photography, perhaps a typical shot of a dinosaur running through the forest. To review what has to be done to get to this point, let's quickly go over all the steps that provided this nice-looking creature element in the first place. First the wireframe model was built, most likely by hand with a digitized maquette as a guide. This model was then "chained" with an inverse-kinematic (or IK) skeleton, along with appropriate constraints for the best animation controls possible. The various patches must be seamed or "socked" together, and a means for secondary animation such as muscles flexing and bulging also is provided. Many different textures must be painted on the 3D model such as color, bump, specularity, and dirt maps. Shaders must be developed to apply and control these textures on the surface correctly.

Next the model is placed in the same 3D space as the jungle location using one of several methods for creating a match-move scene. This provides a virtual camera and ground plane that matches the real scene precisely. If we stopped here and just composited A (our creature) over B (a jungle bg plate), it most likely would stand out dramatically as a fake-looking CG. A Technical Director must place appropriate lights and

171

shadows on the creature to match the physical light sources in the background plate. Now the creature is lit nicely and has a nice contact shadow to connect him with the ground.

This leads us to compositing. The final step of putting a shot together is, in many ways, the most important one. Even the best modeled, textured, animated, and lit CG creature is going to look fake if any one of many subtle aspects are wrong in the composite. The following section describes general practices, tips and tricks, and common-sense reminders to make the subtle improvements that can benefit almost every shot.

As with everything discussed in this book, there always are exceptions. Most of these examples, however, hold true for both simple and complex composites.

TIPS, TRICKS, AND REMINDERS

WATCH YOUR BLACK LEVELS

This simple rule also is one of the most critical. It refers to matching all the brightness levels of your CG element against the corresponding brightness values in the bg plate. Are the blackest blacks in your creature and bg the same value and color? How are the middle tones? Are the highlights and specularity of the CG no brighter than the brightest highlights in your plate? If your bg plate of forest has soft, hazy highlights and deep blacks in the shadows, make sure your CG element has the same. A good trick to better judge these levels is to artificially increase your monitor's gamma level beyond the normal setting. You also might want to view just the luminance information (black and white) if possible, ignoring hue or color information.

DEPTH CUEING AND FOCUS

Watch how the appearance of real objects changes as they travel away from you through the air. They, of course, get smaller at the appropriate rate for their speed, distance, and size. Their colors become less saturated and more "flashed" with the predominant hue of the surrounding scene. The color also begins to shift to blue and magenta at extreme distances. In most cases, the objects also pass into or beyond your initial focal plane. If the foreground action is in sharp focus, make sure your object has the same sharpness as areas of background at similar distances.

All these factors often must be adjusted over time (animated) to match changes in moving bg-plate footage.

EDGE SHARPNESS

CG objects sometimes have a distinct cut-out appearance that can be eliminated with edge blending. This can mean a simple and subtle softening of alpha-channel edge information, or it can mean creating a more involved, blended-edge element between the CGI and back plate (using a sobel filter technique, for example).

INTERACTIVE ELEMENTS

What would happen to the jungle if a 20-ton t-rex were running through it? Leaves, branches, and trees would be displaced, kicked up, and broken down. This might seem obvious, but the more you can add to "put your object in the scene," the more convincing the final shot will be. Shiny surfaces are prime candidates for interactivity. Is there anything reflective in your scene that needs to include an appropriately distorted image of your CG object?

CAMERA ACTION

A real camera photographing a huge beast impacting the ground with each stride certainly would not remain stationary. "Camera shake" and vibration can be added by very slightly translating and rotating (shaking) the final comp in rhythm with the beasts footsteps. Hopefully, when the bg plate was photographed, the camera followed the appropriate action of the yet-to-be-created object. If this is the case, be sure to take the camera's motion into account when placing your object in the scene. This, too, requires a little bit of subtlety. If a critter is running across your field of view, the camera usually wants to follow the action, not lead it. This should happen as if the camera person was trying to follow an action he did not know about ahead of time.

FILM GRAIN

Look at a tight crop of your CG element. Match the amount, size, and color bias of your film grain with that of your plate. Most stocks tend to have the most amount of grain in the blue channel, so match individual red, green, and blue grain levels accordingly. Most professional compositing software tools today have film-grain features that provide very precise control over size, density, and color.

TERMS

After Effects (4.0)

This is the leader in powerful and affordable desktop compositing software for both Mac and Windows 95/NT systems from Adobe. With its multiprocessor capability and hardware acceleration, it is at least the equal of any SGI workstation-based compositing solution. Plug-in support includes Eye Candy from Alien Skin Software, Atomic Power Evolution, Final Effects from MetaCreations, and BorisFX from Artel Software. CineLook from DigiEffects is a plug-in that simulates the look of film for video. ICEfx acceleration technology from Integrated Computing Engines significantly speeds up the ICE plug-ins.

alpha channel

This is the fourth RGBA information channel that contains 8-bit grayscale values used in compositing. It was co-developed by Ed Catmull and Alvy Ray Smith at the New York Institute of Technology in 1977. Why "alpha?" According to Smith, image composition uses simple linear interpretation in which the Greek letter "A" (alpha) controls the amount of interpolation between two images.

Not all file formats use a built-in fourth alpha channel. Alias, for example, creates a separate 8-bit image for the alpha information. Why? Only Alias knows!

Altamira Composer

This is sprite-based image-compositing software for Windows, marketed for Web-based image creation. Originally from Altamira Software Corporation, it was founded by Dr. Alvy Ray Smith in 1991). It was recently acquired by Microsoft's

FACTOID

Ed Catmull, Tom Porter, Tom Duff, and Alvy Ray Smith received a technical Academy Award in 1996 from the Academy of Motion Picture Arts and Sciences (AMPAS) for "pioneering inventions in digital image compositing" (basically, for the invention of the alpha channel)

Advanced Technology Division and is available as Image Composer 1.0 at www.microsoft.com/imagecomposer.

articulated matte

As opposed to a garbage matte, this technique very carefully outlines the object to cleanly separate it from its surroundings during a composite. This is a task performed by a rotoscope artist.

Avid Technology Inc.

This is the maker of the second commercial nonlinear editing system (after EditDroid), which was developed in 1989 and runs on the MacII computer system. Today, the Avid non-linear editing system has become the de facto standard and has by and large supplanted the traditional editing of film. Avid provides a wide variety of compositing, 3D titling (Marquee), and nonlinear editing products for Mac, SGI, and Windows NT platforms. AVID acquired Elastic Reality in 1995 and Parallax(Matador) in 1996. It also acquired Softimage from Microsoft in June 1998 for $194 million. Avid is located in Tewksbury, Massachusetts, and can be reached at 800-949-AVID or www.avid.com.

Notice the clean lines of the articulated matte.

bg

This is short for background. This term usually refers to a live-action image upon which a foreground CG element is composited.

black levels ▶ see the "Tips, Tricks, and Reminders" section at the beginning of this chapter.

BlueICE ▶ see ICE

blue screen

This is photographing a subject against a pure color screen (usually blue or green) with the intention of later replacing that color with an image created or photographed elsewhere. The best color-difference algorithms, found in products such as Ultimatte, give the compositor great control over eliminating color-spill and fringing artifacts. Typically, two separate mattes are created and are combined for a final composite. The first is the critical edge matte; the

175

second is the center or fill matte. Just what color-difference screen is appropriate depends on many factors. Fast film stocks tend to have large grain patterns (especially in the blue channel), hindering a good extraction. The color palette of your subject matter to be photographed also plays an important role in this decision. Choose an extraction screen color as different from your subjects predominant hues as possible. You wouldn't want to shoot Gumby against a green screen, would you? For more personal work on the Mac platform, a version of Ultimatte called Knockout (1.0) is available as a standalone application, and Mask Pro (2.0) is available as a Photoshop plug-in extension.

— *see also*   composite

blue spill

This occurs when a foreground subject is "contaminated" with color from the surrounding screen or reflected light. This unwanted effect can sometimes be handled very nicely by color-difference matting techniques such as Ultimatte. In the worst cases, however, keying is made impossible and articulate roto-mattes are required.

— *see also*   blue screen

Boris AE

This is a set of plug-ins for Adobe After Effects. Fast and fun to use, its open architecture provides unlimited access to underlying functionality. Just a few of the features include very good keying tools, 3D DVE, spotlight effects, color correction, and 2D particle generation. The set costs about $500 from Artel, which can be reached at 888-772-6747 or www.artelsoft.com.

box filter

This is a relatively quick and cheap blur function that is most useful when used at low pixel widths to average with their neighbors. High box-filter widths create linear or box-like artifacts, which do not usually look natural.

CBB

This stands for "could be better." Very often, production time pressure forces a shot to be finaled when some additional small improvements or tweaking still could be done. Such shots are more often labeled CBBs in case there is time at the end of the project to go back and perform the additional work.

center matte ▶ see blue screen

Chalice

This 2D compositing software uses an "interactive data-flow diagram paradigm" (a fancy way of saying an intuitive interface with dependency structure). Written in conjunction with Side Effects Software and RFX, Chalice is available for UNIX and NT from Silicon Grail. Film resolution tracking color correction and extractions can be controlled through mathematical expressions. Chalice is optimized for the DEC Alpha. Chalice costs about $3,000. Silicon Grail is located in Hollywood, California, and can be reached at 323-871-9100 or www.silicongrail.com.

chatter

This is the undesired result of painting elements by hand, frame by frame. Edges appear to flicker unevenly because of the imprecise nature of manual painting. Automatic spline-shape interpolators such as Matador's Roto-Splines, Avid Elastic Reality, or the Mac-based Puffin Commotion are used to avoid this artifact.

chroma keying

This is a compositing method that originated in analog video compositing and whose keying is based on hue differences. On television news programs, the weather person often is chroma keyed in front of a colored backing to insert maps and graphics.

Chyron Corporation

Chyron is the maker of Concerto compositing software for Windows, Liberty paint and animation software, and a host of other digital media products. Chyron is located in Cupertino, California, and can be reached at 408-873-3830 or www.chyron.com.

CineLook

This is a set of plug-ins for AfterEffects that takes input such as video, computer animation, or film and enables you to add grain, to correct color, and to add film artifacts such as dust, scratches, stains, hair, and more. Broadcast versions are available for the Macintosh and Windows NT platforms. A film-res version also is available for the Mac. Sirius can be contacted at `sirius.com/~wsmedia/frames/cinelook/cinelook.html`.

Cineon FX

SGI-based compositing software from Kodak. Typhoon is the O2-based entry-level system, Storm is a dual-processor version for high resolution and remote rendering, and Tornado runs on multi-proc Onyx2 supercomputers. This product hasn't been available since 1998 when Kodak pulled support for it. Its very powerful dual-monitor setup and flow chart GUI approach to interface design are made for productive work sessions.

Cineon also refers to the image file format used by the system, which has the capability to store data in 16-bit log format. This provides a very deep response curve that preserves the subtle color details and gradients found in film. You can find more about this product at `www.kodak.com/US/en/motion/postProduction/cineon`.

clip

This is a term held over from traditional film use that usually refers to a small series of sequential images. Some nonlinear editing and compositing systems, such as Avid and Flame, deal with images in this way. In certain systems, the terms "image sequence," "shot," and "element" are used instead.

color spill

This is contamination of a foreground object in a blue screen (or green screen) element by the light and color meant for the screen. This also is called blue spill and fringing.

comp

This is common slang and abbreviation for composite.

Composer (4.5)

This full-featured film-resolution compositing software from Alias|Wavefront is available only for the SGI. Features include lens warping, motion blur, multiprocessor rendering, time distortion, and "True Track" motion tracking. This product is based on scanline compositing algorithms and a data-flow diagram interface. You can learn more about it at www.aw.sgi.com/pages/home/pages/products/pages/composer_film_sgi/index.html.

composite

This refers to assembling a final raster image by layering two or more elements together. Composites sometimes can involve hundreds of layers including scanned background plates, CG-rendered elements, roto-mattes, and multiple model and miniature elements. For the result to appear as if all the separate elements were photographed together, attention must be paid to the many different subtle details discussed at the beginning of this chapter. These details include using color correction and adding artificial film grain and motion blur to match real photography.

— *see also*   blue screen and composite video

component video

This is an electronic term for how the video signal is delivered to the monitor. Component refers to when the channels are split into different red, green, and blue signals as opposed to a composite video signal.

composite video

This is an electronic term for how the video signal is delivered to the monitor. Composite refers to when the image is combined into one signal as opposed to a component video signal.

Concerto (1.3)

Such a deal! This resolution-independent compositing software for Windows 95/NT (originally from Axis Software) is now available from Chyron Corporation. Plug-ins are available such as "Final Effects" from MetaCreations, "BorisFX" from Artel Software, "Hollywood FX" from Synergy International, and "Power Pack" from WAVES.

This gives you a multiprocessor plug-in environment for the only affordable price. You can contact Chyron at www.chyron.com.

contrast

Contrast is the range of values between an image's brightest whites (DMax) and its darkest blacks (DMin). High contrast denotes a great difference between the two; low contrast means the values all fall more in the mid-tone range of brightness with no bright highlights or deep shadows.

Contrast is strongly related to the apparent richness of an image. Low contrast is associated with a "washed-out" look, and high contrast generally (but not always) is perceived as "snappy."

— *see also* black levels

Obvious contrast differences in an image (low contrast on the left, high contrast on the right).

corner pinning

This is a technique that warps and stretches an image in such a way that it keeps the lines between the four corners linear but stretches and compresses the image. It would be like stretching a box into a rhomboid; all the lines connecting the corners are still linear. This is used in certain tracking and stabilizing preparations to better match two different plate elements.

crop

A cropped section is a smaller subarea of an image selected for copy, duplication, or output.

cut ▶ see dissolve

data-flow diagram interface

A popular GUI method used in some compositing software (such as Composer and Chalice), this isolates individual processes, elements, inputs, and outputs. Although the arrangement varies, the interlinking of these separate "nodes" shows a clear "flow" from the start to the end of an entire composite process in one glance.

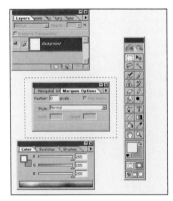

The selection to be cropped from the image (represented by the dashed line).

Digital Fusion

This is compositing software for NT made by Eyeon Software. It is resolution independent and multithreaded. Plug-ins are available from 5D Monster. Digital Fusion V2.5 is about $2,500; Digital Fusion Post is the high-end (about $5,000) postproduction version available with the Ultimatte plug-in. Eyeon can be contacted at 800-862-0004 or www.eyeonline.com.

Discreet Logic

Formed in 1991, this company makes several high-end painting, video editing, and compositing software products based on the SGI hardware platform. Products include inferno* and flame* 6.0, a high-end effects and compositing package; effect*, paint*, and light* for multimedia content creation; and frost*, a real-time 3D broadcast graphics system with vapour* virtual studio module, Paint* 2.0 vector-based painting, and an animation system for NT.

In February 1999, the Academy of Motion Picture Arts and Sciences recognized Discreet Logic's flame* and inferno* products for their influence on the advancement of the motion picture industry with a Scientific and Engineering Award.

Discreet Logic was acquired by Autodesk in August 1998 for about $520 million in stock. Terms of the buyout were modified in early 1999 after an SEC review. The company is located in Montreal, Canada, and can be reached at 800-869-3504 or www.discreet.com.

dissolve

To dissolve is to fade out one image into another image. This is different from a cut, which is a single-frame transition between scenes.

Domino

This is a real-time, 12-bit, film-resolution compositing and effects product from Quantel. The core Double4 workstation can be purchased separately, or (at almost $1 million) the complete proprietary hardware/software film effects system can handle everything from scanning to film out. Domino contains a full suite of advanced tools including tracking/stabilization, color correction, keying, grain tools, restoration, and wire removal. You can learn more about Quantel at www.quantel.com.

— *see also*   Quantel

double expose

To double expose is to combine a secondary image on an already-exposed negative either in-camera or through optical printing. This also is an optical term for superimposing a partial or ghostlike image over the main image on a set by means of an angled, partially transparent mirror. Often abbreviated as DX.

DVE

This stands for digital video effects. This term is used most often in a broadcast video postenvironment to describe real-time 2.5D effects. This distorts 2D textures so they appear to be moving or interactive in 3D space when, in fact, they are not.

DX ▶ see double expose

edge blending

Composited elements, especially ones created in CG, typically have a hard edge to them that makes them look like cut-outs. A subtle blur applied to the edge only, combining foreground and bg plate, can soften this edge and can help the CG blend into the plate better.

edge matte

This is an outline of an existing matte generated by taking the area a few pixels outside the existing matte and a few pixels inside the existing matte. The number of pixels selected inside and outside the current matte determines the width of the edge created. A sobel filter often is used as a cheap method of achieving this effect.

— *see also*   blue screen

EDL

This stands for edit decision list. This is generated by a nonlinear editing software package to record cut lengths, dissolve timings, and so on, for specifying what to do with the physical film. It also can be input into a compositing system such as Flame or Henry to assemble the many different clips that make up a sequence of images, such as a commercial or a music video.

effect*

This is Discreet Logic's entry-level compositing software tools. It is available in several packages including the products that used to be Flint and Illuminare Composition. It includes resolution-independent keying, animated effects filters, 3D lighting, reflection tools, and color correction. It starts at about $900 for Mac, Windows, and SGI.

Effetto Pronto

Effetto Pronto V1.1 is a new compositing tool available for the Mac from Videonics, which was acquired from KUB Systems in 1998. (Effetto Pronto is Italian for "fast effects.") It can be used in connection with the Pronto and Rapido PCI interface cards for real-time, resolution-independent character generation, compositing, effects, keying, 3D DVE, and texture mapping. It has full third-party filter support for Photoshop, After Effects, and Commotion. It is similar to After Effects but with true 3D space control. It costs about $5,000. Videonics is located in Campbell, California and can be reached at 800-338-3348 or at www.videonics.com.

Elastic Reality

This is the de facto industry standard for warping and morphing effects. It also contains many other standard compositing, color correction, matting, and 2D animation tools. Starts at about $1,300 from Avid, which can be reached at www.avid.com.

fettle

A term used more often in the United Kingdom, it means to tweak, fuss with, or otherwise noodle with something. It also is a tool feature name with Quantel products such as Henry and Editbox.

fill matte ▶ see blue screen

A closeup showing the film grain.

film grain

This is the silver halide flake structure of film emulsion seen as color noise in the pixels of an image scanned from an exposed film source. It usually is more prominent in the blue (RGB) color component because of the layered nature of film stock. Proper matching of film grain is a subtle necessity for matching CG images to their live-action bg plates in a composite. Film stocks that are very sensitive to light (high speed) have a larger, more numerous film grain structure.

— *see also* "Tips, Tricks, and Reminders" section at the beginning of this chapter.

flame*

flame* 6.0 is the latest release of Discreet Logic's high-end effects and compositing package optimized for the SGI Octane platform. The cost is over $250,000. New features include a full 12-bit image format, 3D distortion tools, and a new extremely accurate tracking feature.

Capabilities include real-time high-resolution playback, up to 2K resolution at 8-bit per channel color depth, true 3D object manipulating, warping and time-stretch tools, precise keying, painting, automated rotoscoping and matte generation, image processing, film grain tools, and much more. Hundreds of SPARKS third-party plug-ins are available for a wide range of additional capabilities.

— *see also* inferno*

flash

This is an optical term for exposing light onto a film element to desaturate its colors and to decrease black levels. It also refers to adding or exposing an average color of the background plate over the CGI element in a scene to better blend the color value ranges of the scene. In addition, it is also the name of a product available from Macromedia.

Flint (5.0)

This is the native name for Discreet Logics's SGI O2-based effect* compositing software. If offers real-time and resolution-independent compositing, editing, graphics, and painting.

Originally the product name for entry-level SGI workstation-based compositing software, it was marketed as effect* (option 3) before being reintroduced as a new product in February 1999.

— *see also*   effect* and Illuminaire

fringing ▶ see color spill

garbage matte

This is a roughly defined area used to hold out unwanted imagery in a composite element. Blue-screen photography usually needs a garbage matte to hold out the areas of the stage surrounding the actual blue screen coverage area.

generation loss

In optical compositing and film printing, every time an element is subject to another process, it loses sharpness and overall quality. A generation is one of these steps such as a pass through an optical printer. Digital image-manipulation methods are not subject to this result, of course.

glow

Simulating glows can add natural realism to many types of CG. One inexpensive trick is to pull a luminance key from the highlights of an object, apply a blur, and then DX (double expose) or screen the element over the original image. The effect is most effective when used subtly.

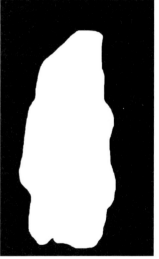

The rough outline of an image.

grain ▶ see film grain

green screen

This is a variation of the more common blue screen technique. A green screen might be required when a subject's predominant color is blue hues.

— *see also*   blue screen

Henry

The Henry Straight-8 ($590,000) and the Henry V-8 ($900,000) both feature real-time effects editing, compositing, color correction, and graphics all integrated into a single tool set. This is available from Quantel, which can be reached at www.quantel.com.

holdout matte

Another term for matte or garbage matte. It also can represent a matte in which the area of an image is to be removed. That area is "held out," and many times, turned to black.

ICE

This is the abbreviation for Integrated Computing Engines of Waltham, Massachusetts, makers of accelerated 2D compositing and effects software and dedicated hardware. CineLook and CineLook FilmRes add film-look effects to video and CG imagery. BLUEice and ICEfx are hardware-accelerator technologies that greatly decrease the rendering time needed for these effects when used as plug-ins for packages such as Adobe AfterEffects by Adobe.

Illuminaire

Composition and paint software tools are now marketed as part of the effect* product for Windows 95/NT and Mac. This product features motion tracking, keying, and 3D shadow-casting space much like flint* and flame*. It was acquired by Discreet Logic from Denim Software in 1998.

inferno*

This is the top-of-the-line ($500,000) compositing and effects system from Discreet Logic. Version 3.0 offers all the basics of flame* with added resolution up to 4,000 lines, a 3D color keyer, and deformation modules.

inverted matte

This term is used to remap all the values in the matte to the opposite end: 0 becomes 255, 255 becomes 0, and all the values in between.

key/keying

To key is to extract a foreground object (such as a person) from a monochromatic background color (such as a green screen) to replace that screen color with a live-action scene, a miniature set, or a CG environment created elsewhere. Keying in video is the same idea as matting in film.

— *see also*   chroma keying, blue screen

KnockOut (1.0)

This is new dedicated, masking, standalone software for the Mac from Ultimattte. It exports Photoshop mask file formats.

Liberty

This is a very robust package that includes painting, effects, color correcting, image processing, motion tracking, and compositing features, from Chyron Corporation.

— *see also*   Chapter 2, "Painting and Graphic Design," Chyron, Liberty 64

light*   ▶ see Discreet Logic

mask

This is an alternate name for matte. In painting and illustration systems, a mask is analogous to those used in airbrushing, for example, to protect areas of an image while working and affecting only other areas.

Mask Pro

Mask Pro 2.0 is a Photoshop plug-in extension that dramatically speeds up mask creation. It is available from Extensis Corp. located in Portland, Oregon. You can contact Extensis at 800-796-9798 or www.extensis.com.

matte (matting)

In digital imagery, a matte is a grayscale single-channel image used to hold out a portion of a composite element when it is placed over a background plate. This makes the element appear to be behind a portion of the plate image. The pixel values of a matte channel therefore represent the opacity of the corresponding image data.

Media Illusion

This full-featured, high-end effects and compositing software is available from Avid for the SGI platform. Version 5.0 includes uncompressed nonlinear editing features of Media Composer and integrated Elastic Reality.

paint* ▶ see Discreet Logic

Panoptica

This is a unique software product used to generate flawless background plates; to remove, add, and retouch artifacts; to reshoot scenes with a virtual camera; and to accelerate creation of complex visual effects. It is available from the Harlequin Group, which can be reached at www.harlequin.com/products/fvpp.

plate

This is a photographed image or sequence of images captured on film, digitally scanned into the computer, and used as one element in a CG composite. This most typically refers to a background or bg plate.

— *see also* clean plate

Primatte

This is a chroma keying software available as a standalone for SGI workstations or as a plug-in for Adobe After Effects, Avid, Discreet Logic, and Kinetix products. Available from Photron USA, which can be reached at 408-261-3613 or www.photron.com.

Quantel

This is the maker of the Domino film effects compositing workstation and the Henry complete video post solution for real-time editing, composition, and effects. Quantel can be reached at 203-656-3100 or www.quantel.com.

— *see also* Chapter 2, "Painting and Graphic Design"

roto-mattes

This 8-bit (grayscale) matte channel information is used to hold out portions of an image in a composite. It is generated either by a matte (rotoscope) artist painting frame by frame or by automated spline software.

— *see also*   garbage matte and articulate matte

Shake 2.0

Shake is a high-speed compositing software optimized for large image resolutions yet without the need for specialized hardware. With a data-flow diagram paradigm, it runs on both NT and UNIX. Features include resolution independence and a host of real-time 2D animation and effects tools. It costs about $9,900 from Nothing Real, which can be reached at 310-664-6152 or www.nothingreal.com.

Silicon Grail

This is the maker of Chalice 2D compositing software. They can be reached at 213-871-9100 or www.sgrail.com.

sobel filter

This is an edge-detection filter often used on the alpha channel to create a "halo" or "rim" element in a composite to aid in edge blending.

soft/softness

This is a general term meaning that a raw image element does not have enough resolution.

super/superimpose ▶ see double exposure

tracking ▶ see the sidebar article by Gary Jackemuk

Ultimatte

This is a patented standalone color-difference extraction software for UNIX and Windows NT, available from Ultimatte Corp. It originally was developed as an analog video keying technology by engineer and inventor Petro Vlahos in 1980. It initially was used extensively at Francis Ford Coppola's Zoetrope Studios in the early 1980s.

Ultimatte is available as a plug-in for just about every major compositing software package including Adobe After Effects, Avid Media Composer, Chyron Concerto, and

Liberty, Discreet Logic, and Softimage D|S environments. Ultimatte Corp. also makes the Mac OS-dedicated masking software KnockOut. They are located in Chatsworth, California and can be reached at 818-993-8007 or www.ultimatte.com.

Zbig Chromakey

This is advanced chroma key and compositing software from Zbigniew Rybczynski. Features include automatic reflections of background objects and very fine pixel-level control of even the toughest and most unevenly lit screens. It is available as a standalone product for NT, as a plug-in for Adobe After Effects and Discreet Logic effect* on Mac and NT, as a spark for other Discreet Logic products, and for Digital Fusion Eyeon software. It is coming soon for Softimage DS and Alias|Wavefront Composer. Zbig Vision Ltd. can be reached at 201-239-1818 or www.zbigvision.com.

Accom Inc.

Abekas

AHI Research Center

Ampex

Ampex Digital Opticals

Auspex

Barracuda

Bernoulli box

bpi

buffer

CalComp Technology Inc.

Celco

ColorScan

Cyberware Technologies Inc.

Cyrax 3D

data glove

Dicomed

Digital Disc Recorder

digitize

DMax

dot matrix printer

dot size

dpi

drum scanner

DST

dye sublimation printer

Electronic Still Store

Epson

exabyte

eXtreme fx

FEElit

floppy

Geometrix

GRAIL

head-mounted display

Howtek

Iconics

Imageware Corporation

Imagica

Imapro

inkjet printers

InSpeck Inc.

Kodak Professional

laser printer

Liquid Crystal Display

logical input device

Management Graphics, Inc.

Minolta

motion capture

mouse

NTSC

Paint Effects

PAL

PAL-M

Paraform Inc.

peripheral

pica

point cloud

Polhemus

PostScript

ppi

puck

QIC

Rand Tablet

Scitex Corporation LTD.

SECAM

SyQuest Technologies Inc.

telecine

VistaVision

VPL Research

Wacom Technology

wax transfer printer

ZIP drive

Input & Output

There's not much point to CG without output, and it certainly would be limited without input. To that end, I've listed some of the basic methods here with the usual emphasis on historical context. In the early days, university researchers had no alternative but to program in Assembly or Fortran with instructions recorded on paper tape or punch cards full of holes. We've come a long way with the mouse, the GUI interface, various Wacom devices, DataGlove, spaceball, and other wacky and inventive ways to get software to do what we want. The biggest breakthrough in input technology for software has to be Maya Paint Effects, which Alias|Wavefront is developing to enable users to paint realistic effects in a 3D scene in real time.

At the same time, our display and output options also have increased dramatically. Long gone are the days of filming of a monitor a frame at a time or being satisfied with monochromatic pen plotter drawings. In addition to the old staple of video and film output, we have rapid prototyping technologies such as sterolithography that enable us to hold in our hands the 3D objects we create. This is a very dramatic experience the first time you do it. Speaking of film for input and output, it finally seems that the 100-year-old medium will go the way of the 78 rpm record and be replaced by all digital methods of both capturing and projecting imagery. George Lucas is leading the way, needless to say, starting with the digital projection screenings of *Star Wars Episode 1: The Phantom Menace* in New York and Los Angeles in the summer of 1999. The next Star Wars film, *Episode 2*, will be the first major studio film to be captured with the new custom digital cameras instead of film.

It is, of course, still about the content, and hopefully people all over the world will use these new options to challenge established methods and ideas.

TERMS

Accom Inc.

This company makes Abekas digital disc recording and effects products as well as the new Elset Post virtual set products that allow for real-time composite playback of broadcast-quality composite output. Accom acquired Scitex

Digital Video Inc. in early 1999. It is located in Menlo Park, California, and can be reached at 650-328-3818. You can find more information at www.accom.com.

Abekas

This is the standard in desktop digital disc recording technology from Accom. The new professional Abekas 6000 is a disk-based, broadcast-quality, digital video server with 10 hours of local storage capacity and up to eight digital video I/O channels.

AHI Research Center

Founded in 1962, the center is headed by Dr. D.C. Engelbart, who is best known for his invention of the mouse input device. The center specializes in custom software and hardware development, and it supports innovative interactive human-computer research.

Ampex

Founded in 1944, Ampex has been at the forefront of electronic and digital image-storing technology with literally thousands of patents and 11 Emmy Awards. Products have included the Electronic Still Store (1977), the ADO (1981), the D-2 composite digital video recording format (1988), and the DST data storage (1992) tape format. Ampex is located in Redwood City, California, and can be reached at 650-367-4111. You can find more information at www.ampex.com.

Quote

"Ampex Electronic Still Store used big Maytag-like 300 meg removable disk drives (like cake platters); Was 4 or 5 ft high, 19" racks, plus the controller, plus the two disk drives. For two 30-second chunks of composite video… Mostly designed for networks (especially sports) to jump on cue to a still or short audio-less clip. How much did that stupid thing cost Will?"

—*Doug MacMillan*

"I think it cost $500,000 for about 60 seconds of record time. The best part was the punch-hole paper tape system software installation. I remember one late night Rob Marinic trying to scotch tape the only copy of the paper tape."

—*Will Anielewicz*

Ampex Digital Opticals (ADO)

Introduced in 1981, the Emmy Award-winning (1983) ADO® was a breakthrough technology in broadcast digital special effects. It allowed rotation and perspective of video images.

Auspex

Auspex is a manufacturer of large-capacity file servers used for data storage. They usually are connected to SGI Challenge servers. Auspex is based in Santa Clara, California, and can be reached at 408-566-2000. You can find more information at www.auspex.com/.

Barracuda

The Barracuda is a high-speed disc drive from Seagate. You can find more information at www.seagate.com.

Bernoulli box

The Bernoulli box is a large, removable storage disc technology used in the 1980s and manufactured by Iomega. It no is longer manufactured. You can find more information at www.iomega.com.

bpi

Bpi stands for bits per inch. It is a measurement of magnetic tape storage density.

buffer

A buffer is a temporary storage space of computer memory for image data. The buffer then is used to either modify or display the image data or to forward it to some output device.

CalComp Technology Inc.

CalComp makes computer graphics peripheral devices such as CAD plotters, printers, and digitizers. CalComp recently shut down operations and transferred all its business to various affiliated companies worldwide. You can find more information at www.calcomp.com.

Celco

Celco stands for Constantine Engineering Laboratories Co., makers of the CRT-based eXtreme line of film recorders. Celco is based in Rancho Cucamonga, California, and can be reached at 909-481-4648. You can find more information at www.celco.com.

ColorScan

ColorScan is Howtek's line of high-resolution drum scanners. Howtek is located in Hudson, New Hampshire, and can be reached at 603-882-5200. You can find more information at www.howtek.com.

Cyberware Technologies Inc.

Cyberware was founded in December 1982 to develop its patented laser-based 3D digitizing technology in which a full-color image is created along with the geometrical data to complete a highly accurate 3D copy of the subject. Applications for the scanner include fine art sculpture work, portrait busts, and 3D copies of museum pieces. Facial and full-body scans also are used increasingly in medical research and in entertainment special effects. Cyberware is located in Monterey, California, and can be reached at 831-657-1450. You can find more information at www.cyberware.com.

Cyrax 3D

This laser-mapping technology from Cyra Technologies in Oakland, California, converts scans of large-scale, live-action sets and environments to highly accurate 3D CG models or 2D drawings. Cyrax can be reached at 510-633-5000. You can find more information at www.cyra.com.

data glove

The data glove was first started as a project in the late 1970s by Thomas Zimmerman and his friend Sam Wantman to build an electronic air guitar. They wired encoders to a glove that, when calibrated to a hand position, tracked the wearer's gestures through the air and modified some data based on that motion. Zimmerman and Jaron Lanier adapted the glove for CG use in 1982 prior to joining the Atari Research group (1983) and later forming VPL Inc. (1984). The glove then was marketed for use in manipulating 3D CG objects within virtual reality environments.

Dicomed

In business since 1968, Dicomed manufactures professional imaging workstations, digital camera backs, scanners, and film recorders including the StudioPro and FieldPro portable high-resolution digital image-capturing products. The studio BigShot digital cameras for Hasselblad camera bodies work in 8 or 12bit color depth and 4k×4k resolution saved as TIFF image format to a PowerMac host PC. LittleBigShot offers lower resolution for smaller budgets. Dicomed is located in Bloomington, Minnesota, and can be reached at 800-888-7979. You can find more information at www.dicomed.com/about.htm.

— *see also*   Imapro

Digital Disc Recorder (DDR)

A DDR is a convenient storage device that replaces slow tape-based systems for playing back animation. Single-frame pickups can be made anywhere within the record to correct mistakes in the footage, and playback can be a series of edited sequences from random areas of the total disc partition.

— *see also*   Accom and Abekes

digitize

To digitize is to input physical (analog) data into digital form for processing in the computer. Digitizing can be done by scanning 2D artwork or film as well as by inputting 3D data with some form of camera, laser, or magnetic stylus system.

DMax

DMax stands for maximum density or dynamic range. It indicates an image's capability to resolve highlight and shadow detail. It is expressed in a logarithmic scale, usually between 2.0 and 4.0. The term is borrowed from print technology's ink levels when applied to a surface.

dot matrix printer

This old, nearly obsolete technology uses electrostatically charged needles that make a physical impression on paper by way of an ink ribbon.

— *see also*   inkjet printer

dot size

This is the smallest discrete diameter of a printer's impression.

dpi

This stands for dots per inch. It is a measurement of desktop printer output resolution; 720 dpi is a typical consumer color printer resolution.

— *see also*   ppi

drum scanner

This high-resolution photographic scanner utilizes a spinning cylinder to capture almost 10,000 dpi.

DST

This mass storage computer tape product was first introduced by Ampex in 1992.

— *see also*   Ampex

dye sublimation printer

This 256-color printer uses a heat-transfer process to create continuous tone and near-photographic reproductions.

— *see also*   wax transfer printer

Electronic Still Store ▶ see Ampex

Epson

Epson makes a wide range of desktop color printers. The company is located in Torrance, California, and can be reached at 800-463-7766. You can find more information at www.epson.com.

exabyte

This 8mm magnetic tape is used for storing digital data. One cassette the size of an audio tape can hold between .5 and 20 gigabytes of data, depending on the compression scheme used. Headquartered in Boulder, Colorado, the company has offices worldwide and can be reached at 800-774-7172. You can find more information at www.exabyte.com.

eXtreme fx

This is Celco's CRT digital color image recorder.

FEElit

This new, tactile-feedback mouse technology enables users to feel a GUI's buttons and menu items. It is brought to you by Immersion Corporation, which is located in San Jose, California, and can be reached at 408-467-1900. You can find more information at www.force-feedback.com or www.immerse.com.

floppy

This is a generic term for commercial rewritable media common to the consumer market. Examples include floppy-based drives (Iomega ZIP), hard disc drives (Iomega JAZ, SyQuest), optical technologies (CD-ROM, DVD), and newer PC/flash cards.

Geometrix

Geomtrix makes the breakthrough 3Scan video-based 3D digitizer and the new camera scene-tracking software. The low-cost tabletop technology is a fast, cheap, and accurate way to create full-color, textured polygon mesh objects. It is a great alternative, in many cases, to the slower and more costly laser-based scanning. Geometrix is located in San Jose, California, and can be reached at 408-999-7499. You can find more information at www.geometrixinc.com.

GRAIL

GRAIL was developed at the Rand Corporation (by Thomas Ellis and others) in the early 1960s to develop a more intuitive working system for programmers. It was combined a Rand Tablet input device, a computer, CRT, and software. Long before the Apple Newton and the newer personal digital assistants (PDAs), GRAIL enabled freeform handwriting of letters and symbols to be recognized and interpreted by the computer. The hand-drawn letters and

words were recognized and replaced with their corresponding text equivalents, and abstract symbols served defined
functions. A squiggly line drawn over a word, for example,
meant to "erase" that word.

head-mounted display

Made popular in virtual-reality simulations, this display
basically consists of two small video monitors, one
mounted in front of each eye in an otherwise light-tight
helmet. The scene viewed by the wearer is most often calibrated to a neutral head position within the virtual world so
that, when a person turns his head, the scene also pivots
correctly to give the impression that the person is "in" the
virtual environment. Current commercial examples include
the Datavisor from n-Vision. You can find more information at www.nvis.com.

Howtek

Howtek makes high-resolution drum and flatbed scanners.
This Hudson, New York, company can be reached at
603-882-5200. You can find more information at
www.howtek.com.

Iconics

Iconics made scanners and framebuffers in the 1980s.
Today, Iconics provides industrial automation software for
Microsoft Windows operating systems. Located in
Foxborough, Massachusetts, Iconics can be reached at
508-543-8600. You can find more information at
www.iconics.com.

Imageware Corporation

Founded in 1991, Imageware makes the Surfacer software
for manipulating 3D scanned model data. The software creates NURBS patch data from other data such as point
clouds or polygons. Surfacer also can export data in either
IGES or STL formats. Imageware was acquired by SCRC
in October 1998. Located in Ann Arbor, Michigan,
Imageware can be reached at 734.994.7300. You can find
more information at www.iware.com/.

Imagica

Imagica makes precision 4K resolution film scanners. The latest digital film scanner is the IMAGER3000V, which supports both 4 perf 35mm and 8 perf Vistavision with up to 12 bits of color depth per channel. Imagica is located in Los Angeles, California, and can be reached at 310-306-4180. You can find more information at www.imagica-la.com.

Imapro

Since 1979, Imapro has made high-resolution film scanners and recorders as well as Windows-based image retouching and manipulation workstations. In February 1986, Imapro was acquired by the Agfa Division of Bayer Corporation. Located in Ottawa, Canada, Imapro can be reached at 613-738-3000. You can find more information at www.imapro.com.

inkjet printers

This is the most common "average" printer technology because of its relative low cost, speed, and quality. It deposits (or "jets") ink droplets directly onto the paper.

InSpeck Inc.

InSpeck makes software and camera-based 3D digitizers capable of full-body scans with halogen light. Products range from the standard 3DCapturor to the 3DBody-Builder for full-body scans. The company is based in Quebec City, Canada. You can find more information at www.inspeck.com.

Kodak Professional

Kodak Professional makes high-end digital cameras that capture images with a CCD instead of by exposing film. Image resolutions of up to 2,000×3,000 can be transferred directly to the computer for manipulation by any one of many software packages such as Photoshop or Painter. Kodak Professional is a division of Eastman Kodak and is located in Rochester, New York. The company can be reached at 800-235-6325. You can find more information at www.kodak.com/go/professional.

laser printer

The laser printer was first developed by Gary Starkweather at Xerox PARC and was released in 1977. These days, monochrome home models can be found for only a few hundred dollars. Resolutions typically are 1800×600 dpi, and the machines print at least eight pages per minute. Color laser printers have come down to the $2,000 price range and usually can handle at least four pages per minute.

Liquid Crystal Display (LCD)

LCD is a technology utilizing polarized crystals in an electric field. Their small size and lightweight construction make them ideal for head-mounted displays.

logical input device

An input device can be any number of physical means for a user to specify data of some kind to a software application. Examples include a keyboard, a mouse, and a data tablet.

Management Graphics, Inc.

This hardware and software company developed the Solitaire and Sapphire film recorders. The Solitare[rm] Cine III Image Recorder is the latest CRT-based film recorder. Q-Bit is Management Graphics' Mac-based software used to drive TARGA files out to the Solitaire and Sapphire film recorders. Jet Stream is Management Graphics' color image server used to drive the Solitaire and Sapphire film recorders. It utilizes a PostScript Level 2 interpreter and allows users to image TIFF and TARGA files. Management Graphics is located in Bloomington, Minnesota, and can be reached at 612-854-1220. You can find more information at www.mgi.com.

Minolta

Minolta makes the laser-based Vivid 700 3D digitizer for SGI or the PC. You can find more information at Minolta's "how2scan" page (www.how2scan.com) or at their main Web page (www.minolta.com).

motion capture

Various points on a person's body are registered, tracked, recorded, and transferred to software to drive the animation of corresponding points on a CGI figure. Extremely realistic human motion is therefore imparted to the digital creature. Two main systems currently are in use, and both have advantages depending on the type of motion being captured and other restrictions such as environment. Optical systems use cameras to record small points attached to the body, and they have no restrictions of movement except if a given point becomes occluded to any camera. The tracking data is then lost for that duration. New software advances, however, can easily interpolate across these dead spots in the tracking data. Optical systems also are not subject to the interference of metallic objects as magnetic systems are; therefore, they can be setup virtually anywhere.

Magnetic systems use physical tethers attached to main pivot points on the body and therefore do not suffer from point occlusion. A main advantage with most magnetic systems is that the data being read and interpreted to the CG animation software often is in real time. This means that "performance" animation can be directed live by a director; most optical systems need many hours of processing time to translate the captured data into a usable form for the animation system. Suppliers of motion-capture technology include Ascension Technology (Burlington, Vermont), Motion Analysis (Santa Rosa, California, www.MotionAnalysis.com) and Polhemus (Colchester, Vermont, www.polhemus.com). Lamb & Company is particularly experienced at motion capture and has a very useful FAQ page online at www.lambsoft.com/mocapfaq.html.

mouse

Douglas Engelbart (from the Stanford Research Institute) first demonstrated the mouse to the public in December 1968 in San Francisco, California. It later was adopted as the input device on the early PC projects Alto and Star at Xerox PARC in the 1970s, but it was not popularized until it was attached to the Apple's first Mac in 1984.

NTSC

In 1953, the National Television Standards Committee developed the North American television broadcast standard of 60 half frames (fields) per second, each containing 525 lines of resolution. Only 480 effective lines are used for display; the remaining occur during blanking. (This is affectionately known as "Never The Same Color" or "Never Twice the Same Color.")

Paint Effects

This new painting input technology is coming soon from Alias|Wavefront for its Maya Complete and Maya Unlimited software. Paint Effects will be fully integrated into the Maya 3D user environment and will allow for real-time creation of organic elements such as plants, hair, lightning, and fire. In addition, it will provide complete interaction with lighting, shadows, depth values, and animation within Maya scenes. You can find more information at www.aw.sgi.com/.

PAL

PAL stands for phase alternate line. This is the television video standard in most of Western Europe, using 625 lines of resolution at 50 interlaced fields per second. It was developed in the early 1960s.

— *see also* NTSC, SECAM

PAL-M

This is a variation of the PAL video format used only in Brazil. Its 525/60 standard is similar to NTSC.

Paraform Inc.

Paraform makes PolySurf, a high-end software solution for allowing interactive NURBS creation from polygonal databases. It is based on software licensed from Stanford University and is available for the Windows NT and SGI platforms. Paraform also has a new full-body 3D laser scanning service facility open in Los Angeles and can be reached at 650-846-2100. You can find more information at www.paraform.com.

peripheral

Any additional equipment attached to a computer[md]such as a mouse, an external CD-ROM drive, a scanner, or a modem—is called a peripheral.

pica

A pica is a unit of measurement in desktop publishing and hard-copy printers. It is equal to about one-sixth of an inch or 12 points.

point cloud

This raw data set of laser-scanned information must be interpreted and converted to usable patch data such as NURBS.

Polhemus

Polhemus makes 3D digitizing and motion-capture tracking products including the real-time optical Star*Trak system. Desktop-scanning solutions include its newest hand-held laser scanner, the FastScan for Windows NT. Polhemus is located in Colchester, Vermont, and can be reached at 800-357-4777. You can find more information at www.polhemus.com.

PostScript

Introduced by Adobe in 1985, PostScript is a device-independent programming language optimized for printing text-based and graphic images. Early laser printers such as the Apple LaserWriter were among the first to take advantage of this technology.

ppi

This stands for pixels per inch. It describes the number of pixels that a scanner's optics can resolve. When used in scanner specification as a pair of two numbers, the first is the optical resolution and the second is the incremental distance change between scan lines. Typical flatbed scanner resolution is between 600 and 1,200 ppi. This sometimes is used synonymously with dpi (dots per inch).

— *see also*   dpi

puck

A puck is a hand-held, mouse-like device most often used with cross hairs to register and digitize flat artwork into the computer.

QIC

QIC stands for Quarter-Inch Cartridge. These magnetic tape-storage formats have capacities between 40MB and 13GB. They are available from Quarter-Inch Cartridge Drive Standards, Inc., located in Santa Barbara, California. The company can be reached at 805-963-3853. You can find more information at www.qic.org/index.html.

Rand Tablet

The Rand Tablet was developed at the Rand Corporation (by Thomas Ellis and others) in 1958 to explore the possibilities of interacting directly with CRT displays. It was combined with a computer, CRT, and software into the GRAIL system for a more intuitive working system for programmers.

Scitex Corporation LTD.

Scitex is a leader in digital graphic art tools including scanners, printers, and desktop publishing tools. The company is located in Herzlia, Israel, and can be reached at 800-800-2500. You can find more information at www.scitex.com.

SECAM

SECAM stands for *sequential couleur a memoire* (sequential color with memory). This broadcast television standard was used in France and Russian republics, using 625 lines of resolution at 50 interlaced fields per second. Developed in the early 1960s, the luminance and sound signals of SECAM are compatible with the PAL standard.

— *see also*   NTSC, PAL

SyQuest Technologies Inc.

SyQuest makes removable storage cartridges that compete with Iomega JAZ drives. The company filed chapter 11 bankruptcy in November 1998. Its assets were sold to

Iomega Corporation, and SyQuest continues limited operations now known as SYQT, Inc. You can find more information at www.syquest.com.

telecine

This refers to film-to-tape transfer. It is a machine that transfers 24fps film images onto video tape at various international standard speeds for use in television broadcasts.

VistaVision

This standard 35mm film motion picture format is oriented horizontally and is exposed on an area eight perforations wide (as opposed to the standard 35mm format that runs vertically and exposes four perfs). Today, VistaVision is used for its greater resolution in capturing plate images to be used for optical compositing in visual effects work. ILM especially has long been a proponent of this film format for use in its effects photography.

VPL Research (1984–1992)

Founded by Jaron Lanier, Jean-Jacques Grimaud, and Thomas Zimmerman, this company designed and sold some of the first commercial virtual-reality products including the Dataglove, which was designed by Lanier and Zimmerman in 1982.

Wacom Technology

Wacom produces a wide range of input devices for the Mac, PC, and SGI hardware platforms. Tablets come in various sizes from 4×5" to 9×12". The latest line of Intuos pens has 1,024 levels of sensitivity and registers not only height but tilt angle and direction of movement across the tablet surface. Other new products include an ambidextrous wireless mouse and a DualTrack feature for the tablets that enables the use of two input devices simultaneously. The DualTrack feature currently is designed to work only with Alias StudioPaint on the SGI platform. Wacom is located in Vancouver, Washington, and can be reached at 800-922-9348. You can find more information at www.wacom.com.

wax transfer printer

This type of printer uses colored wax paper transferred with tiny heated metal filaments for fast full-color output. Thermal wax transfer printers only produce primary colors, however, and rely on dithering to create implied blends and tones (unlike dye sublimation printing, which provides true continuous tone color with its varying heat intensities). Printers such as the ColorPoint 835 PS can operate in either of these two modes, all built into one unit.

ZIP drive

This is a popular 100MB (and new 250MB floppy type) data cartridge from Iomega Corp. Iomega is located in Roy, Utah, and can be reached at 800-697-8833. You can find more information at `www.iomega.com`.

Abel Image Research

Alias Research Inc.

Amiga

Apple Computer

Atari Inc.

Blue Sky Studios

Bo Gehring Associates

Buf Compagnie

Computer Creations

Computer Film Company

Computer FX Ltd.

Computer Graphics Laboratory Inc.

Computer Image Corporation

Cranston/Csuri Productions

deGraf/Wahrman

DemoGraFX

Digital Effects

Digital Pictures

Digital Productions

Electric Image

Evans & Sutherland Computer Corporation

Ex Machina

Fantastic Animation Machine

Image West

Industrial Light & Magic

Information International Inc.

Japan Computer Graphics Lab

Kleiser-Walczak Construction Company

Kroyer Films

Lamb & Company

Links

Mathematics Application Group, Inc.

MAGI/Syntha Vision

mental images

MetroLight

The Moving Picture Company

NCSA

New York Institute of Technology

Ohio State University

Omnibus Computer Graphics Inc.

OptoMystic

Pacific Data Images

Pixar

Historically Significant Companies

Protozoa

reZn8

Rhythm & Hues

Robert Abel & Associates

Robert Greenberg and Associates

Santa Barbara Studios

Side Effects Software

Silicon Graphics, Inc.

Softimage Inc.

Sogitec Audiovisuel

Stanford

Symbolics Graphics Division

Synthavision

Systems Simulation Ltd.

Thompson Digital Images

University of Bath

University of Illinois

University of Utah

Vertigo Software Corporation

VIFX

Wavefront

Whitney/Demos Productions

Xaos

Xerox PARC

Z-A Production

What qualifies as historically significant? My intent for this chapter is to provide an accurate history for the earliest and most significant companies related to computer graphics research and production. The companies listed here were all formed prior to 1987, a date I chose that represented the last of the second-generation companies.

The universities and research centers listed are by no means the only ones that existed at the time, but they are the largest and the most directly and significantly related to early CG development. An entire (large) book could easily be written solely about the academic contributions of the 1970s and 1980s, something that is quite beyond the scope of this humble chapter.

I will forever be indebted to every person who graciously contributed their time and energy to make these histories possible. Their generosity has resulted in making this, and the "Computer Graphics Time Line" chapter, the first ever comprehensive and accurate description of CG history. I only hope it will be as rewarding for you to read as it was for me to research.

Abel Image Research

Abel Image Research (colloquially known as AIR Software) was the subsidiary of Robert Abel and Associates that sold its software commercially.

AIR rendering software was built primarily by Roy Hall, with modeling and animation code based on early Abel production software by Bill Kovacs, Kim Shelly, Mike Sweeney, Michael Wahrmanand, and others including Hank Weghorst and Marcel Sameck, Isaac Leibermann, Josh Aller, Steve Grey, Charlie Gibson, Liza Keith, and Christina Hills.

Approximately eight production companies worldwide bought AIR software including Electric Image in the UK and Steiner Film in Munich, Germany. (It was used there by employees such as Ken Wesley and Tom Nowak.)

After an initial unsuccessful bid to sell AIR to one company, Bill Kovacs of Wavefront (who had left Abel & Associates in 1983 before AIR was actually formed) offered to buy AIR. A week later, to eliminate a competitor, Wavefront Technologies of Santa Barbara, California, bought AIR for $1 million. The purchase also coincided with the demise of Abel's recent parent company Omnibus in April of 1987.

Alias Research Inc.

(1982 to present)

Will Anielewicz, Andrew Pearce, and Kevin Tureski contributed to this synopsis.

Alias Research Inc. of Toronto, Canada, was founded in 1983 by Stephen Bingham, Susan McKenna, David Springer, and Nigel McGrath with the goal of creating software for computer animation in film and video production. Stephen was a television producer, a director for the National Film Theatre of Canada, and an advisor to the government on the use of computer graphics for the visual display of quantitative data. Susan worked as an independent producer in the industrial video and film arena and had some experience in fundraising in the industry.

Nigel ran a local business, McGrath & Associates, that specialized in computer graphics slide production. David was head of the CG lab at Sheridan College and led the software development. The founders obtained a grant of $61,000 from the National Research Council (NRC), borrowed equipment from McGrath & Associates, and secured scientific research tax credits (SRTC) for some funded research work on anti-aliasing that would be needed for their own product, ALIAS/1.

The four principals soon were joined by employees five and six: Will Anielewicz (recently of Omnibus and currently at ILM) and Mike Sweeney (on software development). It was Will and Mike who, unbeknownst to management, made a

FACTOID

The name "Alias" was arrived at during a brainstorming session when Susan said "What we need is an alias for the company."

FACTOID

Alias' first office was in an elevator shaft. Rent was $150 per month in the always-under-construction "Much Music" building, Canada's version of MTV.

conscious decision to make the Alias renderer the best look-ing (as opposed to the fastest), a feature that still accurately describes the current code.

By summer 1985, the product was complete. The company took it to market with the first activity being a small booth at SIGGRAPH 85 in San Francisco. (Coincidentally, Wavefront launched their product, Advanced Visualizer, the same year.) The most unique elements of the Alias/1 system were its use of Cardinal splines (supported by Silicon Graphics' GL language) instead of polygonal lines, the GUI with pop-up menus instead of a command-line interface, and the integration of multiple functions (model-ing, animation, rendering, paint, film recording) within a single interface. Alias/1 also provided the first paint system for the SGI IRIS 2400.

Originally, Alias/1 was targeted at the postproduction mar-ket primarily for advertising usage. One of its earliest cus-tomers, however, was General Motors. The fact that Alias/1 was based on splines was of great interest to GM, who wanted to use the system for design work. Alias was reluc-tant to enter the design market because it was so distant from what Alias was founded to do. By November 1995, however, they had signed a deal with GM to incorporate basis spline (B-spline) technology. Over the next year or so, Alias sold mostly to postproduction customers—its original target market. As is common with emerging technologies, there was a broad range of early adopters with a surprising number doing architectural visualization and scientific visualization. With the introduction of Alias/2 with B-spline geometry in late 1987, however, sales to industrial design companies started to take off. With Alias V3.0 in 1992, the same executable was marketed to industrial design as Alias Studio and to the entertainment markets as PowerAnimator. V3.0 also was the release that introduced NURBS, which has become a standard for both markets.

In 1996, Alias in-house artist Chris Landreth's short ani-mation *The End* was nominated for an Oscar in the Best Animated Short category.

FACTOID

Here's a little known fact: The name of the Alias image-viewing utility "wrl" came about when Will Anielewicz added to the existing code of "rl" and wanted to change its name... Hence, it became the self-initialed w(ill)rl utility name we all know and love today. Will developed his skills in obscurity at Omnibus. One of his dozen-or-so variants of an extrusion program was called " newtube2," and its help went approximately as follows:

newtube2: useage: file x y z xbang ybang zbang xtang ytang zbang

file: a ppt file to extrube about x y z

xbang ybang zbang: do the obvious

xtang ytang ztang: use only if you wrote the code

Animators had to chain together dozens of UNIX programs using Cshell. In fact, Keith Ballinger, a TD, programmed ease-in/ease-out values with his TI-58 calculator. Others looked up the values in tables and typed them in with a text editor.

The Alias Renderer

"Ray casting (as Alias called it) is the casting of 2.5D rays into 2.5D buckets of triangles. We call the rays (and geometry) 2.5D because they are in the projected screen space of the image, so they are 2D, but they still have a bit of Z depth information, which we can use to generate a real 3D intersection point. Alias ray casting is like ray tracing in that we can compute volume intersections (fog, particles, glows, and so on) with the speed of a 2D intersection test, but it is unlike ray tracing in that no secondary rays are (or can be) generated due to the nature of the geometry already projected into 2.5D. The ray casting algorithm is closest to the ZZ-buffer (yes, two Z's) presented at SIGGRAPH in 1993, "Hierarchical Z-Buffer Visibility" (the paper was unrelated to A|W).

People also tend to think of rendering as a post-process, separate task. The Maya renderer is completely integrated so that geometric, dynamic, or other properties of the scene can affect the shading. (Connect the Y coordinate of a sphere to the red channel of a shader, and you've got a sphere that gets 'redder' the higher it is translated.)"

—Andrew Pearce

In 1998, a Scientific and Engineering Academy Award from the Academy of Motion Picture Arts and Sciences was presented to John Gibson, Rob Kreiger, Milan Novacek, Glen Ozymok, and Dave Springer for the development of the geometric modeling component of the Alias PowerAnimator system.

For animators, the latest tools include the most advanced inverse kinematics (IK), a completely integrated particle system, and unique 3D model interpolation and deformation controls.

Alias Research and longtime competitor Wavefront Technologies both were bought by SGI in 1995 and now are known by the new combined name of Alias|Wavefront.

Alias|Wavefront released a next generation complete 3D animation system called Maya in February of 1998. Maya is available for SGI IRIX and Windows NT. Maya v2.0 is expected to ship in the summer of 1999. Alias|Wavefront can be reached at 800-447-2542. You can find more information at www.aw.sgi.com.

—*see also*   Wavefront, Silicon Graphics Inc.

Amiga

The Amiga was a color computer introduced by Commodore Computer in 1985 after beginning development as the Amiga Lorraine. Models included the 500, 1000, 3000, and 4000. Original software included Sculpt-3D and Deluxe Paint II. A unique feature of the 1000 model was its built-in composite video output. This enabled you to record to a VHS deck whatever you saw on the screen in real time. With masked brush shapes and color cycling, you really could get some amazing effects out of D-Paint II with this setup. (I should know, I created my first short film in 1986 that way! —Author)

Commodore also produced the earliest alternative input devices for video games. The JoyBoard (1983) foot controller had a motto of "You lean, you tilt, you bend, you turn." The Power-Stick (1983) was a one-handed thumb controller.

The Amiga is a perfect example of how the best product does not always win the marketplace. The Amiga is still an active platform today, thanks to a loyal following of long-time users. Surf the Web for lots of great software and newsgroup discussions, starting at www.amiga.com.

Amiga Testimonial!

"Amiga—the cool thing about the Amiga was/is (I have two in my house right now…) that it had built-in graphics and sound co-processors and could do true multitasking on the Motorola 68000 series, which DOS, MS-DOS, WindowsX, and MacOS never did on that CPU… or any other, for that matter. What a box!" —John Andrew Berton, ILM VFX Supervisor

Apple Computer

(1976 to present)

Founded by Steven Jobs and Steven Wozniak in 1976, Apple was incorporated on January 3, 1977. Apple began with the introduction of the Apple I, followed by the Apple II later in 1977 and the Apple III in 1980. Although definitely not a computer graphics company, Apple did bring many of the GUI interface and desktop publishing graphics concepts to the masses over the years. Several good books have been written about the history of Apple Computer, but I offer some highlights here.

Jobs and his scientists were very impressed by the interface technology they saw demonstrated during their visit to Xerox PARC in December of 1979—so much so that Jobs completely rethought the direction of a graphic interface project they were working on, code named "Lisa." Jobs was soon taken off the Lisa project, however, and began work on another project named "Macintosh." A year after the introduction of the Macintosh in 1984, Jobs was voted out of Apple by the board (and the then-president he himself had hired, John Scully).

As a side note, Microsoft had also just released Windows 1.0 and successfully negotiated a deal protecting its right to use a similar GUI design.

FACTOID

The Macintosh was the first GUI-based personal computer for the masses. (The Mac was, of course, based on the brilliant Alto of Xerox PARC.) It was introduced in 1984 with a price of $2,495 and a bus speed of 8MHz! It included a built-in 500×384 black and white screen, 256KB of RAM (that's K not M), and no hard drive. (Who remembers switching between floppies over and over again? I see those hands!)

217

The Mac II was introduced in 1987, along with the Apple LaserWriter and other third-party software such as Pagemaker. Together, they all formed the first affordable desktop publishing personal computer system. Portable PowerBooks were first introduced in 1991, along with the ill-fated "Newton" hand-held personal digital assistant (PDA).

The introduction of PowerMac in 1994 proved to be a powerful addition to the Mac line, but more poor marketing decisions caused rough financial times. Today, with Jobs back at the helm of his old company as interim CEO, Apple is profitable again and has introduced new products at both ends of its line of personal computers. At the entry level is the iMac, a low-cost, Internet-savvy PC that's as much fun to look at as it is to use. On the high end, the blazing fast G3 line includes built-in 3D acceleration. In early 1999, Apple announced its licensing of the SGI OpenGL 3D graphics standard, an important step in getting serious about the 3D graphics market. Apple can be reached at 800-538-9696. You can find more information at www.apple.com.

Atari Inc.
(1972 to present... sort of)

This video game manufacturer was founded in 1972 by Nolan Bushnell (B.S. University of Utah 1969) and was sold to Warner Inc. in 1976. With the introduction of Pong (also created by Nolan Bushnell), a simple ball-and-paddle-style video game, Atari led the video game revolution of the late '70s and early '80s before falling on hard times. The Atari 2600 (1977) home video game console, with a blazing 1.19 MHz clock speed and 128 bytes of RAM, still has a very loyal cult following. Many devoted Web sites and emulators are available for nostalgia buffs (like me). Enduring video game classics such as Centipede, Missile Command, Pong, Breakout, and Tempest are still being updated and rereleased today with more modern 3D graphics.

Atari First

The Atari Lynx Handheld Video Game (December 1989) was the world's first color, portable game machine. The Jaguar Video Game Console (1993) was the world's first 64-bit game console. The Jaguar lost its war against competitors Sega and Nintendo and was discontinued.

The short-lived Atari Research Center (ARC) included researchers such as Scott Fischer, Jaron Lanier, Brenda Laurel, and Thomas Zimmerman. (Pioneers in virtual reality (VR), Thomas and Jaron developed the DataGlove on their own.)

In 1984, Warner divided Atari Inc. The home division (Atari Corp.) was sold to the founder of Commodore, Jack Tramiel. The arcade division (Atari Games/Tengen) became its own company. Atari Games then was bought by Time-Warner in 1993 and was later sold to WMS in 1996. Atari Corp. was merged with JTS Corp. in 1996 and was then acquired by Hasbro Interactive (a subsidiary of Hasbro, Inc.) on March 16, 1998. You can find more information at www.atari.com.

FACTOID

Nolan Bushnell, creator of Pong and the founder of Atari Inc., also is the founder of Chuck E. Cheese Pizza.

Blue Sky Studios

(1987 to present)

Located just outside Manhattan, Blue Sky Studios was formed by a handful of key people from MAGI/Syntha Vision. Today, the company is best known for its beautifully realistic ray traced rendering and innovative character animation.

Blue Sky was founded in May of 1987 by six people (in alphabetical order): Alison Brown (administration), David Brown (president), Michael Ferraro (systems architect), Carl Ludwig (VP of R&D), Dr. Eugene Troubetskoy (chief scientist), and Chris Wedge (vice president of creative development).

FACTOID

The company was briefly known early on as Blue Sky Productions and more recently as BlueSky I VIFX. Right now, it is once again good ol' Blue Sky Studios.

Other early key employees included Jan Carlée (Animation Director) and Tom Bisogno.

Michael Ferraro developed the entire backbone of the modeling/rendering and animation environment, and he also designed the user interfaces and system interfaces. The programming language he had designed integrated vector/matrix math into a simple interactive language. The language also included constructs to build procedural geometry and textures with an eye to re-implement SynthaVision's ray tracing as an object-oriented production environment. (Mind you, this was well before C++ was well known, and Java wasn't even a glimmer in someone's eye.) This work also included the development of what became the API and the job-control environments for running on a network of computers, at that time still pretty much an unheard of approach. As Blue Sky's first TD, Michael used the language he had designed to procedurally model and animate objects. For the next seven years as chief technical director, he trained and supervised the TDs and remained the "computer scientist" of the group. Not bad for someone formally trained as an artist (BFA/Syracuse MFA/U.Mass). Michael went on to co-found "Possible Worlds" with partner Janine Cirincione.

A major unsung pioneer of CG, Dr. Troubetzkoy developed the concept of ray tracing into the foundation of the company's proprietary software, CGI Studio™. Today, this rendering system is considered by many in the industry to be the world's finest. Dr. Troubetzkoy developed the geometry and intersection calculations alongside Carl Ludwig, who handled the lighting, rendering, and surface physics development. The software traces rays directly to NURBS patches without subdividing into polygons like all other production code. Dr. Troubetzkoy developed an extremely efficient method for evaluating these intersection calculations (27 coefficients!) to represent mathematically perfect surfaces. Boolean operations also are used directly with NURB surfaces, circumventing again the many polygon approximation artifacts inherent to other renderers. Let it also be known that Dr. Troubetzkoy's brilliance is matched only by his modesty, which is the sole reason his important contributions to ray tracing have gone relatively unrecognized.

Later, Blue Sky's CG character work for the feature film *Joe's Apartment* won several top prizes at international festivals including Imagina, the Annecy International Animation Film Festival, the Ottawa International Animation Festival, and the World Animation Celebration.

Blue Sky and Chris Wedge's latest release, *Bunny*, a seven-minute short animated film, uses a hybrid radiosity technique. This is a time-consuming global rendering process that creates extremely realistic images. *Bunny* won the Academy Award for the Best Animated Short Film of 1998.

Whatever the statistics of a given project, this short film was the culmination of 12 years of a company's clear direction: the finest imagery possible with no compromises. Blue Sky's unique imagery is clearly going to set a new standard for the year 2000 and beyond.

20th Century Fox acquired a controlling interest in Blue Sky Productions in 1997 and merged the company with LA-based VIFX (which was acquired by Fox a year earlier), renaming the company Blue Sky/VIFX. The VIFX portion was sold by Fox to Hollywood CGI house Rhythm & Hues in April of 1999. Today, Blue Sky operates once again as a separate entity known as Blue Sky Studios.

A still from the Bunny animated short. © *Blue Sky Studios. Used with permission.*

BLUE SKY FACTOID

Blue Sky's very first jobs included a recycling campaign for the Glass Institute of New York in 1988 and a film job for Famous Players, a theater chain in Canada. The glass job featured procedurally generated skies, clouds, sunset, and water with a glass logo.

Sidebar

Although radiosity and ray tracing are very time consuming to calculate, the Blue Sky software used clever Monte Carlo techniques (instead of patches) to render the seven-minute film. (It still took an entire month to process the bulk of the film on a 160-processor DEC farm!)

Bo Gehring Associates

Louis (Bo) Gehring began work at Magi in 1972, starting the SynthaVision division with Bob Goldstein. While there, Bo created several CG tests for special effects in Steven Spielberg's *Close Encounters of the Third Kind* before the idea was dropped in favor of Doug Trumbull's traditional miniature and practical effects approach.

Instead of returning to New York and Magi, Bo stayed in Los Angeles and originally formed his company as Gehring Aviation in 1977. Based on his experience with computer-controlled machine tools, he sought to capitalize on the new need for computer-driven motion-control cameras for visual effects work. At this time, the only systems in existence were John Dykstra's at George Lucas's ILM (developed for *Star Wars*) and those at Robert Abel's company.

About this time, creative advertising agency icon Harry Marks (formerly VP at ABC and then one half of Sullivan & Marks) recruited Doug Trumbull to do effects work for him. Trumbull moved on to motion picture work, so Harry then turned to his fellow UCLA alum Robert Abel to help create visual effects for ABC. Bob Abel then left for Hollywood when he began his initial work on the first *Star Trek* film. It was then that Bo Gehring got the call from Marks to step in and create visual effects where Abel and Trumbull had left off.

Milestone

Bo Gehring Associates' first feature film work in 1977 was the little known *Demon Seed*, a sci-fi B-movie about a computer that becomes sentient and wants to reproduce with his creator's wife (a late-night classic to be sure). Bo provided vector graphics for computer displays on set, making this one of the very earliest examples of CG in a feature film.

In 1983, Bo Gehring Associates had about 35 employees. It was then that they developed the amazing Scene Tracking Auto Registration (STAR) automatic scene-tracking electronic rotoscoping system. Conceived by Bo and written by none other than Jim Clark of SGI fame (with the front end written by Bo himself), the technique was based on discussions Bo had with others while at Magi as early as 1974. Both simple and revolutionary, the idea was to be able to automatically track as little as four points (six were ideal) in a filmed scene, allowing the camera matrix program to extrapolate match-move information for compositing CG imagery perfectly into a live-action scene. Film footage was rear-projected on a vertically mounted CalComp 30×40-inch translucent plotting surface. An Oxberry-based camera rig was used to increment the rear projection images one frame at a time.

Most recently, Bo Gehring worked as Director of Audio Technologies at Reality By Design, Inc. in Woburn, Massachusetts, until April of 1999.

Buf Compagnie
(1982 to present)

Pierre Buffin and Henry Seydoux founded Buffin Seydoux Computer Animation (B.S.C.A.) in 1982. In 1988, they finished a six-minute 3D animation about insects living in a computer, the first "long animation" in France. Other early employees were Patrick Albert, Olivier Gilbert, Georges Lagardere, Arnauld Lamorlette, Christophe Hery, Francois Blanchet, Christian Zumbiehl, and Matthieu Schonholzer.

Buf is an important test site for the mental ray software, having completed realistic CG effects with that software on *Delicatessen, City of the Lost Children,* and *Batman and Robin.*

Computer Creations
Tom Klimek headed the company, which was located in the unlikely location of South Bend, Indiana. (Jim Lindner was the New York sales representative, and Gail Resnik was an employee.) Jim Lindner and Suzanne Gavril, former marketing executives at Xerox, later broke with Computer Creations and formed Fantastic Animation Machine in Manhattan.

They used the first digital disk recorder system, the ESS-1 made by Ampex, and used code they had written on PDP-11 minicomputers for rendering. In the later '80s, they did a huge project for Williams video games, but I am unsure how the company fared after that.

Computer Film Company (CFC)

CFC was founded in 1984 by Andrew Berend, Mike Boudry, and Nick Pollock. Andrew came from a motion-control background and previously had formed Computer FX Ltd. and had worked for the Moving Picture Company. Mike was the hardware guy, and Nick was software. Neil Harris joined in 1986 as a software programmer also.

The intent at CFC from the very beginning was full-frame digital manipulation and compositing of live-action footage. This was a unique charter among startup CG facilities until very recently. That is to say, the company was not primarily concerned with vector or raster computer-generated imagery.

In 1985, CFC began researching what was available at that time for computer hardware, input scanning, and film-recording equipment. They happened upon another startup company called Benchmark Technologies in London. Benchmark was in the middle of designing a computer system of its own. CFC was able to collaborate, optimizing the new hardware for their own specialized uses. A homemade film scanner and film recorder would later be hooked up to the system.

By mid-1987, a number of private investors were pooled together (thanks to a government tax break arrangement similar to the break in Canada at the same time), and CFC moved out of the garage and into a derelict factory building (complete with leaking roof and broken floor boards).

The homemade scanner was done by now, built mostly from scratch but based initially on a DataCopy CCD camera. The Benchmark computer system was working, and the software also was well along and ready for the first productions. A film recorder was still a problem, and several of the early commercial systems were considered and rejected.

(The Matrix QCR was not deemed good enough, and the Celco CFR-700 cost a prohibitive $300,000.) Eventually, they built a little phone booth-size clean room in the building to house the film recorder.

Although the majority of early jobs consisted of television work, in 1987, CFC completed work on one of the first ever full-frame digital film composites for a feature film (definitely the first outside the United States). The film was called *Fruit Machine* in the UK and was released as *Wonder World* in the United States. It featured a scene in which a character dives into a pool of dolphins and then transforms into a dolphin himself. Without any affordable disc storage at the time, CFC took advantage of their double-headed film scanner to manipulate one frame at a time.

A single frame of the foreground element was scanned along with a single frame of the background element, both stored in framebuffer memory simultaneously. The image manipulation was completed with the final composite then being sent to the film recorder. The process then was repeated one frame at a time, helped in part by the fully scriptable and repeatable functions of their custom digital painting software. By this time, CFC had about nine employees including management, a producer, and Janek Sirrs, who was quite possibly the world's first full-time digital compositor.

CFC moved out of the factory in 1988 into a facility in central London. It also was at this time that their work attracted the attention of Kodak's Electronic Intermediate Systems group, which visited CFC to learn about their technology. The key to CFC's work from the very beginning was their software's capability to do subpixel accurate motion tracking, a feature that did not become common in commercial packages until very recently. Another major advantage at CFC was the constant working relationship between R&D and production.

By 1988–89, larger and faster disc storage was in use and the scanning/recording work process was decoupled into the more traditional arrangement familiar today. In 1990, the first major Hollywood film CFC worked on was

Memphis Belle. CFC replaced about a dozen "less than per-fect" traditional optically composited scenes of flying bombers with much better quality digital composites. They also digitally restored and colorized some old black and white WWII footage.

Mike visited Los Angeles in 1991 and started looking into potential business there. CFC then opened an office in Los Angeles in 1992. This office has gone on to contribute significant work to dozens of major feature films including *The Hudsucker Proxy*.

CFC has been honored twice with Technical Achievement Academy Awards—once for their contribution to digital film scanning and once for their pioneering work in digital compositing.

In August of 1997, CFC sold 100 percent ownership to MegaloMedia, which also owns London's Frame Store post house and the Saatchi & Saatchi company. Today, alongside Domino, Cineon, Matador, and Flame systems, CFC still uses their original Benchmark computer systems, a true testament to how far ahead that technology was when it was first designed more than a dozen years ago.

Andrew left CFC to help set up Cambridge Animation with Peter Florence. Mike Boudry left CFC to "retire" in 1998.

Computer FX Ltd. (CFX)

(1982 to present)

Computer FX Ltd. (later called CFX Ltd. and today called CFX Associates) was formed by Andrew Berend, Ian Chisholm, and Craig Zerouni in 1982. They began by purchasing the first Interactive Machines Inc. (IMI) vector display computer, a real-time, monochrome system that competed with the E&S products. This was the first real-time animation system in Europe. Craig wrote some code to generate realistic water and reflections before anyone else in the UK. They also built a framebuffer and render engine based on the Texas DSP chip.

Film output was accomplished by filming directly off the monitor through different colored gels, which were mounted on a wheel. The camera and the gels were controlled by the IMI itself. The animation software had a scripting system that controlled the animation files themselves, the camera, and the color wheel. Because the number of colored gels was limited (to six, I think), sometimes a person had to stand there in the dark and change filters between shoots. (Some of this hardware also was built by Mike Boudry.)

Andrew Berend left in late 1984 to join Mike Boudry and co-found the Computer Film Company (CFC).

QUOTE

"Just as CFX was realizing that the wireframe business was evaporating and that our own home-grown raster hardware/software wasn't going to get good enough fast enough (we were always small), two guys named John Penney and Greg Hermanovic phoned us up.

They said they were from Omnibus Computer Graphics, the world's first publicly listed computer animation company, and they were looking to franchise their software around the world. They wanted to start with England because they could speak the language and because it was arguably the next most advanced market after North America.

After a lot of talking and thinking we decided okay, we'll buy the stuff. Terms were arranged (I think the number was in the region of $100,000 Canadian), and a reel of software (just like you've seen in those '50s science fiction films) arrived. We installed it. As franchisees, we were entitled to the source code, so that's what we got. We installed it and got to understanding it.

Meanwhile, Omnibus, belching after having eaten Robert Abel and Digital Productions back-to-back, fell over. Kaputt. Out of business. The world's first shareholders in computer animation found out what a great business this is. But we had never paid for the software we had, which we were now happily using in production.

Eventually, the receivers called us up and demanded payment. We refused on the grounds that, without support, it wasn't worth nearly as much. Eventually, we settled for about $20,000 Canadian, I believe. But we still had the source code.

Greg surfaced from under the wreckage of Omnibus with his partner Kim Davidson and called us up, offering to support Prisms (what Omnibus called the software), which is now available from Side Effects Software. We agreed.

So not only was CFX the world's first customer for Side Effects Software, we had source for a few years until we agreed to give up getting updates (we were always fair and reasonable!). And we used the source—I once ported the command line and channel manipulation portion of Prisms to an Amiga, which we used to control our own motion-control rig."

—Craig Zerouni (craig@sgrail.com)

227

CFX constantly tried to reinvent the medium, partnering with a traditional animation company called Shootsey to try to sell agencies on the idea of mixing the two media. That never went anywhere, but they also built a motion-control rig of their own.

QUOTE

"One of our first rendered jobs went to 1-inch tape (remember that?) via a Sony BVH-2000 (or 2500, whichever it was that allowed single-frame edits). The framebuffer would fill with the image, then a person had to hit "edit" on the Sony, and it would preroll, run forward, record the frame, and then stop. Then a person had to tell the computer to render the next frame. That person was me. I had to stay awake, hitting two buttons every five minutes in the correct order for about 36 hours straight to get it done on time. The truth is, I did fall asleep for a few hours around 5 a.m., so I lost some time, but I don't think it matters now if I admit it.

To do one job, I recall, we had no way of getting digital video back and forth to a post-house, so we ended up taking our 100-lb. Abekas A60 and putting in the back of a taxi as a method of getting the D1 back and forth. It took two or three people to do this plus a little wheely cart thing we had. It was, like everything else about this business, completely mad."

—Craig Zerouni

Computer Graphics Laboratory Inc.
(1981 to 1992)

This was the commercial production company set up by the NYIT Computer Graphics Lab. Commercials included many glitzy sports promos for CBS, spots for Volkswagen and Chevrolet, and the "Live From Lincoln Center" opening (which still is showing today). Many technical directors and animators worked here including Pat Hanrahan (Pixar), Ken Wesley (ILM), and Glen Maguire. Two young animators, Glenn McQueen and Rex Grignon, are now animation supervisors at Pixar and PDI, respectively.

Computer Image Corporation (CIC)
Based in Denver, CIC was the brainchild of Lee Harrison and was in the business of making analog computer graphics in the early 1970s. Unique machines created at CIC included Animac, Caesar, and Scanimate. Lee received the first-ever Emmy for Technical Achievement in 1973 for his work. (See Appendix D, "Scanimate," by Ed Kramer for more details about this.) Lee Harrison passed away in 1998.

Employees included Kirk Paulson and Phil Zimmerman. Jim Johnson was a Director and Technical Director there for more than six years from 1980 to 1986. Jim Johnson (JJ) is now Executive Producer at Deep Blue Sea in Miami, Florida.

Cranston/Csuri Productions (CCP)
(1981 to 1987)

Cranston/Csuri was founded in August of 1981 by Charles Csuri of Ohio State University and investor Robert Kanuth of The Cranston Companies in Columbus, Ohio. Jim Kristoff (also a past treasurer of Ohio State) came with Kanuth and served as president, while Wayne Carlson of Ohio State was VP and head of R&D. Michael Collery was Director of Animation, Don Stredney developed the medical imaging market for CCP, and Dr. Tom Linehan developed the educational market for CCP. Along with Shawn Ho (rendering), Paul Sidlo (Creative Director), and Bob Marshal, the first employees numbered about 10 total.

Hardware included PDP 11-780 and 750s, a Megatek vector display, and an IMI Pyramid (3 or 4mips) and VAX 780 (1 mip!). One of the first production ethernet networks connected everyone. Rendering at that time was done to memory not to a hard disc and was output to a Celco 2000 film recorder. Also used was a rare but extremely cool digital disk recorder called an Ampex ESS. (The Ampex was way ahead of its time in 1983. The Abekas was not released until about 1987.)

The primary rendering pipeline originally was developed by Frank Crow with his scn_assembler. Shawn Ho made significant advances to this by adding new features such as reflection mapping, and he worked out a way of simulation refractions. (It was limited, however, to rendering scenes with less than 10,000 polygons.) Wayne Carlson wrote most of the modeling code, and Bob Marshal did lots of systems-type stuff and miscellaneous production software. Michael Collery wrote compositing software and other miscellaneous stuff, and Julian Gomez came along and wrote

Twixt on the E&S Picture System. The animation software was used on the "IMI" (vector-based graphical display device), and the modeling software ran on the Megatek. Mark Howard (head of engineering) designed and built the "Mark" series of framebuffers from scratch(!).

The first work done at CCP was station IDs and flying logos for ABC News in New York and later for ABC Sports. The relationship between CCP and ABC Sports President Roger Goodman lasted for many years. It did not end until 1984, when they reluctantly had to turn down the work for that year's winter Olympics. Because CCP already was booked with work, Jim Kristoff suggested that ABC use a new company on the west coast that was building an excellent reputation—Pacific Data Images.

Also in 1984, Cranston/Csuri acquired $3 million of additional investor capital from several organizations. Although owning only a minority share in the company, the new investors controlled the board and did not agree with President Jim Kristoff's plans for the future. Chief among the disagreements was the idea of licensing CCP software and the idea of opening a production office in Los Angeles.

During its existence, CCP produced almost 800 animation projects for more than 400 clients worldwide.

SIDE BAR

In 1986, Tom Longtin created Gears on the VAX 11/780 with a Sun workstation and Pyramid Technologies computers. It won wide praise for it's smoothly turning and twisting intermeshing gear heads. NCGA in particular recognized it that year.

QUOTE

"Paul Sidlo was really a great broadcast designer and developed a large and loyal client base, which he took with him when he started reZn8. I think we did the first CGI TV commercial (nonvector) in the USA, which was a spot for the USFL football team called the LA Express. There had been earlier CGI commercials produced for foreign clients by Digital Effects, but we were the first in the U.S. We did the first CGI (nonvector) network fall campaign for NBC, the first CGI Super Bowl open, and the first news open. We did two really cool spots for TRW back in the days of the big-budget/high-art/low-content TV commercials. (Abel did some really nice TRW spots using vector graphics and motion control.) We did the second Dow scrubbing bubbles commercial (the first was done at Magi). We won lots of awards and had a great deal of success in television."

—Michael Collery

In 1985, the in-house software was finally licensed to the Japan Computer Graphics Laboratory (JCGL) for use in the Japanese market. After years of a stalemate over the Los Angeles office issue, Kristoff suggested that the board of investors sell out to him and a new group of investors, who then could do as they pleased. The idea was given initial approval, and Kristoff secured financial support from Mitz Kaneko (with the Japan Computer Graphics Laboratory in Tokyo) and other investors led by a friend of Mr. Kaneko's. At this point, a number of promising new employees were hired and began training, conditionally to staff the soon to be opened LA office of Cranston/Csuri. When Mr. Kaneko's friend unfortunately passed away soon after, the new investors balked, the CCP board changed its mind, and the deal was promptly canceled.

Jim Kristoff then resigned, and Wayne Carlson replaced him as president. In the final months of 1987, the software ultimately was purchased by Lamb & Company in Minneapolis when Cranston/Csuri Productions went out of business.

Where Are They Now?

At its peak, CCP employed some 80 people, many of whom are active leaders in the field of CG today.

- Chuck Csuri left CCP in 1985 to return to his OSU duties. He is actively pursuing new technologies to create new forms of computer graphics fine art.

- John Berton (a longtime ILM Technical Director and most recently a VFX Supervisor on *The Mummy*) was a TD who did a CG logo for a Twisted Sister music video.

- Jeff Light wrote the code that ran the Celco at CCP and is now Motion Capture Supervisor at ILM.

- Paul Sidlo founded reZn8.

- Jim Kristoff and Dobbie Schiff went on to Los Angeles to form MetroLight.

- Here are some other employees and where they went: Shawn Ho (SGI), Julian Gomez (Lego), Michael Collery (PDI), Andy White (ILM), Tom Hutchinson (ILM), Susan Van Baerle (LambSoft), John Donkin (Blue Sky), and Scott Dyer (Windlight/Nelvana).

deGraf/Wahrman
(1987 to 1991)

Formed as a partnership in October of 1987, and deGraf/Wahrman was incorporated in 1988 by Brad deGraf and Michael Wahrman. Additional funding assistance was provided by Tom McMahon (Symbolics Graphics Division).

Here's a description of dWI as related by co-founder Michael Wahrman:

"The founders of dWI were two very idealistic computer animators with what was considered at the time to be extensive computer animation experience. Brad deGraf had been head of technical direction at Digital Productions, which had recently gone out of business due to the Omnibus acquisition and subsequent demise. I had helped design the production system at Robert Abel & Associates and had produced the recent short film *Stanley and Stella*, which had just premiered at SIGGRAPH.

We shared common goals and beliefs. We wanted to use computer animation in entertainment and film as well as in real-time animation, and we believed that the industry was on the cusp of accepting the technology for character animation and digital sets. We felt we could run a small, low-overhead company that could take on projects that required some development and that could not be considered at the larger effects houses. We felt we should stay away from commercial production, as that area was well served by existing companies that specialized in that area. We wanted to focus on what we loved and did well.

We also had friends who wished us well and helped us get started. Among them was Symbolics, Inc., who lent us a Symbolics 3600 and all their software. They also let us make a deal with them in which we would run a render farm in their factory. Silicon Graphics lent us one of their very first systems that did shaded graphics, the 4D70GT, and supported us in the creation of a real-time system for character animation. These were such early days in the field that it is possible we made up the term 'Performance Animation' or 'Performance Character Animation.' That's how early it was."

Mike the Talking Head (officially christened Mike Normal) was the first real-time character (A.K.A "vactor" performance animation). The same technology was used to create the animated head of the bad-guy-robot-gone-crazy Cain in *Robocop 2*, which was directed by Irvin (*The Empire Strikes Back*) Kershner.

In the words of co-founder Brad deGraf:

"Michael Wahrman and I did [Mike the Talking Head] at deGraf/Wahrman in 1988, live at the SIGGRAPH Electronic Theatre in Atlanta. Mike was a virtual caricature of the late Mike Gribble, the host of that show, and the Mike of Spike and Mike's animation festival. Also, in 1990, deGraf/Wahrman did *The Funtastic World of Hanna-Barbera*, the first CG ride-film. It was a fully 3D chase/ride through Bedrock and Scooby-Doo's castle with cel animated characters for Universal Studios Florida."

The Funtastic World of Hanna-Barbera was the first CG ride-film, and all the backgrounds, environments, and vehicles were 3D CG with traditional 2D cel animated characters. (Rhythm & Hues also helped out with this production in the end.)

Full a more complete history and credit list of dWI employees, see Michael's Web page at www.wahrman.com/michael/dwi.html.

DemoGraFX

(1988 to present)

This research and technology company was formed by Gary Demos after leaving the Whitney/Demos bankruptcy. It began with contract work for various projects, including setting up the original Triple-I Digital Film Printer (DFP) at Pacific Title in 1991 and connecting it via HPPI to an SGI network. The DFP had been literally just sitting in a warehouse when Digital Productions (who had leased it from Triple-I) went out of business in 1987.

DemoGraFX presently specializes in high definition (HD) television technology. HD might well provide the next evolutionary step in both video and film. With nearly 2,000 lines of resolution and a new 24p (progressive) format, HD content will be served well by experienced technologists such as Demos and his co-workers at DemoGraFX. You can find more information at `http://home.earthlink.net/~demografx`.

Digital Effects

(1978 to 1986)

Digital Effects was founded by Judson Rosebush and Jeff Kleiser (Kleiser was Animation Director and President) along with Don Leitch, David Cox, Moses Weitzman, Jann Printz, and Bob Hoffman (who was later at Omnibus and RGA).

It was the first CG house in Manhattan.

QUOTE

"Our original setup was a 1200-baud modem connection to an Amdahl V6 running APL in Bethesda, Maryland, using a Tektronix display to preview wireframes. (Polygons refreshed at one per second—that's one polygon per second!) The perspective data was written onto 9-track tape and was mounted on an IBM 370/158 to do scan conversion. Another tape was written as hi-con images onto 9-track and was shipped to LA for film recording on a Stromberg Carlson 4020 film recorder. Processed film was sent to NYC where I deinterlaced it onto hi-con (high contrast) film and made a print to separate out the colors and have matte rolls that I could mount on an optical printer to do multiple passes with color filters onto color negative, which was then processed and printed at Technicolor downstairs. Total time to see a color image: 1 week tops."

—Jeff Kleiser

Quick additions to in-house computing were a Harris 800 and a Dicomed film recorder. They also built a framebuffer to see color images quickly and wrote a paint system for it.

Digital Effects was one of four companies to create CG for the film *Tron*. They produced the opening title sequence in which pieces of Tron fly in over a bright light source to form his body, and they also did all the scenes involving the flying cuboid character Bit who could say "Yes" or "No."

In the end, the many partners and employees wanted to operate the company differently, and the politics and personalities were causing work to go elsewhere. The best solution was to simply shut down the company and have people go their separate ways.

Jeff Kleiser next went to Omnibus/LA as the Director of their new Motion Picture Special Effects division. He later co-founded Kleiser Walczak Construction Company.

The Judson Rosebush Company was founded in 1986 and is located in New York City. It is a creative multimedia studio currently producing commercial and entertainment CD-ROM titles and Web sites. You can find more information at www.rosebush.com.

Digital Pictures
(1980 to 1997)

Digital Pictures was co-founded by Chris Briscoe and Paul Brown in 1980 as the UK's first specialist computer animation company. Liam Scanlan was the first employee, and Peter Florence and Steve Lowe soon joined as co-directors.

QUOTE

"Digital Pictures was eventually sold to a company called Molinaire, which was itself owned by WH Smith. Moli was a TV post house, so buying DP made sense. WH Smith was (and is) a chain of bookstores and what they were doing buying TV companies is not clear, nor was it then." — Craig Zerouni

QUOTE

"When I first started, we were working on Data General Eclipse 3300s, two of them. Each machine was about 7 feet high, 2 feet wide, and 3 feet deep and had 32KB main memory and a 300MB disk drive, which was about twice the size of a domestic washing machine. I'd say they were maybe four or five times more powerful than an Amiga 500. We rendered tests directly to a framebuffer, usually one to two days for a five to ten second test, and rendered directly to a Matrix film plotter. There was no disk space to store rendered images as files. Each frame would take 30–90 minutes to render and 10 minutes to plot. Color consistency isn't guaranteed across film baths, so if we missed or gashed a frame, we started over after we'd got the film back from the labs. Our renderer, which was a fine one, was written in-house, did no ray tracing or texture mapping, had no reflection maps, but did have shadows as long as we didn't use re-entrant polygons in our models. Intersecting surfaces were a no-no. We modeled and animated by writing Fortran 5 code. The last job done on the Eclipses was at a stage when they were so knackered that I was entirely losing disk data about three times a day and was archiving my code every 20 minutes or so. I could recover it after I'd reformatted the disk every time it went down. One of the disk drives busted, so I was booting one machine, starting a render, removing the drive, and plugging it back into the other machine so I could start a render on that one. My 8-second sting took a week to render. The air conditioner was being overworked so much that it would freeze up every couple of hours, melt, and dump gallons of water into the machine room. We had buckets all over the disk drives and mainframes. I didn't get to go home for 10 days."

—Kim Aldis

Paul Brown is now a professor of communication design at Queensland University of Technology, and Steve Lowe is a successful director of commercials in London. Liam Scanlan is the Head of Technical Directors at ILM in Marin County, California.

Digital Pictures closed its doors for good in 1997.

Image created by Digital Productions Company. Image courtesy of Harold Buchman.

Digital Productions
(1981 to 1987)

Digital Productions was formed in 1981 by Gary Demos and John Whitney Jr. Elsa Granville was employee number three and the Director of Human Resources; Brad deGraf (Head of Production) and Larry Yaeger (Director/VP of Software) were hired very soon thereafter. Producers included Sherry McKenna and Nancy St. John. Jim Rapley and Art Durinski joined DP after having worked on *Tron* at Triple-I. Producer B.J. Rack later went on to work with James Cameron on the original *Terminator* film. The renderer was based on the Movie-BYU software originally.

So why the famous Cray? Knowing precisely what kind of performance they would require to start a production company, Demos initially called Ivan Sutherland and discussed just what the cost would be to build a big mainframe. (Remember that SGI did not yet exist, and there would be no "workstations" as we know them for almost another 10 years!) The only reasonable option, it seemed, was the next generation Cray, the XMP.

Disk farm for the Cray. Larry Weinberg immediately recognized the shortcomings of the Cray. Images courtesy of Harold Buchman.

The plan was to lease the yet-to-be-released Cray XMP, but they took on an older Cray-1S initially to get a head start writing code. Capital funding was provided by Control Data Corporation (CDC) and Ramtek, and it went toward renting the Triple-I DFP (Digital Film Printer) and the Cray 1S. (CDC was a big mainframe manufacturer originally founded by Seymour Cray.)

DP's first major computer graphics project was for *The Last Starfighter*—$4.5 million worth of state-of-the-art, high-resolution CG animation. Beginning in Oct 1983, Digital Productions traded in the "older" Cray-1S for the very first Cray X-MP supercomputer. The Cray was fronted by a VAX 11/780 and was used to produce nearly 300 shots totaling 25 minutes of screen time. The team used E&S PS400s for modeling, IMI vector motion systems for motion preview, and Ramtek framebuffers for display. When Triple-I had wrapped the *Tron* work and decided not to continue in the CG film business, DP leased the Digital Film Printer (DFP) and hooked it up to one of the high-speed channels of the Cray. The Cray-driven DFP could scan 35mm film at four seconds per frame and could film out the 2000×2560 rendered images at 12 seconds per frame.

For the first time, highly detailed computer-generated images were integrated with live action as realistic scene elements rather than as monitor graphics or deliberately "CG" looking images. Gary Demos, from the very beginning, always had the drive to produce only the highest-resolution, highest-quality imagery possible.

Kevin Rafferty (ILM) led the team that digitally encoded (modeled) many of the forms designed for the film by Ron Cobb. The technique used was to have top, front, and side views of the model drawn orthographically on blueprint-like paper. A mouse/cursor (or "puck") with crosshairs then was used to input the lines of the drawing one point at a time. Details even included little 3D digital stunt actors inside the Gunstar's cockpit.

Picture Cards

For *The Last StarFighter*, practical explosion elements were licensed from John Dykstra's company, Apogee, and were scanned into the computer. Code was written to pull mattes from the explosion elements (often were shot against black), which were then applied to square polygons and placed into the 3D scene. Scripts to play the running footage on these "picture cards" (as Gary Demos called them) were written by Brad deGraf. Another effect of note was the fractal code written by Walter Gish and used for the moon and cave scenes (dually inspired by the work of Loren Carpenter and Mandelbrot).

QUOTE

"In another room is Ron Cobb, master of detail, carefully designing every last square inch of those spaceships. There was not one grommet on any of those ships that didn't have a purpose that Ron could describe."

"I remember one time I was animating the scene where Alex had just blown away the Rylon cargo ship, deep in the tunnels of the asteroid. The shot begins with the Gunstar facing away from the camera, pointed into the dead end of the tunnel. Alex has just made his first real-life kill. The storyboard called for the Gunstar to "turn around sadly." So at this point, I'm not exactly a seasoned animator, just a couple semesters of hand-drawn fishes and some computer-generated T-bone steaks under my belt. I show Ron the motion test for the sad, turning Gunstar, which is sort of slow and has a little kind of "Aw, shucks" kick to it. Ron's response was to turn to me, look me in the eye, and say very sweetly and kindly, "Well, Paul, I think maybe that's a little bit *too* sad, don't you?""

—Paul Isaacs (pauli@sgi.com), Digital Production Technical Director of
The Last Starfighter, July 1983 through May 1985

As *The Last Starfighter* production wrapped up (on time and on budget) in April of 1984, a critical financial squeeze occurred. DP was forced to purchase the $17 million Cray-XMP instead of continuing the lease. This critical drain of cash put DP in the vulnerable position of being the target of a hostile take over by Omnibus in 1986.

Craig Upson and Larry Yaeger worked on the Jupiter destruction sequence with Boss Film for the film *2010: Odyssey 2.*

Bill Kroyer designed, animated, and TD'd the flying owl in the award-winning opening title sequence of *Labyrinth* (1985–86), which was produced by Alan Peach.

Bill Kroyer and Chris Baily animated Mick Jagger's " Hard Woman" rock video in 1985. The 4.5-minute-long animation was co-produced by Nancy St. John and Alan Peach. Because of the tight deadline, the team concentrated on the character animation. Rendering was restricted to extremely simplified tube-like forms.

Digital Productions also began creating many different kinds of noteworthy projects at this time. New work included Clio award-winning commercials and test footage for special projects including *Dune* (1984) and the *Star Trek: The Next Generation* (1987) television pilot.

Commercial Work

Although the tests did not result in any work for those projects, DP created some 300 commercials in 1985 alone. The key to this success was the strict sign-off policies and client-control skills of Sherry McKenna, the Executive Producer. Sherry had come from Robert Abel's company and was tasked with producing some 60 overlapping commercial projects in-house at any one time, each with a deadline of about two months. The storyboards for a job were part of the contract, and any changes requested meant a new contract, a new budget, and a new schedule. The hi-res model designs were signed-off on by the Art Directors, and low-res versions were then be used to generate motion tests. At the same time, local and model lighting tests were approved as well as global scene lighting. The next step was to generate low-res rendered animation scenes of the complete job. These were approved by the client before committing to final hi-res rendering. Because of this strict incremental process, the final job seldom had to be rerendered more than once.

QUOTE

"Where else would geeky programmers ever have had the chance to meet the likes of Jim Henson, Mick Jagger, DEVO, The Tubes, etc., etc.? I remember sending my parents a copy of an article about the company that appeared in *TIME* magazine, written about our first-ever use of a Cray supercomputer to produce special effects instead of military/defense applications... Lots of daytime meetings, arguing about software architecture that never mattered since we were hacking our way through it every night at 2 a.m. instead."

—Emily Nagle Green (egreen@forrester.nl), software design and marketing at Digital Productions, 1982–1987

DP also set up a division of the company in 1985 to provide computing services and graphics production to the business and scientific community. The feature-film and commercial-production cycles had down time that could be filled by this other new area of CG. Cray time was sold to such companies as General Motors, Ford Motor Co., and the National Science Foundation. Stefen Fangmier (ILM), Craig Upson (Protozoa), Phil Sherwood, and Emily Nagle Green worked for this part of the company. By now, the total Digital Production employee count was up to about 100.

The Omnibus Takeover

In about 1985, CDC and Ramtek were both breaking up or going out of business themselves, and they wanted out of the digital movie-making business at any cost. Anxious to cut their losses, the board went along with a hostile takeover bid by Omnibus, breaking their agreement with Whitney Jr. and Demos. Backed by the Royal Bank of Canada,

The CRT was used as a flying spot to illuminate the film, and there were three photo multiplier tubes to record the density of the negative. Image courtesy of Harold Buchman.

Omnibus arranged for a leveraged buyout that would burden them with nearly $25 million in debt. Unable to prevent what they saw as sheer folly—and unable to afford a costly legal battle to protect their company—John Whitney Jr. and Gary Demos left to start up Whitney/Demos Productions. Digital Productions was renamed Omnibus Simulation in June of 1986, and it declared bankruptcy (along with Omnibus and Abel) only nine months later on April 13, 1987.

QUOTE

Electric Image (EI)
(1983 to 1998)

Paul Docherty left his position as Head of Graphics at Molinare, London's leading post house, and set up Electric Image in 1983. The company was funded by private shareholders, a number of which were previously Paul's clients.

Paul and his then Technical Director Stewart McEwan (whom Paul had hired out of Molinare) spent two years producing real-time video-based animation for the television market on Dubner equipment. They then bought the first two SGI terminals (at that stage, SGI only made terminals) sold out of the U.S. and used them as a front end to a DEC VAX 11-780. The disk drives were two removable platter "washing machines" that stood about 3 feet high and held a massive 450megs of data.

At the time, the only other companies doing raster animation in the UK were Digital Pictures (with their own code) and Electronic Arts (using various Movie-BYU software bits).

Paul did a source code co-development deal with Abel Image Research (Robert Abel's software division), in which Electric helped with some of the PAL video issues and worked closely with the Abel team to debug the code. The development team at Abel at the time included Roy Hall, Hank Weghorst, Kim Shelley, and a number of other Cornell luminaries.

EI began using the Abel system for television work and eventually added an Oxberry Matrix 35mm camera for film work.

Like most companies of this early era, the EI team had to work pretty much from scratch creating custom renders, color lookup tables, modeling utilities, and so on—without the benefit of the academic superstructure that already existed in the U.S.

EI created commercials, television IDs, program inserts, small bits for European features, and pretty much anything anyone asked for. The animation team included Ian Bird (who now runs the London animation house Eye), Mike

Milne (who heads up facility house The Frame Store's animation section), and Ian MacFadyen and Stephen Coren (who run Drum, a small London animation house). The technical side included Stewart McEwan (who now runs the multimedia software section of Dorland Kindersley) and David Benson (now at ILM).

The company was responsible for many European "firsts." They were the first to use C and UNIX for commercial graphics production (most everyone else was using VMS and Pascal). They also provided the first bit of serious ray tracing on UK television (an ident for Yorkshire Television), the first real-time display SGI graphics terminals, and the first UK dynamics animation package (written by David Benson). Heavy use of clever compositing and geometric projection tricks (picked up from Abel initially) gave the company's work a distinctive look and built up a reputation for quality.

With the collapse of Omnibus/Abel/Digital Productions (or "Omnivore" as the guys at Abel dubbed it) in 1987, EI was now on its own as far as software development. The company continued to develop the Abel system and was joined by Paul Newell from Abel (now at Rhythm & Hues), who helped keep the code developing and added a new animation system called (for no apparent reason) DREK.

In 1991, the company began to shift toward commercial software, using TDI Explore augmented by Wavefront's Dynamation and Kinemation.

Shortly thereafter, Simon Maddocks (now at ILM) joined and eventually became Head of Animation. David Benson developed a clever ray tracer for the AT&T Pixel Machine, one of the early parallel-processing systems. EI became the first UK company to be able to render depth of field, motion blur, and other realistic effects without going bust in the process. Joakim Arnesson was a Technical Director there briefly as was current fellow ILMer Ben Snow.

QUOTE

"The various shareholders felt we should have a gimmicky name for the VAX/SGI/AbelGraphix combination, so at a late night pub session, Colin Reynolds drunkenly suggested Doris. After a few more pints, we decided that DORIS stood for Digital Optical Raster Imaging System, and that's what we told the press it was called."

—Paul Docherty

About this time, EI became one of the founding shareholders in The Frame Store along with Director Steve Barron (*Teenage Mutant Ninja Turtles, Merlin*). The new company had the first Quantel Harry and has since grown into one of Europe's largest digital post houses.

In 1996, EI produced all the digital effects for the feature film *Space Truckers* (120 shots, about 15 minutes in all). Although modest by current standards, it was a substantial project at that time, especially in European terms.

In an effort find some stability in the feast or famine effects market in London, EI hired Bob Auger and started Electric Switch, one of the first MPEG compression facilities in Europe and currently the European market leader in DVD authoring. Using Switch's compression hardware, the company pioneered the transfer of MPEG1 video clips of rushes to locations around the world.

In 1997–98, EI produced about 80 shots for *Lost in Space* and produced a four-minute ride-film for the new GM pavilion at Disneyland. Unfortunately, various legal and technical problems caused shareholders in November 1998 to pull the plug on EI and concentrate on the new DVD company.

The company's 16-year life span made it one of the longest lasting computer animation houses in European history.

Evans & Sutherland Computer Corporation (E&S)
(1968 to present)

Incorporated in 1968 by Dave Evans and Ivan Sutherland, E&S was the first computer graphics company ever formed. Based in Salt Lake City, Utah, E&S produced vector graphics workstations initially for military flight-simulator use. Later it produced them for many commercial companies as well such as Robert Abel's and Cranston/Csuri. E&S' first products were the LDS-1, LDS-2, and then Picture System-2 vector systems, all of which were used with another host system such as the VAX-11/780.

Current products include the MindSet Virtual Studio, Accel|Galaxy 3D, and FuseBox 3.0 for NT. E&S sold a minority share of (nonvoting) stock to Intel in 1998. E&S can be reached at 801-588-1000. You can find more information at www.es.com.

Ex Machina

(1989 to present)

Ex Machina was created in 1989 by the merger of two French CG production companies: Sogitec and the production division of Thomson Digital Image (TDI). With the birth of Ex Machina, TDI itself then continued to be involved only in developing the Explore Software.

Ex Machina has been involved in many different areas of CG production including both commercials and films of all formats (IMAX, 70/35mm, stereo, HVISION, and so on). Clients are mainly from Europe and Japan, with most of the large-format films such as IMAX being produced for North American clients.

TDI's Explore software has been used at Ex Machina since its inception. Its R&D department even wrote some of the tools shipped with the commercial package such as the particle system and the script-based modeler "build."

Like other major production companies, Ex Machina also has relied on developing its own custom software. Its in-house character animation system "Appia" was developed in 1991–92 and first was used during the production of *World of Materials*, directed by Jerzy Kukar. This was a 10-minute 70mm stereo movie for a Korean International Festival. (Ex Machina also was involved in training CG artists for a Korean CG company that did one part of the film.)

Later, Softimage was introduced for animation. (Explore is still used for modeling and rendering and Appia for secondary animation.) More recently, NT workstations with 3D Studio MAX were brought into production.

The VFX department was created in 1991 for *Simeon* (directed by Euzhan Palcy), for which Ex Machina bought a scanner from RFX. The compositing software "depict" was developed and was extensively used in conjunction with scanning (RFX) and shooting (MGI|Solitaire) hardware to create some ghost appearances. At this time, Christian Guillon was at the head of the department. Matador also was chosen as the primary 2D tool, although it has been supplemented more recently by After Effect running on Macintosh platforms.

Fantastic Animation Machine (FAM)
(1983 to 1992)

Jim Lindner and Suazanne Gavril, former marketing executives at Xerox, broke with Computer Creations and formed Fantastic Animation Machine in Manhattan. They made animations chiefly with a 32-bit Ridge microcomputer on proprietary software (C and UNIX).

Image West
(1975 to 1985)

Begun as a subsidiary of Omnibus Video of Canada, Image West used analog video animation equipment such as Scanimate, which manipulated video imagery and captured artwork. Cliff Brown was President, and David Sieg was Chief Engineer. Animators included Peter Koczera, Ed Kramer, Russ Maehl, and Roy Weinstock. Image West Art Directors were Sonny King, Henry Kline II, and Gary McKinnon.

Image West's only connection to feature film work was for the original *Star Wars* film in 1977. The Yavin planet countdown imagery was done by John Wash and Jay Teitzell. A great deal more of the screen graphic imagery for *Star Wars* was completed with traditional animation, analog effects, and other non-CG techniques.

Image West was bought from Computer Image's bank at a bargain in the 1970s. They were in the midst of splitting from Canadian parent company Omnibus Group.

—*see also*   Omnibus

QUOTE

"Digital image-making state of the art was a PDP-11, a $50,000 framebuffer, and a bunch of assembly or Fortran programmers hacking away from scratch. Triple-I, NYIT, and MAGI were about the only people going that route. Image West had always had the advantage of "real time," meaning that, despite the limitations of the analog rescan technology, it could run right before your eyes and be adjusted on the fly. Its big downfall was complete lack of repeatability due to all those knobs and patch wires (such as with Scanimate). After reviewing all the options, Cliff Brown and I decided a good approach would be to build a system based on the analog rescan technology but using digital computers to track and store the setups needed to repeat a job. I did not realize at the time how large a project this would be (later to become the VersEFX)."

—David Seig, Image West

Image West moved from Hollywood to Studio City, California, in 1983.

The company faced increasingly hard times competing with the trend of completely digital effects, 3D CG, and digital video effects boxes such as the ADO. The new VersEFX system that they had partnered with SFP to build (the French TV production company) had gone to France, and they were trying to build one for themselves. Hybrid video technology was not going to able to compete with the all-digital systems, however, so they made a deal with Symbolics to get one of their S-series systems with both paint and 3D capabilities. Unfortunately, they never could return to the revenue levels they had been working at with the Scanimates. In desperation, they attempted a public offering on the Vancouver stock exchange. That attempt failed, and the company closed its doors in 1985.

Industrial Light & Magic (ILM): Computer Graphics Division

The Computer Division of ILM originally was formed in 1979 when Ed Catmull was selected by George Lucas to start an in-house research group. Richard Edlund (who at the time was an ILM Visual Effects Supervisor and later formed Boss Film) flew to meet with Ed at NYIT for a secret meeting to discuss the offer. Ed and Alvy Ray Smith went to great lengths to keep the offer a secret from their patron, Dr. Alexander Shure, even going so far as to rent a manual typewriter to draft a proposal letter to Lucas (for fear of the otherwise unsecure email system at NYIT).

QUOTE

"This was the first facility I had ever designed that involved raised computer flooring. Half of the building was on a level two feet lower than the other half, so we used raised computer flooring to make the two floor levels equal. This gave us about 20 inches under the floor for cables, power, and air conditioning." — David Sieg, (http://vhost2.zfx.com/~dave)

At the time, Lucasfilm headquarters were in a building called the Egg Company in LA across from Universal Studios. (*Star Wars* was created at the original headquarters in Van Nuys.) Ed then flew out to meet with George and was hired soon after. Because *The Empire Strikes Back* was still in production (up in Marin County), its financial success was anything but certain, and Lucas was cautious about committing to a large-scale research effort right away. Thus, the offer that was made was only for Catmull himself, even though a great many of his group at NYIT wanted to come with him to California.

Things developed quickly, however, and Alvy Ray Smith soon joined Ed to move into their first official space, a converted laundromat in San Enselmo, California. At the start, there actually were three distinct group efforts: the graphics group itself was headed by Alvy, a video-editing group was headed by Ralph Guggenheim, and a digital audio group was headed by Alan Moore (from Stanford). Malcolm Blanchard and David DiFrancesco also joined the group soon after.

A few years later, the Graphics Group moved to a new custom office space up north in Bell Marin Keys, Novato. In 1983, the permanent space for ILM in San Rafael was finished, and the Graphics Group moved into "C" building on Kerner Boulevard.

The crew that worked on Young Sherlock Holmes. Young Sherlock Holmes *copyright © 1985 by Paramount Pictures. All Rights Reserved.* Young Sherlock Holmes *courtesy of Paramount Pictures.*

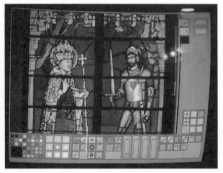

CG elements of the knight, Young Sherlock Holmes *copyright © 1985 by Paramount Pictures. All Rights Reserved.* Young Sherlock Holmes *courtesy of Paramount Pictures.*

Also during this time, many Lucasfilm corporate and management changes took place. The original President Charlie Weber was replaced by Bob Greeber, who was then replaced by Doug Norby. The Egg Company Lucasfilm location in LA was closed down, and development on Skywalker Ranch was ongoing.

The Graphics Group settled into several basic research projects. The film I/O project was headed by David DiFrancesco, who designed a laser-based film scanner and recorder as one unit. From the very beginning, it was clear that no one had ever solved the numerous challenges of perfecting a laser-based film recorder. There was some work being done and military research, but even mighty Kodak at the time was not sure it could be done. In 1980, the first tests were done (on 5247 stock). By 1983, the Pixar image computer was integrated in the heart of the new scanner/recording system.

Young Sherlock Holmes

In 1984, this was the first production to use the new machine. It completed for the very first time ever a complete digital composite of a CG character onto live-action imagery. The digital film printer went on to complete work on a dozen ILM film projects and eventually was retired in 1991. David DiFrancesco (then and still at

John Lasseter at the monitor, doing filmouts for Young Sherlock Holmes. Young Sherlock Holmes *copyright © 1985 by Paramount Pictures. All Rights Reserved.* Young Sherlock Holmes *courtesy of Paramount Pictures.*

Pixar) was able to get the machine back by trading it for Pixar Image computer hardware. He then was able to fulfill a wish to donate the historical hardware to the George Eastman House International Museum of Photography's Permanent Apparatus Collection.

Tom Duff, Sam Lefler, Bill Reeves, and Eben Ostby worked on the company's animation system architecture.

Working on Young Sherlock
Holmes. Young Sherlock
Holmes *copyright © 1985
by Paramount Pictures. All
Rights Reserved.* Young
Sherlock Holmes *courtesy of
Paramount Pictures.*

Real-time 2D line drawing was accomplished with a PERQ vector system from 3-Rivers (two million vectors in 1/30 of a second). The new Stanford University Network (SUN) computers were a full 32-bit system based on the Motorola 68000 chip. The UNIX was ported to the SUN, and the Graphics Group made a deal that allowed SUN to use the port in exchange for receiving a 30 percent discount on their hardware in perpetuity.

When George Lucas decided in 1985 to sell off the division and begin a new production-oriented department, Catmull called on Doug Kay and George Joblove. Kay and Joblove were running their own production company in LA and were asked to come in and basically start from scratch when every single employee left together to start Pixar Animation Studios.

Close Call!

Ironically, when first offered the opportunity from Dr. Catmull, Kay and Joblove turned him down. Dr. Catmull quickly called Doug back on the phone and politely told him, "You're crazy! This is an opportunity of a lifetime! Come back up here for another interview, we'll do it all over again." Kay and Joblove agreed, returned, and promptly changed their minds.

The computer division (Pixar) guys were not out of the space until about May of 1986. Right after that, the very first hires for the new ILM Computer Graphics department were Lincoln Hu and Bruce Wallace (who was only there about a year). Next to come on board were Jonathan Luskin, Jay Riddle (modeler/animator), and Les Dittert (scanning and related software). Computer support consisted of Randy Bean, Jay Lensi, and Ken Beyer. The SUN computers were still used along with a DEC VAX 750 fronting an E&S PS2. Animation consisted of the precursor to Pixar's MENV system with rendering by REYES, the precursor to RenderMan.

Various other hardware components were used until the first SGIs arrived in early 1988 in the form of a 4D/70 and a 4D/80 running Alias v1.0 and Renderman 1.0.

The Very First ILM/CG Projects

CG animatics for the Star Tours simulator ride were done in the spring of 1986 by Joblove and Kay. Star fields and a hyperspace effect were completed by Jonathan Luskin, but they were not used when the E&S picture system proved too unstable to use in the filming process.

Next up was a grid effect for the *Star Trek: The Next Generation* television pilot, which actually aired in 1987.

Howard The Duck (1986) was the first feature film the new CG department worked on. This was the first use in a motion picture of digital wire-removal technology. CG work was done by Bruce Wallace. (See the Time Line chapter for details.)

Star Trek IV: The Voyage Home (1986) contained cyberware scanned heads.

The *Body Wars* simulator ride (1988) required so much rendering power that Lincoln Hu ported Renderman to run on the Cray supercomputers at their headquarters in Minnesota. Many cold weeks were spent in the winter of 1988–89 running the job on the XMP, YMP, and Cray-2 systems, transferring the data at a furious rate to and from San Rafael.

"Titanic" simulation was created on a borrowed Wavefront license in late 1987. Jay Riddle modeled, Charlie Mullen (then head of animation) animated, and Jonathan Luskin TD'd. The documentary-style sinking for television is something we've see done again many times by many other companies in the ensuing years.

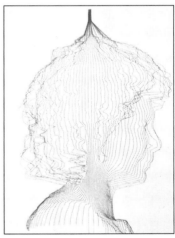

An example of wireframe screen capture. Star Trek: The Voyage Home *Copyright © 1985 by Paramount Pictures. All Rights Reserved.* Star Trek: The Voyage Home *courtesy of Paramount Pictures.*

Doug Smythe arrived in the summer of 1987, followed by Scott Anderson, Steve "Spaz" Williams, Stephen Rosenbaum, Eric Enderton, and Sandy Karpman. More SGIs arrived, and more staff came on board slowly until about 1990, when the big ramp up for *T2* doubled the number of CG production seats from about 15 to about 30 total people. At this time, Scott Anderson, Mark Dippe, John Berton, Tom Hutchinson, Jim Mitchell, and Eric Armstrong came on board.

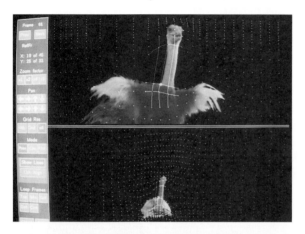

Compared to the 450-person strong 1999 ILM/CG department, the initial *Willow* (1987–88) meeting of the same group in 1987 easily fit around a six-foot-diameter conference table. This movie featured the pioneering "morf" work of Doug Smythe. The seamless multiple transformation sequence was accomplished with original software designed and written by Doug specifically for the film. There was no existing literature or body of work to reference, although years later Doug finally did see the SIGGRAPH piece that Tom Brigham created at NYIT. Tom and Doug shared a Technical Achievement Academy Award for the invention of "morphing" in 1992.

Creating the movie Willow. Willow ©*Lucasfilm Ltd. &*™. *All Rights Reserved. Used Under Authorization. Courtesy of Lucasfilm Ltd.*

For approximately eight total shots, the morf'ed elements were filmed out and optically composited.

Next up were *Cocoon the Return* (1988), *Indiana Jones and the Last Crusade* (1989), and *The Abyss* (1989). *Back to the Future, Part 2* (1989) used digital wire removals, and software was by Doug Smyth, Less Dittart, and Tien Truong. *Back to the Future, Part 3* (1990) involved intensive digital and optical compositing.

Various underwater particle effects for *The Hunt For Red October* (1990) were followed in 1991 by the movie that put CG on Hollywood's wish list: *Terminator 2: Judgment Day*. If *The Abyss* opened the door, *T2* broke it down. CG was now a viable effects method for high-volume, high-quality realistic visual effects creation.

ILM Photoshop Quote

"The first ILM project I used Photoshop on was a Pacific Bell smart Yellow Pages commercial in fall 1988, where I used it for preproduction art. The first production where it was actually used to make stuff for the film itself was *The Abyss*. I used it there to take dozens of stills of the sets and stitch them together to make reflection environments. I also used it to paint animated roto-mattes for the shot of the pod falling down and splashing on the floor."

—John Knoll

By now, multiple ILM projects were in production at one time, and the CG department was still cutting its teeth on key effects techniques previously handled by more traditional methods. The year 1991 saw both the procedural spider swarms in *Arachnophobia* and the huge production of *Hook*. CG Supervised by Stefen Fangmeier, *Hook* used a unique combination of three different techniques for its pixie dust effects. Wes Takahashi created traditional cel animation, Tom Hutchinson used a CG particle system, and Terrence Masson used Layerpaint to create 2D effects animation.

Memoirs of an Invisible Man (1992) and *Death Becomes Her* (1992) both created realistic human-based effects never before seen on the big screen.

Also in 1992, *The Young Indiana Jones Chronicles* began its first season on ABC. Shot on 16mm film, the series featured extensive use of digital matte painting. Interestingly enough, the first season's digital work was not actually done at ILM; it was subcontracted out to Veritel in San Fransisco. Doug Snyder, a Photoshop retouch artist, was hired by Varitel Select to do the first year of *Young Indy's* digital matte paintings in Photoshop. Varitel Select was a digital print-ad/photo-retouch branch that Varitel Video operated briefly before going out of business.

From the very beginning, ILM's award-winning commercial work got its start with projects such as the character animation of *Hummingbird,* M&M Mars aliens, and Heinz ants. Morfing also began it's commercial use in Meryll Lynch Bear to Bull, the Diet Pepsi football "puddle," and Toyota Lips. Today, CG Commercials (CGC) continues to crank out the best work in broadcast, garnering accolades from around the world.

ILM's SGI-based commercial software includes Alias|Wavefront's PowerAnimator (for modeling) and Maya (for dynamics), Discreet Logic's Flame and Inferno, and Pixar's RenderMan and Softimage (for character animation). All commercial software is integrated into the main ILM proprietary software pipeline. It is the proprietary software that's responsible for the vast majority of ILM's work. TDs light with Ishade and composite with Icomp. Both animators and TDs also rely heavily on Cari (Caricature) for secondary animation, shapes description, simulation, and scene planning. Additional Mac-based production software includes After Effects, Commotion, Electric Image Form Z, and Photoshop.

Modern work by ILM/CG throughout the 1990s has been well covered in popular media, so I'll just list some of the key projects. They have included: *Jurassic Park* (1993), *Forrest Gump* (1994), *The Mask* (1994), *Casper* (1995), *Jumanji* (1995), *Dragonheart* (1996), *Twister* (1996), *101 Dalmations (1997), Star Wars Trilogy Special Edition* (1997), *The Lost World* (1997), *Men In Black* (1997), *Flubber* (1997), *Saving Private Ryan* (1998), *Mighty Joe Young* (1998), *The Mummy* (1999), and *Star Wars Episode 1: The Phantom Menace* (1999).

ILM continues to be the undisputed world leader in feature film visual effects. Its cutting edge CG is balanced by the best model shop, motion control, and camera crews in the world. In addition to numerous Scientific and Technical awards, to date, ILM has received 14 Academy Awards and 12 additional nominations. (Of course, if you count *Phantom Menace* that would be 15... if that's not too presumptuous.)

SCI-Tech Award

In 1993, a Scientific and Engineering Academy Award was presented to Mark Leather, Les Dittert, Douglas Smythe, and George Joblove for the concept and development of the Digital Motion Picture Retouching System for removing visible rigging and dirt/damage artifacts from original motion picture imagery.

Information International Inc. (III or Triple-I)
(1962 to 1982)

The company originally was founded to create image-processing equipment and digital-image scanners. Triple-I developed one of the first and best digital film printer and scanner systems and hired Jim Blinn from JPL to work with Gary Demos on developing the TRANEW software that ran on the legendary and unique Foonly F1 computer.

The Foonly F1 Computer

"The F1 was originally built by Triple-I in hopes of getting a large contract with the government for an Optical Character Recognition system. Its design became the DEC KL-10, but it was built on five wire-wrap pages that were machine wrapped. This meant that it was a one-of-a-kind system, a prototype that never went anywhere. It required a DEC KA-10 (five tons of stuff that barely could do 1MIP!), which ran a hacked-up version of the TOPS10 operating system just to boot it. When it was up, it probably ran at something like 6MIPS. The disk systems were old DEC washing-machine-style drives that barely held 50MB, and they crashed at least every month! TRANEW rendering software was written by Gary Demos, Bill Dungan, Rich Schroeppel, Jim Blinn, and a host of others while Triple-I had the machine. Triple-I had married the F1 to a modified PFR-80 film recorder, one of the first in the motion picture industry. Omnibus bought the F1 system because it had produced the majority of the CGI in the film *Tron*, and it seemed like a good way to jump-start feature film production. We did scenes from *Explorers* and *Flight of the Navigator* on it, but it was painful."

—David Sieg (dave@ns.zfx.com)

When Triple-I did not get the government contract, management (Al Fenaughty and Terry Taugner) brought Whitney and Demos over from Evans & Sutherland to form a "movie group" in an attempt to cut their losses by using all that equipment for something else. John Whitney Jr. initially had been introduced to Triple-I because his father (John Sr.) knew Triple-I's founder Ed Fredkin.

The Motion Picture Project (also called the Entertainment Technology Group) was formed at Triple-I in 1975 by Gary Demos, John Whitney Jr., Tom McMahon, Karol Brandt, and Art Durinski. They were later joined by Craig Reynolds and many others.

The first project Whitney Jr. and Demos were charged with was a series of tests for the film *Close Encounters of the Third Kind.* The concept was for little glowing cubes to fly around during the start of the film's finale. The film's DP, Vilmos Zigmund, shot some plates with a crane including some small spheres whose position would be input to a 3D tracking program to extrapolate the matchmove by which to render the 3D elements into the scene. (Malcom McMillan, a UCLA mathematician and key Triple-I programmer, wrote this code.)

Most of 1976 was spent producing broadcast logo packages for foreign markets because the domestic networks were not ready to commit to the new idea of CG flying logos. NBC, in particular, was one early client Triple-I approached with the idea, only to be rejected in favor of a traditional spinning practical model.

Software

Both Frank Crow and Jim Blinn worked at Triple-I briefly in 1977, developing algorithms later published in their thesis work. The Actor/Scriptor Animation System (ASAS) was developed by Craig Reynolds, Art Durinski, and others. The modeling tools were written by Larry Malone (Nichimen) using tools such as the Tektronix 4014 storage tube display terminal running Tekshow software.

Lucasfilm Tests

Other 3D CG tests were done for *Star Wars*, *The Black Hole*, and *The Empire Strikes Back*, but they did not end up in the finished films. One particular test for Lucasfilm involved Art Durinski building a beautiful 60k poly count X-Wing fighter. Rendered at 4k×6k resolution, Lucas was only impressed after the ever-amazing Mal McMillan wrote some additional code to "dirty" it up from its original pristine CG condition. It eventually was shown on the cover of *Computer Magazine* in 1979.

A lower-poly-count version was created for an animation test Gary Demos did of a five-ship formation complete with anti-aliasing and motion-blur. Unfortunately, the $7,000 per minute production cost required by Lucas was much too low for Triple-I to consider real production. Also in 1978, scanning and filmout tests were performed with Richard Edlund at Lucasfilm, but the nature of the CRT technology and 5247 film stocks did not yield great results.

The year 1980 saw the production of seven minutes of digital imagery for *Looker*, another Michael Crichton film written after the author's visits to Triple-I during Westword and FutureWorld productions. Full-body 3D scans were made of an actress from software developed once again my Malcom McMillan. The film was about a company that created computer-generated actresses from full-body scans... Déjà vu?

About this time, it was becoming clear to both John Whitney Jr. and Gary Demos that Triple-I was not going to allow the expansion or spin off of the Motion Picture Group as they had originally hoped. John and Gary were instrumental in the pitching and preproduction of the next big CGI film, *Tron*, but they left in April of 1981 before its production to form their own company, Digital Productions.

Tron

Triple-I created the Sark's Carrier, solar sailor, and the Master Control Program (MCP) scenes for the film. (See the Time Line chapter for more details.) Some key people on the project included Art Durinski, Larry Malone, Craig Reynolds, Bill Dungan, and Jeremy Swartz.

After completing *Tron* and a 3D (stereoscopic) project for Kodak/Epcot called *Magic Journeys*, Triple-I ceased its computer graphics business. Some employees joined Digital Production; others joined the new Symbolics Graphics Division.

Japan Computer Graphics Lab (JCGL)
(1980 to 1987)

In 1978, Mits Kaneko of MK Company obtained from MGM Studios the animation rights to Marjorie Keenan Rollings' Pulitzer-awarded book *The Yearling*. Mits Kaneko decided to use computer animation on the 52 episodes of the subsequent 30-minute television series because of the rapidly rising cost of animation artists and the film-recording process. In April of 1980, after two years of development and artist training, JCGL was established with Mits Kaneko, Toho Company (a movie distribution company), Kodansha (a book publishing company), Toppan (a printing company), and Telework (a television production company).

JCGL started production in June 1980 with 38 artists, four programmers, and three hardware maintenance people. JCGL's system for television animation production consisted of a huge custom-designed optical printer to print extra frames of the same image for reducing rendering time. Additional hardware consisted of two Dicomed 48-S film recorders, two Vax 780 super mini computers , four PDP 44s, eight PDP 11s for ink and paint stations, two DeAnza scanners for scanning animation papers, 18 Genisco buffers for image buffering, and one PS 300 for vector drawing. The MK-1 software was based on NYIT's Tween and Tweep software for vector-animation generation, scanned-image inking, and coloring capabilities. Additional software developement was provided with the help of the Tokyo Institute of Technology Image Lab lead by Professor Takeshi Agui.

The production of *The Yearling*, however, failed with only one completed episode. Because of various creative challenges, the production schedule became almost double what had been estimated. The completed episode (which actually was the second episode of the series) was broadcast in April 1982 and became the world's first animated television program completely processed with a computer. The rest of the 51-episode production was completed using a conventional hand-drawn, hand-painted method.

Mits Kaneko decided to move to 3D computer graphics production for commercial films and special effects on feature films. Jim Kristoff of Cranston/Csuri Productions (CCP) helped integrate 3D production software with the existing JCGL hardware, and the transition went well. JCGL went on to win prizes from such organizations as Nicograph, NCGA, and INA. JCGL led Japan's CG production for seven years, but the company was dissolved in 1987 when its VAX-based system could not compete any longer with cheaper, more modern systems(SGIs).

Kleiser-Walczak Construction Company (KWCC)
(1987 to present)

One of the first Wavefront-based production companies, KWCC was founded in 1987 by Jeff Kleiser and Diana Walczak.

Jeff Kleiser went to Colgate University as a CG major using VISIONS, an early Fortran code from Syracuse. He made several experimental films and a few commercials by outputting to a DEC graphics display terminal and shooting 35mm film off the screen. He worked at Dolphin Productions (1976–77) as a Scanimate operator, at Digital Effects (1978–1986) as Animation Director and President, and then at Omnibus as Director of the Motion Picture Special Effects Division in LA.

Diana Walczak is a sculptor and CG enthusiast from Boston University who met Jeff at SIGGRAPH 1985. She then joined him at Omnibus for a Marvel Comics character test in 1986. Diana's body sculptures were digitized into the computer a section at a time to have separate animatable pieces.

Jeff (still working for Omnibus) was in Canada scouting locations for the feature film *Millennium* when Digital/Omnibus/Abel (DOA) went down. He and Diana formed KWCC to take a one-week job that would pay for the down payment on a new house in Hollywood. (What better reason is there to start a company?)

Their first Synthespian, created for SIGGRAPH '88, starred in "Sextone for President". The 30-second piece demonstrated facial animation based on interpolating Diana's digitized sculptures with TALK software written by Larry Weinberg. TALK could mix any percentage of any facial shape at any frame, even with arbitrary polygon ordering. This technique of phoneme interpolation today is a standard way of producing 3D facial animation. The narration made heavy use of irony as the character lobbied for SAG (Synthetic Actors Guild) rights.

In 1989, Hewlett-Packard supported KWCC's next character, Dozo, in the ambitious "Don't Touch Me." This three-minute animation utilized early optical motion capture from Motion Analysis. Frank Vitz joined the KWCC team to wrangle the always late and always buggy motion capture data.

After more than five months, only about 20 percent of the motion capture data was delivered, forcing KWCC to make very creative use of piecing together and repeating many short fragments of motion. The rendering was done all over the country anywhere there was Wavefront rendering code. All the final imagery was output to big 9-track data discs and was stacked six feet high. It was output to film, delivered to a NY airport, picked up by an HP employee, and handed in to the SIGGRAPH office one minute before the midnight deadline for the Electronic Theatre submissions. The work was very well received for its innovative blending of technologies.

QUOTE

"Diana and I formed KWCC to build databases using her sculptures and a 3D digitizer from Polhemus. Soon we were approached by Viewpoint Datalabs, who wanted to market our data along with theirs, but we were more interested in developing Synthespians (Synthetic Actors) than working in the database service market."
—Jeff Kleiser

In 1992, KWCC based itself in Lenox, Massachusetts, to provide the 3D CG animation for Douglas Trumbull's Luxor trilogy of ride-films. Frank Vitz again wrote custom code for one of the films to transform the flat CG into a curved torus-like screen.

KWCC also created two important television series in conjunction with Santa Barbara Studios. *Astronomers* (for PBS) had 12 minutes of cosmic simulation, and *500 Nations* depicted entire Native American cities.

Feature film work has included *Stargate, Clear and Present Danger,* and *Judge Dredd,* the latter of which featured some of the earliest realistic digital stunt doubles in a feature film.

KWCC also recently created various creatures for *Mortal Kombat: Annihilation* and some effects for *Carrie II.* They have just delivered three years of extensive work on the Spiderman ride for Universal Studios Florida. Spiderman is a stereo-image ride with extensive character animation and visual effects.

Employees and collaborators have included Ed Kramer, Eileen O'Neil, Jeff Williams, Frank Vitz, Derry and Patsy Frost, and Randy Bauer.

Currently, KWCC has offices in New York, Hollywood, and Massachusetts. The MOCA center in North Adams, Massachsetts, can be reached at 413-664-7441. You can find more information at www.kwcc.com.

Kroyer Films

Bill Kroyer was a traditional animator at Disney from 1977 to 1979 and returned to Disney as an Animation Director on *Tron* in 1981. He later worked at Digital Productions, animating the Rolling Stones "Hard Woman" video, and created the realistic CG owl for the opening credits of the feature film *Labyrinth.*

Kroyer Films was founded by Bill and Sue Kroyer in 1986, just before DOA went out of business. The company specialized in the use of 3D computer graphics, plotted out on paper as hidden surface line art to be colored and used along with traditionally created cel animation. Output was on an HP plotter hooked up to an SGI 3130 (a machine with only 4megs of ram that cost $42,000!).

Their unique, hybrid 3D/cel technique was used for the first time in the short-lived TV series *UltraCross*. CG futuristic motorcycles were added to the otherwise cel animated show. (The show was canceled when the merchandizing toy deal fell through.)

With a method proven and the time to spare, Kroyer and his team next produced the short film *Technological Threat* in 1988. The film realized the conflict and resolution of a traditionally animated character with that of a computer-generated one. Great storytelling, design, and execution added up to an Academy Award nomination for the film that year.

A still from the animated short, Technological Threat. *Image copyright, © 1999 Kroyer Films, Inc.*

Next up was the full-length animated feature film *Fern-Gully: The Last Rainforest*, which was completed on February 10, 1990. In addition being a very enjoyable film for both kids and adults, the project was notable for several reasons. Backed by the Australian team that made *Crocodile Dundee*, the entire production was accomplished in just two years from storyboards to premiere. Kroyer ramped up from 15 to 200 people and created 40,000 computer-plotted cel frames to augment the bulk of the traditional animation.

Unfortunately, as successful as *FernGully* was, Hollywood studios at that time were not willing to go up against Disney and commit to an animated feature film.

Kroyer then found a unique niche in creating elaborately animated title sequences for films such as *Honey, I Shrunk the Kids*, *Troop Beverly Hills*, and *National Lampoon's Christmas Vacation*.

Finally, in 1994, studios began jumping on the feature animation bandwagon. By then, however, Kroyer had downsized considerably. Bill and Sue both decided to shut down their company and join the fledgling Feature Animation department at Warner Brothers for *Quest For Camelot*. Although that partnership did not last because of creative differences, the Kroyers were able to freelance and develop their own film project.

Bill presently is on staff at Rhythm & Hues as a Director, having come on board in 1998. Sue Kroyer is working on her own short film titled *Curl Up And Dye*.

Lamb & Company
(1980 to present)

Larry Lamb is President of Lamb & Company. He also is President of the affiliated software company LambSoft. Lamb is a pioneer in the world of 3D animation and computer graphics production. He founded Lamb & Company in 1980 and has been at the forefront of innovation in technology development for computer animation and digital effects for advertising and broadcast for close to two decades. His contributions to the industry include both early adoption and testing of new software systems and the development of proprietary software code on a large scale. He serves on the board of trustees of Minneapolis College of Art & Design (MCAD) and the Larry Lamb New Media Advisory Board of the Walker Art Center in Minneapolis.

Larry Lamb has operated a continuous but informal test lab for new computer graphics tools since the company was founded. Lamb & Company is the most senior CG facility in the Midwest and is one of the oldest, longest standing CG companies in America. As such, its history parallels the development of computer animation itself. The first "cool" tool adopted by Larry Lamb (he says it was before anyone else and we believe him) was a servo-controlled Oxberry animation camera. By 1982, everyone in this niche had to have an Oxberry motion control camera. Hey! Graphics move!

Today, Lamb & Company is well-known for its character animation. Long before there were characters that moved, however, there were flying logos. Lamb & Company created some of the world's first when it acquired the first license of Wavefront software. Wavefront enabled Lamb & Company to do production internally without relying on film or outside film-support services. The Wavefront Preview software complemented the Oxberry equipment by enabling staff to previsualize the work being done on the computer-controlled animation camera. Lamb & Company used the Wavefront system to previsualize the Oxberry animation. This way of working was a "preview" of the coming shift to computer graphics in the industry at large.

About the same time, Larry bought the core animation technology developed at Cranston/Csuri, one of a handful of "original" computer animation companies that passed into history. This substantial body of "prior art" in animation technology served as the basis for Lamb & Company's internal development efforts. Larry also was an early adopter of Silicon Graphics hardware as the platform of choice for animation and, much more recently, added NT machines to the mix.

In 1989, Lamb & Company began to pursue new ways of doing computer animation and began experimenting with motion capture as a means of augmenting keyframe animation. The goal was to develop a computer "puppet" to do high volumes of animation quickly. Two driving needs at the time were the need to produce volume and the need to present personality in the characters. Existing CG looked too algorithmic, stiff, and just plain computer generated. As part of the exploration of tools to accomplish this, Lamb & Company became the first customer for Virtual Technologies' Data data glove. Just having the acquisition device did not constitute an animation solution. It was used as a tool to test motion-capture theories as a microcosm system for larger motion-capture efforts. In the early 1990s Larry became the first purchaser of a Discreet Logic FLAME digital paint and compositing and special visual effects system. In 1992, Larry also purchased a full-body motion-capture suit from Ascension Technologies as part of an experimental effort to reduce production costs on a major new animation. It took Lamb & Company six months to create the first long-format, computer-generated 3D network TV program in the U.S., *The Incredible Crash Dummies* (Fox). The need to produce 23 minutes consisting of 82 scenes with 13 characters on the computer at a time when the computer power was much more limited than today continued the quest for productivity and creativity management tools at Lamb & Company. The next set of breakthroughs dealt with blending keyframe animation and motion-capture data and being able to apply motion data to characters that weren't exactly the same as the performer in shape and size. The company proved the technology during the experimental production *Huzzah*. This production was the first complete capture of an actor's single performance. Huzzah has won numerous international animation awards. In 1997, Lamb & Company spun off LambSoft (www.lambsoft.com), a software technology development company whose goal is to productize motion editing and compositing software created as part of the company's long-term efforts at blending motion capture with keyframe animation.

This history was reprinted with the kind permission of Larry Lamb from www.lamb.com. You can contact Larry at contact@lamb.com or 612-333-8666.

Links

(1982 to present)

Founded in 1982 as Toyo Links, this company has been known since 1987 as simply Links, an Imagica Company. Links created a short film called *Bio-Sensor* in 1984 that was notable for its use of innovative story telling. Art Durinski, along with his wife and producing partner Mitchinko, joined the company from Omnibus in 1986 and stayed for about a year and a half. Much of the work Links did was for Sony Corporation including their international logo that served as inspiration for many later large companies. (Art and Mitchinko left in 1988 to form their own consulting firm, the Durinski Design Group in LA, where they continue to work today.)

The Links 1 computer animation system was developed here by Koichi Omura. You can find more information at www.links.imagica.co.jp.

Mathematics Application Group, Inc. (MAGI)

(1966 to 1987)

MAGI was founded by Phil Mittelman (RPI) and two other fellow scientists in 1966 as a spin off of United Nuclear Corporation. The original purpose of the company was to carry out nuclear radiation penetration studies to calculate shielding requirements and other such top-secret government tests. (The name MAGI also was a joking reference to the fact that it was founded by "three wise men.")

In its early days, MAGI's largest business was creating "junk mail" databases for direct mail and marketing uses. Three other MAGI divisions included a CAD/CAM group that was busy in manufacturing and defense contracts; Computer Slides Corp., which handled the presentation business projects; and the smallest of them all, SynthaVision.

First Ray Tracing

The very first ray traced image was produced in 1963 and was output on special test equipment (similar to an oscilloscope) developed at the University of Maryland. The "egg in a box" geometry had complex hidden surface problems that were easily handled by the new ray tracing technique.

MAGI/SynthaVision

Begun in 1972 by Robert Goldstein and Bo Gehring, SynthaVision was the software division of MAGI that was marketed commercially for a short time under the company name of Computer Visuals Inc. The original software (Fortran2 and Fortran4 running on an IBM 360/65) used by MAGI scientists for tracing particle radiation needed to be only slightly modified to trace light rays instead and make—ta da!—computer graphics. (Well, maybe not quite that easily.) To help put the then-current technology in perspective, a box of tab cards (fully a cubic foot worth) were necessary to describe a few seconds of simple animation.

The software techniques were unique in their use of solid modeling techniques.

Unlike systems used at other studios, Synthavision used not polygons or patches but "combinatorial geometry" (Boolean union, difference, and intersection) of mathematically defined solid shapes such as cubes, cones, and spheres. A simple flying saucer, for example, would be modeled as the intersection of two perfect spheres. A sphere would never suffer from low-resolution, straight-edged profiles because it is defined as mathematically perfect. The ray tracing technique, originally developed by Bob Goldstein in the late 1960s, evaluated these Boolean combinations once per ray. (The key paper was published in "Simulation" in 1968 and was referenced in Turner Whitted's 1981 SIGGRAPH paper, which introduced ray tracing to a much broader audience.) The core math and physics developers at this stage included Herb Steinberg and Dr. Eugene Troubetskoy. Marty Cohen and Larry Elin (a nonscientist and Phil Mittleman's son-in-law) served in Executive Producer-type roles.

MAGI showed some of its military simulation work at SIGGRAPH conferences in the late 1970s including a diving submarine, tanks, and a mine shaft.

CG UFOs for CE3K!

In 1975–76, Bo Gehring and others traveled to Hollywood to produce CG tests for Steven Speilberg's film *Close Encounters of the Third Kind*. Carl Machover built a film recorder for the project. One of the earliest of its kind, this film recorder used a 9" CRT to expose imagery onto 35mm film at 4000×2500 lines of resolution. Doug Trumbull also arranged to use a facility in Minneapolis to output the imagery to 65mm film. The intent was to realize the spaceships in the end landing sequence entirely with CG. In the end, Trumbull favored the traditional approach, and the CG tests were no longer pursued.

In 1981, Dr. Troubetskoy replaced this technique with more efficient techniques that did these Boolean combinations over entire scan lines at once. This higher efficiency was necessary to produce the very high Vistavision resolution images (2280×1200) needed for *Tron*.

Dr. Troubetzkoy (a nuclear physicist) was the director of advanced projects at MAGI. He previously was a consulting physicist for the United Nuclear Corporation and was a senior research associate in nuclear physics at Columbia University.

MAGI was a pioneer in putting high-resolution computer graphics directly out to film. Its Celco film recorder (way ahead of its time) was the second ever made. (The first was used by the government for Landsat imagery.)

Carl Ludwig (Director of Engineering) had begun his involvement in computer animation while serving as a consultant for Celco. There he developed a special film recorder to output footage for the groundbreaking Disney film *Tron*.

FACTOID

The first flying-logo CGI ad is attributed to MAGI. It was an ad for IBM in 1969.

FACTOID

After a 1981 visit to MAGI, Benoit Mandelbrot got a Celco for IBM and used it to output fractal images for his classic book *The Fractal Geometry of Nature*.

Tron

Steven Lisberger (the creator of *Tron*) had just finished the animated television film *Animalimpics* when he saw a CG demonstration by Larry Elin. MAGI wemt on to create the memorable Light Cycles and Recognizer sequences in *Tron*.

The MAGI CG on *Tron* was created by a small core team of people including Chris Wedge (animation), Nancy Campy (production coordinator), Tom Bisogna (artist), Ken Perlin (software), and Tom Miller (night shift). Of MAGI's approximately 150 total employees, Synthavision only ever totaled about a dozen people.

Beautiful as the imagery was, Synthavision software did not render frames with anti-aliasing. The solution was to render at a higher resolution and then scale/filter down to a lower resolution to soften the edges. Even simple techniques such as blurring were nonexistent. If you wanted to do a blur, you would run your frames a second time through the Celco film recorder with tissue paper over the CRT to fuzz the element you wanted to blur.

Memories!

"Shortly after Ken Perlin was hired, I was hired into the CAD/CAM division to help build an interactive modeler for Synthavision's CSG (ray traced Boolean ops on quadratic solids). It was to be used by the movie division and sold to the mechanical engineering market. This was an ambitious task. All of the rendering and animation programs were still written in 80-column punched card format, compiled, and run as batch jobs on IBM mainframes. Later, they were run on 32-bit minicomputers, and animation pencil tests were output to film and looked at on an upright Movieola. There weren't any framebuffer or color displays."

—Michael Ferraro

To relate an interesting perspective on the mindset of the time, all the computer graphics people who contributed to the movie *Tron* were in New York for its premiere. All the people from MAGI, Triple-I, Abel, and Digital Effects were sitting around a table at Sardies. The topic of conversation soon centered on the fact that the "entire CG business was sitting right here" and "had anyone heard about some company trying to break into the CG business in California? They are going to call it Pacific Data Images or something like that…" "How do they expect to get into such an established business as ours? It'll never be successful." Ah, but history would play out very differently as we all know too well!

MAGI in LA

As *Tron* finished up, the second wave of people came on board, hired largely by Ken Perlin. Josh Pines played a key role in programming for film scanning and recording, but he also brought an important film/movie-making sense to the otherwise technical group. Christine Chang primarily was an artist, Tom Miller graduated to the day shift, and Mike Ferraro began a self-imposed, if unofficial, transition from the CAD/CAM division. The main New York office was busy pursuing commercial work, but Hollywood was calling!

In early 1984, MAGI opened an office in LA, hoping to capitalize on the success of *Tron* to get more feature film work. Phil Mittelman recruited Richard Taylor (who supervised the effects for *Tron* while at Triple-I) as Director and Dan Fitzgerald as Executive Producer to head this office. Jeremy Shwartz and Larry Malone (both later at Symbolics) also were there. Jan Van Vliet (now President of Available Light) and his wife Cathy used Christine Chang's digital paint program for 2D animation. Their first (and only) project was for the Disney film *Something Wicked This Way Comes* in 1984. The ambitious goal was to use computer graphics to create a magical circus that would appear to set up all by itself. Unfortunately, the images that worked so well in *Tron* did not cut so realistically with live action, and the project was dropped. Executive management had oversold the still primitive technology and was unable to get any more film work. By 1985, MAGI/LA closed its doors.

QUOTE

"In the meantime, Tom Bisogno and I created what became known as the 'After Hours Movie Group' and produced a short film shown at the SIGGRAPH film show in the early '80s. It was titled *First Flight* and was the first use of the procedural lighting/atmosphere effects that MAGI later became known for. The 'After Hours Movie Group' for the most part included Tom, myself, and for a while Jodi Slater."
—Michael Ferraro

Where the Wild Things Are

John Lasseter (then a traditional animator at Disney) got his first exposure to computer graphics by working as the official Disney-Magi liaison for a joint 1983 post-*Tron* test for *Where the Wild Things Are*. Based on the popular children's book by Maurice Sendak, the short film had a young boy in his pajamas running with his dog up a flight of stairs. The characters were traditional cel animation, and the environment was all 3D CG. Disney footed the bill for production, and MAGI paid for the substantial R&D needed to create the hardware and software.

Ken Perlin supervised and wrote code for the project, which also included the now-well-known Disney animator Glen Keane. Jan Carlee and Chris Wedge modeled the environment and animated the camera move. Christine Chang wrote the digital ink-and-paint software that was used to color the Disney animators' scanned-in drawings, complete with shadow and highlight elements. (This technique was used much later to great effects at ILM in *Who Framed Roger Rabbit*.) Josh Pines built the scanner, and Gene Miller and Tom Bisogna worked in production.

Soon after, John used this test as his calling card to join Ed Catmull's graphics department at Lucasfilm, which subsequently was spun off (in 1986) as Pixar.

An interesting side story that happened about this time concerned another Disney animation project. *The Brave Little Toaster* was being storyboarded by Lasseter and Jo Ramf, but when Ron Miller (then head of Feature Animation at Disney) was ousted so was the project. For those of you who know the film (and if you have kids, you should!), all the characters are household appliances including a lamp, a radio, and a vacuum cleaner. The cel animated characters would have been created in 3D CG by MAGI; however, Tom Wilhite left Disney and formed Hyperion Animation to independently produce the film, and the MAGI work never was to be.

A MAJOR MILESTONE

This amazing project (Where the Wild Things Are) was the first example of full-feature, film-resolution CG digital compositing.

Fun and Rewarding Times

The whole spirit at this time was of around-the-clock creative energy. Each person was egging one another on to constantly push the barriers further beyond what was done the day before. The night crew often left on the screen their most rewarding images for the day crew to see them. This produced no end of awestruck reactions like "How did they *do* that?". Of course, not to be outdone, the day shift repeated the process only to amaze the next night crew and cause the cycle to be repeated. The group of 11 co-workers were referred to as the "22-legged beast" because of their tight lunch-going groups reminiscent of the Warner Brothers cartoons with a single mass of characters atop animated legs.

In 1983–84 at MAGI, Ken Perlin developed his now-famous "Perlin Noise and Turbulence" techniques of creating solid and procedural textures that are now commonly used everywhere in the CG industry. (It earned him an Academy Award for Technical Achievement in 1997, too).

The Beginning Of The End

The Synthavision division was sold off in 1984 to a holding company in Toronto, Canada, run by Bob Robbins and Leo Grey. The company's new president was David Boyd Brown, who later went on to become President of Blue Sky.

The first main project for Synthavision after the buyout was a laser video disk arcade game called Robot Rebellion. It required the player to pilot a small LV1 robot to the core of a mining asteroid to overcome a mine full of crazed robots and booby traps and to regain control of the colony by punching in a color code learned along the way. Hazards included CG fire created with Ken Perlin Language (KPL) texture code.

THE FLY

Sythavision's work can be seen in David Cronenberg's *The Fly*, in which the main character, Seth Brundel (played by Jeff Goldblum), plays a visual sequence on his computer that explains that his DNA has been mixed with a housefly. The work is not credited in the film.

The finished project was shopped around to gaming companies such as Bally and Atari. Unfortunately, this occurred as the downturn in arcade gaming began. Like many other computer graphics production companies of the 1980s, Sythavision collapsed under the enormous overhead costs and capital debt from the purchase of hardware technology.

Scrubbing Bubbles Curse?

"The very last project Sythavision did was a commercial featuring DOW Chemical's Scrubbing Bubbles in their first CG incarnation. These, I'm told, are the same characters that Cranston/Csuri were working on when they folded later. We all watched PDI with interest when they took on Scrubbing Bubbles. Fortunately, they survived the curse."

—Paul Griffin

Synthavision's parent company went out of business in the fall of 1986. The CAD/CAM division of Magi had been sold to Lockheed Aerospace in 1982–83, and MAGI Computer Slides Corp. was purchased in 1986 for $4 million and was renamed MAGICorp.

Where Are They Now?

Phil Mittelman formed the UCLA Lab for Technology and the Arts. Blue Sky Productions was then founded by David Brown (President), Alison Brown (Administration), Dr. Eugene Troubetzkoy, Mike Ferraro (PossibleWorlds.com), Carl Ludwig (Director of Engineering), and Chris Wedge. Jan Carlée (Animation Director) also would later join Blue Sky.

Josh Pines, Ken Perlin, Jan Carlee, and Christine Chang began the CG group at R/Greenberg Associates. Ken Perlin went on to NYU and remains there today. Josh Pines now heads the digital scanning department at ILM, Christine eventually went to Don Bluth and more recently to Pixar, Jan Carlee eventually joined Blue Sky, and Mike Ferraro eventually left Blue Sky to form his own production company, Possible Worlds. Tom Miller now is Head of CG at Fox Animation Studios.

mental images

(1986 to present)

mental images was incorporated in April of 1986 by Rolf Herken with financial backing from private investors. Today, those same initial investors split company ownership 50 percent with the employees and partners of mental images.

The formation of mental images always was intended as a software development company specifically focused on rendering code. Their notoriety as a production house, especially from 1987 to 1991, was strictly pursued to further their experience in production to better improve their rendering code. The production personnel included John Berton, John Nelson, Tom Noack, and Stefen Fangmeyer,

Still from the animation "MENTAL IMAGES." Copyright, mental mmages, 1987

who served as Director of Production until 1988 when he went on to ILM.

From 1986 to 1989, the first generation of mental ray® was written, begun initially by Robert Hodicke. Hardware was one Solarity computer along with the first two SGI 3030's in Europe. The initial commercial software used was the first Wavefront license in Europe. To jump start mental images, it was decided to produce an in-house short animation. The three-minute short entitled *Mental Images* was produced by a core team of about eight people working 18 hours a day for seven months. The film won worldwide acclaim for its beautiful surreal imagery including recognition in 1987 at SIGGRAPH, NCGA, NICOGRAPH, and Prix Ars Electronica.

Stills from the animation "M.A.A.D.D." Simulation of fur and caustics. Images rendered with mental ray. Copyright, mental images, Berlin, 1998.

From 1990 to 1993, the second generation of mental ray (v1.7-1.9) was developed with free-form curve and surface technology for Wavefront Technologies, Inc.

In 1993, mental images was commissioned to develop a complete interactive design visualization system based on mental ray for Mercedes-Benz. Also in 1993, mental images and Softimage Inc. of Montreal, Canada, entered into a rendering technology agreement. Under the terms of the agreement, Version 1.9 of mental ray was integrated into Version 3.0 of Softimage|3D.

In 1994, Dassault Systemes of Suresnes, France, and mental images announced a long-term research and development agreement between the two companies. Under the terms of the agreement, mental images is responsible for the development of the general-purpose CATIA Rendering Component (CRC) for Dassault Systemes' current and next-generation CATIA lines of products.

mental images also is involved in major European strategic research projects in High-Performance Computing and Networking (HPCN). These projects are funded in part by the European Commission. The company was project leader of the ESPRIT Project 6173 "Design by Simulation and Rendering on Parallel Architectures" (DESIRE) from 1992 to 1995. It also is leading the follow-up project, ESPRIT Project 22765 (DESIRE II), from 1997 to its date of completion in 1999.

"Dusty room." Sunlight through a stained glass window scattered off from dust particles in the air lights the room. Image rendered with metal ray. Copyright, mental images, Berlin, 1998.

Modern production companies rely on mental ray for the most realistic CG imagery in a variety of industries. Buf Compagnie's feature film work and the Riven game from Cyan are notable examples.

From 1994 to 1998, the third-generation of mental ray, mental ray Version 2.0, was developed and led by project leader and software engineer Thomas Dreimeyer, who today leads the v2.1 release.

In 1997, Autodesk Inc. and mental images entered into a research and development agreement in the area of advanced modeling and surface approximation technology for use in Autodesk's 3D Studio MAX and 3D Studio VIZ lines of products. The first product containing such technology, 3D Studio MAX Release 2.0, was released in October 1997. 3D Studio VIZ Release 2.0 followed in June 1998. In April 1999, Autodesk and mental images entered into a larger agreement to make future versions of mental ray available to all Autodesk products including 3D Studio MAX R3.

Still from the animation "MENTAL IMAGES." Copyright, mental images, 1987.

At the same time, Avid Technology, Inc. (having acquired Softimage a year earlier) and mental images entered into a similar long-term license and research and development agreement.

Since April 1999, mental ray 2.0 and higher versions also are available on an OEM/VAR basis from mental images to interested third parties in all fields.

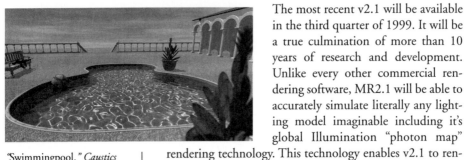

The most recent v2.1 will be available in the third quarter of 1999. It will be a true culmination of more than 10 years of research and development. Unlike every other commercial rendering software, MR2.1 will be able to accurately simulate literally any lighting model imaginable including it's global Illumination "photon map" rendering technology. This technology enables v2.1 to render, frame to frame, only those portions of the scene that have changed. This is fundamentally different from all other software, which essentially renders 24 discrete still frames for every second of film animation.

"Swimmingpool." Caustics in a swimming pool seen through a wavy water surface. Image rendered with mental ray. Copyright, mental images, Berlin, 1998.

Today, Rolf remains President and Director of R&D, the "nucleus and DNA" of the mental images corporate body. mental images remains small and specialized and constantly recruits the best and brightest mathematicians and software engineers in the world.

NOTE

Major portions of this mental images history have been reprinted with the permission of Rolf Herken from the company's Web site www.mentalimages. com/). mental images is located in Berlin, Germany.

MetroLight

(1987 to present)

Ron Saks (formerly of Abel's) was hired by Cranston/Csuri Productions (CCP) in anticipation of opening an LA office. Richard "Dr." Baily was hired in LA first, followed by Paul Sidlo and a few more people. All the new hires went out to Ohio in the summer of 1986 to learn the various custom CCP software. A bunch of people soon went back to LA to an office in the back of Abel's old building. These people included Tim McGovern (Abel), Jon Townley, Steve Martino, Mark Steeves, Richard "Dr." Baily, Neil Eskuri

(Disney), Al Dinoble (Cinesite), Larry Elin (MAGI/Abel), and Steve Klevatt.

When CCP folded, Ron Saks remained in Ohio and took a teaching job there. Jim Kristoff, Dobbie Schiff (Jim and Dobbie are married), several of their family members, and Mits Kaneko all contributed the original funding to then start MetroLight.

Other key people who soon joined MetroLight included Con Pederson (Abel), Tom Hutchinson (ILM), Jim Hillen (Disney Feature Animation), John McLaughlin (Sony Pictures Imageworks), Gary Jackemuk, Jim Rygiel, Joe Letteri (ILM), Jeff Doud (Click 3X), Yung-Chen Sung, Rebecca Marie (Hammerhead), Scott Bendis (Interplay), Billy Kent, Patrice Dinhut, Kelley Ray (Sony), Mark Lasoff (Station X), Sean Schur (ILM), and Joey Alter

Initially, new SGI 3130 computers were purchased for the new company, running software from a relatively new company called Wavefront. At this same time, Robert Abel & Associates had just gone out of business with the company's landlord acquiring much of the production equipment upon its closing. MetroLight then purchased this gear for itself (including Evans & Sutherland computers, Mitchel cameras, motion-control equipment, and other hardware).

MetroLight's first job was an intro for *National Geographic* directed by Jeff Doud. The rendering was done at 1k at 1:1.33 aspect ratio for both film and television markets. Jeff was hired soon after to work at MetroLight as an Art Director and is now at Click3x in Atlanta.

For their first attempt at feature film work, MetroLight shared a Special Achievement Visual Effects Academy Award for 1989's *Total Recall*. The project required animating 3D CG skeletons in a life-size, walk-through X-ray machine. Initially, an early optical motion-capture system from Motion Analysis was tested on Arnold Schwarzenegger. (The system required that the production crew stick ping-pong balls all over him!) Eventually, though, because of many technical problems with the system, a backup plan was put into use.

FACTOID

Before MetroLight was chosen as the official name, it originally was called North Light Studios (until it was discovered that this name already was taken).

The rear camera used behind the X-ray in the motion capture setup was used to capture footage that was rotoscoped for the keyframes used in the final character animation. Director Paul Verhoven, then new to CG technology, was very accommodating to the MetroLight crew, although he vetoed the idea of putting muscles on the X-ray skeletons. The hope was that this would help differentiate Arnold's large physique from the other "normal"-size human skeletons, but it was not to be.

In May of 1988, MetroLight decided that it wanted a more robust rendering software solution than the one provided by Wavefront at the time. Yung-Chen began work on in-house code, only to lose all his data four months later in a series of software backup failures. The second time around, the code (finished in spring of '89) was fast and was enough to carry them until about 1991–92 when they began using Pixar's RenderMan. At this same time, Alias was selling its product modularly, and MetroLight decided on Alias' superior modeling package instead of writing their own code for this task. Alias PowerAnimator eventually replaced Wavefront Preview. Alias|Wavefront's Composer recently was replaced with Silicon Grail's Chalice for compositing. Alias|Wavefront's Maya is now being introduced as the all-around tool of choice (although Con Pederson was still using Abel software up until very recently!).

From the very beginning, MetroLight had two separate divisions, each ultimately with about 65 employees. These divisions were the main 3D production division and MetroCel, the 2D ink and paint division. Mits Kaneko directed the overall development of the MetroCel 2D software, Mark Steeves ran the MetroCel division, and Charles Scalfani was the lead programmer. MetroLight's Annie digital ink-and-paint software was ready for production work by about 1991, and it was used in such television shows as *Ren & Stimpy*.

In 1994, the Annie software was sold to the interactive company 7th Level, which was going public with the backing of a certain investment banker named Michael Milken.

Over the years, MetroLight also has contributed to a number of large-format films including the Korean *Star Quest* (with DreamQuest providing practical effects) and an Imax Intel show. Two such large-format projects are currently in production: one for a summer 1999 release in Universal's new Florida theme park and another in Orlando for Sigfreid and Roy, produced by L Squared.

A large part of Jim Kristoff and MetroLight's vision for the future of their company is character animation. To this end, they are just finishing work on the sequel to *Dragonheart*, due for a fall 1999 direct-to-video release.

The Moving Picture Company (MPC)
(1980 to present)

This section on MCP history was contributed by Craig Zerouni(`craig@sgrail.com`*).*

As the UK's leading video post house in 1981 (and it arguably still is), MPC employees had reputations as technology junkies. They recently had built a motion-control rig under the direction of Andrew Berend, a London Film School graduate. The computer that controlled the rig was built by Interactive Motion Control (IMC). One of the partners at IMC was Bud Elam, who later won an Academy Award for Technical Achievement for motion-control technology. (His co-winner was Ray Feeney, who started RFX.)

In 1981, they also had just installed a computer animation system that consisted of a Hewlett-Packard desktop machine programmed in Basic, which drove a plotter. The plotter had no pens. Instead, it had a fiber-optic light source where the pen went. This was pointed at the camera film plane. The lens opened, a colored gel rotated in front of the lens, and the plotter drew a wireframe layer directly onto the film emulsion. The color would then change, and more lines would be drawn. Of course, this all took place in a black box. This multilayered approach took minutes to do a single frame. There was no way of knowing what you had until you unloaded it, took it to the labs, waited overnight, went back to the labs, brought it back, laced it up, and viewed it on the Movieola.

National Center For Supercomputing Applications (NCSA)
(1985 to present)

Founded in 1985 by Nancy St. John and Craig Upston (Co-Managers), the NCSA is located at the University of Illinois at Champaign-Urbana. The NCSA is known for creating pioneering scientific visualization software tools that scientists themselves could use. Stefen Fangmeier (ILM Visual Effects Supervisor) was there briefly as a TD.

New York Institute of Technology (NYIT)
In 1974, Dr. Alexander Schure, a wealthy entrepreneur, began to assemble the Computer Graphics Laboratory (CGL) at the New York Institute of Technology. His vision was to create a feature-length animated film with the aid of the day's most sophisticated computer graphics techniques. NYIT, itself founded by Dr. Schure, has grounds encompassing numerous estates situated in the beautiful wooded hillsides of Old Westbury, New York. Some of these estates were owned by members of the Rockefeller family, who also happened to have a seat on the board of Evans & Sutherland. Because of the close association of E&S with the University of Utah, Dave Evans recommended that Alex seek out Edwin Catmull to head the new CGL at NYIT.

Ed Catmull had just finished his Ph.D. at the University of Utah and had taken a job at a CAD/CAM company called Applicon. It was not a hard sell to get Ed to leave Applicon for NYIT, however, so he and fellow Utah graduate

Malcolm Blanchard packed their bags for New York. Alvy Ray Smith and David DiFrancesco (both fresh from Xerox PARC) joined the team a few months later in what was called the "Gerry Mansion." Alvy and David had heard of Dr. Schure's plans from Martin Newell at Utah (whom Alex had just hired briefly as a consultant). Dr. Schure had recently come through Utah and literally ordered "one of everything" to jump-start his NYIT project. This equipment included a DEC PDP-11, a new E&S LDS-1, and the first random access frame buffer, also from E&S. Later, the CGL group also received the very first commercial DEC VAX.

VAX Almost Smashed!

The VAX would never made it inside the building if not for Alvy Ray Smith's quick actions. It seems that, when the computer was lowered off the back of the delivery truck, another truck parked behind and uphill had its brakes slip, and it started it rolling towards the brand new machine. Alvy quickly jumped in the driver-less truck and stopped it just before it could smash the VAX back into the very truck from which it was just unloaded.

The CGL quickly attracted other technology experts and artists including Christy Barton (from E&S), Tom Duff, Lance Williams, Fred Parke, Garland Stern, Ralph Guggenheim, Ed Emshwiller, and many others.

Throughout the 1970s, the people of the CGL thrived in a pioneering spirit and created milestones in many areas of graphics software. Many of the "firsts" that happened at NYIT were based on the development of the first RGB full-color (24-bit) raster graphics.

Here are a few of the more notable firsts:

- First RGB anything (because they had the first RGB framebuffers in the world).

- First RGB paint program (invented by Alvy Ray Smith, and called Paint).

- First soft-edged fill (Alvy Ray again).

- First computer-controlled video editing.

- First TV commercial with raster graphics.

- First pixel dissolve.

- First networked computer system (Christy rolled our own for us).

- The alpha channel was invented by Ed Catmull and Alvy Ray Smith.

- First hidden-surface algorithm within a pixel (Ed).

- Lance Williams invented mipmapping. (Texture mapping is still done this way today.)

- Garland Stern implemented the first scan and paint system. (This is how the Disney/Pixar CAPS system now makes 2D animation—different system but same idea.)

The atmosphere at the CGL was very open, and many invited tours came through the lab year-round. Other universities such as Cornell and companies such as Quantel were among those to visit and take notes about what was being developed. The personnel structure was virtually nonexistent, with never any heavy handed management from Dr. Catmull. People did what they were best at and helped each other out whenever necessary.

Strangest Job Title Ever!

Alvy Ray Smith later accidentally came across an organization chart for the lab put together by Dr. Shure. Ed Catmull was running the lab, of course, but there were people listed above and below him that no one had even heard of. Alvy was particularly amused to find that his official title was "Information Quanta." This term was very much in keeping with Dr. Shure's somewhat unique, non-standard form of communicating.

Ed Catmull's Tween, Alvy Ray Smith's Paint program, and the 2D animation program SoftCel all were in keeping with the original charter of the CGL, which was 2D CG. There also were many breakthroughs in image techniques involving fractals, morphing, image compositing, Mip-Map texture mapping, and many others.

The key to this pioneering effort was the seemingly unlimited financing evidenced by Alex Schure. One such example took place when Alvy Ray Smith spoke with Alex about how good it might be to have not just the one but three framebuffers. This way, Alvy explained, the three 8-bit buffers could be combined to create the first RGB color framebuffer ever! Sometime later, Alex not only delivered the two additional framebuffers, he delivered an additional three, which gave the CGL team a grand total of six. At $60,000 each (plus the $80,000 for the first), this means that, in today's dollars, Alex had just delivered about $2 million worth of equipment on a simple request.

More Utah people joined the CGL including Garland Stern, who would write the vector animation system BBOP. David DiFrancesco also began what would turn out to be a long association with film recording at this time.

Tubby The Tuba!

At the same time the CGL was up and running, Alex had about 100 traditional animators working on a film called *Tubby the Tuba*. Unfortunately, when the film finally screened two years later, everyone's worst fears were realized... it was worse than awful.

Several different departments existed at NYIT by now in different neighboring mansions: an audio group, a video/post production lab, and a computer science department as well. One successfully completed project was a half-hour video (2" with a single frame recorder) called *Measure for Measure*, which combined conventional cel animation with TWEEN imagery.

In 1979, when Ed Catmull left to start the Computer Graphics Division at Lucasfilm, many at the Computer Graphics Division wanted to come with him. In fact, Alvy, Tom Duff, and David DiFrancesco all left and went elsewhere while waiting to join Ed in California when the time was right. Ralph had promised to stay at NYIT a full year, and he honored that commitment. He even turned down an offer from Alex Schure to head the CGL group so he would be free to leave after that year was up.

A New York City commercial office known as CGL Inc. also was established to market and sell the technology developed in Old Westbury. CGL Inc. also produced numerous commercial graphics jobs for the broadcast market.

The Works

The remaining historical text for NYIT/CGL was contributed by Paul Heckbert.

Shortly after Catmull left NYIT, Alex's son, Louis Schure, became lab director. At about the same time, the NYIT lab began preparing to make the first 3D computer animated movie called *The Works*. Its science fiction screenplay was written by Lance Williams. A number of people were hired to work on the project. The principal robot designers and modelers were Lance, Bill Maher, Dick Lundin (designer of the famous robot ant), Ned Greene, and Carter Burwell. Some of the animators were Rebecca Allen and Amber Denker.

The Works

A great deal of effort at NYIT went into the development of the film *The Works*, which was written by Lance Williams and was worked on from about 1979 to 1986. For many reasons, including a lack of film-making expertise, it never was completed. Sequences from the work in progress still stand as some of the most astounding animated imagery of the time.

Software development during the early '80s was guided by Lance Williams, Paul Heckbert, Fred Parke, and Pat Hanrahan.

A number of excellent graphics software developers did pioneering work there during those years:

- **Jim Blinn** MAT: yacc-based modeling language

- **Jim Clark** E&S picture system library from the '70s; Jim later went on to found Silicon Graphics and Netscape

- **Lance Williams** Z-buffer and texture mapping techniques; Coons image warp; mesh modeling tools; face modeling and animation; DEKINK: antialiasing, recording tools

- **Tom Duff** SOID: Z-buffered quadric surface rendering with texture mapping; bump mapping; MAT: yacc-based modeling language

- **Garland Ste** BBOP: interactive keyframe animation system

- **Dick Lund** dynamics simulation and robot modeling and animation tools

- **Ephraim Cohen** ZOOM: filtered image resampling; EPT: paint program

- **Thad Beier** SSOID: CSG on quadric surfaces

- **Mike Chou** SOID's environment mapping

- **Frank Crow** antialiased line drawing

- **Andrew Glassner** antialiased line drawing

- **Tom Sherm** antialiased line drawing

- **Robert McDermott** geometric modeling tools

- **John Schlag**   image processing software

- **Paul Heckbert**   POLY: z-buffered polygon renderer with texture mapping; Coons image warp; beam tracing; z-buffer rendering for fisheye projection; early splatting, a form of volume rendering; face modeling and animation

- **Fred Parke**   face modeling and animation

- **John Lewis**   fractal modeling

- **Peter Oppenheimer**   fractal modeling

- **Ned Greene**   sky modeling from photographs; z-buffer rendering for fisheye projection; mesh modeling tools

- **Jules Bloomenthal**   realistic tree modeling; DEKINK: antialiasing, recording tools

- **Kevin Hunter**   early marching cubes

- **Pat Hanrahan**   EM: interactive modeling system; beam tracing; winged edge library

- **David Sturman**   animation database and tools

- **Tom Brigham**   image morphing

- **Tracy Peter**   audio synthesis

- **Mike Kowalski**   audio synthesis

- **Carter Burwell**   audio synthesis

- and many other amazing graphics hackers and graphics hacks.

The workhorse hardware during the early '80s was six DEC VAX 11/780's as main computers; about three E&S Picture System II's for animation preview; about eight E&S and Genisco framebuffers for 512×486×24-bit raster graphics; about six programmable Ikonas graphics processors, the largest with 12MB of image memory (an ungodly amount in that day: 2048×2048×24-bits) viewed with rare thousand-line color monitors; several IVC 2000 2" videotape recorders; and a Dicomed film recorder.

Although The Works was never completed (the group was ahead of its time; it wasn't until 1995 that the first 3D computer animated movie—*Toy Story*—came out), some major milestones of computer animation came out of the effort: The Works trailer (the hit of the SIGGRAPH '82 film show), 3DV, Inside a Quark, and segments for the 1984 Omnimax movie *The Magic Egg*. The lab's animation demonstrated the first extensive use of texture mapping and environment mapping in animation and some of the first 3D character animation. Some pictures from the early '80s are available at www.cs.cmu.edu/~ph/nyit.

After this peak, the party began to wind down in the mid- to late '80s. Bloomenthal left for Xerox PARC in 1985; Heckbert left for PDI and Pixar in 1985; Hanrahan left for Wisconsin, DEC, and Pixar in 1985; and Williams left for Apple in 1986. The dispersal of its lab members helped spread NYIT's ideas to many other sites.

Ohio State University

Portions of the Ohio State entry were excerpted with permission from "A Short History of ACCAD": by Wayne Carlson.

Charles A. Csuri

In 1963, Charles Csuri joined OSU as a Professor in the Department of Art. A former All-American football player and painter, he soon became interested in computers as an aid in creating new forms of art and animation.

By 1967, with the assistance of a fellow faculty member from the Department of Mathematics (and a mainframe computer), Csuri created several interpolated line drawing sequences including one of a hummingbird in flight. Csuri produced more than 14,000 frames that exploded the bird, scattered it about, and reconstructed it. These frames were output to 16mm film, and the resulting film *Hummingbird* was purchased by the Museum of Modern Art in 1968 for its permanent collection as representative of one of the first computer-animated artworks.

The CGRG

Beginning with a National Science Foundation grant for $100,000 in 1969, The Computer Graphics Research Group (CGRG) began working with a PDP 11/45 mini-computer and Vector General Display. The CGRG was truly multi-disciplined and included faculty and graduate students in art, industrial design, photography and cinema, computer and information science, and mathematics. Additional grants from the Air Force Office For Scientific Research and the Navy continued at the center until 1990. The CGRG projects specialized in computer animation languages, geometric and terrain modeling, motion control, and real-time playback systems.

FACTOID

In the early 1970s, Mark Gillenson (now at IBM) developed a technique of blending images of facial drawings. This was one of the earliest examples of the now-familiar technology called morphing.

Animation Systems

Early animation language projects focused on a new concept of user friendliness termed "habitability" by Tom DeFanti. This was promoted as an interface to the real-time systems consisting of dials and joysticks.

- GRASS (Graphics Symbiosis System) animation programming language was written by Tom DeFanti in 1972.

- ANIMA motion language was written by Manfred Knemeyer in 1973.

- ANIMA II was developed with contributions from Ron Hackathorn, Alan Myers, Richard Parent, and Tim Van Hook.

- TWIXT was designed by Julian Gomez as a "track-based keyframe animation system."

Other Important Developments

Procedural animation was developed in the late '70s by Wayne Carlson, Bob Marshall, and Rodger Wilson.

Frank Crow arrived from the University of Texas and continued the work with shadows and anti-aliasing that he started at the University of Utah. He later went to Xerox PARC.

Character Animation

A great many individuals at Ohio State created award-winning, character-based short animations including *Tuber's Two Step* by Chris (Blue Sky) Wedge and *Snoot and Muttly* by Susan Van Baerle and Doug Kingsbury.

Cranston/Csuri Productions Inc.

In 1981, Chuck Csuri approached investor Robert Kanuth of The Cranston Companies to form a production company based on the great array of custom software written at the CGRG.

Mark Howard designed and built a framebuffer that was used extensively for real-time animation testing at the CGRG and Cranston/Csuri Productions until the latter went out of business in 1987.

The ACCAD

In 1987, Chuck Csuri and Tom Linehan (now President of the Ringling School of Design) converted the Computer Graphics Research Group into The Advanced Computing Center for the Arts and Design (ACCAD). With funding from a long-term Ohio Board of Regents grant, ACCAD was established to provide computer animation resources in teaching, research, and production for all departments in the College of the Arts at Ohio State. The ACCAD homepage is www.cgrg.ohio-state.edu.

Also in the late 1980s, Scott Dyer (Windlight co-founder, now at Nelvana) and a group of ACCAD personnel connected with the new Ohio Supercomputer Center for the purpose of developing flexible software solutions in the burgeoning field of scientific visualization.

Alumni Works

For a more complete listing of CGRG, Cranston/Csuri, and ACCAD alumni and their work, visit these Web sites:

www.cgrg.ohio-state.edu/accad/people/alumni.html

www.cgrg.ohio-state.edu/accad/research/

www.cgrg.ohio-state.edu/accad/gallery/films.html

Charles A. "Chuck" Csuri currently is the Director and Professor Emeritus of the Departments of Art, Art Education, and Computer and Information Science at Ohio State University.

Wayne Carlson has been on the faculty at OSU since 1988 and is an Associate Professor in the Department of Industrial Design with joint appointments in Art, Art Education, and Computer and Information Science. He also is currently the Director of the ACCAD.

Omnibus Computer Graphics Inc.
(1982 to 1987)

The Omnibus Group Inc. began as a group of Canadian companies in marketing and communication founded in London, Ontario, in 1972. It expanded with affiliated and shareholding offices in Toronto (Omnibus Video Inc.), Los Angeles (Image West Limited & Downstream-Keyer Inc.), and Sydney, Australia (The Picture Company). John C. Pennie joined in 1974 as President.

Image West was developed by Omnibus beginning in 1975 and was located in Hollywood, California. (See the Image West company entry for more details.)

Omnibus Video Inc., started in 1981, was headed by President Jack Porter (who for 14 years was president of Sheridan College in Toronto) and was located in the Yonge-Eglinton area of Toronto, Canada. The NYIT TWEEN system was acquired and used by animator Robert Marinic (now a CG Supervisor at ILM), who was one of nine employees there at the time.

Omnibus Computer Graphics Inc. was started in early 1982 with W. Kelly Jarmain as Chairman and J.C. Pennie as President and CEO. In 1983, they installed a DEC VAX 11/750 and produced the first CG commercial in Canada. In 1983, an IPO (which raised $4.2 million) made

Omnibus the first publicly traded CG company. The plan was to expand and operate three main facilities: Toronto, New York, and Los Angeles. The original Toronto location was for computer operations and for Canadian broadcast and agency work. Its Production group was run by Dan Philips (now head of CG production at Dreamworks). The New York facility, for video broadcast and recording, was on 57th street West under a lease from Unitel Video Inc. The Los Angeles location was intended primarily for motion picture film work. All three were linked by satellite by the end of 1984. (The satellite link amounted to modems for many months and finally a WAN that was painfully slow and unreliable.) As part of the initial expansion in mid-1984, several larger VAX 11/780 systems were installed at the Toronto facility.

Omnibus/LA (which was now majority-owned by Santa Clara-based Ramtek) hired David Sieg from Image West as VP of R&D and a team of programmers from CalTech working with Al Barr, Brian Von Herzen, and many others. In addition to developing their own software (called Prisms), Omnibus obtained several exclusive software license agreements with Robert Abel & Associates and Triple-I. (The deal with Abel originally was signed to last seven years, the Triple-I deal until the year 2001. This is a moot point given the abbreviated future of the companies.)

To start up the Omnibus/LA facility, they bought the F1 computer system and older film printers (called PFRs) from Triple-I (which had just shut down their CG group) and started working out of the Triple-I offices in Culver City. Omnibus/LA soon moved to the Paramount Studios lot in Hollywood, sharing facilities with Unitel Video. Art Durinski was hired as Creative Director and staffed the initial dozen employees. Among these employees were a number of students from UCLA where he had been teaching.

FACTOID

Kevin Tureski relates his first day on the job at Omnibus in Toronto:

"I remember walking in past reception to where the animators worked. There was Eric Ladd hunched over a massive drafting table. He was digitizing by hand the x, y, and z coordinates of a horse. Someone had drawn about five sectional slices of a horse on 4 foot by 3 foot graph paper, one slice per paper. Eric was calculating the x,y values from the grid and was writing down the coordinates on a piece of paper, later typing them in, manually creating several .ppt files. There was no digitizing tablet to be found anywhere. Later, on a tour of the edit suite, I saw Mike Johnson feeding paper tape containing the boot program through the ESS, a still store capable of holding 30 seconds of video on its RK05 disks."

Star Trek III

The first feature film contract Omnibus worked on was for Paramount Pictures' *Star Trek III*. Omnibus (one of three companies to contribute effects) created a number of video graphics displays seen on the bridge of the Enterprise and Klingon starships. About 30 to 40 computer-generated video clips comprised almost an hour's worth of imagery. Artists included Technical Director Dan Krech and Animator Dan Philips.

Jeff Kleiser came on board in the LA office as Director of the Motion Picture Special Effects division. He directed animation for the feature film *Flight of the Navigator* and the original *Captain Power* television pilot for Landmark.

Flight of the Navigator showcased the first feature film use of 3D morphing and animated texture mapping. (Environmental film footage was transferred to video, was digitized, and was used to simulate the chrome surface of the spaceship.)

Explorers would require a dream sequence illustrating a fly-over of a city represented by a 3D CG circuit board. Without the capability to render different-colored vector graphics, Art Durinski designed the effect to be output in multiple black and white layers, each of which was filmed out and optically colored and composited at Industrial Light & Magic. (ILM was the primary traditional effects house on the movie.) Bob Hoffman coded and animated on both Navigator and Explorers.

DOA

In June of 1986, Omnibus bought Digital Productions. Omnibus was approached by their majority owner Control Data, which was desperate to get out from under the increasing debt of DP. In September of that same year, Omnibus also bought Robert Abel & Associates for $7.3 million. Abel likewise was on the verge of bankruptcy and was led to believe that Omnibus was a legitimate bid from a publicly held and stable company. The management at

---

*THE FIRST
D.O.A. DOMINO
TIPS*

The *Captain Power* project was meant to save Digital Productions from bankruptcy. When Jeff brought the project to Omnibus instead, DP was forced to sell out. The rest, as they say, is history.

Omnibus saw the purchases as a way to consolidate the best of everything (and all their customers) into a single monolithic parent company. Unfortunately, nothing was as it appeared, as everyone soon found out.

Gary Demos and John Whitney Jr. had no choice but to leave Digital Production when their contract agreement with Control Data was violated by the sale to Omnibus. They both left to form Whitney/Demos. Art Durinski was privy to the financial state of the recent deals early on and decided to leave the company and go to Toyo/Links in Japan.

QUOTE

"The Omnibus management knew nothing about computer animation but kept muttering about 'Economies of Scale.' The reality was: three separate sales forces, three separate production crews, three separate facilities, philosophies, software systems, and hardware systems, none of which were likely to ever work together. What is ironic is that the next *Star Trek* movie was about to go into production and had tons of CGI work in it. We had good contacts with the right people, and we did some amazing tests (I have videotape!) of the Enterprise that blew the modelmakers away. But they were too scared Omnibus would go under to give us the contract that would have saved us."

—David Sieg (dave@ns.zfx.com)

Diana Walczak began working on human figure tests for Marvel Comics, and Jeff Kleiser was in Vancouver, Canada, scouting locations for the film *Millennium* when the end came. In early 1987, with a debt of $30 million, Omnibus defaulted on investments and closed Abel, DP, and Omnibus on April 13, 1987.

President J.C. Pennie later headed The Virtual Reality Company until it went under in 1993.

Kim Davidson and Greg Hermanovic purchased the rights to the Prisms source code and started Side Effects Productions, which later became Side Effects Software.

Kevin Tureski went to Alias and was Director of Engineering for Alias|Wavefront's PowerAnimator from its inception. He now is responsible for various bits and pieces of Maya.

An Omnibus Japan still exists today and uses the 3D Omnibus orb logo.

QUOTE

"Auctions were held for the remainder of the equipment including people's desks with papers still in them. I bought an Ikonas framebuffer for $50 that had been bought 18 months earlier for $35,000. I still have it today. It still works."

—David Sieg

OptoMystic

— **see** Whitney/Demos Productions

Pacific Data Images (PDI)

(1980 to present)

Incorporated in August 1980 by Carl Rosendahl, PDI originally began in a small office in Los Altos. Carl grew up in LA and graduated with a degree in Electrical Engineering from Stanford in 1979. Wanting to combine entertainment with his technical experience, computer graphics seemed a natural solution. Times being what they were (so early in the CG evolution), Carl formed his own company rather than seeking employment at one of a very few established companies.

Richard Chuang and Glenn Entiss made it a company of three in 1982. Later, after moving to a Sunnyvale industrial complex until 1984, PDI moved into another larger building owned by Carl's father. They remained there until moving to their present location in Palo Alto in 1997. PDI has grown from employing fewer than 20 people in about 1984 to employing more than 300 today.

The first PDP-11/44 was used for programming much of the original proprietary code written by Richard and Glenn (and Carl, too).

Richard concentrated on the renderer and later on lighting tools. A DeAnza framebuffer also was used early on. Their very first jobs were doing broadcast graphics for Jose Diaz of Brazilian Globo Television.

Many early commercial jobs that kept the company busy were from the Harry Marks creative agency.

By the late 1980s, PDI was using Ridge UNIX workstations (similar to those by Solarity) and controlled about 60 percent of the high-end commercial broadcast market. Clients included virtually every network and cable channel along with hundreds of affiliate local stations. From the very beginning, it was clear that PDI (and Carl, in particular) had a uniquely keen business savvy that enabled the company to thrive through a time when CG company bank-ruptcies otherwise were the norm. At least two key strategies were instrumental to PDI's continued financial success. First, unlike most companies that were going heavily into debt to finance "glamorous" feature film work, PDI concentrated through the 1980s on the lucrative commercial market. Their early reputation in broadcast graphics work made the transition to film work easy. The second important factor that kept the books in the black was the wise decision to purchase and use "last year's" models of computer equipment and to depreciate it in just a few short years.

It also was at this time (1989–90) that Carl and Tim Johnson began to visit various Hollywood studios to try and begin a dialog about creative content partnerships. It was a proactive decision in response to what they saw as a future trend of CG as a commodity, possibly limiting the uniqueness of what PDI might have to offer in the future. As would be expected, the studios were much less forward-thinking and no deals came to pass.

In 1990, however, PDI opened a feature film production office in LA for work on its first film project, the Japanese-funded *Solar Crisis*. New equipment included a film scanner built by none other than Les Dittert and a Management Graphics film recorder. (The effects work was optically composited.) Soon after that, PDI got a big break with some lesser-known but still important work on *Terminator2: Judgment Day*. PDI did a number of different "invisible" effects such as wire removal and digital plate reconstruction. Work continued on many other features including the several *Batman* films. In 1994, PDI closed the LA office, and several key employees (including Jamie Dixon and Thad Bier) stayed in LA to form HammerHead.

Meanwhile, back at home base in Sunnyvale, PDI was continuing to set new standards in broadcast commercial CG techniques. In 1991–92 the technique of morphing was used with great success on numerous projects. The first was a Plymouth Voyager commercial, followed soon by the

Exxon tiger and the famous Michael Jackson video "Black or White." A perfect subject that was perfectly executed, the "Black or White" video only served to increase the demand for this new technology in broadcast work.

Along with the strong 2D effects work being produced, PDI also began very early to experiment and create 3D character animation. Waldo, the first ever 3D CG real-time animated "muppet," was created for the *Jim Henson Hour* in 1988. (See the Time Line chapter for more details.) The Crest Toothpaste "Singers" (1988) and DOW Scrubbing Bubbles (1989) commercials were followed by the *Last Halloween* television special in 1991 (based on the M&M Mars candy commercial campaign started by ILM). In 1994, PDI broke a long-standing stop-motion tradition by introducing a 3D CG Pillsbury Doughboy with the "Mambo" spot. The doughboy would in fact continue to be created by PDI for another four years. Gradually, more subtle enhancements crept into the spots including motion blur, which originally was intentionally left out to more closely resemble the look of stop-motion animation.

The year 1995 saw Carl knocking on Hollywood studio doors again, this time with better results. In March 1996, PDI signed a co-production deal with Dreamworks to create original, computer-animated feature films. *Antz*, of course, was the first of the films produced under this deal. *Shrek* is in production now for a late 2000 release; *Tusker* will follow probably in 2002.

PDI Shorts

PDI always has gone beyond pure commercialism with its support of short animated films for their own sake. Some of the earliest memorable SIGGRAPH clips include *Happy Drinking Birds*, *Chromosaurs*, *Opera Industrial*, *Cosmic Zoom*, *Burning Love*, *Max's Place*, *Locomotion*, and *Gas Planet*. Recent shorts such as *Gabola the Great* and *Sleepy Guy* are no exception. Their next short, *Fat Cat*, is due out soon.

Other fun projects have included the long-running Bud Bowl half time series and *The Simpsons* 3D episode.

In 1998, Richard Chung, Glenn Entis, and Carl Rosendahl were awarded a Scientific and Technical Achievement Award for the concept and architecture of the PDI Animation System.

Employees included Thad Bier (Hammerhead) and Scott Anderson (ILM, Sony). Carl and Richard are still with PDI, and Glenn Entis left PDI to become President of Dreamworks Interactive. You can find more information at www.pdi.com.

Pixar

(1986 to present)

Pixar was formed in 1986 when Steven Jobs (of Apple and NeXT computer fame) purchased the Lucasfilm Computer Graphics Division from George Lucas. George had decided about a year before that he did not want to continue a hardware development effort in-house. He also did not at that time want to pursue computer-generated animation (as did the employees). He therefore agreed to allow Edwin Catmull, Alvy Ray Smith, and the rest of the employees of the Lucasfilm Computer Division to seek out investors so they could spin off into their own company. Many different options were explored over the course of that year. In the end, the negotiations went down to the very last minute with the outcome not always certain. The deal that was finally made called for $5 million dollars to purchase the division with an additional $5 million for immediate capital investment.

Founding members included (in alphabetical order): Tony Apodaca, Loren Carpenter, Ed Catmull, Rob Cook, David DeFrancesco, Tom Duff, Craig Good, Ralph Guggenheim, Pat Hanrahan, Sam Lefler, Darwyn Peachey, Tom Porter, Eben Ostby, Bill Reeves, Alvy Ray Smith, and Rodney Stock.

SIDEBAR

Here the story of how Pixar got its name: It was 1981 and the Computer Graphics Group at Lucasfilm was developing the hardware and software for a digital imaging "scanning/manipulating/filming computer-machine." David DiFrancesco was the hardware guy, Loren Carpenter was the software guy, and Alvy Ray Smith managed the project. When it came time to write up a formal proposal about the new device, it seemed appropriate to come up with a catchy name for the middle component of the system, the computer that did the image processing between the scanning and the filming.

One night over dinner (at Franks Country Garden restaurant in Bel Marin Keys, California), four men got around to discussing the topic of a name. Present were Rodney Stock (a hardware consultant), Jim Blinn (who worked at Lucas for a short time), Loren Carpenter, and Alvy Ray Smith. Because the hope was for this clever device to actually "make pictures," the name Picture Maker was suggested. This quickly was rejected in favor of Alvy's suggested contraction of Pixer. Loren then made the suggestion to change it to Pixar (it had a nicer ring to it), and the rest is history.

Loren relates that there occasionally are some attempts to put a greater meaning to the word after the fact (such as "Programmed Image transformation[X] And Render") but the true story has now been told.

Suddenly, the new company Pixar was no longer part of a larger profitable effects studio. Rather, it was a business all its own. In the first few years, the Pixar Image Computer sold well to a few (very different) client markets. For instance, Philips bought more than 20 systems to use in the medical image-processing market, and Disney made a significant partnership with Pixar to develop the graphics end of what would eventually become Disney's CAPS system. Roy Disney himself wanted to get his company back into feature animation in the right way, and this was seen (wisely) as an investment in the future technology of 2D animation production.

Ed Catmull and Pixar soon realized, however, that the 2D image-processing power of the Image Computer was not a moneymaker. They felt its days were numbered because of the ever increasing power and low cost of new general-purpose PCs. Ed chose, however, not to drop the hardware development business right away, mainly because the CAPS deal with Disney was entirely based on the Pixar Image Computer, and he did not want to leave them high and dry. Ed also knew it was only a matter of a time before they could port the CAPS development to the new SGI platform; it was just a matter of waiting it out while they continued to lose money. Just then, Ed received a call from one of their chief competitors in the image-processing market, a company called Vicom. Vicom was taking the position that to make that market more successful, all the competitors should join forces with one product. "Would Pixar be willing to *sell* their hardware outright to Vicom?" Ed: "Let me think about that and get back to you..." (Ed smiles to himself). Ed happily sold the Pixar Imaging Computer hardware business to Vicom for $2 million, hoping that they could keep it as a viable product just long enough for the Disney CAPS system to transition over to SGI, which is exactly what happened.

Pixar was still a struggling company with small profit margins and occasional layoffs during particular hard times. It is a testament to the belief of the key partners and employees of Pixar that they hung on during the hard times without giving up their hope to make CG animated movies. John Lasseter himself turned down several offers from Disney to come back and direct a film for them.

About this same time (1990 or so), the Commercial Division was started to cut some teeth on real production experience. The Listerene, Life Savers, and Tropicana spots immediately stood out as being in a creative class by themselves. Produced in conjunction with Colossal Pictures, they blended what was (and continues to be) Pixar's trademark realistic rendering "look" with outstanding character animation and humor. It was at this time that Andrew Stanton and Pete Doctor joined the company as animators. The hope was to get the hang of commercial production and then step up to make a half hour television short film based on Tinny from the *Tin Toy* short film. Then, in 1991, Ed Catmull made a three-picture deal with Disney to create fully CG-animated films. Disney's point of view was that if Pixar was ready to commit to a half hour show, then doing an 85-minute feature film really shouldn't be that much of a stretch. (Yeah... sure!) The first film, to be called *Toy Story*, was given a budget of only $17 million. Although the final cost was considerably more than that, it still was considerably *less* than the cost of a traditionally animated Disney feature film.

TRIVIA

Toy Story was rendered with a render farm consisting of some 300 Sun computers, each with roughly the processing power of one original Cray 1 Supercomputer. (*A Bug's Life* used 1,400 SUN computers, each with a processor upgrade that was three to four times faster than the ones used on *Toy Story*! You do the math.

Pixar Short Films

Pixar is back in the short film business after too long an absence. Their 1998 animation *Geri's Game* won the Academy Award for Best Animated Short Film. It follows a long history of shorts that set a high standard of excellence in both imagery and story telling. After *Andre and Wally B.* (1984), while still part of Lucasfilm, there was *Luxo Jr.* (1986), *Red's Dream* (1987), *Tin Toy* (1988), and my personal favorite, *Knick Knack* (1989). See the Time Line chapter for more details about some of these films.

The Future of Pixar

Today, Pixar is overhauling the very foundations of its production environment: its Marionette animation software, its RenderMan, and its film recording. The software tool sets will be rebuilt from the ground up into the next generation of animation and rendering software. David DiFrancesco has culminated his 20 years of pioneering film-recording technology knowledge into PixarVision. This new laser-based recording system is meant to be the finest and fastest in the world, operating with 35mm,

65mm, and VistaVision film stocks at between four and eight seconds a frame. The system was tested on *Bugs*, but it should see full use on Pixar's next film *Toy Story II*, which is due out in the fall of 1999. (Early problems with the PixarVision laser film recorder eventually were tracked down to the air-conditioning system that keeps Pixar's vast render farm cool. The AC system was so large that the vibrations caused the whole building to vibrate just enough to throw the delicate film recorder's quality off!)

In 1998, Eben Ostby, Bill Reeves, Sam Leffler, and Tom Duff were awarded a Scientific and Engineering Academy Award for the development of the Marionette Three-Dimensional Computer Animation System.

Pixar is planning to relocate south a dozen miles to Emeryville sometime in mid-2000. Their next film due out in 2001 is *Monsters, Inc.*, to be directed by Pete Doctor and David Silverman. Pixar currently is located at Point Richmond, CA. You can find more information at www.pixar.com.

Protozoa

(1990 to present)

Protozoa is a pioneering performance animation company that provides complete systems, production, and Web-based animation content.

Protozoa founder Brad deGraf previously (along with partner Michael Wahrman of deGraf/Wahrman) had created the first real-time character performance, Mike the Talking Head, at Siggraph 1988. Brad also was part of the team that Jim Henson contracted at Digital Productions in 1988 to digitize Kermit the Frog. Protozoa and its founders have been leaders in the medium ever since.

Moxy, the first-ever live 3D character for television, was created and originally produced by Protozoa's founders while at Colossal Pictures in 1993 (and later by Turner Productions). Turner also licensed Protozoa's Alive for the Cartoon Network.

Ziff-Davis Television bought Alive and Dev Null from Protozoa to co-host *The Site* on MSNBC. They produced more than 20 minutes a week for over a year, viewed by 55 million homes worldwide. This makes Dev easily the most widely seen virtual character in the world.

Protozoa also created *Floops*, the first live 3D episodic cartoon, which has been published twice weekly on the Web for over six months using VRML 2.0 (Virtual Reality Modeling Language). *Floops* won Best of Show at the 1997 VRML Excellence Awards.

Other successful projects include:

- *Dilbert* in 3D! Forty-seven episodes in VRML were sponsored by Intel for their Mediadome Web site.

- The BBC licensed Alive for production of a series in 1998.

- MTV premiered Virtual Bill, the digital president, during the State of the Union address in 1998.

- Sinbad performed Soulman, his digital alter ego, live on his late night talk show *VIBE*.

- The Blue Man Group commissioned Protozoa to create Virtual Blue Man for live shows.

- The Disney Channel commissioned a pilot, designed by Protozoa, for a series for 1998.

The company has numerous international licensees—Germany (2), Spain (site license) Italy (site license), South Africa (2), Britain (2)—a growing reseller/representative network, and a full sales pipeline.

Protozoa is located in San Francisco, California. You can find more information at www.protozoa.com.

reZn8

(1987 to present)

This company was founded by Paul Sidlo, the former Creative Director for Cranston/Csuri Productions from 1982 to 1987. reZn8 has won countless awards for broadcast design and animation including three Emmys. Its unique dedication to original creative content has earned the company a unique and respected reputation.

Rhythm & Hues

(1987 to present)

While working at Robert Abel's company, Randy Roberts suggested to John Hughes that they spin off a new company. Once the venture got going (as six people in John's living room with one SGI), Randy actually ended up directing independently for a few years, ultimately joining R&H in 1993.

The company was founded in a former dental office in Santa Monica by John Hughes, Charles Gibson, Pauline T'So, and Keith Goldfarb (from Bob Abel's) along with Larry Wienberg and his wife, Cathy White, from Omnibus.

Other early employees included Frank Wuts, Cliff Boule, and Peter Farson (from Digital Productions).

Their very first job (April 23, 1987) was a film project to realize the MGM/UA logo for that studio. This was especially unusual at a time when virtually all CG production work was for broadcast television. The following years were spent creating many different commercial and logo projects, starting with their second job for a New Zealand station.

The year 1990 saw some incredible breakthrough work for the feature film *Flight of the Intruder.* Remember that, at the time, *The Abyss* had just come out a year before and *T2* was still a year away (1991). R&H created more than 30 full-daylight shots of photo-realistic aircraft, cluster bombs, and smoke—all with proprietary software. This was truly breakthrough work that unfortunately was not as recognized as it should have been because the film itself did poorly. With four out of the six original employees being code writers, the in-house software effort had begun from day one. Eventually, four main components were written: animation, modeling, rendering, and compositing. Before all the code was production-ready, however, Wavefront software was used based on an agreement John had made earlier with the company started by his former co-worker Bill Kovaks. While working at Bob Abel's on and off from 1976 to 1987, John had his own company called Motion Control Systems (MCS) with partner Jim Keating. Jim, at that time, wrote the model component of the Wavefront code. In exchange for sole rights to that software, Wavefront gave a number of licences to John's new company, R&H. Bill Kovacs actually wrote his preview code while consulting for John's earlier MCS company, but he retained sole ownership of that software for himself.

Rhythm & Hues' work on *Babe* won an Academy Award for best Visual Effects. (It was VFX Supervised by Scott Anderson and VFX Produced by Nancy St. John.)

In March of 1999, R&H bought the visual effects CG company VIFX (which was located just two blocks away in Hollywood). VIFX's founder and President Richard Hollander's new position is as head of the film effects group, bringing some 80 of VIFX's employees with the purchase. Bill Kroyer also has recently joined the company as a Director, and Richard Taylor is still there today also. R&H now employs more than 300 people.

Robert Abel & Associates
(1971 to 1987)

If you talk about CG history with anyone who's been in the biz for at least 10 years, one name will inevitably come up very early in the conversation. In fact, Bob Abel's name itself is virtually synonymous with the pioneering early days of computer graphics. Talk to him yourself and you'll quickly realize that this is a man to whom the tool is much less important than the creative result.

Abel's introduction to new technology came at an early age as a preteen in the 1950s. His uncle Earl Kanter, a World War II draftee and "high-IQ" Harvard student, began experimenting with electronics and early computers. This high-tech childhood set a foundation for things soon to come.

Robert Abel in 1983 with most of the 33 Clios that he won for Best Visual Effects. Image copyright, Robert Abel & Associates, Inc.

In 1957, a young Abel was doing pasteup work for the legendary Saul Bass. A trip that Abel made to one man's garage would soon change his life. Saul was working on the opening titles to Hitchcock's *Vertigo* with a man by the name of John Whitney. Whitney was using analog computers and homemade motion-control rigs to create artwork of various kinds. Abel got on very well with the older artist—so much so that Abel was hired as a graphics design consultant on one print job for Foodmaker, the parent company of Jack-In-The-Box.

Abel remained busy doing a great variety of things that ran the gamut from the realistic to the surreal. Abel shot an award-winning documentary for David Wolper, spent a tour in Vietnam as a combat photographer, and contributed to multiscreen music festivals and rock concerts.

All this solidified in 1971 when that icon of advertising, Harry Marks, provided Abel and his old friend Con Pederson with the opportunity to create a new look for ABC television. From 1971 to 1973, in 6,000 square feet of vacant space behind an accountant's office, the fledgling Robert Abel & Associates began to take shape. There was no phone, no sign on the building, no advertising, and no secretary—just Abel, Con, an optical guy named Dick Alexander, and a cameraman named Dave Stuart.

Larry Cuba joined RAA for a short time at the start of 1976, hoping to program the new motion-control computers. He left just four months later, however, to create the famous Death Star graphics for George Lucas' *Star Wars*.

Abel assembled a team to work on *Star Trek: The Motion Picture*, but the work eventually was discontinued at Abel's and was completed by Doug Trumbull and others.

The "Sexy Robot." *Image copyright, Robert Abel & Associates, Inc.*

Among Abel's early associates were Richard Hollander, John Hughes, Richard Taylor, and Wayne Kimall. By 1979, Abel's was a full-service effects company with a miniature shop and six different motion-control rigs to augment live-action footage. A real breakthrough came when they wanted to have a way to preview motion control moves. To this end, Bill Kovacs was hired to modify an E&S real-time vector PS-2 flight simulation computer. A deal was made to acquire the source code for the $100,000 machine in exchange for promising to E&S that Abel's would not go into the flight simulator business. Eventually, with new employee Ray Feeney's help, the resulting "Abel/Kovaks box" drove six axes of movement in both the camera and the motion controlled object for virtually unlimited range of motion combinations.

RAA sold its own software under the division Abel Image Research. Bill Kovacs left to found Wavefront, and Frank Vitz took over his job as head of R&D at Abel's. (Frank ended up as VP of Production while they produced the "Gold Series" ads for Benson and Hedges and the "Brilliance" commercial for the Canned Food Council, or "Sexy Robot" as the CG character was called.)

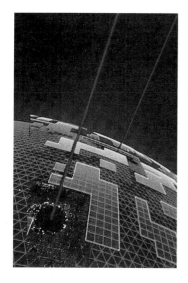

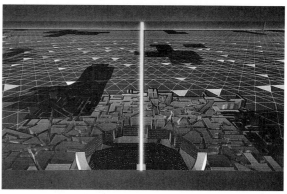

The approach of Jeff Bridges from the real world down into the micro-electronic world is 40 seconds long, and it is called "Flynn's Ride." Tron copyright 1982, Walt Disney Productions. Images copyright, Robert Abel & Associates, Inc.

Disney awarded a CG effects job for the film *The Black Hole* to an independent company called Neo Plastics, which was run by C.D. Taylor and Mick Hagerty. They, in turn, hired John Hughes to create a vector graphics grid/black hole simulation. John rented Abel's E&S system and shot the images off the screen, optically compositing the CG with artwork and additional traditional animation. Unfortunately, once he had the job, he also realized that he had to deliver it in a mere 14 days. Not only did John actually finish the job in just nine days, Disney liked it so much they had him repeat the effect for the film's opening sequence and one-sheet poster.

Kenny Merman and Frank Vitz headed the team that produced the opening titles and "Flynn's Ride" sequences of the movie *Tron*.

A still from the "Gold Series" Benson & Hedges commercial. Image copyright, Robert Abel & Associates, Inc.

Other major projects included:

- The 7-Up "See the light" campaign
- The "Gold Series" ads for Benson and Hedges
- The *Amazing Stories* opening sequence
- The Randy Roberts designed "Brilliance" commercial for the Canned Food Council

At its peak, RAA occupied some 45,000 square feet and employed 240 people. With the best of intentions, Robert Abel & Associates was sold in September of 1986 to Omnibus Computer Graphics of Canada for $8.5 million. The hope was to gain much needed capital investment from an established, publicly traded company. As soon as January of 1987, it was clear that all was not right with the new parent company. Sure enough, on April 12 of that year, all the Omnibus people left en mass in the evening. The next day, with word that Omnibus had defaulted on mountains of dept, all of Abel's had one last party before packing up for good.

A 2.5D composite called "Birds and Fish," created for TRW in 1981 by Kenny Merman. Image copyright, Robert Abel & Associates, Inc.

Hundreds of talented people passed through Abel's, many of whom are leaders of the CG field today: Clark Anderson, Richard "Dr." Baily (Image Savant), John Grower (Santa Barbara Studios/Wavefront), Charles Gibson (R&H), Keith Goldfarb, Steve Grey, Rich Hoover, John Hughes (Rhythm & Hues), Pauline T'So (R&H), Bill Kovacs (Alias|Wavefront), Sherry McKenna, Tim McGovern (MetroLight, Sony Pictures Imageworks), Kenny Merman, John Nelson, Con Pederson (MetroLight), Randy Roberts, Richard Taylor, and Michael Wahrman.

Robert Abel himself went on to explore other varied independent projects in various interactive multimedia. He continues to work actively today, speaking frequently at many CG and visual effects-related conferences.

Robert Greenberg and Associates
(1981 to present)

Chris Woods set up a computer graphics department in 1981. Early on, some folks (including Jonathan Luskin) did some research, but not until 1985 did the CG department really get off the ground. The initial crew was all from MAGI/Synthavision: Josh Pines and Ken Perlin wrote the R/GA rendering code, Jan Carlee and Christine Chang were joined later by Tom Miller, Jim Goodman, Kevin Bjorke, and Job Francis.

Integral to RGA up to that point was a world-class optical and motion-control effects department headed by Joel Hynek and Stuart Robertson.

The Los Angeles production office, run by George Joblove (Technology/ILM) and Ellen Sumers (Producer/Boss Film), and RG/LA operated for a few years in the mid-1990s.

Santa Barbara Studios (SBS)
(1990 to present)

Santa Barbara Studios was founded in 1990 by John Grower and began specializing in procedural natural phenomenon effects using Wavefront Technologies' Dynamation software. Employees included Bill Kovacs, Will Rivera, Eric Guagliani, Bruce Jones, Phil Brock, Eric DeJong, Mark, Wendell, Diane Holland, and Matt Rhodes.

Large format work has include the 70mm 3D film *Shooting Star* and IMAX space films *Destiny In Space* and *Cosmic Voyage*.

Television series contributions include *Other Worlds: A Tour of the Solar System* and two collaborations with the Kleiser-Walczak Construction Company on *The Astronomers* and *500 Nations* (the latter of which depicted beautifully realistic reconstructions of Native American cultures).

FACTOID
The first film project (of many) to which Ken Perlin's noise function code was applied was the film *Weird Science* in 1985. (Now there's an obscure factoid for you!)

Recent feature film work has included *An American Werewolf in Paris*, *Spawn*, *Star Trek: Generations*, and *Star Trek: Insurrection*.

Side Effects Software

(1987 to present)

Side Effects Software makes the procedurally based 3D system Prisms and its modern version, Houdini. The company was founded by Kim Davidson and partner Greg Hermanovic after the demise of Omnibus Toronto. Greg was Director of Research at Omnibus, and Kim programmed and was the Director of Animation.

When Omnibus went under in 1987, Greg and Kim bought the rights to the Prisms software they had developed from the Royal Bank of Canada (the majority dept holder of Omnibus at the time of Omnibus' collapse). They started up a production house called Side Effects that later split into Side Effects Production and Side Effects Software. (The production side eventually was renamed Spin Productions to reduce confusion.)

Greg Hermanovic, Kim Davidson, Mark Elendt, and Paul Breslin were presented with a 1998 Academy Scientific and Technical Achievement Award for the development of the procedural modeling and animation components of the Prisms software package. Prisms has been used in dozens of major feature films such as *Apollo 13*, *Titanic*, *Contact*, *Independence Day*, *The Fifth Element*, and *Ghost in the Shell*.

Side Effects is thriving today, having renamed Prisms in September of 1996 as their new, updated Houdini software. Houdini also has recently been made available for the Windows NT platform and has been ported to Linex. Side Effects presently has offices in Santa Monica, California, and Toronto, Canada. The company can be reached at 416-504-9876. You can find more information at www.sidefx.com.

FACTOID

Jim Clark, founder of Silicon Graphics, went on to found Netscape Communications Corporation, the Web's most popular graphical browser. Netscape was acquired by AOL in November 1998 for $4.1 billion (yes, that's billion with a "b").

Silicon Graphics, Inc.

(1982 to present)

Founded in 1982 by Dr. Jim Clark (Ph.D., University of Utah, 1974), Silicon Graphics is the manufacturer of RISC processor-based IRIS graphics workstations, which are popular in visualization and high-end CG animation/visual-effects companies. Jim Clark, while at Stanford University, invented the Graphics Engine, the first Very Large Scale Integrated (VLSI) graphics chip.

SGI produced its first computer, the IRIS 1000, in 1983 and went public in 1986. (IRIS stands for Integrated Raster Imaging System.) SGI then acquired both Alias and Wavefront in 1995 and Cray Supercomputers in 1996.

In 1997, SGI announced a new joint effort with Microsoft and Intel to develop a next-generation processor line for its graphics workstations, a new SGI Intel/NT. Just introduced in spring of 1999, the SGI 320 and 540 workstations are Windows NT-based and cost between $3,400 and $5,995. The 540 supports up to four Pentium II Xeon 450MHz processors and up to 2GB of graphics memory.

Family Tree Of Hardware

In 1983–84, SGI's first 1000 series workstations were really terminals because they required a VAX host.

IRIS 2400
3030
3130

4D-Series
PI-35 (Personal Iris)
Crimson
Challenge Server
Indy
Indigo2
O2
Octane

Revenues for fiscal 1998 were $3.1 billion. SGI can be reached at 800-800-7441. You can find more information at www.sgi.com.

FACTOID

The IRIS Model 3030 in 1986 came with the following specs:

- 2MB of RAM expandable to a whopping 16 megs!

- A 16Mhz 68020

- A 40MB hard drive

- All in a 29"×18" 200lb. chassis.

Softimage Inc.

(1986 to present)

Formed by Daniel Langlois (one of the three animators on the short film *Tony de Peltri*) in 1986, Softimage is based in Montreal. Its first interactive 3D software product, Creative Environment 1.0, debuted at the 1988 Siggraph in Atlanta. Softimage led the way in advanced IK character animation tools for high-end 3D users with the Actor module. The work on Actor started in late 1990, and it was first shown in public at Siggraph 1991 in Las Vegas. It was first released in version 2.51 of the Softimage Creative Environment in early 1992.

Dominique Boisvert, Rejean Gagne, Daniel Langlois, and Richard Laperriere were awarded a Scientific and Engineering Award from the Academy of Motion Picture Arts and Sciences in 1998 for the development of the Actor animation component of the Softimage computer animation system.

The company did well by being promoted at a time when industry leader Alias was floundering due to management and marketing troubles. Softimage was acquired by Microsoft in 1994 and was sold to Avid in June of 1998 for $285 million. Current products include Toonz 2D cel animation production software and Softimage|DS, which runs on SGI, NT, and Intergraph platforms. Proposed next-generation products include Sumatra for 3D animation and Twister for rendering.

Softimage can be reached at 800-576-3846 or 514-840-0324. You can find more information at www.softimage.com.

Sogitec Audiovisuel

The Ministere de la Culture, managed by Jack Lang, gave some funds to start new CG technologies in France. Sogitec is a big industrial group that acts mainly in the military field as part of Dassault Electronic. The Sogitec CG department was created in 1982–83 by Xavier Nicolas, Daniel Poiroux, and Alain Grach to try to create images using a customized version of a flight-simulator software. The first short animated film they created was called *Maison Vole*.

Early employees included Veronique Damian and David Salesin. Sogitec became a subsidiary of Dassault Aviation in France and is now involved in simulation but not in CGI directly.

Nicolas joined with TDI's production unit in 1989 to form Ex Machina.

Stanford

The Stanford Computer Graphics Laboratory can be found online at www-graphics.stanford.edu.

Symbolics Graphics Division (SGD)
(1981 to 1992)

Symbolics, Inc. was formed in 1980, headed by Russell Noftsker and his right-hand man and CTO Jack Holloway (both from Triple-I). Hardware architecture was based on work by researchers at the M.I.T. Artificial Intelligence Laboratory and the Lisp Machine project in 1974 (thanks to the close proximity of the Symbolics Cambridge Research Center).

The Symbolics LM-2 was introduced in 1981, the 3600 in 1982, the 3640 and 3670 in 1984, and the 3675 and 3645 in 1985. At its peak in 1985, Symbolics had more than 650 employees and 35 sales offices in North America, Europe, Japan, and the Middle East. Symbolics had more than 1,500 systems installed around the world. Color graphics system hardware included 8-bit or 24-bit high-resolution framebuffers, 32-bit broadcast resolution framebuffers, CAD buffers, digitizing frame grabbers, genlock options (for synchronization to video), color monitors (standard, premium, NTSC-resolution, and CAD buffer monitors), graphics tablets, and NTSC encoders and decoders.

SYMBOLICS FIRSTS

Symbolics produced the first workstation that could genlock, the first to have real-time video I/O, the first to support digital video I/O, and the first to do HDTV.

The Symbolics Graphics Division (SGB) was created by former members of Triple-I when that company ceased computer graphics production work in about 1981. Founded initially by Tom McMahon (General Manager from Triple-I), he soon was joined by Craig Reynolds, Dave Dyer, Larry Malone, Jeremy Schwartz, Larry Stein (hardware), and Bob Coyne (software). Matt Elson, Jay Sloat, and Ken Brain were artists, TDs, and trainers. Tom first worked out of the small Woodland Hills office, commuting often to the Massachusetts research center. Chatsworth was home for a short while before finally relocating to Westwood, California, in 1983.

Stanley and Stella: Breaking the Ice

As many as 50 people worked on this memorable project and shared responsibility. Some key people included Phillipe Bergeron (hero animation), Joseph Goldstone, Kevin Hunter, Larry Malone, Craig Reynolds (flocking and schooling code), Jim Ryan, and Michael Wahrman (Producer). Richard "Dr." Baily was hired by Michael Wahrman to model the two main characters based on sketches. He also composed and recorded the original soundtrack, which later was replaced by another one. It was a big hit at the 1985 SIGGRAPH in particular.

SGD's first general manager was Howard Cannon from the Cambridge office, followed by Sheila Madsen, John Kulp, and then Tom McMahon. Tom went on to design most of the hardware and video systems for the company including all the framegrabbing, genlock, and high-definition capabilities that SGD pioneered with Sony and others.

In-house tools included S-Geometry for modeling and S-Dynamics for animation. S-Paint was a LISP-based 32-bit paint system designed by Craig Reynolds, Tom McMahon, Bob Coyne, and Eric Weaver.

Around 1990, Symbolics started to fail and began to lay off employees. Even though SGD had a successful ongoing business with a good customer base, it still relied on its parent company for workstation and operating system technology as well as for other corporate infrastructure such as HR, finance, customer service, and so on.

Symbolics declared Chapter 11 bankruptcy in 1995 and was bought back by its original founder Russell Noftsker.

QUOTE

Tom McMahon relates the following events:

"Eventually, SGD was the target of a takeover and transition to Japanese management. SGD's Japanese distributor (Nichimen) had a thriving business based on the SGD product line of videographics hardware and the animation and rendering software. They couldn't afford to see us get blown away lest they be left without a source of supply. So they started buying up an insurance policy. They made Symbolics some offers it couldn't refuse given its poor financial health.

In a sequence of financial transactions, Nichimen bought rights to certain hardware technologies. They also started picking up the payroll for SGD employees in exchange for certain worldwide distribution rights. In the end, we had the people but Nichimen ended up owning most of our hard-earned technology.

We already had begun looking at how to port these tools off of Symbolics workstation platforms. SGI became the porting target. By 1991, we were well into the rewrite and port, but Symbolics needed to pull the plug on us.

I worked out a pretty amazing salvage deal with our old friends at Triple-I. I negotiated a contract where I could take *all* of SGD's key employees back to the employ of Triple-I but under a funding arrangement with Nichimen. Nichimen got their security blanket, and the employees kept their jobs. (A blanket layoff and the entire extermination of SGD were the alternatives at the time.)

At Triple-I, we proceeded to port all the SGD products to SGI machines, but things started going sour there, too.

We spun out of Triple-I and started yet another new company (with Nichimen seed funding) called Del Rey Graphics. Del Ray was co-founded by Al Fenaughty, President and CEO of Triple-I, along with Jack Holloway, one of the Foonly designers at Triple-I. But that didn't work due to a hostile takeover by Nichimen. My partners and I ended up selling the whole thing to Nichimen and what is left of this very long thread is now called Nichimen Graphics."

Synthavision

— see MAGI

Systems Simulation Ltd.

(1977 to 1988)

John Lansdown founded System Simulation in London with his colleague George Mallen and others from the Computer Arts Society. Through it, he developed major innovations in computer animation such as special effects for advertisements and television titles; effects for the feature films *Alien* (1979), *Saturn III*, and *Heavy Metal*; and the realization of the original animated Channel 4 logo. John created what was then the world's largest computer-generated mural (reviewed in *Building Design* as a "waste of electricity," although few today would question the bright power of his creative output).

John Lansdown

"John Lansdown was Emeritus Professor of Computer Aided Art and Design and formerly Head of the Centre for Electronic Arts (formerly called the Centre for Advanced Studies in Computer Aided Art and Design) from September 1988 until July 1995 when he retired from full-time employment.

In 1968, he was one of the founders of the Computer Arts Society and was its honorary secretary for more than 25 years. He was engaged in using computers for creative activities (such as architecture, art, and choreography) since 1960 and wrote over 300 publications on computer uses in art and design." —excerpt by permission of Huw Jones

A true pioneer of computer graphics in the UK, John Lansdown died of leukemia on February 17, 1999.

John Lansdown chaired the company until 1988. For a full biography of John Lansdown by Huw Jones, see this site: www.cea.mdx.ac.uk/CEA/External/Staff96/John/obit.html.

Thompson Digital Images (TDI)
(1984 to 1993)

The *Institut national de l'audiovisuel* (INA) was interested in computer graphics and associated themselves with the French defense contractor Thompson CSF to create the Paris-based Thomson Digital Image. Managed by Pascal Bap and Jean Charles Hourcade, TDI developed the 3D animation software Explore and also did production work.

Known particularly for their Explore Interactive Photorealistic Renderer (IPR) interface, TDI even opened a sales branch called Rainbow Images in San Jose. The production division merged in 1989 with Sogitec to form Ex Machina. TDI (the software company) also was at one time half owned by IBM.

In 1990, TDI released the first versions of their software for the PC. The software division was then bought by Wavefront in 1993. Wavefront in turn was bought by SGI and merged with Alias.

University of Bath (UK)

This section was submitted by Phil Willis, Eurographics Professional Board chair and current Department Head of Mathematical Sciences at the University of Bath (www.maths.bath.ac.uk).

Special Display Architectures

"In the mid-1970s, we developed the ZMP parallel processor for real-time display (25 frames per second) of color scenes for aircraft flight simulation. This architecture was patented.

In the early 1980s, we developed the color Quad-encoded display for instantaneous pan and detail-revealing zoom into images of 4k by 4k resolution displayed on a 512-line monitor. Overviews correctly showed subpixel data as anti-aliased averages. The same system could also be used to reveal different symbology at different levels of zoom. As far as we are aware, it was the first display system to achieve either of these. The hardware required to do this was carefully chosen and designed but quite modest."

References

"Improvements in display apparatus for controlling raster scan displays." R.L. Grimsdale, A.A. Hadjiaslanis, P.J. Willis. UK Patent Specification 1-532-275, November 15th 1978.

"Zone management processor: a module for generating surfaces in raster scan colour displays." R.L. Grimsdale, A.A. Hadjiaslanis, P.J. Willis. IEE Computer and Digital Techniques 2, 1, February 1979, pp 21-25.

"Quad encoded display." D.J. Milford and P.J. Willis. IEE Proceedings Part E: Computer and Digital Techniques, 131, 3, May 1984, pp 70-75.

Ultra-Resolution Pictures

"We have a long history of working with pictures of very high resolution. In 1983, we completed a paint program for the binary Perq display, which offered a roamable drawing area of approximately 7000 by 7000, displaying a 640 by 640 subset.

We moved on to use the HLH Orion UNIX workstation's new color display (the design of which was in part influenced by us; we later took delivery of the preproduction prototype). With our own software, we produced what we believe to be the first color picture with a resolution of a billion pixels (32k by 32k) in about 1986."

References

"Manipulating large pictures on the Perq." P.J. Willis and J.B. Hanson. Displays, July 1984, pp 170-173.

"UltraPaint: a new approach to a painting system." P.J. Willis and G.W. Watters. Computer Graphics Forum, 6, 2, May 1987, pp 125-132.

"Scan converting extruded lines at ultra high definition." G.W. Watters and P.J. Willis. Computer Graphics Forum, 6, 2, May 1987, pp 133-140.

University of Illinois—Chicago

This history is reproduced with permission from the EVL online database at www.evl.uic.edu/EVL/EVLLAB/history.shtml.

The Electronic Visualization Laboratory (EVL) is a graduate research laboratory specializing in virtual reality and real-time interactive computer graphics. It is a joint effort of UIC's College of Engineering and School of Art and Design, and it represents the oldest formal collaboration between engineering and art in the country, offering graduate degrees to those specializing in visualization.

The EVL started its life in 1973 as Circle Graphics Habitat, part of the effort by then Vice Chancellor Joe Lipson to utilize interactive computer graphics and low-cost video (which had just become available) to make an impact on undergraduate education. This reflected a commitment to using technology in education and a belief in its transformative power, which have again become important in the '90s. The Lab's earliest home was in the Chemistry department, which already boasted the most advanced computer graphics available for state-of-the-art chemical modeling—a Vector General Calligraphic Display (PDP 11/45). The earliest goal was to develop computer-based introductory material for the chemistry curriculum with the basic premise that this would constitute a self-paced learning environment specifically designed for the varying entry levels of students at an urban university.

Circle Graphics Habitat brought together Tom DeFanti and Dan Sandin. The media development system they designed used DeFanti's Graphics Symbiosis System and the Sandin Image Processor. The Graphics Symbiosis System (GRASS) was a computer graphics language that DeFanti had developed for his Ph.D. thesis. The Sandin Image Processor was a patch-programmable analog video synthesizer. A combination of the two systems was the basis of a video production facility for the generation of educational materials. Sandin was a faculty member of the sculpture department, where he taught video and was involved with the making of electronically based, interactive, kinetic sculpture. Circle Graphics therefore also brought together chemists, engineers, and artists. An equally important early goal for the Lab was to use the systems created to make art. The GRASS and Image Processor systems were used to make real-time animations that were distributed on the experimental video circuit. The Lab also organized a series of Real-Time Interactive Installations and Performances—performance in the music tradition rather than in the newer sense of performance art.

Electronic Visualization Events 1–3

The first EVE (1973) event was actually an IEVE—Interactive Electronic Visualization Event. The performers were faculty and students of Chicago Circle (UIC) and of the School of the Art Institute. The performances took place in the rotunda of the Science and Engineering South building. In the evenings, images—manipulated using the GRASS system and analog processor—were projected onto large video screens and shown on monitors to the accompaniment of live music.

"Real time," with respect to these performances, meant that the images changed instantaneously as the controls were manipulated. In effect, the performers "played" both musical instruments and visuals. The performances were improvisational in a variety of musical styles. Preparation involved not only technical and programming issues but extensive jamming. The interactivity of Interactive Electronic Visualization Event was supplied during the day when the audience could come and play with the equipment. Subsequently, the "I" was dropped, and EVE2 and EVE3 continued as performances, which were interactive for the performers but not for the audience.

EVE1 was the prototype, establishing the possibility of such an event. EVE2 (1975) involved a lot more planning and quality control of content but was also held in the rotunda with live musical accompaniment. EVE3, in 1977, still emphasized the real-time possibilities of this medium. However, the performers felt that the logistics of organizing a complicated live performance and a large-scale physical event were beginning to interfere with aesthetic goals. Therefore, the performances were recorded in front of a small studio audience and were edited on a _" deck. The finished show took place in the auditorium of the First National Bank, and the computer graphics and sound were played back on a light-valve projector. By the end of the '70s, calligraphic systems were being replaced by raster graphics systems with framebuffering. Except in the video games industry, computer graphics became very static. The possibility of interacting in real time with graphics is only becoming a possibility in the '90s.

In 1976, Larry Cuba came to the lab to create his wireframe Death Star simulation for George Lucas' *Star Wars* film. (See the Time Line chapter for all the details.)

The EVL currently is actively working on new projects, information about which can be found at www.evl.uic.edu/EVL/index.html. Tom Defanti's home page is www.eecs.uic.edu/eecspeople/defanti.htm.

University of Utah

Dr. David Evans founded the Computer Science Department at the University of Utah in 1968. It was started in part by Bob Taylor's ARPA funding a $5 million grant.

The number one problem of the day (according to Ed Catmull at least) was hidden surfaces. Many continually evolving algorithms, such as Watkins' algorithm (which subdivided the picture), were never actually implemented but served as inspiration for more practical solutions such as Catmull's more expensive techniques that actually subdivided surfaces. (This work was presented in his thesis work "Characteristics of 10 hidden surface Algorithms" in 1974.)

At the time, Ivan Sutherland did not like Catmull's "brute-force" approach, but the advent of much cheaper memory and storage made it extremely effective and increasingly practical. Indeed, it is just such a technique that is used as the basis for most all CG systems today. Catmull, as part of his interest in solving curved surface problems, had briefly attempted techniques of bending polygons before making his discovering of how to very efficiently and quickly subdivide cubic patches.

How to Light Things?

Henri Gouraud had been working for some time on linear interpolated shading when he visited Martin Newell and his brother in England who were working on similar research. A stumbling block with the early implementation was mach-banding artifacts, which also hindered the Newells. This allowed Gouraud to travel to Utah to finish his paper on "Continuous Shading of Curved Surfaces" in 1971.

TOM STOCKHAM

Image processing guru Tom Stockham was a brilliant teacher at the University of Utah who brought together the disciplines of image processing and computer graphics. The Academy of Motion Picture Arts and Sciences honored his extraordinary contributions and his related work in audio processing in February of 1999 with a Technical Achievement Award.

Other important individuals at Utah over the years included Frank Crow, Fred Parke, Jim Blinn, Jim Clark, Lance Williams, Garland Stern, Ron Resch, Alan Kay, John Warnock, Patrick Baudelaire, Jim Kajiya, Christy Barton, Gary Watkins, and many others.

A good online source containing University of Utah Computer Science history can be found at http://www.cs.utah.edu/~riloff/cs-history/html.

Vertigo Software Corporation

This history of Vertigo Animation Systems was submitted by Bill Diack (bdiack@aw.sgi.com) and Rikk Carey (rikk@best.com).

Key employees included Fred Daniels, Mike Parker, Bill Diack (A|W), Tim Piper, Bill Etra (Sun), Rikk Carey (SGI), Gary Hooper (A|W), John Gross (PDI, A|W), Dave Dignam (SGI, Gigapixels), Mike Kelley (Apple, SGI), and Paul Wagschal. Other employees included Rod Paul (Omnibus NY, R&H, Dreamworks), Floyd Gillis, Dave Gordon, Carl Frederick (OMNIBUS NY, then ILM), Matt Arrott, and Nancy St John.

Approximately 1,000 units were sold, with a total revenue of approximately $50 million

Company "firsts" included the first digital framebuffer, the first multiprocessing rendering system, the first complete 3D animation system, the first extrusion modeler, the first friendly 3D animation user interface, and the first integrated animation system.

The history of Vertigo, a 3D animation company based in Vancouver, Canada, is marked by a sequence of four distinct eras:

Vertigo Production Company, 1979–83

Vertigo Systems International, 1983–87

Vertigo/Cubicomp, 1987–90

Vertigo Again, 1990–present

Vertigo Production Company

Vertigo began, unlike the startups that predominate our industry, as a company in a totally different field in search of solutions for which computer graphics was an excellent fit. The company was formed in 1979 in Vancouver, Canada. Two real estate developers (Fred Daniels and Mike Parker) building prefabricated houses for the Asian market were looking for ways to communicate the complexities of assembling their product in the field in a clear, unambiguous way. Because their product sold into a variety of countries speaking different languages, a visual approach was ideal.

A video production group was formed, and the bold idea of harnassing computer graphics to demonstrate the assembly of their product was adopted. In those days, there were no off-the-shelf animation systems one could buy, and computers powerful enough to render were still in the $500,000 price range or higher.

By 1982, development had begun on a scanline polygon renderer written by Steve White from the University of British Columbia. (Later, Steve became software architect for the Neo-Visuals animation system—a turnkey computer animation system that debuted at SIGGRAPH 1985 and had the interesting quality of being written in Fortan.) The computer was a VAX-11/750 that was "borrowed" at night from a timeshare company two floors upstairs.

The company hired artists who had to learn computer graphics on the job. Very soon, the company began work on computer animations for the Canada-wide market such as flying logos for national ad campaigns, instructional videos, and a memorable 30-second flythough of Vancouver for a local radio station. Time was billed at $1,000/second of finished work, and the upstairs computer with 4MB of RAM was churning images on a nighly basis.

Vertigo employed many animators, many of whom are still active in the industry. Matt Arrott went on to Silicon Graphics and later became Director of Engineering for Dreamworks. Rod Paul went to Rhythm & Hues and then DreamWorks. Kirk McInroy ended up at ILM. Nancy St. John (producer) went on to Digital Productions, ILM, and later worked on feature films such as *Babe* as an independent producer.

In 1983, Vertigo began development of a quadric surface constructive solid geometry renderer for its producton work. The interesting thing here is that the developer on this project, Dave Gordon, went on to Omnibus. (Later in 1988, the Omnibus software became the nucleus of the Side Effects animation system.)

Vertigo Systems International

In mid-1983, Vertigo sensed that, with the introduction of UNIX-based workstations from SUN and the formation of Silicon Graphics, a market for a 3D turnkey computer animation system was possible. A feasability study was launched with favorable results.

Such a system would allow a production company to purchase a complete package of tools for completing a job without the cost of maintaining a programming staff. Around this time, the Robert Bosch company of the Netherlands introduced a custom-built computer that performed very rudimentary modeling, animation, rendering, and video recording control. The system was selling well but had a high price tag ($350,000).

By the spring of 1984, Vertigo felt they could offer a product based on the Sun 100 computer (apparently the first workstation to run the powerful UNIX operating system, retailing around $25,000) with a custom-built display device.

Vertigo management realized that there was a large market for a UNIX workstation-based computer graphics software package that utilized a vector display device and provided the high-end capabilities of production software. A decision was made to proceed with development of the V-2000 animation system. The goal was to provide a much richer tool set with higher quality than was available on the Bosch system and at a much lower price point. Software was easily upgradable as opposed to the hardware-based Bosch system, which typically required hardware changes in order to add features—and such changes were often impossible.

Design began in earnest in mid-1984 and development commenced in October of 1984. Under Bill Etra (who had developed numerous real-time graphics effect devices including co-development of the Rutt-Etra synthesiser used in 1977's *Logan's Run*), three development teams were set up. A turnkey software group was led by Rikk Carey (a rendering expert from Don Greenberg's group at Cornell), a hardware group was led by Tim Piper (who had worked on real-time flight simulator hardware), and an interfacing group was led by Doug Girling. Soon afterwards, Gary Hooper and John Gross joined Carey, and this threesome led the effort to design and build the Vertigo animation system.

Like several other animation system companies, Vertigo was struggling internally with trying to be both a product company and a production company. There was concern that the Vertigo production group would pose unfair competition toward the customers of the Vertigo animation system. Furthermore, the production team could not tolerate formal product development schedules and processes. They wanted tools yesterday and expected full-time support. This tension caused frequent in-house politics and feuding. Eventually, the management team separated the two entities and focused most of their resources on the product. Afterwards, the production team dwindled and slowly transformed into an effective product testing and demo group for the product.

During early 1985, Roy Hall was hired by the production group as a consultant. He wrote a polygon renderer and later became a member of the Wavefront development team. Several consultants (including Charles Poynton and

Paul Fuscher) were hired to help with hardware layout. At
SIGGRAPH 1985, Alias Research of Toronto unveiled a
"slidemaker." It really was just a renderer with the modeller
and animation system promised "shortly." Wavefront
unveiled its offering, displaying PreView, their animation
tool, but no renderer or modeller. Meanwhile, Vertigo had
an extrusion modeller and a renderer but decided to wait
and unveil the finished product when all the pieces were
complete. The official unveiling was at SIGGRAPH 1986.

By summer 1986, the Vertigo system was shipping with the
following components:

- A turnkey 3D animation system complete with
  procedural spline-based modeling (EXTRUDE),
  polygonal modeling (MESH), scene choreography
  (CHOREO), material design and assignment, rendering, and recording. The system utilized a SUN
  3/160 processor for computation and an SGI IRIS
  2400 for graphics display.

- A multiprocessing renderer utilizing custom hardware boards, which were inserted into the SUN
  backplane using a custom multiprocessing operating system developed at Vertigo and based on the
  Harmony operating system from the University of
  Waterloo.

- A framebuffer with D1 video input and output
  (the world's first digital video framebuffer).

The first customer was San Francisco Production Group
followed by Limelite and ARRI (Munich, Germany).
Imagery produced by the Vertigo package was soon being
seen regularly on television and corporate video. Some customers produced character animation, which was performed either via posing an articulated object at selected
"key" frames and allowing Vertigo to compute the smooth
animation between frames or via object metamorphosis
consisting of modified copies of the object at various frames
with which the software would smoothly interpolate the
shape over time.

In 1987, however, Vertigo was running out of money, and sales were not yet strong enough to support the company. Things quickly unraveled, payroll was missed, the doors were shut, and the employees waited around to see what would happen. Surprisingly, the core engineering team stuck it out and eventually participated in the deal to be acquired by Cubicomp.

Vertigo/Cubicomp

In late 1987, Vertigo was purchased by the Cubicomp Corporation of Hayward, California. Cubicomp was founded in the early 1980s in a garage in Berkeley, California, by Edwin P. Berlin, Jr. to provide a turnkey computer animation system on an IBM personal computer. The Cubicomp product, called PictureMaker, featured polygonal modeling, scene choreography, and rendering at a much lower price point than on comparable workstation-based software systems. At the time of the aquisition, the combined installed based totalled some 750 units worldwide.

Vertigo moved from the historic Pender Street office to a new modern office in the West End of Vancouver. The team was reinvigorated by the new office, excitement, and owners and quickly got back on track.

In 1988, the Vertigo product was rewritten to take advantage of the new RISC-based workstations from SGI (the 4D series). All 3D modules of the system were integrated with new extended functionality and enhanced workflow was provided. A new hardware product providing D1 and D2 video support, the VideoPak (with development led by Dave Dignam), was released. Boolean modeling and ray tracing were added in 1989. A notable advance for character animation purposes was the addition of free-form deformations that permitted animatable lattice deformations to be applied to static or animated objects. In addition to bend and twist deformations, the lattices also permitted arbitrary animation of lattice points to enact simple muscle bulging.

In 1988, Cubicomp submitted a version of *Night Cafe*, a computer-generated character animation piece (the one with the dancing salt and pepper shakers). This made it into the 1989 SIGGRAPH Electronic Theater. *Night Cafe* was put together by Sharon Calahan, an artist employed by the Vancouver office who now works at Pixar.

By this time, Rikk Carey had left for Silicon Graphics; John Gross, Sharon Calahan, Shawn Neeley, and Barry Fowler for Pacific Data Images; Venu Venugopal and I.V. Nagendra for Alias; Bill Etra for Sun; Mike Kelley for Apple; and Dave Dignam for SGI. Of the original 1984 team, Bill Diack, Ron Woods, and Gary Hooper remained.

Vertigo Again

This section was written by Rick Stringfellow.

In 1990, out of the ashes of Cubicomp, a couple of ex-Vertigo employees and a group of investors purchased the code. With little money and little experience, this team managed to finish the next release of code, which sold well. Existing Vertigo users, fearing that this would be the last cut, bought up the software. Surprised by its success, the team then continued to expand and rebuilt the company. For a number of years the successes continued, as did the releases of versions. New features were added, and the team grew back to the size it was in the early days. In 1993, the decision was make to ditch the old renderer in favor of supporting the industry standard RenderMan. The team undertook this directly, creating a seamless link to RenderMan. An interface was created to allow easy interactive editing of shaders and renders to RenderMan without writing out the usual ASCII RIBs. Finally, this enabled Vertigo to break into the film market. Disney BVVE took the system along with a great deal of support from Vertigo. This relationship grew into Vertigo eventually producing shots for Disney movies in Vancouver. Even with this success and turning into a public company, Vertigo again began to run short of cash and lost its capability to compete with teams such as Softimage and Alias|Wavefront. In a final attempt to get out of the way of these bigger competitors, the team started to move the entire development to the Mac using Apple Quickdraw3D, at the same time spinning off smaller components into 2D applications such as

Photoshop and Illustrator. Vertigo still exists and still functions on the SGI. (See Chapter 4, "Animation," for more details.)

Rick Stringfellow was Head of Animation, Product Manager, and Designer of versions 9.4, 9.5, 9.6, and the Mac port. Rick can be reached at Radical Entertainment at `rstringfellow@radical.ca`.

VIFX

(1985 to 1999)

VIFX was co-founded by partners Richard Hollander, Greg McMurry, Rhonda Gunner, and John Wash.

The company's first job was to produce video display graphics for the feature film *2010: Odyssey 2*. Virtually all the 3D CG in the early years was produced using Cubicomp equipment. Richard was inspired by a NASA/Kodak article about CCD technology and promptly designed and built a 1k by 1k input scanner for production use. The first digital composites it was used for were on the feature film *Bill and Ted's Excellent Adventure* in 1989.

In about 1990, the company began creating more ambitious motion picture visual effects and was then known as VIFX/Video Image. Feature film visual effects work for 20th Century Fox and other studios was wide-ranging and extensive. The work included *Batman Returns, Mighty Morphin' Power Rangers, Down Periscope, Volcano, Face/Off, The X-Files, The Relic, Star Trek: Insurrection, Blade,* and *Pushing Tin*.

VIFX was sold to 20th Century Fox in 1996, and partners Greg McMurry and Rhonda Gunner left the company.

In 1998, the Fox animation production *Planet Ice* was changed from an all-3D CG feature to being traditional cel animation. This left VIFX with an opportunity to sell itself yet again to Rhythm & Hues in the spring of 1999. About 80 people, including Richard Hollander, transferred to the new company following the merger.

John Wash no longer is with the company, but he does continue to consult. Richard Hollander currently is President of the film effects division of Rhythm & Hues. He also co-chairs the Motion Picture Academy of Arts & Sciences' Digital Imaging Technology Subcommittee with Ray Feeney.

Wavefront
This history of Wavefront was written by Mark Sylvester, Ambassador: Alias\Wavefront.

Overview

Larry Barels, Bill Kovacs, and Mark Sylvester founded Wavefront Technologies in 1984. The company created its first product, an animation software application called PreView, and shipped it to Universal Studios for use on the television series *Knight Rider* and to Lamb & Company for use in previsualizing and controlling a motion control camera rig. During the next several years, the product line expanded to include modeling, rendering, compositing, and material-editing capabilities. The company enjoyed early relationships with key partners that shaped the direction of the products and the marketplace. Those early partners included Disney (*The Great Mouse Detective*), NASA (the Shuttle accident re-creation), NBC (the 1986 Olympics), and Failure Analysis (legal animations, including the World Airways crash at Logan Airport in Boston).

The company's first real competition came in 1987 with the advent of Robert Abel & Associates' software division, Abel Image Research (AIR). This company, originally founded on a code base developed by Bill Kovacs, was started to capitalize on the momentum Wavefront was enjoying in the marketplace. This software was incomplete, undocumented, and very expensive, but AIR had the best marketing materials in the industry with an award-winning animation reel done by Robert Abel. Unable to compete against this body of work, a deal was struck in 1988 that had Wavefront purchasing the assets of AIR. The AIR software was never incorporated into the Wavefront code bases, even though urban myths have contrary opinions.

The company originally was financed by the founders for the first year. Then it went through several rounds of venture funding, culminating in an IPO 10 years later in 1995. Initial revenues were in the several hundred thousand per year range and ended in 1994 with annual revenues around $26 million.

The company went from three founders and four employees to 12, then 28, then 50, then 90, and then 160 at its highest point in the late '80s. Expansion into Europe happened in 1987 with the creation of Wavefront Europe, located in Belgium. At that time, the Belgian government also became an investor. The next year, concurrent with the AIR acquisition, Wavefront moved into Japan and then throughout the rest of Asia.

In the early '90s, a round of funding with CSK, a major Japanese computer company, resulted in the founding of Wavefront Japan, a wholly owned subsidiary. CSK at one time owned 14 percent of Wavefront.

How the Company Got Started

Wavefront originally was designed as a production company to create visual effects for commercials and feature films. The initial fundraising efforts were ineffective until the business model was changed to that of a software company that could sell the same software the production company would create to produce the commercials. During the first year, the company's production department, headed by John Grower, now president of Santa Barbara Studios (*Star Trek: Insurrection, American Werewolf in Paris*), created opening graphics for Showtime, BRAVO, and the *National Geographic Explorer* television show. These projects enabled the new software to be tuned to meet the needs of the animators and provided the company with early marketing materials.

In March of 1985, the company attended its first tradeshow, NCGA, and (with Alias) participated in Silicon Graphics' booth. At this show, the first systems were sold to NBC (New York), Electronic Arts (London), Video

PaintBrush (Australia), Failure Analysis (Mountain View, California), and NASA (Houston). This put the company in two markets, Broadcast and Engineering Visualization, and on multiple continents, forcing management to deal with multiple opportunities across diverse geographies.

In 1993, Wavefront entered into discussions to acquire another of the pioneering computer graphics companies, Thomson Digital Images (TDI). TDI had developed a similar set of technologies—in modeling, animation, and rendering—and had innovated in the area of NURBS modeling and interactive rendering. These technologies coupled with extensive distribution in Europe and Asia made for an ideal fit with Wavefront. The acquisition was treated more as a merger, but more than half the employees of TDI left immediately. It took nearly two years to blend the distribution channels in Europe and Asia because Wavefront had a toehold in those areas already. Fierce competition between the channels was clearly in play.

What Markets Did Wavefront Serve?

Wavefront started with the intent of working with the film and high-end commercial market. As a result of its first major tradeshow, however, it was accepted into the visualization, engineering, broadcast, and postproduction marketplaces as well. The fact that the system was designed to be open-architecture allowed for this market expansion. The majority of the software, as designed, served both markets well. Some modifications were made for data import and numerical accuracy to satisfy the military (NASA) and forensic animation (Failure Analysis) requirements. Because of the open architecture of the system, third-party developers were able to create ancillary applications and market them through a program called Ripples. This open approach was a hallmark of Wavefront and tended to draw users that were more technical and interested in customizing the application.

The original business plan talked about military, educational, medical, electronic game, simulation, film/entertainment, engineering, and product visualization marketplaces. The only one that never materialized was the simulation market. The company expanded into the scientific market in the late '80s with a product called The Data Visualizer. This product, aimed at nonpolygonal databases, was a success until Silicon Graphics and IBM developed competing products that were offered for free in bundles to sell high-end server hardware into the scientific marketplace. The Data Visualizer built on Wavefront's reputation for open systems and fast graphics interaction.

The company made one foray into the desktop marketplace with a project co-developed by Silicon Graphics called The Personal Visualizer. This product was created to give CAD users a point-and-click interface to high-end photorealistic rendering. Initially targeted to SGI hardware, the product eventually was ported to Sun, IBM, HP, Tektronix, DEC, and Sony platforms. The strategy was to bundle the software on every system sold and then follow with module sales into the installed base.

The company had its greatest success in the postproduction marketplace with sales into the major networks. The software was extremely fast, productive, and reliable. It was able to keep up with the industry's incessant demand for more speed. The other major success for the company was in engineering visualization. Based on the idea that the software would be a complement to CAD, the Wavefront system specialized in file translation and had native translators for every major CAD package. At one Autofact tradeshow, Wavefront was in the booths of 22 vendors, showing interactive visualization of parts, mechanisms, and assemblies created with a plethora of CAD packages. This, coupled with the system's open architecture for reading any type of ASCII data, enabled it to also serve in the post-simulation visualization space, which included NASA and virtually any company that wanted to view results derived from supercomputers and proprietary software. In 1995, nearly half of the company's installed base was in this marketplace.

In 1993, the company entered the electronic game market with a repackaging of its core application, The Advanced Visualizer, into a tailored offering called GameWare. This bundle focused the marketplace on Wavefront for game development and was very successful. This effort lasted for one year until the merger of Alias and Wavefront, when the program was canceled so PowerAnimator could be sold to game developers instead.

Major Customers

In the film market, Disney was the premier customer along with Warner Digital and Boss Film (both now defunct), Industrial Light & Magic, Film Magic (Hong Kong), TRIX (Belgium), and Electronic Arts (London). In video production, NBC, CBS, ABC, and CNN (Turner Broadcasting) were the premier partners. In engineering visualization, there was Harvard, National Center for Atmospheric Research (NCAR), NASA (six locations), Alcoa, and the National Center for Supercomputing Applications (NCSA). The military visualization marketplace included the CIA, FBI, Naval Surface Warfare Center, U.S. Air Force, and the National Security Agency. At the high point, there were nearly 8,000 Advanced Visualizer users.

Market Dynamics

For the first few years, the company enjoyed rapid growth in the film, video, and engineering marketplaces. Because most customers were doing mostly the same types of things, the company was not stressed with specific product requests that were not generally applicable to all types of users. The visualization market was mostly in place to create marketing videos and presentations, so the tools to "create pretty pictures" were most desirable. It was after the effort of The Personal Visualizer and the growing demand for CAD Visualization that the company had to begin custom engineering to develop CAD translators.

These efforts at CAD visualization were significant because Wavefront was the first to take on this arena. But the efforts of porting to every platform that carried CAD applications, the fact that it took nearly one year per port, *and* the fact that most facilities eventually would run CAD on Sun, HP, or IBM and then use Silicon Graphics for Visualization really took the competitive wind out of the company's sails.

Because so much effort was spent on CAD compatibility and trying to negotiate porting deals with hardware manufacturers, the focus on film and video application advancement was lost.

This loss of focus enabled Alias to make inroads into the entertainment market. It also created a vacuum in the entertainment space, especially in animation, that Softimage filled. Softimage originally was billed as a blend of the best of Alias and Wavefront software. Designed by artists *for* artists, it languished and was not taken very seriously until Softimage released the product Actor, which was the first inverse kinematics package that enabled animators to do real character animation easily. (Actor was recognized this year with a Technical Achievement Award by the Academy.) This propelled Softimage into the spotlight of the entertainment marketplace. Remnants of this period still exist in the entertainment market today, with Alias used for modeling, Wavefront (Dynamation) for simulation animation, Softimage for character animation, and RenderMan for rendering. (Alias also received a Technical Achievement Award for the modeling component of PowerAnimator, the recognized industry standard.)

For Wavefront, this meant a retrenching into engineering visualization with a renewed focus on CAD translation and less on porting. Porting efforts started to dwindle post-1992 with the demise of the Personal Visualizer. The reliance on revenue from the visualization market allowed for the development of the Data Visualizer and continued emphasis on motion data import into The Advanced Visualizer. The efforts to continue to work with the engineering visualization market were terminated post-A|W-merger because the Alias sales force had no expertise nor management acumen in this marketplace.

In 1994, the activities that led to the release of GameWare invigorated the company's marketing efforts, returned them to the spotlight, and increased the competition between Alias and Wavefront. The company teamed up with Corypheus Software to produce a real-time simulation environment for use on Onyx systems, giving greater control to game developers. (Called Activation, this product was terminated because it conflicted with Alias's efforts in the game business postmerger.) Several Wavefront executives and technical personnel went to Corypheus postmerger.

In early 1995, another effort was undertaken to capture the architectural market. ArcVision was designed to take existing CAD translation software and bundle it with preset color and environment controls, using IPR (Explore's renderer front-end) to offer a low-cost solution to small firms that wanted to experiment with different color and lighting schemes using existing CAD architectural databases. This project was terminated postmerger because the Alias management had bad experiences in this market with their Sonata purchase and did not believe the market was viable. It never really got off the ground because it was scheduled to be launched at Siggraph 1995.

In June of 1995, the merger of Alias Research, Wavefront, and Silicon Graphics was completed.

In 1998, a Scientific and Technical Achievement Award was awarded to Jim Keating, Michael Wahrman, and Richard Hollander for their contributions that led to the Wavefront Advanced Visualizer computer graphics system.

Also in 1998, a Scientific and Engineering Award was presented to Bill Kovacs for his creative leadership and to Roy Hall for his principal engineering efforts that led to the Wavefront Advanced Visualizer computer graphics program.

Whitney/Demos Productions
(1986 to 1988)

Whitney/Demos was founded by John Whitney Jr. and Gary Demos after their company, Digital Productions, was taken over by Omnibus. Funding assistance included Tom McMahon from the Symbolics Graphics Division and other private investors.

Initial production was based on Thinking Machines' Connection Machine II fronted by a Symbolics workstation along with other computer systems. Their first project was to team up with fellow ex-Triple-I employees from the Symbolics Graphics Division to produce the film *Stanley and Stella: Breaking The Ice*. Unfortunately, before they could collect the remainder of an initial $5 million loan, the majority of the CG production industry collapsed (thanks to the Omnibus fiasco), and the investors balked.

The Name Game

After declaring bankruptcy in June of 1988, Gary Demos went on to form his own research company, DemoGraFX. John Whitney Jr. elected to stay and take the company through the bankruptcy proceedings himself. John continued the company under various names, initially starting fresh as OptoMystic. When another company's name was found to be similar to that of OptoMystic, he changed the name to Digital Animation Laboratories and later sold the assets of the company to US Animation Labs. In December of 1996, US Animation Labs split in two. It kept the production side as Virtual Magic and sold the company name and software side to Toon Boom Technologies. Today, John runs his remaining original assets of Digital Animation Laboratories under the name Digital Editions Inc.

Xaos

(1988 to present)

Xaos originally was called Eidolon by Arthur Shwartzberg and Michael Tolson when they both left a studio in San Fransisco called Synthetic Video, where Arthur was Director of Marketing and Michael was a co-founder.

Renamed and incorporated in early 1989, Tolson held the office of President, Schwartzberg was VP/General Manager, and a new third partner, Mark Malmberg, was named Secretary, Creative Director, and Head of Production.

While Arthur's strength was in marketing, Tolson was largely self-taught and was a visionary both creatively and technically. He wrote the bulk of Xaos' early software from scratch with contributions to software development at the time from programmers Michael Beese and Eric Texier. Malmberg received an M.F.A. from UC-Berkeley in 1981 and had been working for General Graphics Services in San Francisco.

All the software used for the first four years or so was written in-house, from image and object formats to animation tools and renderers. Using this proprietary script-based software, Xaos quickly became known for complex, organic imagery. This was quite contrary to the norm of the period, which largely consisted of rectilinear, beveled-chrome logos created with commercial software derived from industrial design applications.

The animation crew in late '89 consisted of Hayden Landis (now at ILM), Ken Pearce (now at PDI), and Tony Lupidi (now at EA), followed by the additions of Henry Preston (ILM) and Roberta Brandao. This group was supported by the engineering teem of Tolson, Texier, and Michael Beese. Executive Producer from late '89 through '96 was Helene Plotkin (now producing *Toy Story 2* at Pixar).

During the '89–90 period, Xaos produced more than eight minutes of animation for the film *Lawnmower Man*. While certainly a B-movie, *Lawnmower Man* topped the sales charts for a week and was, in fact, a milestone in its extensive use of computer animation. Also produced were a similar volume of show graphics for the MTV series *Liquid Television* including the title sequence for which Malmberg and Pearce shared a Primetime Emmy for Design.

Tolson and Schwartzberg soon left Xaos to spin-off Xaos Tools, but the venture did not fare well. Arthur left Xaos Tools in 1996, and Michael followed in late 1998. Xaos Tools has gone through bankruptcy but should continue in some form at least for a while.

Xaos continued to grow under Malmberg's presidency, garnering numerous awards for such projects as animation for the feature film *The Pagemaster* (starring Macaulay Culkin), a fully animated music video for the Grateful Dead ("Infrared Roses"), numerous commercials and film titles, and a pair of IDs for the SCI-FI channel that were mini sci-fi movies in themselves, complete with miniature motion-control models and an intergalactic battle sequence. Another Emmy followed in 1996 for a set of MSNBC IDs designed and produced by Xaos.

Xaos continued its role as an industry leader, becoming in 1996 the world's first high-end 3D CG animation company to officially move fully to Windows NT. This move, quite "against the grain" of the SGI-loyal industry, initially was the inspiration of Lupidi, whose background includes having helped establish the historic Amiga lab at Ohio State nearly a decade earlier.

Teaming closely with Intel, Kinetics, and Intergraph, Xaos entered the "large-format" world in 1996, producing its first two "15-perf 70mm" projects on prerelease Pentium Pro (then code-named "P6") machines running the first 3D Studio MAX beta. In the ensuing years, Xaos has become a leading supplier of animation for the IMAX/large-format industry.

During the mid- to late '90s, Xaos benefited from the substantial programming expertise of Cassidy Curtis (Brown University graduate), Sumit Das (previously of "The Cave" in Illinois, now at PDI), and Kevin Rogers (now at Disney).

Virtually all the hallmark pieces Xaos produced have been marked by exceptional art direction combined with unique and powerful software.

In late '97, Schwartzberg rejoined the company as President, and Malmberg took this opportunity to focus on creative direction and to work with Christina Schmidlin, Executive Producer, in the development of the large-format market.

FACTIOD

PARC initially followed the pure research model of such facilities as IBM's Yorktown Heights research Center, AT&T Bell Labs, MIT Lincoln Labs, and The Stanford Research Institute's Augmentation Research Center (where Douglas C. Engelbart created the mouse). PARC also spawned the follow-up DEC Systems Research Center, founded later by Bob Taylor just across the Stanford campus from PARC.

FACTOID

SuperPaint recorded and stored its first image at 486×640 resolution (a picture of Dick Shoup holding a sign saying "It works, sort of"). The work was completed with assistance from Robert Flegal, Jim Curry, and Patrick Beaudelaire on April 10, 1973.

In late November 1998, Malmberg left Xaos, citing differences in management style, after dedicating 10 years to the direction and growth of this unique company. Malmberg now works at Radium, S.F. as a creative director specializing in C.G. along with his industry pals and Radium founders Jonathan Keaton and Simon Mowbray. Xaos continues to produce innovative animation and effects for the feature, large-format, and commercial markets.

Today, with Schwartzberg at the helm, Xaos is in the midst of a rebirth of sorts. Plans call to roughly double in size from 25 to 50 employees in the next year. It is this "boutique" sensibility that is the intended format to carry them into the next era of creative content markets. The key to this plan is strengthening their already strong presence in the large-format film market and expanding their commecial presence. You can find more information at www.xaos.com.

Xerox PARC (Palo Alto Research Center)

The Xerox Palo Alto Research Center (PARC) opened on July 1, 1970, in Palo Alto, California, just outside the Stanford University campus.

Jacob Goldman, chief scientist and founder of PARC, initially divided the facility into three separate units:

1. The Computer Science Lab

2. Systems Science Lab

3. General Science Lab

Although computer graphics was never a goal of PARC per se, Bob Taylor himself was very familiar with this new area of computer science research. He had overseen the Information Processing Techniques Office of ARPA (the Defense Department's Advanced Research Project Agency), which funded many early university graduate programs such as Dave Evans' graduate program at the University of Utah back in 1965.

The person who brought CG research to PARC under Taylor was Dr. Richard Shoup of Carnegie Mellon University. Shoup had been at the short-lived Berkeley Computer Company (BCC) from 1968 to 1970 and was given a full year upon starting at PARC to explore what it was he wanted to do. What he ended up doing was developing SuperPaint. Along with artist Alvy Ray Smith, Shoup experimented, designed, and built the first digital paint system with a non-random access, 8-bit framebuffer.

Shoup left to form Aurora Systems and was awarded a Technical Emmy Award in 1983 for SuperPaint.

Other CG-related breakthroughs at PARC included the following:

- In February 1975, the first GUI is demonstrated with multiple windows and pop-up menus. These later would be incorporated as a standard in Mac (and later Windows) operating desktop systems.

- The first Alto PC was powered up in 1973 (displaying an image of Sesame Street's Cookie Monster). Its bitmap display was a vertical format 8×11-inch screen with a resolution of 606×808 pixels. With a maximum of 128k of main memory and a 2.5 meg disc, more than 2,000 were manufactured by 1978 at a cost of about $12,000 each. Upgraded as the AltoII in 1975 and the AltoIII in 1976, it actually was the first PC installed in the White House (in 1978). There's some irony, perhaps, in the fact that the world's first WYSIWYG computer was used in the heart of Washington politics.

- The Smalltalk object-oriented language by Alan Kay (1974) developed the WIMP (Window manager, Icons, Mice, and Pop-up) interface concept.

PARC is still an active research center today. Youc an find more information at www.parc.xerox.com/parc-go.html.

QUOTE

"My big technical contribution (I was really there as an artist) at Xerox PARC to Shoup's SuperPaint was invention and implementation of the RGB to HSV transform for artistic selection of colors. Other than this contribution, all other programming of Super Paint was Dick's."
—Alvy Ray Smith

Z-A Production

(1987 to present)

This history of Z-A Production was contributed by Maurice Benayoun.

Z-A was founded in 1987 in Paris by three people: Stéphane Singier (Chief Manager), Thierry Prieur (Technical Manager), and Maurice Benayoun (Art Director).

Computer Graphics series by Maurice Benayoun. Year of production, 1993. Copyright, Z-A/ Canal +/ Ellipse/ France 3/ Club d'Investissement MEDIA.

Backgrounds

Stéphane Singier was an architect and film producer, Thierry Prieur was an architect in CAD/architecture, and Maurice Benayoun (me) came from a fine arts and video background. After an initial period of time dedicated to architectural visualization and advertising, the Z-A team decided to explore the potential of 3D computer graphics for television programs. After two years of project development and research, *The Quarxs* pilot came into being. Conceived and directed by Maurice Benayoun, it included graphic design by François Schuiten. *The Quarxs* was first created on a PC 486 using Opium (French 3D software). Already at this point, *The Quarx* started to receive many awards at international competitions (the first one being first prize in the Truevision competition at Siggraph 91 in Las Vegas). Two years later, the series was made in HD 35mm on SGI computers using Softimage. This was to be the first 3D series with a completely original script broadcast on TV during prime time on Canal + (8h300) and during the Christmas schedule. This series was to become a hallmark and reference point for all future 3D graphics series (of which there were 12 episodes, each lasting three minutes). A feature film is in still in the pipeline!

In addition to the animated projects for television, Z-A has worked on special effects, television openings, (receiving numerous awards. For example, 1st and 2nd prize at Imagina) scientific and architectural simulations, and so on. (They have received numerous awards such as first and second prize at Imagina.) More recently, however, Z-A has been working on several Japanese CG ventures (television, theme parks, and so on) and French and European productions. Within this relatively short space of time, Z-A risks becoming one of a rare breed of companies that have contributed historically to the evolution of the digital age in Europe.

In addition to using Softimage, Z-A continues to develop its own software for animation. One of the most interesting is probably Persona. Interfaced with some classical 3D animation software, Persona is a complete toolbox for filtering captured inputs such as gestures (with magnetic trackers, for example), sounds (music, voice), mouse, joystick, and so on. Persona the animator can easily convert plain gestures in cartoon-like, robotic, elastic animation. For all virtual reality applications, Z-A R&D (David Nahon, Tristan Lorach) has developed in-house software including the Zasoundserver, which is a tool for real-time sound mixing and 3D sound effects for

16 channels and up to eight outputs suitable to virtual environments. Mostly developed in OpenGL, some of these developments have been achieved thanks to the partnership of SGI Europe (Patrick Bouchaud, Kimi Bishop).

Ann Lewis Dark Savour, Computer graphics singer for JVC Victor video clip. Copyright JVC Victor, Japan.

In 1992, Z-A founded a subsidiary called Stratosphere specifically for the field of architecture visualization and communication. Managed by Thierry Prieur, Stratosphere works on international architectural projects, Shangai

Opera Theater, airports for Aeroports de Paris, Electricite de France, and Grand Stade (Saint Denis France).

At the heart of Z-A's creed is its development since 1994 of extensive know-how in the field of virtual reality and "tele-virtuality." This has occurred mostly through the implementation of artistic projects such as *Is God Flat?* and *Is the Devil Curved?* and *The Tunnel under the Atlantic* that linked the Centre Georges Pompidou in Paris to the Museum of Contemporary Art in Montreal (ISEA 95).

World Skin. *Interactive installation by Maurice Benayoun. Copyright, Z-A.*

In 1998, *World Skin*, a CAVE installation presented at Siggraph 98 (Orlando), received the Golden Nica interactive art award at Ars Electronica. All these artistic as well as philosophically challenging installations combined virtual reality, the Internet, intelligent agents, photographic cameras, and printers. These works, conceived by Maurice Benayoun, were able to give Z-A a leading edge in Europe with regard to interactive installations, museums, cultural theme parks, exhibitions, and events. Such information concerning the "collective interactive experience" led Z-A to develop interfaces such as the Hypercube for la Cité des Sciences et de l'Industrie de la Villette, still on show during a one and a half year network exhibition. One million visitors have confirmed the interest in the user-friendly potential of Hypercube. At present, Hypercube is being refined as a standard interface for computer desktops, Web browsers, and electronic program guides (EPG) for television.

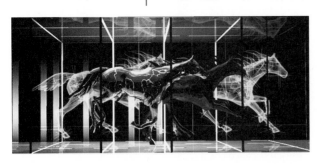

Gallop Racer II. *Opening sequence of a Japanese video game with horses animated by motion capture. Copyright Tecmo/ pH studio.*

During Hypercube's development, Z-A created an intuitive profiling tool (Z-A Profiler) based on behavior analysis to enable people to find their way through information without having to ask or reply to predefined questions. The Z-A profiler has shown to be efficient in combination with the tunneling system adapted for travel agencies (in collaboration with France Telecom). You just dig into pictures of landscape, and you very quickly arrive at the proposed holiday destination of your dreams. Completely anonymous, this profiling system will be adapted to the Hypercube interface to become an intuitive browser for info-trips.

Currently, Z-A is working on a new CAVE/Internet work for the ICC biennale (Tokyo October 99) as well as interactive installations for EXPO2000 Hanover, Virtual Garden (a theme park in France), two Centre Georges Pompidou exhibitions, pilots for 3D CG series, and some other things that haven't been divulge just yet. Maurice Benayoun can be reached at www.benayoun.com64 or at rue de la Folie Méricourt 75011 Paris, France. You can find more information at www.Z-A.net.

Programming and Mathematics

Programming is naturally the basis of all other CG endeavors, but it's already been written up very well in texts such as *Computer Graphics: Principles and Practice* by James Foley, Andries Van dam, et al. More to the point, the intent for this book is to be just an introduction to concepts and ideas. It is left up to the readers to pursue the specialty of their choice in the many great texts already out there.

Thankfully (for us artist types), modern CG production does not require a CS degree. Any serious technical directing work, however, especially on feature films, often requires a very thorough understanding of pseudo-code concepts. UNIX C-Shell scripting, RenderMan shaders, Python, and the like all are staples of a TD's arsenal of basic tools.

This chapter covers the historical origins of these important programming languages along with the usual terms and concepts.

DR. ED CATMULL
(PH.D., UNIVERSITY OF UTAH, 1974)

A brief synopsis of this one man's continuing accomplishments reads like the foundation of the entire CG industry. Some of Ed Catmull's noted achievements include the development of texture mapping, the Z-buffer method of hidden surface removal, Catmull-Rom splines, and subdivision surfaces. He is the founder of the NYIT Graphics Lab and Lucasfilm's first Computer Graphics Division, and he is the cofounder and current CEO of Pixar Animation Studios.

Catmull grew up in Utah and wanted to be an animator, but he also wanted to be able to make a living, so he switched his career of choice to physics. As a University of Utah undergraduate, he reveled in many wide-ranging electives including an early CG course in Fortran. Upon graduating in 1969, he went to work for Boeing but was soon one of approximately 50,000 employees laid off.

Back at the University of Utah as a graduate student, Catmull joined teachers and fellow students including Alan Kay, John Warnok, Garry Watkins, and Jim Blinn to name a few.

Soon after receiving his Ph.D. in 1974, he was offered a job with IBM and was actually turned down for a teaching position at Ohio State University (due to competing interdepartment politics, not for lack of qualification). Catmull settled in at a local CAD/CAM company called Applicon. Just a few months later, however, on the recommendation of Dave Evans, he was invited by Dr. Alexander Schure of the New York Institute of Technology to begin a computer graphics department there. Catmull left NYIT in 1979 to start the Computer Division at Lucasfilm. He then broke off that group in 1986 to form Pixar, where he remains today as Executive Vice President and Chief Technology Officer.

TERMS

affine

This is a transformation (translation, rotation, and scaling operation) that carries straight lines into straight lines and parallel lines into parallel lines. However, it may alter distance between points and angles between lines.

algorithm

An algorithm is a mathematical procedure for solving complex or repetitive operations.

alpha version

The early (and usually in-house-only) prerelease version of software is called the alpha version. It is followed by a limited beta version and then the official version 1.0.

API

The Application Programmer Interface (API) is the program that the user views and interacts with. It also is the set of libraries, sometimes called a Developer's Kit, that advanced users can access to extend the possibilities of the application (through either plug-ins or standalone programs).

array

An array is an organized arrangement of data. One-dimensional arrays are called vectors; two-dimensional arrays are called a matrix.

Assembly language

This language is a low-level computer code usually not directly written by a human being. It usually is created from a higher-level language such as C, Pascal, or Fortran. Sometimes writing directly in Assembly language is the only way to gain the last CPU cycles in a critical routine.

basis vector

A vector defining a +1 increment of an axis is called a basis vector.

batch process

This means to run a program, such as a renderer, without a GUI interface or additional input. It often is run in the background or is set to execute at a later time when no user interaction is needed.

bias

Bias means to alter the result of a given function to favor either its low or its high values. The bias function originally was written by Perlin and Hoffert in 1989.

— *see also*   gain

binary

Binary is a base-2 numbering system in which information is encoded with only two possible states, zero and one. Although most image formats are binary, text files are left in readable ASCII format. Conversions from binary to ASCII often are done by programs such as BinHex on the Mac.

— *see also*   Mac-binary, fat-binary

bit

This word is a contraction of "binary digit." It is a single storage location in computer memory (represented in binary by 0 or 1), and it is the smallest unit of data measurement. Eight bits make up 1 byte.

— *see also*   binary

block

A block is an arbitrary unit of bytes grouped into some larger unit.

block size

Block size is the number of bytes in a block.

BSP-trees

This stands for binary space-partitioning trees. A subdividing algorithm used in visible surface determination, BSP-trees is similar in concept to octrees and quadtrees. Developed by Kedem, Fuchs, and Naydor in the early 1980s, BSP-trees is based on Shumaker's work of 1969.

byte

A byte is a unit of measurement comprising 8 bits of computer memory. It is the equivalent of one alphanumeric character such as "w" or "@."

Boolean

These logical operators used in solid modeling techniques were named for English mathematician George Boole (1815–1864).

Rules govern the functions of logical (true/false) operations. The OR operator is the union, AND is the intersection, NOT is minus, and XOR is exclusive.

— *see also* constructive solid geometry

TRIVIA

A unit of 4 bits is sometimes called a nibble (as in half a byte).

C

Brian Kernighan codeveloped the C programming language with Dennis Ritchie at Bell Labs in 1978.

C++

An extension of C, C++ is an object-oriented, high-level programming language used by many modern software designers. Bjarne Stroustrop wrote the C++ programming language (originally called "C with Classes") in 1982. It was revised and renamed C++ in 1984 and was widely released a year later. An excellent reference page on C++ can be found online at www.isi.edu/~iko/pl/hw3_cpp.html.

clamping

To clamp is to restrict a given attribute or function to a specified limit.

compand

This is a contraction of "compress" and "expand." A weighted function is applied to an input that distributes a greater amount of information to some areas of that input over others.

compiler

A compiler is a program that translates a high-level programming code, such as C++, into an executable machine language.

convolution

Convolution is a weighted summing operation. The weighted function is called the filter kernel or convolution kernel. It is used in anti-aliasing computations.

CORE Graphics System

The CORE Graphics System is a device-independent graphics standard. It was defined as such by ACM SIG-GRAPH in 1977–79.

— *see also* Graphical Kernel System

Dore

This is a graphics language used in the now-defunct Ardent Titan supergraphics workstation during the 1980s.

Euler's formula

This formula describes the necessary conditional relationship of a simple polyhedron:

$$V - E + F = 2$$

V is the number of vertices, E is the number of edges, and F is the number of faces.

extents

This is a fancy name for a bounding box.

Fortran

This stands for formula translation programming language. A good starting point on the Web for information is www.fortran.com/fortran/market.html.

fractal

A fractal is a complex shape that derives from the continuous repetition of form over a varying scale.

— *see also*   graftal, Mandelbrot set, procedural models

GPHIGS

GPHIGS is an enhanced implementation of the ANSI/ISO Programmer's Hierarchical Interactive Graphics System (PHIGS) standard. It provides standard PHIGS+ functionality for applications requiring dynamic and interactive modeling, viewing, modification, and rendering of 2D and 3D objects. GPHIGS provides the lighting and shading capabilities required for generating realistic models. Supported environments include Cray, DEC, Hewlett-Packard, IBM RS/6000, Microsoft Windows 95 and NT, UNIX, Silicon Graphics Inc., and Sun SPARC. You can find more information at www.sd.tgs.com.

Graphical Kernel System (GKS)

GKS is the first 2D graphics specification to be officially standardized by the American National Standards Institute (ANSI) and the International Standards Organization (ISO) in 1985. GKS-3D was similarly introduced in 1988.

— *see also*   PHIGS

graftals

Graftals were defined by A.R. Smith in 1984 after the L-grammer models of Lindenmayer in 1968.

high-level language

This is the programming language actually written by a computer programmer. It uses more readable syntax and formatting than the low-level machine code interpreted by the computer. Languages commonly used in CG include C, C++, Pascal, Lisp, Fortran, and Java.

HOOPS

HOOPS is a high-level development system that enables developers to build portable interactive 3D graphics applications.

interpolation

Also known as "filling in the blanks," interpolation is a mathematical function that creates missing information by interpreting the existing data. Keyframe animation interpolates information on a per-frame basis between each of the keyframe values set by the user.

Inventor ▸ see IRIS Inventor, Open Inventor

IRIS Inventor

IRIS Inventor was the first C++ 3D development toolkit released by SGI in 1992. It is built on top of IRIS GL and also is known as Inventor 1.0. Open Inventor, also known as Inventor 2.0, was defined in 1994 and is built on OpenGL but has more features.

— *see also*   Open Inventor

isometric

This 3D viewing technique eliminates all realistic distortion. No vanishing points are used, and all lines along a given axis are rendered parallel, yielding a clear technical illustration often used in CAD.

Java

This popular Web-based programming language from Sun was introduced on May 23, 1995. You can find more information at `http://java.sun.com/`.

Julia set ▸ see Mandlebrot set, fractal

L-grammer

This procedural method for describing structured growth models (such as trees) was developed by A. Lindenmayer in 1968.

LISP

LISP is a popular ARPANET language. The DEC-PDP10 ran LISP.

matrix

A matrix is strictly defined as a 2D array. Matrix operations commonly used in CG, however, are actually four-dimensional.

median cut algorithm

This was developed by Paul Heckbert at MIT in 1979 for his undergraduate (BS Mathematics) thesis, "Color Image Quantization For Frame Buffer Display." It basically creates accurate low-bit-depth color representations (8 or 9 bit) of higher-bit-depth original images.

Motif

This is the standard GUI for UNIX operating systems.

object-oriented

This software enables users to define objects such as images, line art, text, and so on. It also is possible to manipulate the objects for placement in page layout or other creative graphics programs.

OpenGL

SGI's Open Graphics Library was introduced in 1992 and has since grown into the industry's leading cross-platform 2D and 3D graphics API. OpenGL® is an independent software-development environment for creating interactive 2D and 3D computer graphics. It is supported on all major operating systems and windowing environments.

OpenGL provides a range of functions including anti-aliasing, alpha-blending, double buffering, interpolated shading, surface lighting and shading, texture mapping, affine transformations, and Z-buffering.

More information can be found on the SGI OpenGL home page at www.sgi.com/software/opengl.

Open Inventor

Open Inventor is SGI's object-oriented 3D toolkit. It offers a comprehensive solution to interactive graphics program-ming problems. It was developed in 1994 and was based on the earlier Iris Inventor standard of 1992. It presents a programming model based on a 3D scene database that dramatically simplifies graphics programming. It includes a rich set of objects such as cubes, polygons, text, materials, cameras, lights, trackballs, handle boxes, 3D viewers, and editors that speed up your programming time and extend your 3D programming capabilities.

— *see also*   Iris Inventor

OPGS

The Open Productivity Graphics System (OPGS) is an implementation of the PHIGS+ integrated set of graphics tools used to develop interactive 2D/3D graphics applications.

PERL

A simple but powerful programming language, Practical Extraction and Report Language (PERL) was created, written, developed, and maintained by Larry Wall (`lwall@netlabs.com`) in 1987. For more information, you can visit the many Web dedicated to this topic. The Perl Institute is a nonprofit organization dedicated to keeping Perl available, usable, and free for all (`www.perl.org`). Other central sources for all things Perl include `www.perl.net` and `www.perl.com`.

PHIGS

The Programmers Hierarchical Interactive Graphics System (PHIGS) was developed in 1988. PHIGS PLUS (PHIGS+) supports advanced lighting and shading of surfaces. In 1991, a machine-independent version called GPHIGS was developed by the French company G5G (Graphisme 5eme Generation).

— *see also*   SPHIGS, GPHIGS

Python

According to `www.python.org`, Python is an interpreted, interactive, object-oriented programming language. Its development started in 1990 at CWI in Amsterdam and continues at CNRI in Reston, Virginia. It often is compared to Tcl, Perl, Scheme, or Java. Python combines remarkable power with very clear syntax. It has modules, classes, exceptions, very high-level dynamic data types, and dynamic typing. New built-in modules can easily be written in C or C++. Such extension modules can define new functions and variables as well as new object types. The Python implementation is portable—it runs on many brands of UNIX and on Windows, DOS, OS/2, Mac, and Amiga.

QuickDraw
This is the Mac graphics standard.

quaternians
Developed by Ken Showmake in 1985, quaternians are used most often in animation packages to represent rotations. In the traditional XYZ rotation notation, "gimble lock" can occur when one axis is rotated through and confused by another. Quaternian rotation is represented by a single orientation value, thus avoiding the gimble lock problem. Unfortunately, it is not a very intuitive way to position something, and it also can never "add up" multiple rotations past 360 degrees. (I will save the 4D complex number nature of the technique for your own investigations.)

run-length encoding
Run-length encoding is a compression's scheme that stores data and repetition coding on a line by line basis of an image file.

SRGP
The Simple Raster Graphics Package (SRGP) was designed by David Sklar for the Mac OS, Windows, and UNIX platforms in the popular book *Computer Graphics: Principles and Practice* by James Foley, Andries van Dam, Steven Feiner, and John Hughes.

spatial partitioning ▶ see spacial subdivision

spatial subdivision
Also known as spatial partitioning, this method is used for breaking down one large problem into many smaller ones for easier analysis. Visible surface algorithms are a typical application of this technique.

SPHIGS

The Simple PHIGS (SPHIGS) Graphics package was designed by David Sklar for the Mac OS, Windows, and UNIX platforms in the popular book *Computer Graphics: Principles and Practice* by Foley, van Dam, Feiner, and Hughes.

unit vector

A unit vector is a vector with a length of 1. This can be derived by scaling a vector by the reciprocal of its length. It sometimes is called unitizing the vector.

UNIX

This operating system is used with the Silicon Graphics computer system. Ken Thompson co-invented the UNIX operating system with Dennis Ritchie at Bell Labs in 1978. You can check out UNIX Guru Universe at `www.usu.com`.

vector

A vector is a direction and a length.

— *see also*   unit vector, basis vector

VRML

The following VRML description is excerpted with permission from *The Annotated VRML97 Reference Manual* by Rikk Carey and Gavin Bell. You can find more information at `www.best.com/~rikk/Book/toc-ch1.htm`.

"VRML, sometimes pronounced "vermal," is an acronym for the Virtual Reality Modeling Language. At its core, VRML is simply a 3D interchange format. It defines most of the commonly used semantics found in today's 3D applications such as hierarchical transformations, light sources, viewpoints, geometry, animation, fog, material properties, and texture mapping. One of the primary goals in designing VRML was to ensure that it at least succeeded as an effective 3D file interchange format. VRML also is a 3D analog to HTML. This means that VRML serves as a simple, multiplatform language for publishing 3D Web pages.

In 1989, a new project was started at Silicon Graphics, Inc., by Rikk Carey and Paul Strauss (code name: Scenario) to design and build an infrastructure for interactive 3D graphics applications.

In 1992, the IRIS Inventor 3D toolkit was released as the first product of these efforts. In 1994, the second major revision of Inventor was released. The reference manual describing the objects and file format in the Open Inventor toolkit eventually was used by Gavin Bell to write the first draft of the VRML 1.0 specification. Gavin, with help from Tony Parisi, Rikk Carey, and a variety of Inventor engineers, revised and finalized the first draft of the VRML 1.0 specification. In October 1994 at the Second International Conference on the World Wide Web in Chicago, the specification was published. In August 1996 at SIGGRAPH 96 in New Orleans, the first version of the VRML 2.0 specification was released. You can find more general information about VRML at www.vrml.org."

Warnock algorithm

This visible surface determination algorithm is based on recursive-subdivision, a technique for breaking down the surface into smaller and smaller areas for easier calculations. It was developed by Alan J. Warnock in 1969 at the University of Utah.

3D	cache	EGA
2D	CGA	emulator
ACM	component video	ethernet
A to D	composite video	Eurographics
AIX	compression	exabyte
analog	core	export
ANSI	CPU	file
ARPANET	crash	file format
ASCII	CRT	gain
AT&T	cursor	GIF
applets	cyc	gigabyte
application	D to A	GIGO
Ardent	default	GNU
artifact	degauss	graphics accelerator
Association of Computing Machinery	densitometer	graphic file format
	desktop	GUI
attribute	dialog box	Hewlett-Packard Co.
AVI	digital camera	HTTP
back up	digital disc recorder	IMI
bandwidth	Digital Equipment Corporation	Intergraph Corp.
beta test		ISO
bounding box	directory	IRIX
British Computer Society	disc array	isometric
	dongle	JPEG
BTS	download	kilobyte
buffer	DRAM	LED

Basic and Miscellaneous Terms

3D

3D stands for three-dimensional. It is the height, width, and depth defined in an XYZ coordinate system. A wire-frame model in a CG animation program has all three dimensions, as opposed to 2D raster paint systems.

— see also 2D

2D

2D stands for two-dimensional. All CGI ends up as 2D raster images upon rendering and prior to compositing.

— see also 3D

ACM ► see Association of Computing Machinery

A to D

This stands for analog-to-digital conversion, the converting of analog signals to and from digital encoding.

— see also digitization

AIX

AIX is IBM's flavor of the UNIX operating system.

analog

Any process that allows for a nondiscreet description of information, such as radio frequencies, a thermometer reading, or a video signal, is considered to be analog. There are no predetermined, discreet steps to restrict a change in increment of any kind. This contrasts with the digital processes that must sample data into regular indivisible units.

ANSI

The American National Standards Institute (ANSI) was formed in 1923 as a nonprofit organization to coordinate and administer the development of U.S. voluntary national standards. It is the U.S. member body of the International Organization for Standardization (ISO) and the International Electrotechnical Commission (IEC). ANSI's membership consists of approximately 1,300 companies, 35 government agencies, and more than 260 technical, trade, labor, and consumer groups. You can find more information at www.ansi.org.

— see also ISO

ARPANET

This precursor to the Internet became operational in September 1969, connecting just four locations: UCLA, the Stanford Research Institute, the University of Utah, and the University of California at Santa Barbara.

ASCII

The American Standard for Computer Information Interchange (ASCII) is made up of alphanumeric-based (text-based) symbols that are readable across most any computer platform.

AT&T

AT&T formed the Electronic Photography and Imaging Center (EPIC) in 1984 to create PC-based video graphics products. In 1985, it released the TARGA video board for PCs. This was the first practical consumer product to work in real 32-bit color space. The center also developed the TARGA (.TGA) file format to describe this image data. AT&T introduced the Pixel Machine for real-time parallel rendering in 1988.

applets

Applets are little applications. Similar to plug-ins, they are intended to work with and complement a larger, more complete application program. Unlike plug-ins, which require a host program to operate, an applet also can often be operated on its own.

application

This term is just another name for a software program.

Ardent

This is the maker of the Titan line of minisupercomputers that were popular for a brief time in the mid-1980s. They used the Dynamic Object Rendering Environment (DORE) modeling and rendering system. The company no longer is in business.

artifact

An artifact is a defect or an imperfection. This usually is the unwanted result or byproduct of some other process. For example, an artifact of image compression often is color banding.

Association of Computing Machinery (1947 to present)

Founded in 1947, the ACM is the world's oldest professional computer society. Its largest special interest group, or SIG, is SIGGRAPH, the only essential professional organization for CG practitioners.

— *see also* SIGGRAPH

attribute

An attribute is any described element of a CG object, such as color, surface texture, or scale.

AVI

Audio Video Interleaved is a special case of the Resource Interchange File format (RIFF) developed by Microsoft. This Windows operating system standard file format describes digital, audio, and video signals. It is denoted with the .AVI extension.

back up

To back up is to make a copy of software on a separate storage medium for archiving and safety purposes. Exabyte (10megs), DAT (20–80megs), DLT (2–3gigs) all are tape formats used to do backups. Backups are often a duty performed by the technical assistants in a company.

bandwidth

Bandwidth is the limit of data allowed to pass through a given medium. Standard 10BASE-T ethernet, for example, has a bandwidth of 10 megabits per second.

beta test

This is the term used for software being tested before wide commercial release. Its purpose is to find final bugs and other problems in interface design and feature sets. This follows initial alpha testing and comes before the first official v1.0 of the product.

bounding box

A bounding box is a simple cubic volume created to exactly enclose the largest dimensions of an object. It is used in place of the actual object during certain operations to greatly speed up calculations. This also is called extents.

British Computer Society

The British Computer Society (BCS) is roughly the equivalent of the ACM. Online information can be found at www.bcs.org.uk. The BCS Displays Group currently is led by Rae Earnshaw at r.a.earnshaw@bradfor.ac.uk.

BTS

The Broadcast Television System (BTS) is co-owned by Bosch and Philips. BTS developed the BTS-Pixelerator, a 3D graphics accelerator that was marketed briefly around 1990.

buffer

A buffer is a piece of computer memory used for temporary storage of information. An important example is the framebuffer, which represents the amount of memory necessary to keep one image alive.

— *see also* Z-buffer

cache

A cache is a hardware or software storage area for frequently used data. Caching data makes for much quicker data retrieval by minimizing slower disc access.

CGA

Introduced in 1981, the Color Graphics Adapter (CGA) was the first low-resolution (320×200 pixels) color video card developed by IBM for its PC computers.

— *see also* EGA and VGA

component video

Component video retains separate chrominance and luminance signals. RGB also can be considered a form of component signal.

composite video

Composite video combines chrominance and luminance signals in such broadcast video formats as NTSC, SECAM, and PAL.

compression

This means to reduce a file's byte size by various means of encoding to save disk space and to reduce transfer times across networks. File compression (such as with the UNIX utility gzip) is an optimized storage solution. Image compression, on the other hand, is more often used in specific image formats. Lossless compression formats (GIF and TIFF) return 100 percent of the data when uncompressed. Lossy compression formats (JPEG and MPEG) suffer some data loss that is not visibly noticeable.

— *see also*   run-length encoding

core

A core file or core dump is created by some UNIX systems to catalog a crashed process. They can be very large and, in most cases, should be removed immediately to free up space. For the true systems geek, they actually contain a complete memory dump and stack tree of the offending process. In that sense, they can be very useful to keep around for debugging.

CPU

The central processing unit (CPU) is the main "number-crunching" computer chip that does most of the work in all computers. Although most home computers and workstations have a single CPU, some supercomputers (such as those from Thinking Machines) can have hundreds in a single configuration.

crash

Any catastrophic error that causes software or hardware to stop functioning properly is called a crash. UNIX system crashes often generate large core files.

CRT

A cathode ray tube (CRT) contains three colorless electron beam guns that illuminate red, green, and blue phosphors on each spot inside the tube.

cursor

A cursor is a symbol, usually an arrow, that defines the placement of an input device such as a mouse or a stylus in the windowing system.

cyc

Cyc is shorthand for cyclorama, and is pronounced like "psych." It is a large, smooth, usually curved surface that is used as a backdrop in stage photography. Monochrome color schemes are used in keying; fully painted versions are used in camera backdrops.

D to A

This stands for digital-to-analog conversion, such as transferring a digital image to a video tape. The discreet digital information bits are then described with a continuous analog video signal.

DDR ▶ see digital disc recorder

DEC ▶ see Digital Equipment Corporation

default

The standard setting of some attribute is called the default. For example, a medium-blue is the default color of Alias shaders.

degauss

To degauss is to remove built-up magnetic field charges from a monitor. This usually is done automatically when the monitor is turned on. Old SGI monitors had a button on the front you could push to hear a satisfying electrical "thump" sound, proclaiming your monitor degaussed.

densitometer

This is an instrument that accurately measures the density of an exposed film image. An area of film that has been exposed to little or no light is "thin;" a fully exposed area is "thick." This information is used to better adjust both the exposure and development process, and it is film stock (emulsion) specific.

desktop

This is a euphemism for a computer's main display screen area. The desktop is where you put folders with files in them before you throw them in the trash.

dialog box

A dialog box is an area of a software program that sometimes pops up to communicate important information to the user, such as "Do you really want to reformat your hard drive? Click OK to confirm!"

digital camera

Both still and video cameras that do not expose images on film like conventional cameras are called digital cameras. Instead, they use CCD technology to record the data directly onto digital tape or hard disk. Consumer products generally use a single CCD; professional models can use three CCDs, one for each RGB color channel for better quality. In all cases, the images can be downloaded directly to a computer's hard drive for use just like any other scanned or painted image.

digital disc recorder (DDR)

A DDR is a desktop or rack-mounted frame storage device to which a person transfers animation to play back real-time tests or to transfer the footage to video. An example is the Abekas from Accom Inc.

Digital Equipment Corporation (DEC)

This company produced the VAX and PDP mainframe computers used in the very early 1960s through the early 1980s. DEC was bought by Compaq Computer

Corporation in early 1998 with only about one-third of the 135,000 employees it had at its peak around 1989. DEC currently makes the popular DEC Alpha PC platform.

directory

A directory is an operating system definition containing multiple data files. A directory can contain any number of files or other directories. (It is limited only by operating system constraints.) Under the Mac OS, this also is called a folder.

disc array

A disc array is two or more disc drives combined to form a single logical device to speed access file I/O.

dongle

A dongle is a hardware encryption device physically attached to the computer to temporarily key software licenses. They were used more widely in the 1980s by companies such as Alias. They are rarely used today.

download

To download is to transfer data from one system to another, as in downloading digitized video images to a hard drive for use in a compositing system.

DRAM

Dynamic random access memory (DRAM), more commonly referred to as just RAM, is the computer's main memory. Information stored in RAM is temporary (unlike information on a hard drive) and is retained when power is interrupted.

EGA

Introduced in 1985, the Enhanced Graphics Adapter (EGA) was the next graphics standard after CGA. Trademarked by IBM, EGA describes 640×350 pixels at 16 colors (from an available 64 colors).

— *see also*   VGA

emulator

An emulator is a product that duplicates the operation of another. You can get emulators for PCs and Macs, for example, that play games such as the old Atari 2600 video games.

ethernet

Ethernet is the most common type of local area network (LAN) used to connect multiple computers together so they can exchange information directly. Types of ethernet include 10BASE-T (twisted pair), 10BASE-2 (thin), 10BASE-5 (thick), 10BASE-F (fiber optic), 100BASE-T (fast), and the new Gigabit Ethernet. Every networkable computer manufactured has a discreet ethernet address designated by the IEEE Society that enables identification across any such network.

Hawaii's ALOHAnet technical paper influenced Bob Metcalfe in developing ethernet, which he put down in a memo in May of 1973. Formal specifications were agreed upon on September 30, 1980, by Xerox, Intel, and DEC for the Ethernet that was then made available by those companies for a nominal licensing fee.

Eurographics

The Euro equivalent to ACM/SIGGRAPH is on the Web at www.eg.org. Information about the Eurographics UK Chapter can be found at info.ox.ac.uk/eg-uk. Rob Fletcher, who can be reached at rpf@york.ac.uk, is EG-UK chair.

exabyte

An exabyte is an 8mm magnetic tape format used for storing digital data. One cassette the size of an audio tape can hold between 0.5 and 20 gigabytes of data, depending on which compression scheme is used.

export

To export is to transfer a file out of one software program for use in another. Standalone modeling programs can export DXF-format geometry files to be read by another animation program.

file

A file is a computer record containing data that resides in a directory.

file format ▶ see graphic file format

gain

A gain is a function to increase or decrease the gradient of a function at a given point. The gain function was originally written by Perlin and Hoffert 1989.

— *see also* bias

GIF

The Graphical Interchange Format (GIF) is a lossless compression format developed by CompuServe Inc. that utilizes only 8-bit (256) color.

— *see also* JPEG

gigabyte

A gigabyte is exactly 1,073,741,824 bytes.

GIGO

This stands for "garbage in, garbage out." It is slang for "If you give a program bad instructions, don't expect anything but the same for its output."

GNU

GNU is a freeware UNIX-like operating system developed by the Free Software Foundation based in Boston, Massachusetts. The GNU project has expanded greatly to include a huge variety of freeware applications such as gimp (a famous image processing program). You can find more information at www.gnu.org.

graphics accelerator

A graphics accelerator is an add-on card that, when installed into a computer, contains dedicated memory and processing specifically designed to speed up the interaction with 3D graphics, especially games.

graphic file format

The graphic file format is the format in which an image's information is encoded and stored as digital data.

GUI

Graphical user interface, pronounced "gooey," refers to the graphical menus and buttons of a computer program that allow user manipulation of the program itself. The first notion of a GUI was developed at the Stanford Research Institute. It later was refined by Alan Kay (Ph.D. University of Utah, 1969) at Xerox PARC. Apple's first Mac in 1984 was the first commercial PC to make a GUI its standard interface.

Hewlett-Packard Co.

Hewlett-Packard makes the Kayak line of Windows NT-based workstations. Very fast 450Mhz Pentium II Xeon processors and hardware graphics acceleration make for a very attractive multimedia platform for around $5,000. Options include the AccelGalaxy OpenGL card from Evans & Sutherland. Located in Palo Alto, California, Hewlett-Packard can be reached at 800-752-0900. You can find more information about the Kayak line at www.hp.com/kayak.

— *see also*   Intergraph Corp

HTTP

The Hypertext Transfer Protocol (HTTP) is the foundation of Web language developed by the World Wide Web Consortium (W3C). It is found in front of URL addresses such as http://visualfx.com. HTTP-ng is the next generation version currently under development.

IMI

Interactive Machines Inc. (IMI) made early vector graphics computer systems similar to Evans & Sutherland's products. The company no longer is in business.

Intergraph Corp.

This company makes Windows NT-based workstations that use the very fast 450Mhz Pentium II Xeon processors. Like the HP Kayak line, hardware graphics acceleration makes for a very attractive multimedia platform. Located in

Huntsville, Alabama, Intergraph can be reached at 800-763-0242 or www.intergraph.com/ics.

— *see also* Hewlett-Packard Co.

ISO

The International Organization for Standardization was established in 1947 and is headquartered in Geneva, Switzerland. The ISO is a nongovernmental, worldwide federation of national standards bodies from some 130 countries. You can find more information at www.iso.ch/welcome.html.

— *see also* ANSI

IRIX

This is Silicon Graphics' version of the UNIX operating system.

isometric

This is a 3D viewing technique that eliminates all realistic distortion. No vanishing points are used; all lines along a given axis are rendered parallel, yielding a clear technical illustration often used in CAD.

JPEG

The Joint Photographic Experts Group (JPEG) is a 24-bit lossy compression format. Its varied compression ratios can be balanced against image quality. MPEG is the JPEG variant format used for moving digital video image sequences. You can find more information at www.jpeg.org.

— *see also* GIF

kilobyte

A kilobyte is exactly 1,024 bytes.

LED

Light-emitting diodes (LED) are those little blinky lights on the front panels of computer equipment. First developed in 1968, they were much more prevalent in the 1970s than they are now (you can see them in old movies such as *War Games*). They are supposed to be a visual signal of some important internal processes going on, but mostly they just look cool.

Linux

Linux is a popular alternative operating system for personal computers. It is fast, stable, open-sourced, and best of all, free. It was developed by Linus Torvalds and was released publicly on November 5, 1991. You can find more information at www.linux.com.

macro

A macro is a simple keystroke assignment that replaces a more complex command string. It is used to reduce the time required to execute lengthy and repetitive tasks.

megabyte

A megabyte is 1,048,576 bytes.

menu

A menu is the part of the graphical user interface (GUI) that contains buttons for selecting and manipulating portions of the software program. The first concept of a graphical menu was proposed and implemented by scientists at XEROX PARC in 1975. The idea caught the eye of Steve Jobs, who implemented the concept into the first Mac computer system.

memory

Memory is a more general term for how much RAM is in your computer. The amount of memory limits the amount of information the CPU can store and process at one time. (Memory generally is measured in megabytes.)

MIPS

MPIS stands for "millions of instructions per second." It is a frequent standard reference for a processor's speed of calculation.

MPEG ▶ see JPEG

National Computer Graphics Association (NCGA)

Formed in 1979, this association no longer is in existence. It used to hold CG conferences much like SIGGRAPH.

NFS

The network file system (NFS) is the de facto industry standard in network connection schemes used today. It originally was developed by Sun Microsystems.

NG

NG stands for "No Good". It often is used as a descriptive comment in effects work.

nonlinear editing

Nonlinear editing originally was conceived by George Lucas and was realized in the EditDroid system developed at his company Lucasfilm Ltd. in 1980. Nonlinear editing describes the process of working in a free and random order of edits rather than linearly as in traditional film editing.

Many different systems are available today such as Avid's Film Composer and Symphony (NT/Mac), Discreet Logic's smoke* for SGI's Octane and edit* 4.0 for NT, Sony's ES-3 EditStation(NT), Fast Multimedia's 601 (NT), in:sync corporation's Speed Razor 4.5, DPS's Perception RT3DX, Media 100 Inc.'s Finish(NT) and Media 100(Mac) products, Quantel's EditBox Platinum, the Sphere v2 from Scitex, and TimeGate by JVC.

NORSIGD

NORSIGD is the Norwegian Association for Computer Graphics. Since 1974, it has developed the General Purpose Graphics System (GPGS), a scene-description language similar to PHIGS.

PCM

Pulse Code Modulation (PCM) is the de facto A to D standard method of converting an analog signal into its digital equivalent.

— *see also*   quantize

petabyte

A petabyte is exactly 1,125,899,906,842,624 bytes. It is the next step beyond gigabyte and terabyte.

PGML

Precision Graphics Markup Language (PGML) is the old name for the new Scalable Vector Graphics (SVG), a language for describing two-dimensional graphics. You can see the official W3 spec at www.w3.org/TR/WD-SVG.

pixel

The term "pixel" stands for picture element. Pixels are the discrete, rectangular, colored dots that make up a computer-generated image. TV images have about 720×486 or 349,920 pixels. Film images can have more than 6 million pixels in every frame.

plug-ins

Plug-ins are third-party specialized minisoftware applications that "plug into" and enhance the capabilities of larger turnkey products. Most large software vendors have formal programs in place for maintaining this partnership with other companies. Some of these include Alias|Wavefront's Conductors Program, the Softimage Software Development Kit (SDK), and Avid Video Extension (AVX). Products such as Kinetix's 3D Studio Max and Adobe After Effects are heavily reliant on a large suite of these enhanced applets. Companies leading the way in creating these specialized plug-ins include The Foundry and 5D, both based in London, and Arete Image Software of Los Angeles, California. Digimation, Kinetex's preferred plug-in author, can be found at www.digimation.com.

prompt

A prompt is the symbol at the beginning (far left) of a line in an operating system. It denotes where your typed text will appear.

pull-down

An example is the 3:2 pull-down technique used to convert 24fps to 30fps. Because film is shot at 24fps and NTSC television uses 30 fps, you must interpolate the 24 individual frames into 30 frames. Every five frames of video will actually only contain four frames of film. Here's how it works:

Because NTSC actually is made up of 60 fields per second, during the film-to-tape transfer (called "telecine") the film frames are combined in alternating combinations of these 60 video fields. The first frame of the film is transferred to two fields of video, the next film frame is transferred to three fields, the next to two, the next to three, and so on.

quantize

This is the same thing as sampling. To quantize is to convert an analog signal to a digital one.

QWERTY

This is the current standard keyboard configuration named for the first six letters in the upper left corner. It was purposefully designed to be less efficient in layout to slow down fast typists and prevent the jamming of old manual typewriters.

Radius

Radius sold its line of monitors to Miro Displays and then changed its corporate name to Digital Origin in early 1999. Now it is concentrating on its digital video-editing software line. Located in Mountain View, California, Radius can be reached at 800-572-3487 or www.digitalorigin.com.

RAM

RAM stands for random access memory.
— *see also*   DRAM

right-hand rule

Right-hand rule is a convention of 3D coordinate systems in both mathematics and computer graphics. All positive world-space rotations are clockwise when viewing the origin from a positive axis.

It is so named because you can visualize the three axes by holding your right hand with thumb (Y) up, pointer finger (Z) extended forward, and middle finger (X) at a right angle pointing left. Pretty cool, huh?

RISC

Reduced Instruction Set Computing (RISC) is an alternative CPU technology developed in the mid 1980s to oppose the conventional CISC chips. Macs use RISC; most PCs (such as Intel) use CISC. Of course, the new EPIC chip due out from Intel sometime after 2000 could make them both obsolete.

SCSI

SCSI stands for small computer system interface. It is a standard port or plug type used to interface peripherals with a computer.

SIGGRAPH

Started as an ACM special-interest committee in 1967 by Sam Matsa and Andy vanDam, the Special Interest Group GRAPHics of the ACM was formed in 1969 but did not hold its first conference until 1974 (in Boulder, Colorado with 600 attendees). Currently, every other year Boulder alternates with Los Angeles, and the conference averages about 40,000 attendees. It is the one conference not to miss if you at all are interested in CG. Events center around courses and paper/panel sessions, an art show, the electronic theater and animation screening room, plus interactive venues and educational "SIGKids" events. Of course, the real reason veterans go is for the free T-shirts and the late-night parties.

SMPTE

The Society of Motion Picture and Television Engineers (SMPTE) is the organization responsible for the standards of television broadcast signals. You can find more information at www.smpte.org.

Solaris

Solaris is the computer graphics hardware system from Sun Microsystems that hopes to compete head-on with industry leader SGI. Solaris offers comparable performance at a lower cost than the equivalent SGI machine.

storyboard

A storyboard is a series of images, usually hand drawn in black and white, created to visualize a script. The storyboard shows camera action, framing, and the separate elements that need to go into the shot: actors, sets or locations, and visual effects.

Scalable Vector Graphics (SVG)

SVG is the newly proposed World Wide Web vector graphics standard from Adobe. It previously was called Precision Graphics Markup Language (PGML).

SVGA

Super Video Graphics Array, introduced in 1988, is a general term used to collectively define many graphics "standards" with a greater resolution than that of VGA.

S-Video

S-Video is video signal technology that keeps the luminance (Y) signal separate from the color (C) information. This results in a better image than with standard VHS signals.

TARGA

TARGA is a contraction of Truevision Raster Graphics Adapter. It is a raster image file format developed by Truevision for both Windows NT and Dec Alpha platforms. Truevision can be reached at 800-522-8783 or www.truevision.com.

TGA

The TARGA image file format that supports 32-bit color: 24 bits for millions of color, and the last 8 bits of storage of masks.

— *see also* TARGA

terabyte

A terabyte is 1,099,511,627,776 bytes.

TIFF

The Tag Image File Format (TIFF) was developed by Microsoft and Aldus. TIFF uses the lossless compression format.

toggle

To toggle is to switch a setting one way or the other, as in on or off, up or down.

Truevision Inc.

Truevision makes video graphics cards such as the TARGA. You can find more information at www.truevision.com. The company can be reached at 800-522-8783 and is located in Santa Clara, California.

tweaking

To tweak is to make minute changes, as in tweaking a composite to get it just a little bit better. Excessive tweaking usually is the privilege of the supervisor and the bane of the producer.

UNIX

UNIX was written by Bill Joy and Sam Lefler at Berkeley and was trademarked by AT&T/Bell Laboratories. It si the operating system of many CG workstations including the SGI. Different flavors of UNIX are very popular, including AIX, IRIX, Linux, XENIX, and others.

VAR

A value-added reseller is a company (such as Kaleidoscope in Ohio or RFX in LA) that sells hardware and software along with "added value" such as installation and support options.

virtual reality

Virtual reality (VR) was all the rage in the early 1990s, typified by film's glamorization of the concept as in *Lawnmower Man*. Without writing a book on just this one topic, VR is basically a broad term for any immersive digital environment, typically experienced wearing a helmet and gloves. The helmet contains small image monitors in front of the wearer's eyes to view the virtual environment, and the gloves serve to interact with objects in that environment. All the equipment is calibrated to the person's movements, so that looking up will look "up" in the CG world viewed through the helmet. The effect can be very convincing even with relatively simple environments. VR originally was championed (and still is) by the military and aircraft-simulator industries to dramatically reduce costs.

VGA

Video graphics array (VGA) is the IBM PC graphics card format standard that replaced EGA in 1987. It has a pixel resolution of 640×480 with 16 colors. It later was used as a medium-resolution graphics standard in 1980s era PCs. It is a term for 4-bit (Standard VGA) or 8-bit (256) color systems.

— *see also* CGA, TGA

VR ▶ see virtual reality

workstation

Workstation is a generic term for a desktop personal computer that generally has professional-quality power, more so than a standard home PC. An SGI O2 is just one example.

worldspace coordinate system

This is the three-dimensional virtual work space defined in a CG environment. An object, with its own local coordinate system for rotations and scaling, is translated around in space relative to some point, the worldspace origin. Units are arbitrarily defined by the user as feet, millimeters, or another linear measure.

WWW

World Wide Web (WWW) is a subset of the larger Internet.

Developed by Tim Berners-Lee in 1990, the initial World Wide Web program was first developed on the NeXT in November of 1989. The linemode browser was released to a limited set of users of one Vax in March 1991 and to central CERN machines in May 1991. That summer, the world at large was given access to the new World Wide Web of data. You can find the official history at www.w3.org/History.html.

Even earlier than this, in the period from 1986–89 (well before the initial CERN proposal), Andy Hunter was a research assistant at the University of Bath (England) and was working on Picture Archive Retrieval. He demonstrated a fully operational system with the following features:

- The user sees a mouse-driven graphical front end.

- The user clicks to retrieve pictures linked from icons.

- Optional text annotation also is retrievable.

- Remote documents can be anywhere on the network.

- The user does not need to know where the actual documents are located.

- Free-form linking allows webs to be developed.

WYSIWYG

Pronounced "wizzy wig," this is a contraction of "What You See Is What You Get." Bravo, the first WYSIWYG word processor, was developed by a XEROX PARC team led by Charles Simonyi in the early 1970s.

XENIX

This is Microsoft's version of the UNIX operating system.

XGA

Extended graphics array (XGA) graphics cards are capable of 1024×768 resolution (8-bit color). XGA-2 improved on XGA by increasing the color depth to 16 bits at 1024×768 resolution.

Computer Graphics
Time Line

This chronological history of computer graphics innovations is by far the most comprehensive and accurate listing ever assembled. It is not, however, complete by any definition. What I have attempted to do is bring together important persons, projects, and events to illustrate the context of a very wide-ranging field.

You will notice many facts and "firsts" listed here, and many other milestones are placed in their true context historically. Some entries are more obscure than others, but all are an important part of how and why computer graphics is what it is today.

THE HISTORY OF COMPUTER GRAPHICS

Computer graphics (CG) software was first created as a visualization tool for scientists and engineers in government and corporate research centers such as Bell Labs and Boeing in the 1950s. From the very beginning, artists also embraced the new technology as a way to visualize images and motion. Later, tools were developed in the 1960s and '70s at universities such as Ohio State University, MIT, the University of Utah, Cornell, the University of North Carolina-Chapel Hill, and the New York Institute of Technology.

The early breakthroughs that took place in academic centers continued at various research centers. They broke into broadcast video graphics and then major motion pictures in the late 1970s and early 1980s.

Computer graphics research continues today around the world, now joined by the development departments of entertainment and production companies. Companies such as Blue Sky, Pacific Data Images, Rhythm & Hues, and George Lucas's Industrial Light & Magic are constantly redefining the cutting edge of computer graphics technology to present the world with a new synthetic digital reality.

In the beginning…

1940s

The very first computer-assisted graphics were created in many different, unrelated fields around the world. A very blurred line is crossed somewhere between mechanical and analog computer-assisted graphics and the first directly digital computer-generated graphics that one would associate with today as being true "CG."

The Very First Radiosity Image

While at MIT in the 1940s, Professors Parry Moon and Domina Eberle Spencer were using their field of applied mathematics to calculate highly accurate global lighting models that they called "interflection reflection." The illumination algorithms were based on those by H.H. Higbie, published in his 1934 book *Lighting Calculations*.

Synthetic color images from the book Lighting Design by Moon and Spencer. Images used with permission from Domina Spencer. The images on the left have low reflectances while the images on the right show high reflectances.

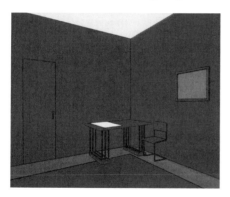

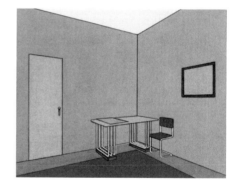

Lacking any display or output mechanism, the image itself was created by painstakingly selecting Munsel paper samples that matched the output data of their mathematical model. (Munsel is a calibrated color system similar to Pantone.) The paper was cut out and ironed together by hand to create the image, which is shown here in print for the first time in more than 50 years.

The images were first presented at the 1946 National Technical Conference of the Illuminating Engineering Society of North America, and they were published two years later (in color) in the book *Lighting Design* by Moon and Spencer (Cambridge, Massachusetts: Addison-Wesley, 1948). The book was used for many years to teach lighting theory at MIT in the architecture curriculum. Dr. Spencer went on to teach at Tufts, Brown, Rhode Island School of Design, and the University of Connecticut where she remains active today.

1950s

John Whitney Sr. devised his own computer-assisted mechanisms to create some of his graphics artwork and short films. One of his sons, John Jr., worked with and learned from his father from childhood through high school.

Pioneering artists Stan VanderBeck, Michael Noll, and others at Bell Labs in New Jersey created computer-assisted graphics using analog computer devices and plotter output. Later, in the mid-1960s, digital computers and film recorders would be used there to produce some of the earliest CG animated films.

Bill Fetter experimented with early vector CAD graphics at Boeing (Seattle) in the late 1950s, using an IBM 7094 computer with punch card input and a Gerber plotter.

1950

- Artist Ben Laposky used analog computers to help him create oscilloscope artwork.

1951

- A vectorscope-type graphics display was used with the Whirlwind computer at MIT. A device similar to a light pen allowed direct input to the screen.

- The General Motors Research Laboratory began studying the role of computer-aided graphical design applications. (This later would result in the development of the DAC-1 in 1959.)

1955

- The SAGE system at MIT's Lincoln Lab used the first true light pen as an input device. It was designed by Bert Sutherland.

1956

- Lawrence Livermore National Labs connected a graphics display to an IBM 704 mainframe computer. It used a film recorder for color images.

- Bertram Herzog at the University of Michigan Computing Center used analog computers to generate CRT graphics studies of military vehicle behavior.

1957

- The first image-processed photo was created at the National Bureau of Standards by Russel Kirsch.

- The IBM 740-780 (paired with a separate IBM 704 computer system) generated a sequence of points on a CRT to represent lines or shapes. Time-lapse film photography was then used to capture the images as they were drawn on the screen.

- The Defense Department's Advanced Research Project Agency (ARPA) was founded.

1958

- Steven Coons, Ivan Sutherland, and Timothy Johnson began working at MIT Lincoln Labs with the TX-2 computer system to manipulate drawn pictures. (This was funded in part by the Air Force.) Ivan Sutherland later began refining the work into his famous Sketchpad system while he was a student at MIT. DEC later commercialized the TX-2 as the PDP-6.

1959

- The first commercial film recorder—General Dynamics' Stromberg Carlson 4020—was developed (produced in San Diego, California).

- DAC-1 (Design Augmented by Computers) was the first computer-aided drawing system, created by Don Hart and Ed Jacks at General Motors Research Laboratory and IBM (although not unveiled until the Fall Joint Computer Conference in Detroit in 1964). The system originally was based on an IBM 7090 computer (later upgraded to a 7094 in 1963), augmented with extra disc space and a specially designed IBM 7969 "image-processing system." Input was with punch cards, but it also was capable of scanning in drawings. The final data could be output to either 35mm film (by way of a CRT), a hard copy plotter, or used to drive computer-controlled machining devices.

Biography: John Whitney Sr. (1917-1995)

A Los Angeles native, Whitney was a pioneer in many forms of experimental and abstract art before turning to computers to aid in his graphics creations. He attended Pomona College in California in the 1940s and was the first in a wave of artists to begin new techniques of computer-assisted graphics.

The integration of analog computer-controlled cameras and artwork at first was more a pioneering use of motion control than of computer graphics. In fact, the devices these early artists used were not even thought of as computers, being more akin to analog music synthesizers. From his experience working in the aircraft industry during World War II, Whitney realized that components of a computerized antiaircraft controller could be used to drive his mechanisms. These synchronized mechanisms ultimately would be used to calculate abstract shapes and change them over time to create beautifully abstract forms and animation.

In the 1950s, Whitney worked in Hollywood as an animation director at UPA, most notably contributing graphics elements for the Saul Bass-designed opening credits to Hitchcock's *Vertigo*. Whitney then founded Motion Graphics Inc. in 1960 and produced animation for both television and film, devising the "slit scan" technique for his early short film *Lapis*. This technique later would be made famous when used by Con Pederson and Doug Trumbull as a portion of the famous StarGate ending sequence of Stanley Kubrick's *2001: A Space Odyssey*.

In 1966, with the help of a grant from IBM and a Fortran programmer named Jack Citron, Whitney made his first digital computer short film called *Permutations*. His next works, *Matrix 1* and *Matrix 2*, were done at Cal Tech, followed by *Matrix 3* at Triple-I in 1971. It was at this time that he met Larry Cuba, who would later be asked by Whitney to collaborate with him in 1975 on his last 16mm film project *Arabesque*, which was funded in part by an NEA grant. Both Whitney and Cuba would work briefly at Robert Abel's effects company before digital computer graphics were begun there.

Beginning in the mid-1980s, a new collaborator named Jerry Reed translated Cuba's Fortran code into Pascal for use on new personal-computer hardware that Whitney could use at home. Whitney continued to create abstract computer animation on his own with the aid of this new PC technology, which freed him from the reliance on large, company-owned mainframe machines and the need for sponsored grants. His work would be displayed in galleries on the same PC hardware on which he created it. His last commercially available collection of works, called *Moondrum*, was released on video in the late 1980s.

Today, his son Michael Whitney is serving as archiver for his father's work and recently organized a retrospective showing at UCLA.

1960s

Much of the nationwide university computer science research conducted during the 1960s was due in part to funding from the government's Advanced Research Project Agency (ARPA). At the time, ARPA took a very hands-off approach to funding. This gave researchers an unpressured environment in which to concentrate on their work without the heavy bureaucracy, paperwork, and political constraints that are more common today. Much to the benefit of researchers, Ivan Sutherland headed ARPA for a time. With good funding, little oversight, and many brilliant young minds inspiring each other, it was a unique and special time that produced the very foundation of today's computer graphics tool sets.

Computer-assisted graphics were being created more widely as a new and unique art form by people such as Charles Csuri, Ken Knowlton, and John Whitney Sr.

Many pioneering artistic films and artworks were created at Bell Labs from approximately 1962 to 1967 by artists and programmers such as E.E. Zajac, Leon D. Harmon, Ken Knowlton, A. Michael Noll, Lilian Shwartz, M.R. Schroeder, and Stan Vanderbeek. An IBM 7094 computer ran a Stromberg-Carlson 4020 film recorder, programmed in Fortran to run Ken Knowlton's BEFLIX animation system.

Herb Freeman had a school of CG development going on at NYU that included Alvy Ray Smith in his first professor's job out of Stanford in 1969. Freeman and his students already had solved the fundamental hidden-line problem. This technique of viewing only the surfaces facing the camera was a critical development.

Nicholas Negroponte taught computer-aided design (CAD) at MIT in the mid- to late 1960s and developed the URBAN5 system. A light pen allowed interaction directly on the CRT in combination with keyboard instructions. Points and symbols were added in orthographic mode with a perspective option entered after the fact to view structures three-dimensionally. An "intelligent" system study, URBAN5 was abandoned by 1968 in favor of other projects.

The Society for Information Displays was formed in the early 1960s, publishing papers dealing mostly with military applications.

At this same time, practical commercial and industrial use of computer graphics began to take hold in many areas of design and manufacturing. Throughout the decade at Boeing, William Fetter and Robert Woodruff (Computing Technology Administrator) lead many important industrial applications of vector-generated CG.

Architectural and urban-planning programs (typically written in Fortran on machines such as the IBM 1130 or 1800) were used at the firm Skidmore, Owings & Merrill in

Chicago and at the University of Texas School of Architecture. A sample workstation consisted of a Rand tablet providing input, with output to pen plotters such as the CalComp.

In the late 1960s, the Electronics Laboratory of General Electric (in Syracuse, New York) produced a prototype visualization system for NASA and the Office of Naval Research. The system produced real-time color raster graphics on a monitor as a training aid to astronauts going to the moon. This same system was used by Professor Peter Kamnitzer of the UCLA School of Architecture and Urban Planning to simulate urban development plans.

Biography: Dr. Dave C. Evans (1924-1998)

One of a very few who could be called a true founding father of computer graphics, Dave Evans is perhaps best know for being the co-founder of Evans & Sutherland Computer Corporation. Evans was at one time chairman of the computer science departments at both the University of California at Berkeley and the University of Utah. At Utah, he started the venerable doctoral program that would give birth to much of the foundation of our industry. Evans first associated with Ivan Sutherland at both Berkeley and the Pentagon's ARPA.

Evans made many contributions to a wide range of computer technologies, and a great many of his students went on to flourish in the brand new field of computer graphics, some becoming true pioneers themselves. Evans' students include Alan Kay (co-founder of Xerox PARC), Jim Clark (founder of Silicon Graphics and co-founder of Netscape Communications), John Warnock (co-founder of Adobe Systems) and Edwin Catmull (see his biography in Chapter 9, Programming and Mathematics").

Dave Evans passed away on October 3, 1998.

1960

- William Fetter of Boeing coined the term "computer graphics" for his human factors cockpit drawings. With help from Walter Bernhardt and others, Fetter input an aircraft drawing's coordinates into a database and plotted out a calculated perspective on an Illustromat 1100 plotter.

- John Whitney Sr. founded Motion Graphics, Inc. in Los Angeles.

1961–62

- Spacewar is the first popular computer graphics game written by students Steve Russell, Slug Russell, Shag Graetz, and Alan Kotok of MIT to run on the DEC PDP-1. (DEC's PDP-1 cost $120,000, and MIT's was one of only 50 ever built.) The large, round CRT display featured graphics controlled by primitive handmade joysticks. The object of the game was to maneuver away from a gravitational "sun" force at the center and to avoid the other enemy ships while trying to blast the other player with your own space torpedoes!

  The original source code (which ran on 4k of memory!) can still be found at www.media.mit.edu/groups/el/projects/spacewar/sources or ftp://ftp.digital.com/pub/DEC/sim/sources/sim_2.3d.tar.Z.

  There is also a copy of the PDP-1 manual at www.dbit.com/~greeng3/pdp1/pdp1.html.

1962

- "Sketchpad: A Man-Machine Graphical Communication System" is presented by Ivan Sutherland as his Ph.D. thesis at the M.I.T. Lincoln Laboratory. The user could input simple lines and curves by drawing directly on the screen with a light pen. The computer, a TX-2, had a whopping 320 kilobytes of memory and a 9-inch monochromatic CRT. Although Sketchpad was strictly 2D, a few years later Timothy Johnson expanded its capabilities into three dimensions as Sketchpad 3. The display CRT was divided into the now familiar four views: top, front, side, and perspective.

- J.C.R. Licklider was put in charge of the new Information Processing Techniques Office (IPTO) at the Defense Department's ARPA. The initial $14 million budget supported projects at MIT, Berkeley, and Carnegie-Mellon.

Biography: Ivan Sutherland

Born in 1938 in Hastings, Nebraska, Ivan Sutherland was truly an early founding father of computer graphics. After completing his Ph.D. at M.I.T. (where he developed Sketchpad) in 1963, Sutherland joined the army and was assigned to the NSA as an electrical engineer. One year later, he was transferred to the Defense Department's Advanced Research Projects Agency (ARPA, later DARPA) and was given responsibility for the newly established Information Processing Techniques Office. At age 26, Lt. Sutherland was given a secretary and $15 million a year and was told to "go sponsor computer research," which he gladly did for the following two years until joining the faculty at Harvard in late 1966. With student Bob Sproull, he developed the Head Mounted Display (HUD) for remote viewing, the first virtual reality display device.

In 1968, Ivan formed Evans & Sutherland with partner Dave Evans. Ivan was now a part-time tenured professor at the University of Utah, where Evans was the founding head of the Computer Science Department. Dr. Sutherland had first met Evans during a visit to U.C. Berkeley as part of his ARPA work.

Sutherland's last research in computer graphics was a paper titled "A Characterization of Ten Hidden-Surface Algorithms," by Sutherland, Sproull, and Schumacker. The paper solved many of the largest problems of the day in this critical area of rendering and display technology.

Later, as co-founder (with Carver Mead) and head of the Department of Computer Science at the California Institute of Technology from 1976–1980, Dr. Sutherland developed and promoted courses involving integrated circuit design, the seed of knowledge that helped create the Silicon Valley industry.

In the early 1980s at Carnegie Mellon University, Sutherland researched on a six-legged walking robot that was large enough to carry a driver (and was controlled by a joystick acquired by brother Bert from his contacts in the Navy as a former fighter pilot!).

In 1980, Sutherland and Sproull started the consulting firm Sutherland, Sproull & Associates. Sun bought the company in 1990, and it then became the nucleus of Sun Microsystems Laboratories.

1963

- Charles Csuri created an analog computer and used it to make transformations of a drawing. He completed a series of drawings based on the paintings of old masters such as Durer, Goya, Ingres, Klee, Mondrian, and Picasso.

- Ken Knowlton's programs BEFLIX and EXPLOR were used to create early computer films at Bell Telephone Labs.

- The first computer art competition was sponsored by *Computers and Automation* magazine.

- The Spring Joint Computer Conference had several people from MIT presenting papers about graphical display technology: Steven Coons, Ivan Sutherland, Tim Johnson, Bob Stotz, Doug Ross, and Jorge Rodriquez.

- John Lansdown pioneered the use of computers as an aid to architectural planning. He made perspective drawings on an Elliott 803 computer in 1963, modeled a building's elevators, plotted the annual fall of daylight across its site, and authored his own computer-aided design applications.

- Edgar Horwood developed a computer graphics mapping system used by the U.S. Department of Housing and Urban Development. HUD published "Using Computer Graphics in Community Renewal."

- Frieder Nake at The Computer Institute of the Stuttgart Polytechnic used the Graphomat Zuse Z 64 drawing machine to produce four-color plotter drawings.

1964

- Ivan Sutherland (a recent MIT graduate) took over at the Information Processing Techniques Office (IPTO) at ARPA. It was suggested by his predecessor J.C.R. Licklider that he take on a deputy, Bob Taylor. (The office's budget reached $30 million by 1969, when it was changed to DARPA.) Sutherland transitioned out of his office by early 1966 to go to Harvard, leaving Bob Taylor in charge. (Bob Taylor later went on to play a key role in staffing the famous Xerox PARC.)

1965

- Dr. David Evans founded the Computer Science Department at the University of Utah.

- The Ohio State University CG program was started by Charles Csuri.

- The first computer art exhibition at Technische Hochschule in Stuttgart was held in 1965.

- Bella Julesz and A. Michael Noll exhibited at the first U.S. computer art exhibition at Howard Wise Gallery in New York (April 1965).

1966

- "Odyssey" was the first consumer computer graphics game created by Ralph Baer of Sanders Associates. It later was marketed at Magnavox.

- With a grant from IBM and a Fortran programmer named Jack Citron, John Whitney Sr. made the first digital computer short film, *Permutations*. An IBM 2250 Graphic Display Console created dot patterns that were then recorded onto black and white 35mm film. The filmed images were then further enhanced with a specially designed optical printer to add secondary motion and color.

- As Associate Professor at Harvard, Ivan Sutherland and his students (Bob Sproull, Jim Clark, and others) took earlier Remote Reality vision systems of the Bell Helicopter project and turned them into what we now call virtual reality environments by replacing the camera with computer images. The first such computer environment was no more than a wireframe room with the cardinal directions—north, south, east, and west—initialed on the walls. The viewer could "enter" the room by way of the west door and turn to look out windows in the other three directions.

- Affectionately called "The Sword of Damocles" because of its ceiling-mounted gear, this first head-mounted display was the first foray into what later became known as virtual reality.

FACTOID COSTS

A typical CRT costs about $40,000. Rand input tablets are about $10,000, and CalComp plotters about $4,000.

- The International Conference on Design and Planning, "Computers in Design and Communication," was held at the University of Waterloo (in Ontario, Canada). Organized by Professors Constant and Krampen of the Design Department, the conference was brought together to enlighten and inform designers of emerging computer technologies.

QUOTE

"At the same time that geometry-based computer graphics (CG) were being invented, so was sampling theory-based computer graphics, often called image processing (IP) or imaging. In the early days, two conferences—one for each half of the discipline—would be held side by side. One of the earliest journals was called the *Journal of Computer Graphics and Image Processing*. Its editors were Herb Freeman (CG) and Azriel Rosenfeld (IP). The earliest paper that I actually have in possession on the IP side is "Processing of Tiros Cloud Cover Pictures on a Digital Computer" by Albert Arking in 1967, but I'm sure the literature is much older. It's easy for the geometry-based guys to leave all this stuff out and vice versa."
—Alvy Ray Smith

1967

- Allen Bernholtz and William Warntz of the Laboratory for Computer Graphics and Spatial Analysis at Harvard University used computer graphics to study layout and sound patterns for hospital floor plans.

- Cornell University's School of Architecture was founded by Professor Donald Greenberg.

- Charles Csuri created his famous *Hummingbird* film. The 10-minute-long, vector-interpolated 16mm animation was later purchased by the Museum of Modern Art as part of its permanent collection.

- 2D morphing techniques were started by Les Mezei at the University of Toronto.

- The MIT Center for Advanced Visual Studies was founded by Gyorgy Kepes.

- The Computer Technique Group in Tokyo, Japan, was funded at the IBM Scientific Data Center. Engineers and designers created many beautiful and varied computer graphics art works, using image processing and geometric transformations. Members included Koji Fujino, Junichiro Kakizaki, Masao Komura, Fujio Niwa, Makoto Ohtake, Haruki Tsuchiya, and Kunio Yamanaka.

- Stephen Coons was Associate Professor of Mechanical Engineering at M.I.T., where he headed the computer-aided design (CAD) group. He invented a method for patch continuity, which is precisely aligning the edges of multiple geometric patches.

1968

- Robert Mallary, professor in the Department of Art at the University of Massachusetts, developed the TRAN2 computer program for calculating three-dimensional sculpture.

- The Computer and the Arts exhibition at London Institute of Contemporary Arts (ICA) was organized by Jasia Reichardt. The first major public computer art show, "Cybernetic Serendipity" also was a book published with the same name.

- The UK's Computer Arts Society (CAS) was founded by John Lansdown at the Royal College of Art.

- The EVENT ONE computer art exhibition was held at the Royal College of Art. It was chaired and organized by John Lansdown.

- CalComp (California Computer Products) held a competition for the best "Computer Plotter Art" with scholarship and cash prizes.

- The first computer animation in the UK was the FLEX-IPEDE made by Tony Pritchett at the Open University.

- Several computer art publications were available in Europe including *Bit International* out of Zagreb and *Page* by the London Art Society, a monthly magazine that actually lasted until the mid-1980s.

- Ivan Sutherland joined the Computer Science Department at the University of Utah.

- The very first computer graphics company was formed by two of the leading researchers of the day, Drs. David C. Evans and Ivan E. Sutherland. Aptly named Evans & Sutherland, it provided a vector system comprised of custom-designed hardware and software previously available only to one-of-a-kind, multi-million dollar military sites.

■ Dicomed was founded as a manufacturer of hardware and software products to apply computer graphics technology to the field of medical radiology. The company's systems operated by scanning x-ray films, converting the information into digital data, enhancing it, and redisplaying the processed image (see the Web site at www.dicomed.com). Still in business 30 years later, Dicomed provides professional high-resolution digital image capturing technologies.

■ Bill Fetter contributed to the first (vector-based) computer-generated television commercial in 1968 while at Boeing.

1969

■ Edward Zajec began a long career in fine art aided by the computer, creating plotter output works using an IBM 60/20 at Carlton Collage in Minnesota. He later spent 10 years as an artist-in-residence at the University of Triese in Italy. He returned to the United States in 1980 to reinvigorate Syracuse University's CG program, which had begun in the early 1970s. You can find more information at http://web.syr.edu/~ezajec/ez-plain.html.

COINCIDENCE!

It should be noted that Edward Zajec (with an "e") is not the same person as the Edward Zajac (with an "a") who worked at Bell Labs. Two early pioneering CG artists, two very closely spelled names!

■ LDS-1 (Line Drawing System) was the first commercial CAD wireframe graphics system released by E&S. It incorporated hardware design from Garry Watkins and design input by Chuck Seitz (University of Utah faculty 1970–73), Bob Shumaker, and others.

LDS-1 FACTOID

A local play-on-words for the LDS-1 was based on the fact that the Mormon church is very prominent in Utah and is more commonly known by the contraction of the Church's full name, "Latter Day Saints" (LDS).

■ John Warnock (University of Utah Ph.D. 1969) developed the Warnock recursive subdivision algorithm for hidden surface elimination.

■ Alan Kay (University of Utah Ph.D. 1969) first developed the notion of a graphical user interface with the Alto project at Xerox PARC (Palo Alto, California). This directly influenced the design of Macintosh computers.

■ Computer artist Lloyd Sumner created Christmas cards under the company name Computer Creations.

- Bell Labs developed the first framebuffer for storing and displaying 3-bit images.

- Gary Demos first became acquainted with computer-assisted graphics thanks to John Whitney Sr., who was teaching at Cal Tech in California. An IBM 2250 ran a custom operating system; images were photographed in Ektachrome and printed on Kodachrome.

1970s

Widespread commercial use of this early technology did not begin until the 1970s when early pioneers saw the potential in the broadcast video market for the new creative tools. Companies such as Image West (LA), Dolphin Productions (New York), and Computer Image Corp (Denver) used these real-time, computer-assisted video graphics machines to introduce new imagery to both broadcast clients and viewers at home.

Relatively affordable commercial random access framebuffers became available in the mid- to late 1970s, opening up the market for CG production. The input for these earliest machines often was banks of patch wires, paper tape, or punch cards—very different from today's mouse and graphics interfaces.

These first million-dollar commercial machines were mostly capable of only limited-video-resolution, raster-based graphics. Although their output was limited in most cases to video-taping or filming monitor screens, their imagery introduced the public at large to the new art form. By the end of the decade, affordable raster technology outpaced the earlier vector graphics mainstay.

Pioneering work was done by Jim Blinn at the Jet Propulsion Laboratory (JPL) in Pasadena, California (started in 1975 by Bob Holzman). David Em (who would work with Alvy Ray Smith at Xerox PARC on Dick Shoup's Superpaint system in about 1974) also later joined Jim at JPL to create some of the early serious computer art in raster form.

FACTOID

Artist and author Jasia Reichardt estimated in 1970 that there are perhaps "1,000 people in the world working with computer graphics" who are not involved in pure research or mechanical design (in other words, CG artists).

1971

- Gary Demos visited NASA AMES and Evans & Sutherland while researching a documentary film about computers for Dimension Films in Los Angeles. It is there that he first met Ivan Sutherland and expressed his ambitious desire to create complex and realistic high-resolution CG images for films. (Gary was only about 21 years old at the time.) Because most of the hardware and software technology that would make this possible did not yet exist, Gary joined E&S in hopes of creating these missing pieces. John Warnock ran the San Jose E&S office before going to NYIT, and Ivan himself was working on his own hidden-surface solutions at the time. Gary helped develop a high-precision data table (table, not tablet, because it was 4 feet by 5 feet) that was accurate to 1/100 of an inch for digitizing images. The table used two pens to define two simultaneous points in 3D space. Programming was done in Assembly code on a PDP-11 with a Picture System 1 for vector display.

- Both Henry Gouroug and Bui Toi Phong worked on shading at E&S. Needless to say, that area was well covered. Gary and the E&S team next tackled the challenge of building the first-ever random access framebuffer. They began with the first 8 DRAM chips every produced, which came from a company in Texas called Mostek.

1972

- PONG was developed by Nolan Bushnell (who later founded Atari).

- The first feature film appearance of *CG: West World* occurred in 1972, a "block pix" scene done at Information International Inc. (III, a.k.a "Triple I"). Led by John Whitney Jr., digitally processed film was used to portray a pixelated android point of view.

1973

- ACM/SIGGRAPH was formed.

- "Interact" at the Edinburgh Festival, a seminal event in establishing the use of computers for the creation of art works, was organized by John Lansdown.

- Edwin Catmull (Ph.D., University of Utah, 1974) developed both the z-buffer algorithm and the concept of texture mapping in 1973–74. (Texture mapping techniques were later refined by Catmull, Alvy Ray Smith, Tom Duff, Lance Williams, and Paul Heckbert at NYIT.)

- The first physical structure designed entirely with computer-aided geometric modeling software was a large Easter egg that is still standing in Vegreville, Alberta, Canada, "The Easter Egg Capitol of the World." The egg was designed by Ronald Resch, a pioneer in the field of computer art and a member of the Computer Science Faculty at the University of Utah from 1970–1979. The programmer that worked with Resch was Robert McDermott (who got his Ph.D. from the work at the University of Utah).

- Frank Crow (Ph.D., University of Utah, 1975) developed anti-aliasing methods for edge smoothing.

1974

- The first ACM/SIGGRAPH conference was held in Boulder, Colorado. There were 600 attendees.

- The New York Institute of Technology Computer Graphics Laboratory (CGL) was founded in 1974. Dr. Alexander Schure hired recent Utah graduate Edwin Catmull to head the new CGL group. (See the Chapter 8, "Historically Significant Companies," for a good history of the NYIT CGL.)

- Phong Bui-Toung developed the Phong shading method at Utah.

- Dr. Ivan Sutherland and associate Glen Flex started a Hollywood company called Picture Design Group with John Whitney Jr. and Gary Demos. One of the first tests they did was for a feature film proposed by Walter Films and Carl Sagan called *Cosmos*. Using an E&S Picture System at UC San Diego, Demos began tests on one-million-star galaxy simulations.

They did other work for educational films and the Museum of Science and Industry, but after about 9 months, Ivan wanted to give up production in favor of going back to academia. Demos and Whitney then went to Triple-I.

1975

- ACM/SIGGRAPH was held in Bowling Green, Ohio, with 300 attendees.

- *Hunger* by Peter Foldes is the "first fully animated figurative film every made using computer techniques" (otherwise known as computer interpolation or in-betweening). Like Charles Csuri's earlier work, these were some of the first 2D geometric interpolation or morphing techniques. Foldes also created the film *Metadata*.

- The venerable icon of early computer graphics, the famous Utah teapot, is designed by Martin Newell at the University of Utah.

QUOTE

"The original design system used for the teapot was very rudimentary and involved squared paper, a ruler, and a Tektronix 4012 (Connected to a PDP-10). Having sketched the key outlines of the teapot from the real one, I guesstimated appropriate locations for control points and wrote down the coordinates. The "design system" had enough smarts to create an approximate revolute from a profile, but beyond that it was little more than a viewer of wireframe representations to verify the design. Individual control points could be moved via a command language, either individually or in groups. For the teapot, no changes were made from the originally estimated control points. Had I known how widely used the model was going to be, I would have taken more trouble to model the real teapot more precisely, but I liked what I got from the process, so I went with it."

—Martin Newell, May 1999

- The TWEEN animation system was developed by Dr. Edwin Catmull at NYIT. Originally written in Assembly language (Ed hated Fortran), TWEEN was rewritten completely in C to run on UNIX about a year later. He then actually renamed the program MO-TRUCK for "motion trucking-thru-the-frames," but no one would use the new name... so TWEEN it stayed.

- After 20 years of research, Dr. Benoit Mandelbrot published his seminal paper "A Theory of Fractal Sets." The study of fractal geometry was revealed to the popular press. (The theory had been around before and contributed to by noteworthy mathematicians such as Julia, Poincare, and Falconer. Mandelbrot gave it a name and codified it.)

- John Whitney Jr. and Gary Demos formed the Motion Picture Project Group at Triple-I.

1976

- ACM/SIGGRAPH was held in Philadelphia, Pennsylvania, with 300 attendees and the first exhibition (with 10 exhibitors!).

- Gary Demos, John Whitey Jr., and a team at Triple-I created the first feature film appearance of 3D CG—a 3D polygonal representation of a hand and of actor Peter Fonda's head (rendered and filmed out at 2000×2560 pixel resolution). The film also featured the first ever digital composite, a sequence of samurai warriors materializing in a chamber room.

- Warner Communications bought Atari from Nolan Bushnell for $28 million.

- Nelson Max's brilliant and beautiful *Turning a Sphere Inside Out* film was shown at SIGGRAPH. Nelson first created a stop-motion clay animation test in 1970 when no modeling or rendering CG tools yet existed for his specific goal. Initial CG tests proved less than fruitful, both at the University of Cambridge (in summer 1971)

Images of a sphere turning inside-out. Provided courtesy of Nelson Max.

and at Carnegie Mellon (in 1972). Eventually, the modeling and rendering were completed and realized on a PDP-10 front-ended Case Shaded Graphics System designed by E&S at the Case Western Reserve University in 1975–76.

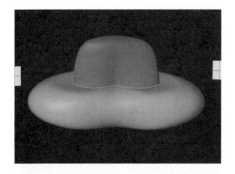

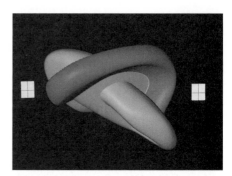

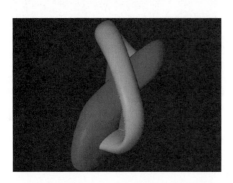

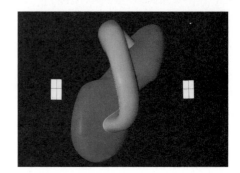

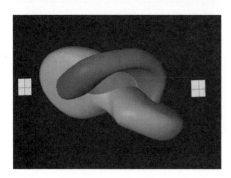

- Jim Blinn developed environment (reflection) mapping while he was a graduate student at the University of Utah. The paper was co-authored with his professor Martin Newell and was published in the Communications of the ACM in 1976.

1977

- ACM/SIGGRAPH was held in San Jose, California, with 750 attendees and 38 exhibitors.

- Nelson Max joined Lawrence Livermore National Laboratories and used CG to illustrate basic biologic research—the first "scientific visualizations."

 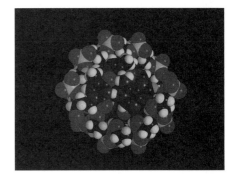

Two images of molecules. Provided courtesy of Nelson Max.

- Star Wars was released by 20th Century Fox.

Star Wars

The Death Star simulation was designed and created by pioneering algorithmic artist Larry Cuba. George Lucas was impressed both by Cuba's early abstract CG film *First Fig* (1974) and by the fact that he had worked with another pioneer of motion control and computer graphics—John Whitney Sr. Ben Burt, the film's sound designer, had been assigned the task of getting the word out around town and tracking down bids for the work.

Cuba designed storyboards from the description of the scene in the script and worked on the job at the University of Illinois—Chicago. A 2D drawing program that Cuba designed with the GRASS language was modified to allow input of a third Z-axis for every point entered on the digitizing tablet, creating the 3D representation of the Death Star surface.

Using the Vector General-based GRASS graphics system designed by Tom DeFanti, Larry worked night and day for 12 weeks to produce 2 minutes of film, of which 40 seconds appeared in the final film sequence.

Quote

"While the GRASS system was capable of real-time animation, the real-time capability came from the Vector General's hardware implementation of basic transformations like translation, rotation, and scaling as well as the projection transformation that turns a 3D object into a 2D drawing. But it was only capable of a parallel projection (that is, no "true perspective"). Since I needed perspective for this project, I was back to using software for the projection and, therefore, was *not* able to animate the scene in real time. I was getting a frame rate of about two minutes of computation per frame, and so the whole shot took about 12 hours."

—Larry Cuba

A rented Mitchell camera filmed the imagery off the computer monitor. The finished footage originally was intended to be shot as a rear-projected element live on stage with the actors in London, but greatly reduced production deadlines made that impossible. Here's the full story as told by Larry Cuba himself:

Quote

"Around two months from my deadline, I was sent a production schedule, and I noticed that the live-action shooting of the shot that my work was to be used in was scheduled a month earlier than the delivery date specified on my contract. So instead of having two months left to finish the shot, I had only one.

Larry Cuba in the lav at the University of Illinois. Image provided courtesy of Larry Cuba.

When I mentioned this to the Assistant Producer, he informed me that it was even worse than that because they required the film to be delivered four weeks earlier than shooting in order to have time to make backup copies (should any-thing happen to the footage during the live-action filming). So appar-ently, since I couldn't send out the shot immediately, we were already dead in the water.

The 'solution' he came back to me with was that they would rearrange the schedule and place that scene (the briefing room scene) on the last day that they had the large sound stage. (They were shooting in England. All communication went from me in Chicago, to the Assistant Producer in LA, to Producer Gary Kurtz in London, then to Lucas, and then the reverse trip back.) This would give me four more weeks to produce the shot (rather than the eight that I thought I had).

So, with my schedule cut in half, I stepped up production. I was getting three hours of sleep a night by sleeping on the sofa in the (over air-conditioned) lab with the computers. Computers generate a lot of heat so computer rooms need to be kept cool or the computers will fail to work.

Working in this way, I was able to finish building the computer model of the Death Star and pro-gram the fly-through sequence just in time for it to be filmed and sent off. But once I started the film run (which had to run continuously for 12 hours), the computer would crash about 30 min-utes into it. Up until this point, the occasional crash was not a problem—reboot and keep going. But now this was a disaster. I couldn't put the shot together filming in 30-minute bursts. (I could if I rewrote the program, but there was no time for that now). We tried everything we could think of to get the system to stop crashing. We even took the hard disk apart and cleaned it, but 30 min-utes after every start, the system crashed.

It was getting late on Saturday night, and I had to put the exposed film in the mail on Monday. By 3 a.m. (my bedtime), I decided that it was useless. On Monday morning, instead of sending out the film, I would have to call Los Angeles and tell them that I had failed to deliver and that our only recourse at this point was to shoot the scene blue screen and optically print my animation in later.

Since there was no more hope, I figured I would at least be more comfortable, so before I went to sleep, I turned off the air conditioning so I wouldn't freeze, and I started the shot from the beginning one more time. (What the heck?) This time it ran continuously throughout the night and Sunday morning, completing the shot just in time."

—Larry Cuba

Traditional hand animation was done for the final four seconds of the bomb entering the Death Star exhaust port and exploding. This was completed by John Wash at Image West.

Other computer-generated and video-display images were created for *Star Wars* by several different people. John Wash, Jay Teitzell, and Dan O'Bannon at Image West created many electronic video graphics effects for the targeting computers and background tactical displays. Larry Cuba also completed several graphics seen in the Death Star guard room when R2D2 and C3PO first tap into the central computer.

SIGGRAPH FACTOID

The 1977 SIGGRAPH convention's electronic film show prematurely ended with Larry Cuba's work. Halfway through his film *First Fig*, all the power went out in the hotel bringing it and the show to an abrupt ending.

1978

- ACM/SIGGRAPH was held in Atlanta, Georgia, with about 1,500 attendees and 44 exhibitors.

- Jim Blinn produced the first in his series of animations for The Mechanical Universe while at JPL.

- Jim Blinn also published his technique of bump mapping, which was completed as part of his graduate thesis at the University of Utah the previous year. His demonstration of the new shading code was shown as a 128×128-resolution, 16-frame loop of a bumpy sphere. His initial method of calculating both the angle and amount of perturbation was later refined and simplified as an altitude description, allowing for incremental grayscale values to define intermediate angles of surface normals.

1979

- ACM/SIGGRAPH was held in Chicago, Illinois, with about 3,000 attendees and 79 exhibitors.

- *The Black Hole* (Disney) was an opening grid/black hole simulation. It was created by John Hughes (Rhythm & Hues), et al. at Robert Abel & Associates.

- Edwin Catmull left NYIT to head the Lucasfilm Computer Division. He soon was joined by Alvy Ray Smith, David Di Francesco, Tom Duff, and Ralph Guggenheim. Lucas' specific directions, according to Alvy's recollections, were to build three pieces of equipment to modernize the technology of film-making:

  - A digital film printer (part of which would later be known as the Pixar Image Computer)

  - A digital audio synthesizer

  - A digitally controlled video editor

  For more details about ILM, see Chapter 8, "Historically Significant Companies."

- Jim Clark designed his "geometry engine," the basis for his future company Silicon Graphics.

- For the movie *Alien*, Alan Sutcliffe at Systems Simulation Ltd. of London created a computer monitor sequence showing a 3D terrain fly-over, rendering computer-generated mountains as wireframe images with hidden-line removal.

- Meteor had vector graphics created by Triple-I.

- Julien Gomez develops TWIXT at Ohio State. The software is used at Cranston Csuri Productions.

- Ray tracing was developed at Bell Labs & Cornell University. Turner Whitted published a paper for SIGGRAPH 1979 describing ray tracing techniques.

QUOTE

"In 1979, the most significant artistic event of my career occurred: Ed Emshwiller and I created the animated art video *Sunstone*. It is primarily his piece, but we worked very closely on this piece, and I am still extremely proud of it. It is in several museum collections of the world including MOMA. Lance Williams and Garland Stern also helped some on it."
—Alvy Ray Smith

1980s

The first digital computers used in CG were those in the Digital Equipment Corporation (DEC) line including the early PDP-1, PDP10, and PDP-11 of the last decade. Because of their cost and high maintenance, however, these were restricted to large-budget university and major production settings. Typical of this work was Jim Blinn at JPL creating the *Voyager* flyby films, the *Cosmos* Series for Carl Sagan, and the *Mechanical Universe* project—all from about 1979 to 1983.

The "workstation," as we know it today, was introduced in the early 1980s by companies such as Apple Computer and Silicon Graphics Inc.

The consumer market for personal computer graphics began with the Macintosh personal computer and its MacDraw and MacPaint software in 1984. The Xerox Alto did, of course, predate the Mac by a decade, but it did not reach personal use in any numbers. Its initial market was government and university settings.

Commercial CG production was boosted by a new generation of digital machines including the early Silicon Graphics workstations such as the IRIS 3130 in 1989. At the same time, third-party companies began providing specialized software to run on these new graphics platforms. For 2D graphic design and image processing, Photoshop was introduced for the Mac in January 1990. Early 3D animation software for the higher-end market included software from Wavefront (1987) and Alias (1984).

The mid-1980s through the early 1990s was a time of tremendous advances in technology and stunning creative breakthroughs. Companies such as Robert Abel and Associates, Triple-I, MAGI/Synthavision, Omnibus, and Digital Productions created such memorable images as Sexy Robot (Abel), Chromosaurs (PDI), and the Benson & Hedges (Digital Productions) commercials.

The U.S. National Science Foundation began to provide supercomputer access to university research programs including the University of Illinois Supercomputing Center.

1980

- ACM/SIGGRAPH was held in Seattle, Washington, with about 7,500 attendees and 80 exhibitors.

- Triple-I produced seven minutes of computer graphics for the film *Looker* under the direction of Richard Taylor, et al. Polygonal models of a complete human body were created.

- Loren Carpenter's fractal extravaganza *Vol Libre* was presented at SIGGRAPH 80.

- Loren Carpenter at Lucasfilm's Games Group & Atari created the popular game Rescue From Fractalus!

- Chris Briscoe and Paul Brown co-founded Digital Pictures, the UK's first specialist computer animation company.

1981

- ACM/SIGGRAPH was held in Dallas, Texas, with 14,000 attendees and 124 exhibitors.

- Nelson Max began making computer graphics for the IMAX film format at Lawrence Livermore National Labs. Steve Levine and George Matthews also had lots of contact with NYIT in the early days. Important image synthesis papers included "Vectorized Procedural Models for Natural Terrain: Waves and Islands in the Sunset." The ray tracing algorithms were computed on a Cray-1 supercomputer and were output with 8-bits pixel to a Dicomed color film recorder.

Stills of waves and islands in the sunset. Images provided courtesy of Nelson Max.

- Omnibus Video Inc. (the precursor to Omnibus Computer Graphics) was founded in Toronto, Canada.

- "Adam Powers (The Juggling Tuxedo Guy)" was part of the Information International Inc. (Triple-I) demo reel shown at SIGGRAPH in 1981.

- Nintendo introduced the Donkey Kong video game.

1982

- ACM/SIGGRAPH was held in Boston, Massachusetts, with about 17,000 attendees and 172 exhibitors.

- Tom Brigham (NYIT) introduced the first full-raster "morph" technique at the 1982 SIGGRAPH conference.

A still of "Adam Powers (The Juggling Tuxedo Guy)." Provided courtesy of Art Durinski.

- Silicon Graphics Inc. was formed by Jim Clark (Ph.D. University of Utah 1974). For more details about Silicon Graphics, see Chapter 8, "Historically Significant Companies."

- Autodesk, formed by Dan Drake and John Walker, released AutoCAD v1.0 at COMDEX.

- Mits Kaneko and the Japan Computer Graphics Lab (JCGL) produced the TV series *The Yearling*. Episode No. 2 was broadcast in April 1982 and became the world's first animated television program completely processed with a computer. (For more details about JCGL, see Chapter 8, "Historically Significant Companies.")

TRIVIA
The same database used by Triple-I for the face of Adam Powers was used for the MCP character in the end sequence of *Tron*.

- The first all-digital, computer-generated image sequence was created for a motion picture film—the *Star Trek II: Wrath of Khan* Genesis sequence. Inspired by Jim Blinn's Voyager flyby animations from JPL, the team consisted of Loren Carpenter with his amazing fractal geometry (based on the work from his *Vol Libre* film, completed while he was at Boeing), Bill Reeves with his particle system fire, Tom Porter's paint system and stars, Rob Cook and Tom Duff's rendering, and David DiFrancesco's film experience. It was conceived and directed by Alvy Ray Smith at the Lucasfilm computer division. (According to Alvy, in the end, it was Loren Carpenter's minute-long camera move that most impressed Lucas.)

- The Disney film *Tron* represented the first extensive use of 3D CGI animation in a feature film. This milestone project was pitched to Disney by Steve Listberger and originally was boarded by Bill Kroyer and Jerry Rees. Bill and Jerry came up with the title Computer Image Choreographers for their roles, which were much more than traditional Animation Directors. The model motion and choreography, along with camera blocking and motion paths, were all sketched out in exacting detail to be passed on and realized precisely by four CG production houses. To reduce confusion among the many different companies (MAGI, Robert Abel's, Triple-I, and Digital Effects), the choreography was laid out in real-world dimensions. (The light-cycle grid was one mile square with motion of the individual cycles calculated in feet per second.) Tests were checked twice a day between the various companies and Disney by modem.

TRON FACTOID

These were the largest-format pencil tests ever! The Disney art and animation team that was previsualizing the CG for *Tron* never had any way to view a traditional pencil test. The first time they got a chance to see their planned motion scenes was only after the CG was created, rendered, and output to 70mm film. Because of technical limitations at Disney, the film was actually rear-projected in the screening room.

In total, only about 15 minutes of computer-generated imagery was created for the film, supervised by Richard Taylor and Harrison Ellinshaw. Although originally budgeted for $12 million, a major deadline change forced the final cost to over $20 million. Disney management had cut production time in half from a delivery in December to one in July. The sole intent was to open on the same weekend as Don Bluth's animated feature *The Secret of Nimh* in hopes of cutting into its box office. The move to a summer release also put *Tron* up against the biggest effects movie season of all time, which included *ET*, *Poltergeist*, *Blade Runner*, *FireFox*, *Conan*, and *The Dark Crystal*.

It should be noted that the majority of effects in *Tron* were accomplished by traditional animation techniques involving tens of thousands of hand-rotoscoped individual frames of artwork. In fact, when asked about the actual volume of roto'd cels created in Taiwan, the unit of measurement Richard Taylor used was "several plane loads full."

1982–83

- *Where the Wild Things Are* (test done at MAGI) was the first instance of digital compositing for motion picture work. The character animation was done at Disney (led by Glen Keane), and the CG backgrounds, rendering, painting, and compositing were done at MAGI/Synthavision. John Lasseter was the official Disney-MAGI liaison. Ken Perlin supervised the project, and the CG work was led by Chris Wedge and Jan Carlee (both now at Blue Sky). Software was by Ken Perlin, Christine Chang, Gene Miller, and Josh Pines. For more details about MAGI, see Chapter 8, "Historically Significant Companies."

1983

- ACM/SIGGRAPH was held in Detroit, Michigan, with about 14,000 attendees and 195 exhibitors.

- The AVCO Finance spot was shown at SIGGRAPH Electronic Theatre. (This was the first raster-based, fully rendered, 30-second commercial spot.)

- Alias Research Inc. was founded in Toronto, Canada.

- The Bosch FGS-4000 (the first true turnkey 3D system) was introduced at NAB in 1983.

- Cube Quest by Simutrek Inc. was introduced, an early 3D graphics video game.

- The movie *Return Of the Jedi* (20th Century-Fox/Lucasfilm Ltd.) contained the holographic Endor moon sequence created by the Lucasfilm Computer Graphics Group. Bill Reeves and Tom Duff used vector graphics to simulate raster graphics.

1984

- ACM/SIGGRAPH was held in Minneapolis, Minnesota, with 20,390 attendees and 218 exhibitors.

- Synthavision, a division of MAGI, was sold to a Canadian investment company.

- Silicon Graphics released its first commercial product, the IRIS 1000 terminal (which ran off a VAX host).

- Wavefront software company was formed in Santa Barbara, California, by Larry Barels, Bill Kovacks, and Mark Sylvester. (For more details about Wavefront, see Chapter 8, "Historically Significant Companies.")

- A modern global illumination rendering technique called radiosity was presented by a team led by Don Greenberg at Cornell University.

- The Apple Macintosh computer was released. It was the first personal computer with a graphical user interface (GUI).

- *The Adventures of Andre and Wally B* was created by the Lucasfilm Computer Graphics Division. Alvy Ray Smith directed John Lasseter in his first CG short animated film.

- *The Last Starfighter* (Lorimar) was the first CG project by the new Digital Productions formed by Gary Demos and John Whitney Jr. after leaving Triple-I. (For more details about Digital Productions, see Chapter 8, "Historically Significant Companies.")

- In *2010: Odyssey Two*, Digital Productions worked with Boss Film Corp.'s Richard Edlund, Larry Yaeger, Craig Upson, Neil Krepela, et al. to combine computational fluid dynamics with CGI to create the planet Jupiter.

1985

- ACM/SIGGRAPH was held in San Francisco, California, with 27,000 attendees and 254 exhibitors.

- Disney's *The Black Cauldron* was the first use of 3D computer-generated elements in a feature-length animated film. A glowing ball was animated on the computer and was output to animation paper via an ink plotter. Traditionally animated effects elements were added to the scene to emulate the how the glowing ball would cast light and create shadows in an environment.

- The first-ever Academy of Motion Picture Arts and Sciences award recognition for computer graphics achievement went to John Whitney Jr. and Gary Demos of Digital Productions. They received The Scientific and Engineering Award for "the practical simulation of motion picture photography by means of computer generated images."

- Robert Abel & Associates' "Sexy Robot" was completed for the Canned Food Council.

- The *Amazing Stories* television series opening was produced at Abel's. David Vogel produced and Randy Roberts directed the 45-second, computer-animation extravaganza for Steven Spielberg. Thirty-seven separate objects were designed, digitized, choreographed, and animated on an E&S Picture System II during the six-month schedule. It was rendered at 1024×768, 24fps for 35mm film output on Gould computers around the country.

- The animated short film *Tony de Peltrie* by Phillipe Bergeron was shown at SIGGRAPH 85. It used digitized clay models and the new user-friendly TAARNA 3D animation system (from the University of Montreal), along with additional keyframe interpolating algorithms by Doris Kochanek described at the previous year's SIGGRAPH. (Phillipe also did hero animation on the Symbolics short *Stanley and Stella* in 1985.)

Max Headroom

Max Headroom was *not* computer-generated. (Really, take my word for it.) Beginning with the 1985 British music video show and TV pilot, he was portrayed by actor Matt Frewer in stylized makeup with added video-editing effects. The U.S. TV series produced in 1987 did feature some other on-screen CG (created with an Amiga) but never Max himself. (By the way, 10 years later actor Matt Frewer stared in the *LawnmowerMan II* sequel… infinitely less good than Max in my opinion.) For all things Max, visit www.maxheadroom.com/altfaq.html.

- Commodore introduced the Amiga color personal computer.

- At the Los Alamos National Lab, the Ultra-High Speed Graphics Project was started. It pioneered animation as a visualization tool and required gigabit-per-second communication capacity. An early massively parallel (128-node) Intel computer was installed.

- In the movie *Young Sherlock Holmes*, the stained-glass knight sequence was the first CG character in a feature film and the first computer-generated images in a feature film to be exposed directly onto the film with a laser.

   One shot also was the first ever all-digital composite of CG with live-action footage for a feature film. (The rack focus shot starts on the knight's hands grasping the sword hilt and then tilts up to his face.) This was done by the graphics group at Lucasfilm LTD.

- The "Money for Nothing" MTV video for Dire Straits was directed by Steve Barron. Gavin Blair and Ian Pearson created the blocky character animation at Rushes Post Production in London with a Bosch FGS-4000. The Quantel painting and rotoscoping effects were done by Viv Scott. Ian and Gavin now own and run a company in Vancouver called Mainframe, out of which they produced the CG-animated television series *Reboot* (1994).

- Cranston-Csuri produced many national broadcast network graphics but closed in 1987. Many of its employees went on to later form MetroLight Studios (1987).

FACTOID

David DiFrancesco built the digital film printer used for *Young Sherlock Holmes*. It was designed as one unit with three main components—a scanner and a printer with a Pixar Image Computer in between. DiFrancesco, a former video artist, later received two separate Academy Awards for his pioneering work: a Sci-Tech Award in 1994 for the scanner portion, and a Technical Achievement Award in 1999 for the printer work.

A still from the stained glass knight sequence. Young Sherlock Holmes *Copyright©1985 by Paramount Pictures. All Rights Reserved.* Young Sherlock Holmes *courtesy of Paramount Pictures.*

1986

- ACM/SIGGRAPH was held in Dallas, Texas, with about 22,000 attendees and 253 exhibitors.

- Softimage was founded in Montreal by Daniel Langlois.

- Complex 2D vector graphics character animation was produced by Digital Productions for the Mick Jagger music video "Hard Woman." Among those contributing to the piece were Brad deGraf, Bill Kroyer, and Kevin Rafferty. The CG was co-produced by Nancy St.John and Alan Peach.

- "The Juggler" was a memorable Amiga demo by independent artist Eric Graham.

- Digital Productions created the three-minute opening sequence for the feature film *Labyrinth*.

QUOTE

"I was at Digital Productions when we produced the Stones' 'Hard Woman' video. I didn't produce it, John Lugar did, but I bid and spec'd out the project and was involved throughout the production. It was funny. That was only a few years away from vector graphics as the dominant method of CG production. They wanted the characters to be "CG," which meant they had to look vector graphic, but at Digital, we were working on proprietary 3D software running on a Cray X-MP Supercomputer. The E&S vector displays we used for developing and approving motion tests were hooked up through another system, so we couldn't just composite 3D backgrounds with vector graphic characters, so we had to 'fake' vector graphics for the characters by rendering skinny 'tubes' in 3D.

Jagger's people had said they only wanted to spend $250,000, and management accepted their price. Our internal team (I think it was Brad deGraf, Steve Skinner, me, and perhaps Kevin Bjorke) bid the project at something like $1.5–2 million, which was almost exactly what it took to finish the project.

It was one of the best pieces Digital Productions ever did. But it didn't keep the creditors away..."

—David M. Ginsberg (davidg@metrolight.com)

- Pixar was formed by Lucasfilm Computer Graphics Division pioneers Edwin Catmull and Alvy Ray Smith along with about 35 others including John Lasseter, Ralph Guggenheim, Bill Reeves, et al. It was purchased from George Lucas by Steve Jobs (Apple/NeXT) for $10 million.

- *Luxo Jr.* (Pixar Animation Studios) became the first CG short animated film to be nominated for an Oscar for Best Short Animated Film.

- In *Flight of the Navigator*, Omnibus Computer Graphics created the silvery reflective spaceship. Contributors included Jeff Kleiser (KWCC), Les Major (ILM), and Kevin Tureski (Alias).

- *The Great Mouse Detective* clock gears, contrary to popular belief, were *not* the first use of 3D computer-generated elements in an animated film. *The Black Cauldron*, which was released the previous year (1985), claims that distinction. The camera was in almost-constant motion, which is why CG was well-suited to create the interior of the clocktower for the climactic moment in the film. Like most of the CG elements from this era (including *The Black Cauldron*) the CG gears were plotted to animation paper, Xeroxed for ink lines, and then hand-painted.

- *Howard the Duck* contained the first digital wire removal for a feature film, and it was the first feature film work for the fledgling ILM/CG department. It was painted by Bruce Wallace at ILM with proprietary Layerpaint software on a Pixar Image computer. Layerpaint code originally was written by Mark Leather and was modified by Jonathan Luskin and Doug Smythe.

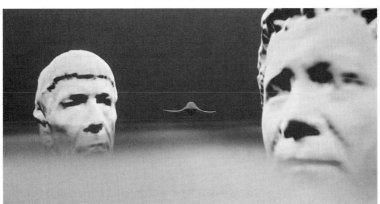

Frame from Star Trek IV showing two scanned heads. Star Trek: The Voyage Home *Copyright©1985 by Paramount Pictures. All Rights Reserved.* Star Trek: The Voyage Home *courtesy of Paramount Pictures.*

- *Star Trek IV* contained the first use of Cyberware 3D scanner for film.

■ Digital Productions was purchased in June and then Robert Abel & Associates was purchased in September by Omnibus Computer Graphics. Omnibus went out of business one year later on April 13, 1987.

1987

■ ACM/SIGGRAPH was held in Anaheim, California, with 30,541 attendees and 274 exhibitors.

■ Rhythm & Hues was formed by ex-Abel staffers and opened in a former dentist office.

■ *Oilspot & Lipstick* (CGI characters and props), a Disney "after-hours" project, was driven by artists and CG staff to show off the computer's capability for character animation. It was released briefly in the animation festival circuit but has never been released since. It was never released on video.

■ *Captain Power and the Soldiers of the Future* was the first television series to include 3D characters done entirely with computer animation. It went on the air (in September) in North America. Soaron and Blastarr were two CG robots that appeared in the 22-episode series. The computer animation was produced by Arcca Animation in Toronto.

About four minutes of computer graphics were animated for each weekly episode using two SGI 3130 workstations running Wavefront software. The motion was then ported over to Synthavision data.

Rendering was done on 13 Sun workstations that ran a proprietary job-control system that picked up new frames in a sequence as they were completed. This might have been the first render farm of its time. The work for the show won Arcca a Gemini Award (the pinnacle in Canadian film production) for Technical Achievement in 1988.

The producer was Bob Robbins. The art director was Earl Huddleston. Paul Griffin (ILM) was the animation director. Other animators included Andy Varty, Sylvia Wong (Rhythm & Hues, ILM), and Les Major (ILM,

SYNTHAVISION FACTOID

"Arcca was the re-formation of Sythavision staff and software to do the *Captain Power* series, which was a creation of Landmark Entertainment (Hollywood) and was financed by Mattel. The show featured toys that were interactive with the television show by registering blast hits on the toy (via a 30hz flicker on TV) or on the TV show character (via a trigger pull during a 15hz flicker from the TV)."
—Paul Griffin

Pixar). Paintbox work was by Rob Smith and Mike Huffman. Jenniffer Julich was in charge of storyboards. Rob Coleman was Arcca's onset liaison/line producer. Mark Mayerson now directs *Monster by Mistake* on DisneyTV and YTV (Canada). On the live-action production side, Doug Netter (Rattlesnake Productions) and Larry DiTillio (the writer) went on to develop *Babylon 5*.

Animating With Sticks and Stones

"Animation for the *Captain Power* series was incredibly arduous sometimes. First you'd plot the model and the path of your animation on graph paper. Then you'd input hundreds or thousands of text lines in a form that Synthavision would understand. If you were out as much as a space or a tab in your input file, it wouldn't run. To review your animation, you played it back by flipping images through a framebuffer that often had pixels as big as postage stamps. Based on this, you'd make a decision as to whether to send your rendered animation to the film recorder. Two days later, it would come back from the lab, and you could see where all the mistakes were and start over again. But it was a beautiful renderer. The quality of the solid-modeled surfaces and the lighting routines made for some great images."

—Paul Griffin

1988

- ACM/SIGGRAPH was held in Atlanta, Georgia, with about 19,000 attendees and 249 exhibitors.

- *Fruit Machine* (*Wonderworld*) was the first all-digital film composite for a feature film outside the United States by Computer Film Company (CFC)/London. Multiple film elements were scanned into a computer, were 100 percent digitally composited, and were filmed back out again. (*Wonderworld* was the film's title when released outside of England.) (For more details about CFC, see Chapter 8, "Historically Significant Companies.")

- Jim Henson and Digital Productions created a real-time 3D digital character for the *Jim Henson Hour*. It was the first of its kind. Steve Whitmeyer was the puppeteer and voice. Thad Bier (PDI/Hammerhead) and Grahm Walters shipped all the equipment up to Toronto one week before SIGGRAPH. The opening to the show was done by Jamie Dixon (PDI/Hammerhead).

QUOTE

"When I first started working in Australia in 1988, we had in-house code running on an Elexsi (an Indian supercomputer). All modeling was done with make files (invoking a series of modeling programs—extrude, clean curve, Boolean, etc.). All animation was done on an E&S PS300. Then we went to a rendering program to produce rendered images. (The render was shade tree-based, and writing shaders in it was similar to writing a RenderMan shader.) After rendering an image, you had to call out to everyone else demanding/begging for access to the framebuffer. There was one screen in the middle of the room connected to it (we worked off dumb text-only terminals hanging off the Elexsi) to view rendered sequences.

We had to shoot each frame onto film and then wait for the film to be processed and returned. Ah, the good old days when you could send a final render off and be told to stay home for the next three days. Ah, the bad old days of coming in at four in the morning to lay files to 1/4-inch tape before deleting and freeing up space for the next lot of rendered images. I still miss that renderer, though, and the kind of support you can get when your in-house programmer can whip up a lattice program in four days (in 1989!). But, then, he was god-like... (and still is!—Hi Bruno, got anything to add?)"

—Kit Devine, Senior Animator at Garner MacLennan Design

- Mike the Talking Head was the first real-time character (a.k.a motion-capture, vactor, performance animation). Michael Wahrman and Brad deGraf performed Mike at deGraf/Wahrman live at the SIGGRAPH Electronic Theatre in Atlanta. (Mike was a virtual caricature of the late Mike Gribble, the host of that show, and the Mike of Spike and Mike's animation festival.)

Frame from Willow *of the goat morph.*
Willow ©*Lucasfilm Ltd. & %o. All Rights Reserved. Used under authorization. Courtesy of Lucasfilm Ltd.*

- *Willow* (MGM/Lucasfilm Ltd.) contained the first feature film use of digital morphing technology.

- The Computer Animation Paint System (CAPS) was developed jointly between Pixar and Disney.

- *Oliver & Company* (Walt Disney Feature Animation) was released. Animated cars and cement sewer pipes in the city construction scenes were clearly distinguishable due to cel-painted CG elements. Nonanimated traffic was particularly easy to spot in comparison because it was painted into the background and had tonality and shadows. CG elements had single-color areas without complex shadows.

- *Tin Toy* (Pixar Animation Studios) became the first CG short animated film to win an Oscar for Best Short Animated Film.

1989

- ACM/SIGGRAPH was held in Boston, Massachusetts, with 27,000 attendees and 238 exhibitors.

- In *Indiana Jones and the Last Crusade* (Lucasfilm Ltd. /Paramount), the "Donovan's destruction" sequence by ILM was the first to use many multiple-scanned film elements, digitally composited and then scanned back out to film with a laser. (By now, it's getting a little silly with all the sub-sub classifications of "firsts" in areas such as these.)

Frame from Donovan's destruction sequence. Indiana Jones and the Last Crusade ©*Lucasfilm Ltd. &™. All Rights Reserved. Used under authorization.*

- In *The Abyss* (GJP Productions/20th Century-Fox), the water pseudopod was created by Industrial Light & Magic.

1990s

The entertainment world as we knew it began to change in the 1980s when motion picture images in *Tron, Star Trek II, The Last Starfighter,* and *Young Sherlock Holmes* gave the audience a taste

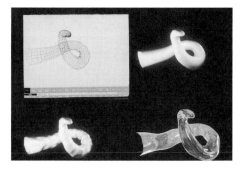

Still from the movie The Abyss *courtesy 20th Century Fox. All Rights. Reserved.*

of the future. George Lucas's Industrial Light & Magic began to continuously raise the popular standard by which all CG was judged by creating such images as the water pseudopod in James Cameron's film *The Abyss* (1989) and the T-1000 in *Terminator 2: Judgment Day* (1990). In 1993, ILM smashed all previous conceptions about computer graphics when *Jurassic Park*'s photo-real dinosaurs took center stage in theaters around the world.

FACTOID

1990

- ACM/SIGGRAPH was held in Dallas, Texas, with 24,684 attendees and 248 exhibitors.

- For the feature film *Flight of the Intruder*, Rhythm & Hues created more than 30 shots of photo-realistic aircraft, cluster bombs, and smoke in full daylight, all with their own proprietary software.

- deGraf/Wahrman did *The Funtastic World of Hanna-Barbera*, the first CG ride film. It was a fully 3D chase/ride through Bedrock and Scooby-Doo's castle, complete with cel-animated characters, for Universal Studios Florida. (Additional CG work was done by Rhythm & Hues.)

- *Robocop 2* (also by deGraf/Wahrman) contained the first use in feature films of real-time performance animation. Among those who also contributed were Ken Cope (animation) and Gregory Ercolano (TD).

- Kroyer Films created the full-length animated feature film *FernGully: The Last Rainforest*. It contained 40,000 3D hidden-line, computer-plotted cel frames to augment the bulk of the traditional animation. It also contained a digital ink-and-paint sequence by the company Sidley-Wright, a feature film first.

- *The Rescuers Down Under* (Walt Disney Feature Animation) was the first complete feature film to be entirely digital. The CAPS system digitally inked and painted every frame of the film. 3D CG was used once again for machinery and vehicles and was still plotted out to be treated just like the rest of the movie.

- *Die Hard 2: Die Harder* (20th Century-Fox) contained the first digitally manipulated matte painting created at Industrial Light & Magic. The matte department supervisor was Bruce Walters, Paul Huston and Michael McAllister helped in design and composition, and Yusei Uesugi was the matte painter extraordinare. Four separate images were digitized from the painting (which was 13 feet wide by 5 feet tall), decreasing in resolution from the center outward. The images were assembled in a

Mac II computer and were manipulated by Uesugi using Photoshop. The image was combined with numerous live-action elements of people, lights, and steam with a camera move programmed by Pat Myers.

- NewTek released the Amiga-based Video Toaster.

1991

- ACM/SIGGRAPH was held in Las Vegas, Nevada, with about 23,100 attendees and 282 exhibitors.

- *Terminator 2: Judgment Day* (Carolco) contained a T-1000 liquid metal cyborg. The 3D character animation directed by James Cameron and realized by Industrial Light & Magic was the breakthrough work that introduced both Hollywood and the public to realistic feature film use of CG.

- Beautiful all-CG commercials by Pixar (produced by Colossal Pictures) for Listerine, Life Savers, and Tropicana set a new standard for broadcast excellence.

- In *Beauty and The Beast* (Walt Disney Feature Animation), the ballroom sequence represents a major new direction in feature-length animated films. The background scene is fully rendered in CG and is not just plotted out to be inked in later.

1992

- ACM/SIGGRAPH was held in Chicago, Illinois, with 34,148 attendees and 253 exhibitors.

- *Aladdin* (Walt Disney Feature Animation) contained the first CGI character in an animated feature film (the first two, actually). The Tiger Head in the desert talked, but the Carpet was more significant. The carpet was more or less roto'd to traditional animation, but it still proved that the computer tools were in place to do good character animation. CG also was used for the lava-flow scene inside the Cave of Wonders. This was easily the most varied and complex use of CG in a Disney Feature Animation film to this point.

- *Off His Rockers* was a short film produced by the Walt Disney Feature Animation Florida unit that had been doing the *Roger Rabbit* shorts. It was directed by Barry Cook, who directed the last *Roger Rabbit*, "Trail Mix-Up," and went on to be co-director of *Mulan*. The film mixed a traditionally animated boy and a CG-animated rocking horse. It was released in theaters and then on video. It was recently rereleased with *Honey, I Blew Up the Kid* on laserdisc.

- In *Death Becomes Her* (Universal), the photo-real human skin and body replacement was done by Industrial Light & Magic.

1993

- ACM/SIGGRAPH was held in Anaheim, California, with 27,000 attendees and 285 exhibitors.

- Wavefront acquired the TDI software company from Thompson Corp. of France. In exchange, Wavefront received a major capital investment from Thompson.

- PDI opened a Hollywood production office but closed it in a short few years.

- Marc Scaparro, Eric Gregory, and Brad deGraf performed Moxy for the Cartoon Network at Colossal Pictures. Produced by Anne Brilz, it was the first live broadcast of a virtual character.

- In *Jurassic Park* (Amblin/Universal), the photo-real 3D digital dinosaurs were by Industrial Light & Magic.

1994

- ACM/SIGGRAPH was held in Orlando, Florida, with about 25,000 attendees and 269 exhibitors.

- The first 100 percent CGI television series, *Reboot*, aired on ABC. It was created by Mainframe Entertainment Inc.

- Microsoft acquired Softimage.

- In *Forrest Gump* (Paramount), photo-real/invisible 3D and 2D digital effects blended new footage with old, changed archive footage, and removed an actor's legs! This was done by the ILM CG Dept.

- For *The Flintstones* (Universal), the first feature film digital hair was developed by Industrial Light & Magic for the saber-toothed tiger.

- In *The Mask* (NewLine), the realistic yet wildly exaggerated "Tex Avery" style of 3D character animation was a first for feature film visual effects. Effects and animation were co-supervised by Steve "Spaz" Williams and Tom Bertino.

Step-through illustration of exaggerated realistic cartoon effects. The Mask *copyright 1994, New Line Productions, Inc. All rights reserved. Photos appear courtesy of New Line Productions, Inc.*

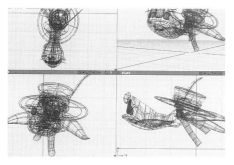

- *The Lion King*'s wildebeest stampede was the first use of crowd simulation in a Disney feature animated film.

1995

- ACM/SIGGRAPH was held in Los Angeles, California, with 40,100 attendees and 297 exhibitors.

- Silicon Graphics Inc. acquired both Alias and Wavefront, merging the two companies.

- *Toy Story* (Pixar Animation Studios) was the first full-length CG animated feature film. Director John Lasseter won a Special Achievement Academy Award.

- *Judge Dredd* (Cinergi) contained early examples of fully 3D digital stunt people for a feature film by Kleiser-Walzack Construction Company completed for the main post-production contractor Mass-Illusion.

- In *Casino* (Universal), Matte World Digital utilized LightScape software to seamlessly integrate a 1970s virtual Las Vegas strip into present-day, live-action footage. This was the first time radiosity lighting was used in a feature film.

- *Batman Forever* (Warner Bros.) contained an early example of a 3D realistic digital stuntman by Warner Bros. Imaging Technology (W.B.I.T.) and Pacific Data Images. It also contained a very realistic, fully 3D cityscape by W.B.I.T.

- *Casper* (Amblin/Universal) contained a record number of on-screen shots with a 3D digital character (more than 400). These shots were completed by Industrial Light & Magic.

- In *Jumanji* (Tri-Star), further development of photoreal, particle-based digital hair technology for the lion sequence was created by Industrial Light & Magic.

- The CG in *Pocahontas* (Walt Disney Feature Animation) consisted of Grandmother Willow, the canoe, and other props.

1996

- ACM/SIGGRAPH was held in New Orleans, Louisiana, with 28,800 attendees and 321 exhibitors.

- Alvy Ray Smith, Ed Catmull, Tom Porter, and Tom Duff received a Technical Academy Award for digital image compositing (the alpha channel).

- *Dragonheart* (Universal) contained breakthrough 3D CGI character animation and lip-synch dialog completed by Industrial Light & Magic. Cary Philips wrote the Caricature "Cari" software for the facial animation. This later won him a Technical Academy Award.

- For *Twister,* breakthrough realistic tornadoes and weather effects were created by Industrial Light & Magic using Wavefront's Dynamation.

- The CG in *The Hunchback of Notre Dame* (Walt Disney Feature Animation) consisted of crowds, props, and 3D effects.

1997

- ACM/SIGGRAPH was held in Los Angeles, California, with 48,700 attendees and 359 exhibitors.

- *Floops* (done at Protozoa by Brad deGraf, Emre Yilmaz, Steve Rein, and others) was the first character distributed as 3D (VRML), was the first episodic cartoon on the Web, and was the first significant animation on the Web (30 minutes worth).

- The *Star Wars/ Special Edition* rereleases (20th Century-Fox/Lucasfilm Ltd.) contained restored and enhanced 20-year-old film footage. About 350 shots were added or modified for all three films by Industrial Light & Magic.

A frame from the re-release of The Empire Strikes Back. The Empire Strikes Back ©*Lucasfilm Ltd. &™. All Rights Reserved. Used Under Authorization*

- *Spawn* (NewLine) contained photo-real fully 3D creature transformations, full-screen digital stunt doubles, and a dynamic simulated cape. All the bone-cracking, digital-drool-slinging realism was provided by Industrial Light & Magic. The film was led by the Ex-ILM trio of Mark Dippe (director), Clint Goldman (producer), and Steve "Spaz" Williams (VFX supervisor and second unit director).

- *Titanic* (Paramount) contained large-scale use of motion-capture and 3D digital crowd extras. The effects work was created primarily by Digital Domain, which won an Academy Award for Visual Effects for the work.

- The CG in *Hercules* (Walt Disney Feature Animation) consisted of the hydra, cloud and background morphs, and 3D effects.

- The British company Quantel sues Adobe for patent infringement on U.S. versions of UK patents covering airbrushing (digital painting with soft-edged brushes), digital image compositing, pressure-sensitive stylus, mixing paints on a window called a palette, and so on. The jury found all five patents at issue invalid and found Adobe innocent of infringement.

1998

- ACM/SIGGRAPH was held in Orlando, Florida.

- An unprecedented number of SciTech awards went to the computer graphics community. Individuals at Alias, Pixar, PDI, Side Effects, Softimage, and Wavefront all were recognized for various components of their systems.

- Several individuals were recognized for their general contributions to computer graphics.

- A Scientific and Engineering Academy Award was awarded to Richard Shoup, Alvy Ray Smith, and Thomas Porter for their pioneering efforts in the development of digital paint systems used in motion picture production. The award reads: "Much of the foundation for the numerous contemporary digital paint products for motion pictures can be traced directly back to the early work of these digital pioneers."

- A Scientific and Engineering Academy Award was awarded to Craig Reynolds for his pioneering contributions to the development of 3D computer animation for motion picture production. The award reads: "The early contributions of Mr. Reynolds in the digital animation arena have become both influential and instrumental in the architecture of many later systems developed at companies throughout the computer animation industry."

- *Geri's Game* (Pixar), an Academy Award-winning animated short film, showcased the newly rediscovered modeling technique of subdivision surfaces.

- *Bingo* (Alias|Wavefront), Chris Landreth's test piece for the initial Maya release, received a Genie Award from The Academy of Canadian Cinema and Television. It was named Best Computer Animation at Ottawa 98 and at Imagina in Monaco. Bingo also received an award from France's *Societe des Auteurs et Compositeurs Dramatiques* (SACD) for Most Innovative Story and Production.

- *Antz* was released (PDI/Dreamworks). Big-name voice talent lent a more adult feeling to this "animated Woody Allen movie." PDI's first full-length 3D CG animated film will be followed by *Shreck* sometime in late 2000 and then *Tusker* in 2002.

- *A Bug's Life* (Pixar/Disney), Pixar's followup to the smash hit *Toy Story*, was 10 times more complex. It utilized beautiful translucent shading techniques and many highly detailed models. BMRT software was used to ray trace the scene of the bottle inside the Mexican hat, which was used as the grasshoppers' bar.

- The CG in *Mulan* (Walt Disney Feature Animation) consisted of the Hun Charge and other various 3D effects.

1999

- ACM/SIGGRAPH is scheduled to be held in Los Angeles.

- Autodesk is merging its newly acquired Discreet Logic (Montreal) division with its Kinetix (San Francisco) division into the new Discreet entertainment division.

- *Star Wars Episode 1: The Phantom Menace* is scheduled to be in theaters all summer. The movie contains almost 2000 state-of-the-art digital effect shots, most of which were created at Industrial Light & Magic in less than two years production time. The Gungan JarJar Binks is the first photo-realistic, all-digital main character in a motion picture. Boss Nass and Watto play supporting digital roles.

  The few shots in the film that were not effects-related also were scanned and color-corrected to produce a full-length digital master. This format is be used later in the summer at premiers in New York and Los Angeles with a new digital video projection system. The Texas Instruments system uses 1920×1080 progressive video resolution to project the film at 24fps directly from digital storage. The direct projection of the digital imagery most notably avoids the third-generation quality degradation of a typical 35mm release print. Combined with the additional lack of a film projector's unsteady film gate and the inconsistencies of film printing lights, the digitally projected feature makes for a sharper, true-color representation of the source imagery.

- Pixar Animation Studios is scheduled to release *Toy Story II*, the much-anticipated follow-up to its breakthrough fully-3D, CG-animated feature film. It is the first film to be completely filmed out with the new custom-built laser-based PixarVision system. (For more details about Pixar, see Chapter 8, "Historically Significant Companies.")

TRIVIA

Four live-action shots in *The Phantom Menace* were not captured on film at all. Rather, they were captured on high-definition digital video. Can you tell which ones?

Frequently Asked Questions About Computer Graphics

Author's Side Note

I think I must have been born with a silver pencil in my mouth…or hand, or whatever. My earliest memories are of sitting on the floor of my room drawing anything and everything. I'd often just copy page after page of comic-book characters such as Thor or the Hulk (the real Hulk, not that thing they've been doing the last 10 years). Having been brought up first on sci-fi books and then on movies by my Dad, this genre held my interest more than any other as a creative outlet. This all came to a head (as it did for a couple million other kids in the world) in the spring of 1977 when I saw a film that just about gave me goose bumps for the rest of my life—*Star Wars*. (And here I am 20 plus years later having worked on the Special Edition. Someone pinch me!)

The whole point of this rant is that I soon started down a very calculated path to what I saw as the only place on the planet I wanted to get a job—Industrial Light & Magic, of course. Back then, there simply were no other companies as far as I was concerned. (The saying remains today that there is ILM and then there is everyone else. But then, I'm biased.)

I had done some programming (a full year as a CS major—ugh!) and was very happy to switch to the B.F.A. program, which had just gotten the first Mac and Amiga computers. I started going to SIGGRAPH conventions in the mid-80s to start learning about "the biz." I worked backwards; ILM used Alias, so I learned Alias. That led me to choose a graduate school with a certain tool set. Soon after, I was out "flying logos" and beveling chrome text with the best of them. This began my long relationship with Alias as my primary tool of choice for the best all-around modeling/animation/rendering software.

After a course at one early SIGGRAPH, I remember asking Craig Good of Pixar just what I needed to do to get a job doing CG in films. (This was probably 1988 or so.) His reply was that I could start by getting a short film in the SIGGRAPH film show. (Oh, is that all?) My naïve thought was that, well, I had done a short film in undergraduate school on the Amiga, so why not? (I did a literal animation to accompany the lyrics of "Red Barchetta" by Rush. I found out the hard way just how long it takes to animate five and a half minutes with DeluxePaintII!) Using my newfound SGI-based tools, I made "Paranoimia" based on the Art of Noise song of the same name. Needless to say, it didn't get into SIGGRAPH.

It did, however, help get me hired at ILM to work on the Spielberg film *Hook*. (Thank you, Doug Kay.) I left ILM for a while and worked with lots of cool people before returning a few years ago.

What is the point of this story? It's how I happened to end up where I am, doing something I've always loved. Talk to a dozen other people and they'll all have different backgrounds (and more interesting stories, most likely). This is a real advantage to the business. Having such diverse personal histories makes for a much more interesting work environment and a better final product because of all the different points of view you encounter. Someone is bound to show you a path that will work for you, too.

—Terrence "Tman" Masson

Q: What are the differences between the old way of making effects (with models) and computer-generated visual effects?

A: Traditional models and miniatures are still very much a part of the visual effects used today. In many ways, more miniature work is being done lately because of the resurgence of big effects pictures. This was brought on in part by the advances of newer digital technologies. The largest single difference between any traditional effect method and CG is based on the nature of the mediums. Models naturally have physical limitations, both in how they are constructed and in how they are photographed. It is important to note that most CG models are created from some traditional reference sculpture, model, or "maquette" made of clay. They are digitized into the CG modeling software and are rebuilt and optimized depending on their end use.

Computer-generated imagery is only limited by a person's imagination (the very real production constraints of time, cost, and personnel notwithstanding, of course!).

Q: When do you use the computer and when is it better to use models?

A: This depends on many factors including time, cost, resources, personnel, and the final stylistic look desired by the director. Many times, a particular technique is chosen because of the individual experience of the Visual Effects Supervisor assigned to the job. Very often, a combination of the two techniques (computers and modeling) is used to take full advantage of the benefits of both. An excellent recent example of this is ILM's transforming black sedan sequence from the movie *Men In Black*. The metallic quality of the car itself and the very intricately animated surface structure and jet exhaust are all things CG can do well. The tunnel through which the car travels was a miniature set that needed to be realized with hundreds of cars and lights and a great deal of motion blur. This was something that it made good sense to capture with real photographic techniques.

Q: What are the advantages and disadvantages of both CG and traditional techniques?

A: As with any artistic endeavor, the final result is only as good as the skills of the people creating it; the tools are always secondary to the talent. That said, practical models have a distinct advantage in their interaction with real light on a set or outdoors. Our eyes are accustomed to viewing images captured in a real space through a lens and onto film. The many subtle nuances of this seemingly simple and commonplace technique are very time consuming and are difficult to duplicate in an all-digital environment.

Creating a completely realistic all-digital reality occasionally is done so well that it goes unnoticed altogether. Most times, the whole point of a visual effect is to blend seamlessly into the context of the film and not stand out at all. An excellent example of this is the film *Mission Impossible*, which featured several such scenes. One of these scenes depicted a helicopter entering a tunnel entrance. No sets or models were used at all, but you'd never know it!

One of the biggest advantages of CG is being able to do a job when it cannot be done any other way. In the Universal film *Small Soldiers*, ILM created more than 300 shots with many hundreds of interacting Commando and Gorgonite action figures, all completely digital and integrated perfectly with the live-action sets. Achieving that volume of photorealistic character animation on a very strict production timetable would not have been possible with any practical techniques. The animators even had to match with the few live-action Stan Winston puppet closeup shots.

Q: What kind of cost differences are associated with CGI and models?

A: In providing entertainment content, several factors have great influence on the method of creating an effect. If you need to create a fleet of battling spaceships for a CD-ROM game and you have only a month to deliver the final shots, CGI is going to look like the only cost-effective solution. Similarly, if your feature film requires a walking, talking, completely realistic alien creature, practical animatronics can only take you so far. Although a CGI creature can take you farther, neither of these extremely high-end effects come cheap. The two full-scale T-Rex animatronic dinosaurs created by Stan Winston for *The Lost World* reportedly cost one million dollars each. Although PC-based video-resolution effects have become extremely affordable for certain markets, a full-length feature film of high-end CG effects still costs tens of millions of dollars.

Q: What does CG still need to improve on?

A: First, natural things such as cloth, fire, hair, skin, smoke, and water are hard to duplicate convincingly with current digital tools. All these things can be created in some circumstances, but they always are very computationally expensive to render or animate, and are time consuming to perfect. We are accustomed to seeing such things every day and can instantly pick up on the slightest thing out of the ordinary. Completely digital pyrotechnics might be the very last effects to be achieved completely convincingly.

Second, imitating a real camera is, in many ways, still just not practically possible with commercial software tools. As soon as light enters a virtual camera, we must begin a long list of slight-of-hand to even begin to get close to how an actual camera exposes images on film through a lens. The nonlinear distortions that a lens creates by bending the incoming light unevenly are the first aspect of reality that we must fake either as a 2D post process or a complicated ray tracing procedure. We also must reproduce dozens of other subtle artifacts such as motion-blur, reflections and refractions, film grain, depth cueing, chromatic distortions, soft shadows, lens flares, and glows (just to name a few obvious ones!).

Q: What kind of training do you need to be a digital artist?

A: You don't need any specific degree to get hired. The great thing about this business is that, because there are so many different types of jobs, nearly everyone has a different type of background. Every artistic, computer science, and engineering program gives you some kind of exposure to some element of computer-graphics technology. The trick is to try and figure out just what kind of job you want to pursue.

Recently (in the last five years), there has been an explosion in the number of colleges, universities, and training centers that offer computer graphics–specific courses. Traditional animation skills benefit anyone wanting to become a character animator. A Technical Director (TD) must be a true jack-of-all-trades and Renaissance person. Other skills that help digital artists excel include the traditional lighting techniques of cinematography, some programming skills, fine-art training, and a thorough knowledge of the film-making process. No matter what area you choose to work in, computer graphics is an artistic field that rewards people with a superior aesthetic sense combined with technical know-how. One application of this that can get you noticed is to create a killer short animated film and then prove you have working knowledge of some kind of scripting or programming.

The bottom line is just to get out there and get a job. Any job can give you experience, and no job lasts forever if you don't want it to. The better you get, the more options you have. Remember that there are tons of people out there to learn from experts who have been doing this for a long time.

Q: Does it matter what kind of software or hardware I use?

A: No and yes. When you are experienced at many different platforms, they all become just tools in the tool box. You use whichever is best suited for the job at hand. (Don't use a screwdriver to pound nails!) Of course, many times, to get a specific job, a particular company by necessity favors someone who is proficient with the tools they happen to use. 3D Studio MAX and LightWave are popular "all-around" CG programs, for example, but for high-end film work, Softimage is many times preferred for specialized character-animation work.

Q: How do you get to be a technical director?

A: Like most other CG roles, TDs are hired on the strength of their reel. So the chicken and the egg conundrum goes digital it would seem. My advice has always been to start out somewhere (usually a smaller company) that allows you to do a little bit of everything. Unlike most other CG professions, a TD must be skilled in many different areas. Ideally, a TD comes with several years of experience in a variety of jobs such as modeling, animating, painting, lighting, film-making, programming, and fine arts. The more rounded a career, the more likely the individual is to have a user's knowledge of the "big picture," the pipeline that builds the effects shot.

After you gain experience, you can specialize in whatever you like, such as high-level scripting or the more aesthetic side of lighting. You absolutely do *not* have to have a Computer Science degree. It might have been a near necessity 15 years ago and might have helped five years ago, but not today (unless you want to program, of course).

Everything has changed in the past ten years. The TD job can be more specialized now, but you always manage to do a little bit of everything (if you're able, and if that is what you like to do).

Q: Where does the overlap occur between programming and art?

A: Despite the name, a TD ideally should spend most of his time lighting and using all the established tools in the pipeline to make the shot look better. The reality is that much time is spent working around problems and coming up with solutions to make a shot work at all. Now don't get me wrong, this challenge can be half the fun. The best part of the job sometimes is being asked, "So just how the &*%#@ are we going to do that?" and being the one to have to figure it out.

It's all the better if you *like* to code shaders and scripts (in something like Cshell or Python most often), which the TD does (sometimes quite often). Most high-end companies' pipelines are script driven, so you couldn't totally avoid it if you wanted to. Everyone gets into this to some degree. Compositors and technical animators even write their own "plug-ins" for new features that do not exist in off-the-shelf programs.

Q: Why so much emphasis on programming and scripting anyway?

Compositing scripts very often are thousands of lines long, and it's not just the comp scripts (which have evolved into more GUI-based programs now anyway). It's taking models, applying textures, and adding procedural animation rules, roto and plate elements, matchmove cameras, and dynamic scene elements—as with Dynamation/Maya—all from other specialists (or your jack-of-all-trades self) just to get an element rendered. If it was easy, everyone could do it.

But fear not C++! There often is a very well-defined team of Research & Development programmers to create all the magical production tools to use. The major tools used to light and composite CG take months and years to code and update. Most simpler tools are show driven and must be written in only days or weeks.

Remember, ILM and most other well-established places have lots of custom code, such as BlueSky, PDI, Rhythm and Hues, and so on. Smaller places must rely on off-the-shelf software and less coding, but cannot do totally without it.

GUIDELINES FOR PREPARING A DEMO REEL AND GETTING A JOB

Many companies in many various fields have different jobs out there. Consequently, there are no hard and fast rules about interviewing. The following universal guidelines will serve you well most of the time and in most circumstances.

- **Include information** along with your reel detailing all your shots with the following information:

  1. For what project was it done? (A film, a game, TV?)

  2. Where it was done? (At which company or at home?)

  3. Which tools did you use? (Include hardware and software.)

  4. Explain exactly what you did and did *not* do for the shot. (Did you just do the modeling or texturing? Just the animation or lighting? Did you do it all?)

  5. If you TD'd a complex shot, break down how you did it.

  A short paragraph for each shot on the reel usually is plenty of information. Be both precise and concise.

- **Your best work** should be the only work you present. If you only have one minute of really good work, that is all you should include. Don't include any amount of mediocre or older work just to lengthen the reel. It will only water down the reel as a whole and will detract from the better work.

- **Keep it short and sweet!** Even if you have 10 minutes of good stuff you want to show, pick the very best three minutes and keep it at that. If you insist on including more lengthy work, you might want to first show short takes and excerpts and then include longer works at the end after an appropriate title card. That way, someone watching it has the choice either to watch just the best highlights or to sit through the whole 10-minute short film you made in high school.

- **Be original!** If you are preparing your own work at home or at school, take advantage of the creative freedom this offers. You'll get more points for developing new and creative work rather than just making an X-wing fly past the camera. When you have a limitless capability to create, what is it that you choose to do and just how do you do it?

- **Music?** This is a tough area to define. The choice of music on your reel says something about who you are and the impression you are trying to make. It also is true, however, that some people keep the sound off when viewing reels so as not to detract from the visual impact of what they are trying to judge. Music is important to me in many ways, so I took great care to choose appropriate music for all my early reels. Think about more than just heavy metal or classical; try to edit each cut to the beat of the soundtrack for an even greater impact.

- **Be honest** about what you have done and what you can do. Believe it or not, some people have consciously tried to pass off others' work as their own. If you don't have 10 years of Softimage experience, don't put it on your resume. (It's still a really small business out there. Word gets around fast and impressions are lasting, so make yours a good one.)

- **Include references** for a potential employer to contact. Be sure to check with the people you include as references first. You don't want to be surprised with what they have to say about you!

- **Study your craft!** This might seem obvious, but the more you know about what people have done before and about what people generally consider to be "good work", the better you'll be at preparing and presenting your own work. Constantly ask yourself the following questions:

  1. What makes really good animation stand out from ordinary animation?

  2. What makes a well-lit scene look realistic?

  3. What is the most effective use of color and composition for a given shot? Why?

     Be well prepared with this information, especially how it pertains to the job and company at which you are interviewing. This will show that you have a broader knowledge than the next person.

- **Be tenacious!** Don't give up, but also be patient and honest about your chances and abilities in a given area. Don't take up basket weaving for the rest of your life if ILM won't hire you. (They get about 20,000 resumes a year, so you're not the only one being turned down, believe me.) Get out and take any job that offers you a challenge and a chance to gain experience.

- **Be humble!** Trust me on this one. You don't know it all, you're not the best animator since the Nine Old Men, and you're not doing the company any favors by interviewing with them.

I've been very fortunate. I've done a bit of everything there is to do in CG over the past dozen years or so, and rarely a day goes by that I do not learn something new from someone around me. I've also worked at quite a few companies, but ILM is a uniquely humbling place to work. The talent and experience level of my coworkers consistently amazes me.

—Tman

TMAN'S WORDS OF WISDOM

Here are a few closing digital fortune cookies for you:

- Constantly strive to improve yourself in every way.

- Always have fun! (If you are not having fun, ask yourself why and think about maybe doing something else.)

- Be a team player. It's a cliché, but it's one for a good reason. Working in this business, you rely on the skill of many others around you. The sooner you realize and acknowledge this, the better off you will be.

- Pass on what you have learned. No matter where you are or what you are doing, someone helped you get there. When you get a chance, help others in the same way others helped you.

Animation Director

Art Director

Character Animator

Compositor

Computer Graphics
Sequence Supervisor

Computer Graphics
Supervisor

Digital Artist

Digital Effects
Supervisor

Effects Animator

Matchmover

Modeler

Production Assistant

Production
Coordinator

Rotoscope (Roto)
Artist

Software Designer or
Developer

Technical Assistant

Technical Director

Visual Effects
Producer

Visual Effects
Supervisor

Computer Graphics
and Job Descriptions

Animation Director

The Animation Director is responsible for supervising a team of animators and for developing the behavior of all the digital characters in a production. For larger, character-based feature films such as *Casper*, *Dragonheart*, or *Episode I: The Phantom Menace*, the most senior Animation Directors might be placed at the same level as the Visual Effects Supervisor. In this case, he might report as much to the Director as to the Visual Effects Supervisor.

Art Director

An Art Director creates detailed storyboards, production designs, and artwork so the Director and Visual Effects Supervisor can communicate the vision of the film to the production team. A very strong fine art and design background and a vivid imagination are required for this critical first step in creating visual effects. An Art Director might have a large team working for him or her including Storyboard Artists, Designers, and Assistant Art Directors. Feature film projects typically have several Art Directors reporting to the Production Designer. Traditional tools, such as the venerable pencil and paper, are just as important, if not more so, than Photoshop.

Character Animator

A Character Animator specializes in bringing life and personality to digital characters. Many individuals in this specialty come from traditional animation training. For feature film work at least, Softimage and Alias|Wavefront PowerAnimator are the most prevalent tools. Many other much-less-expensive software products are used for broadcast and games work, including NewTek LightWave 3D and Discreet 3D Studio MAX. The important part is always the pure performance of the character and not which particular tool was used. Animators typically report to an Animation Lead or directly to an Animation Supervisor, depending on the project's size.

Compositor

A Compositor combines many different rendered and scanned raster elements into a finished image or shot. These elements often include a background image or live-action plate, rendered CGI elements, rotoscope or garbage mattes, and other digital matte paintings. The compositor must integrate all these together by balancing color and black levels, sometimes extracting blue or green screen elements, and by adding the right amount of subtle nuances such as flash and grain. The ultimate goal is to make the composited elements appear to have been captured as a whole. After all, it's all 2D in the end! Excelling at this job requires a thorough understanding of color, light, film, and traditional photographic techniques. When the shot involves animated 3D CGI elements, this task might be performed by the Technical Director. When performed as a separate specialty, a Compositor must work closely with the Technical Director to achieve a common goal. More and more productions thankfully are creating the position of Compositing Supervisor to oversee the larger issues of continuity and technique.

Computer Graphics Sequence Supervisor

This individual is an experienced Senior Technical Director with a thorough knowledge of the tools in use on the production, excellent organizational skills, and a proven aesthetic sense. It is a relatively new role demanded by the greatly increased size and complexity of today's digital productions. The CG Sequence Supervisor works at a level between the Technical Director (who is responsible for individual shots) and the CG Supervisor (who oversees the show as a whole). Although this individual typically reports to the CG Supervisor, direct interaction with the Visual Effects Producer and the Visual Effects Supervisor also is common, depending on the type of project.

Computer Graphics Supervisor

The "CG Supe" generally works with the Visual Effects Supervisor to come up with technical solutions for all the CG work on a production. Working together, they suggest 2D and 3D methodology, choose the most appropriate software techniques for the tasks or implement new ones, and select the size and makeup of the personnel required as well as the exact hardware required to complete the work. On larger feature film projects, several CG Sequence

Supervisors report to the CG Supe. Depending on the scope and style of a production, the CG Supe might be more of a project manager than a technical or aesthetic contributor. In most cases, this person also must work closely with the Producer to keep the project on time and on budget. CG Supervisors typically report directly to the Visual Effects Supervisor and Producer of the show.

Digital Artist

This broad, general term is used both in screen credits for nonsupervisor personnel on a production team, regardless of their specialty, and within a company to describe general 2D or entry-level positions such as wire-removal, rotoscope, or clean-up artists. Its usage has become even more general, encompassing many different specialties and seniority levels. Digital Artists report to the "lead" in whatever specialty role happens to be described, such as roto or matchmoving. They, in turn, take direction from the Technical Director or Compositor for any given shot.

Digital Effects Supervisor

This newer term sometimes is used in place of Computer Graphics Supervisor or Visual Effects Supervisor, depending on the nature of the work performed on a production.

Effects Animator

Often the other half of a Technical Director's job, an Effects Animator usually animates any "hard-surface" elements (except characters): flying spaceships and vehicles, natural effects such as tornadoes and water, and any other fantasy effects such as pixie-dust, laser blasts, and explosions.

Matchmover

Fitting CG elements into live-action scenes requires a Matchmover to precisely calculate in 3D what the camera position, lens type, and real environment were when the plates were shot. This information is then handed off to both the Technical Director and the Animator on the shot. Only then can the 3D CG dinosaurs plant their feet firmly on the ground or the digital set extensions match up to their real counterparts. This process of matchmoving can be achieved using many different techniques, most often using full 3D environment packages such as Alias PowerAnimator or Softimage. More recently, specialized tools such as 3D Equalizer and custom 2D/3D software programs written by the major effects houses have become more widely used. Lead Matchmovers most often accompany the live-action shooting crew to take measurements of the set and to make copies of camera reports to aid in the work later performed by their team.

Modeler

A Modeler creates the essential 3D geometric-shape information in the form of characters, props, and sets used in computer graphics. Although many 3D wireframe models are digitized from real reference models, in most cases, the Modeler uses the scanned wireframe only as a starting point to re-create the surface with specific production needs in mind. Large productions sometimes differentiate between character (creature) modelers and "hard-surface" (spaceship) modelers. AutoDessys Form•Z and Alias|Wavefront PowerAnimator are examples of popular modeling tools for gaming and film-effects applications, but many other versatile tools exist for a wide range of specialized jobs. (See Chapter 3, "Modeling," for more details.) Senior Modelers sometimes supervise other Modelers on larger projects.

Production Assistant (PA)

This is an entry-level position in the production office. The PA assists the Production Coordinator and generally keeps the office running smoothly on a daily basis. A typical experienced PA could be promoted to Production Coordinator and eventually to Visual Effects Producer. Although no formal or strict training is required, it always helps to be familiar with the particular industry such as animation or film production. Memorizing this book also is a sure way to excel at this position.

Production Coordinator

Sometimes called the Production Manager, the Production Coordinator often works as an assistant to the Visual Effects Supervisor or Visual Effects Producer. More generally, this person runs the production office. Specific tasks include managing the PA staff and scheduling the day-to-day events of the production crew. Grace under pressure and superior organizational skills are essential (as well as thorough knowledge of this book).

Rotoscope (Roto) Artist

Traditional rotoscoping dates back to the earliest days of film and cel animation work. An artist would painstakingly draw and paint over live-action footage to mimic its shape and movement or to create a matte for later compositing use. For CG elements to appear "behind" something in a scanned live-action plate, a matte element must be generated that matches the shape of the object in the plate (for example, to have a dinosaur run "behind" a real tree in a background plate). When composited over the plate, the CG element is "held out" where the matte information exists, making it appear to be behind that shape. Different types of mattes include articulate matte work, such as for the many leaves of a tree, and the matting out of larger general areas with so-called garbage mattes.

Recent software tools such as the roto-spline in Avid Matador enable 2D vector-based shapes to be keyframed and deformed over time to lessen the amount of frame-by-frame painting required. Long the mainstay of rotoscope production, Matador on the SGI is just recently being challenged with faster, more intuitive software tools such as Puffin's Commotion for the Mac platform. Lead Roto Artists might organize teams and supervise techniques while reporting to a Technical Director, CG Sequence Supervisor, or CG Supervisor.

Software Designer or Developer

A Software Designer or Developer is anyone who writes the software code and custom tools that the production team uses. These programmers must work with the CG Supervisors to determine just how far off-the-shelf software can take the project and what needs to be written from scratch in-house. During development, the Software Designer works with Technical Directors who use the early versions of the software and help the Designer refine the tools to include the best features and interface. Although most often not considered "in production," a Software Designer is very much part of the team effort that gets a show done on time. A Software Designer might report to a CG Supervisor on a large show or, more typically, to management as part of a facility's more general overall scope of operation. Software design requires extensive training in computer programming languages such as C++ on platforms such as Silicon Graphics workstation running UNIX operating systems. On large Research & Development projects, a software group might be led by one or more Team Leaders to coordinate with production needs and time constraints.

Technical Assistant

This entry-level position is often the backbone of many companies' productions. Specific tasks of a Technical Assistant (TA) often include data backup to such formats as Exabyte and DST tape, render scheduling of CPU resources, and output of animation tests to digital disc and videotape formats for review by the production team. The TA most often reports to a Department Manager as part of general facilities organization. A TA must be fluent in the network and operating systems used (usually SGI and UNIX) while also being very responsible and mature to handle the day-to-day technical operation of the studio.

Technical Director

For delivering a final effects shot in a film or other type of project, the buck stops here. The Technical Director (TD) is responsible for the direction of the technical aspects of an effects shot, although (like Digital Artist) this term might mean different things at different companies. The TD's job is to assemble the many different elements from Modelers, Animators, Painters, Matchmovers, Roto Artists, and others and create the finished shot to the Director's satisfaction. The TD usually reports to a CG Supervisor for technical, scheduling, and personnel issues and to the Visual Effects Supervisor for aesthetic direction. Assistant Technical Directors and Senior Technical Directors all perform different aspects of the same job to varying degrees of responsibility. At smaller companies, TDs are likely to perform an even wider range of duties including many of the roles that usually are specialized in the larger companies. The two other skills most commonly performed by a TD at many companies are compositing and effects animating.

Visual Effects Producer

The Visual Effects (VFX) Producer usually works with a Visual Effects Supervisor to come up with the budget for the effects work. When a VFX Supervisor translates a script into storyboards, the VFX Producer provides specific cost breakdowns and might propose alternatives to the VFX Supervisor or Director, depending on his or her experience. This individual reports to the Producer and/or Director of the film.

Visual Effects Supervisor

Formerly called the Visual Effects Director, this is the only person who gets to say the magic word "Final!" and accept shots as finished. In the absence of the film's Director, the Visual Effects (VFX) Supervisor gives creative and aesthetic direction to the other Supervisors, Animators, and TDs on his crew. For shows that involve a great deal of character animation, an Animation Director often is brought in to handle that specific portion of the show on a level with the VFX Supervisor. The VFX Supervisor reports directly to the Producer and Director of the film. There are as many backgrounds for becoming a Visual Effects Supervisor as there are people with that title. In the past, people with effects-camera and motion-control experience most often graduated to this position. Today, with digital technology so prevalent, many more individuals from computer science and fine arts are coming up through the ranks of TD and CG Supervisor to oversee visual effects.

Previsualization

Article contributed by Colin Green

Previsualization is a facet of the visual effects world that often is overlooked or ignored. In a nutshell, pre-vis is the process of using 3D animation tools to plan complicated visual effects sequences prior to the production of any elements of the shot. Generally, pre-vis focuses on traditional photography—whether this involves shooting live-action sets or locations, green-screen photography, motion-control photography of miniatures, or pyrotechnics—and not on the creation of CGI elements.

Although this might not seem as glamorous as creating a photo-real CGI character that appears in a final cut, it often has a far greater overall impact on the success of the effect. Because the digital artist is involved in the design of a sequence from the beginning and interacts regularly with the Director, the Production Designer, and the Visual Effects Supervisor, he or she is likely to have greater creative participation in the conceptual and technical development of the sequence, long before the shots are turned over to the digital artists involved in finishing the shots.

Although pre-vis is not a new concept—Robert Abel & Associates explored it back in the '80s—it is only recently that the technology costs have come down enough to make the process practical. Now, pre-vis is increasingly being used in the industry, and most major effects films now list pre-vis artists in their credits.

Most visual effects sequences begin their development in the form of storyboards. These hand-drawn sketches are an effective medium for defining the basic action and flow of a visual effects sequence. Because each storyboard represents a single frame at various points in the sequence, however, much is left to the imagination.

Pre-vis is a 3D animated version of the entire sequence, not just certain frames. The set is modeled, and action can be viewed from any camera angle through any lens. In this virtual environment, the director can see precisely what the camera would see with the chosen lens—one significant advantage over storyboards.

The stage and shooting equipment also are modeled, creating a virtual stage. Spatial relationships between objects and the physical limitations of the equipment and the space are established and can be seen in 3D space. In this space, complex motions can be choreographed in detail, uncovering and solving problems in advance. These animated frame-by-frame sequences replace the arrows and written notes indicating motion on storyboards, and they remove all the guesswork from shoot days.

The Director is able to make critical decisions in advance about angles, camera movement, lenses, focal lengths, and cuts, effectively editing the sequence before a single frame is shot. Foreground and background actions that will be shot separately are integrated in pre-vis. This provides a mechanism to compose foreground elements shot on a green screen against a background that isn't there and to frame background plates for foreground action that hasn't been shot yet or that will be CGI. In this virtual world, the Director can try hundreds of variations, perfecting the sequence in a fraction of the time and cost of working it out on stage or in post-production.

After the Director approves the sequence, everyone involved has the same mental picture of how the sequence will work. Physical set design and construction is limited to what is seen in the pre-vis: the designer does not need to overbuild to compensate for uncertainty in how the sequence will be shot. Motion data is exported directly from the CGI software into the motion-control camera, and stage-planning diagrams are printed and distributed to key production staff, minimizing stage setup time. Overall, using pre-vis can eliminate many production bottlenecks and reshoots, potentially saving a great deal of time during the most costly phase of a project.

The value of pre-vis does not end with the shoot. Data created in pre-vis can be valuable to people involved in creating final CGI elements and in compositing the elements together. Pre-vis becomes the blueprint for how the elements were intended to come together and for how elements relate to each other spatially through the lens. In addition, 3D models created in pre-vis can be refined and reused as digital set-extension elements for the final shots.

Ironically, by using the tools of postproduction during pre-production, effects sequences can be shot cost effectively and with a certainty that eliminates the "fix-it-in-post" mentality.

Colin Green

Beginning as a student of architecture at Yale and MIT, Colin went on to found Pixel Liberation Front in 1995 to focus on developing the art of pre-vis for feature film visual effects. He has many years of expertise in this area, having contributed to such films as *Judge Dredd, Starship Troopers, Eraser, Fight Club, Mouse Hunt, My Favorite Martian,* and *Godzilla.*

Scanimate and the Analog Computer Animation Era

Believe it or not, there was a time not long ago when special effects were not created inside digital computers, and no graphics software, UNIX shell scripts, or C++ skills were used to create network TV show openings or flying logos for national ad campaigns. From the early 1970s until the mid '80s, many of the computer-generated effects on TV and even in the movies were made using analog, not digital, technology!

The most widely used analog device during this time was Scanimate, which was created under the leadership of the late Lee Harrison. The story goes that one day, as Harrison turned off his black and white TV, he noticed the picture shrinking to a dot before disappearing. In a flash, he realized that the electron beam in a TV tube could be electronically controlled to display its image on the screen differently. The beam could draw the video image larger, narrower, wider, or taller than in a regular TV, and these changes could vary constantly and smoothly over time. This constant electronic variation of the video image is an analog signal as opposed to the discreet on-off data in a digital device. Harrison's revelation prompted him to hire Ed Tajchman to design and engineer Scanimate in 1969.

A Sine of the Times

Patented in 1972, Scanimate was a wall-sized behemoth of knobs, switches, thumbwheel counters, and patch panels. At its heart was a 950 scan-line resolution cathode ray tube (CRT) with special phosphors for a brighter, longer-lasting image. A camera was trained on a light box with flat artwork of the client's logo. The monochromatic video image of the logo from this camera was fed into Scanimate's special CRT. The Scanimate artist could then plug hundreds of little yellow wires into the patch panels, connecting such electronic components as ramp voltages, summing amplifiers, multipliers, rectifiers, diodes, and oscillators in much the same way as with a "50-in-1" electronics kit. These circuits could animate the client's logo on the screen in an infinite number of ways—stretching, warping, undulating, wiggling, sparkling, glowing, flying over slit-scan grids or star fields—all based on the creativity and electronic virtuosity of the Scanimate artist. If a sine wave oscillator was patched into Scanimate's HORIZONTAL parameter, for example, the logo would move back and forth from left to right. If the oscillator was switched to a square wave, the logo would pop from left to right. If a sine wave was patched into HORIZONTAL and a cosine wave of the same frequency was patched into VERTICAL, the logo would move in a circular path. Available parameters also included WIDTH, LENGTH, INTENSITY, BLANKING, and DEPTH (not true 3D depth, but WIDTH and LENGTH working together).

Scanimate gave rise to a generation of artist/programmers who could quickly create dazzling effects using video's capability to run in real time. A session at a Scanimate facility could cost as much as $1,500 per hour, and the client often sat in the suite while the animator worked. Because the effects could be played in real time, speeds and trajectories could   be controlled by turning a few knobs and triggering the animation again. When the client was satisfied, the animation was recorded on video. This approach never required the long calculation times that were necessary for rendering with the digital technologies of the time. A client such as ABC News could come into the facility in the morning and have an animated graphic for their show ready to air that evening! This kind of time constraint would be difficult even with the advanced digital computer graphics technologies of 1999, yet in the "old days" of analog graphics, it was quite common to complete up to 10 jobs a week from start to finish!

THE GOLDEN DAYS

The aesthetics of television graphics were driven by analog technology in the 1970s and early '80s, and were defined by such Scanimate effects as shining gold logos flying over glowing grids and sparkling star fields. Because Scanimate used a video CRT, optical devices such as star filters, shower glass, or rainbow filters could be placed in front of the lens to make the logos glow or twinkle.

A Scanimate suite was much like a video-editing suite; image sources were combined through a video switcher using wipes, cross-dissolves, luminance keying, and chroma keying. Multiple images could be played back from multiple videotape machines through the switcher. Scanimate could be triggered to run in sync with any tape deck. (This was before the invention of VHS, Beta, or digital videotape. The professional video standard format at this time was reel-to-reel two-inch videotape!) Scanimate animation could be recorded on one tape machine, played back with another pass added on top, and then recorded to another machine.

These video techniques enabled Scanimate trickery to be used, for example, to create 3D gold flying logos. Here's the secret: An artist programmed Scanimate to create an undulating golden texture using oscillators patched into the INTENSITY parameter. (At Image West, we referred to this effect as "Thrill-o-vision!") A 3D logo, physically carved from balsa wood, was attached to a wooden dowel and connected to a stepper motor. The front surface of the carved logo was painted white, and the extruded sides were painted gray. The whole logo was then mounted in front of a chroma key blue background. Patching these signals into the video switcher, the artist defined the logo's white front surface as a luminance key hole. He then replaced it with the moving gold texture from Scanimate. Setting a different luminance key for the gray surfaces, he patched a darker gold texture into the extruded sides. He then created a streaking Scanimate star field and replaced the chroma key blue with that. The artist added another Scanimate pass to make the logo glow and used an Apple II computer to drive the motor to rotate the logo. Voilá! A 3D gold logo rotating through space! All this was recorded to tape in real time with the capability to change speeds, color, or motion as the client and art director supervised.

From Pepto to Star Wars

Scanimate won an Emmy Award for its contribution to the video industry in 1976. Eight Scanimates had been built, six of which were in the United States. Two were in Denver at Video Image Corporation, Lee Harrison's company. (Harrison's team also created an analog animation device known as CAESAR, which was specifically used for character animation.) Two Scanimates were in New York at Dolphin Productions, and two more were in Hollywood at Image West.

One of the most memorable uses of Scanimate was an indigestion effect for a Pepto-Bismol campaign in the late 1970s. It also was well-known for being used to create the opening graphics for hundreds of sporting events including the Rose Bowl, the Sugar Bowl, the World Series, the Super Bowl, and ABC's Wide World of Sports. Scanimate was used to create scores of national ad campaigns for companies such as Yamaha, Hitachi, Ford, and Beechnut. It also was used in movies to create laser and computer effects for *Logan's Run* and *Demon Seed* and for psychedelic music-video sequences in "Sergeant Pepper's Lonely Hearts Club Band." The most famous Scanimate effect of all time was animated at Image West when George Lucas created an onscreen display of the Death Star for his 1977 hit *Star Wars*.

THE BEGINNING OF THE END

In the early 1980s, with the digital revolution poised to wash over the effects industry, there were two attempts to create a digitally controlled analog video system. At Image West, David Seig engineered the VERSEFEX, a system in which full-color transparencies could be used as input. Digital oscillators and 3D perspective were incorporated to animate the same video parameters found in Scanimate. At Computer Image Corp., Ed Tajchman created the System IV, a true digital 3D animation system with accurate perspective and digital keyframing. Its input, however, was still monochrome video, and it carried a price tag of around a million dollars. The System IV was used in production (by this author) at Editel in Hollywood from 1983 to 1985 in conjunction with Scanimate.

With the introduction of the Ampex Digital Optics (ADO) digital video system in late 1981, digital paint systems such as the Quantel Paint Box in 1982, and affordable 3D animation systems such as the Bosch FGS-4000 in 1983, the era of analog effects was rapidly phased out in the United States by the mid-1980s.

It would be impossible to name all the analog animation pioneers from the early days of computer graphics. Many of them, however, have remained active in the CG industry for almost 20 years including Rob Bekhurs, Susan Crouse-Kemp, Richard Froman, Dave Holman, Mike Jackson, Art Kellner, Fred Kessler, Sonny King, Jeff Kleiser, Henry Kline II, Peter Koczera, Ed Kramer, Russ Maehl, Gary McKinnon, Mike Saz, and Roy Weinstock. The late Ron Hays was one of the original pioneers of the aesthetics of video animation, and he is remembered for his elegant direction of effects in the music video for "Sergeant Pepper's."

For a more in-depth look at analog video animation, see "ANALOG to DIGITAL Conversion: A History of Video Animation" by Ed Kramer, published in the Conference Proceedings of the National Computer Graphics Association, Volume II, 1987 pp. 363-382. You also can visit the Scanimate Web page, maintained by former Image West engineer David Seig, at www.scanimate.com, or http://scanimate.zfx.com.

BIOGRAPHY

Ed Kramer has a B.S. in psychology from Duke University (1977) and an M.A. in film production from The University of Texas (1980). He was one of the last Scanimate animators, but he has been among the first to use many video tools for production including the ADO, Via Video, and Quantel paint systems, System IV, Bosch FGS-4000, Abekas, Wavefront, and digital videotape. He has worked for video facilities in Hollywood, New York, and Atlanta and for NASA in Houston. He has written about video animation and has chaired courses at SIG-GRAPH. His film work includes the LUXOR project for Douglas Trumbull and effects sequences for *Clear and Present Danger*, *Jumanji*, *Twister*, *101 Dalmatians*, *The Lost World*, *Deep Impact*, and *Star Wars: The Phantom Menace*. He currently is a Sequence Supervisor at Industrial Light & Magic in San Rafael, California.

Ed Kramer sitting in front of a Scanimate machine in 1982.

Index

SYMBOLS

bones, 104

Boolean, 77, 353

Boris AE, 176

bounce lights, 6-8

boundary representations
(b-rep), 78

bounding box, 367

box filter, 176

BPI (bits per inch), 196

The Brave Little Toaster,
MAGI, 272

Brigham, Tom, 416

brightness, 9

British Computer Society
(BCS), 367

Bryce 3D, 104

Bryce 4, 78

BSP Trees (Binary Space
Subdivision Trees), 78, 353

BTS (Broadcast Television
System), 367

buckets, 143

Buf Compagnie, 223

buffers, 196, 367. *See also*
Z-buffers
    framebuffers, 403

bump mapping, 143, 412

Bunny, 221

Bushnell, Nolan, 218

bytes, 353

C

C (programming
language), 353

C++, 353

cache, 367

CAD translation,
Wavefront, 337

CAD Visualization,
Wavefront, 336

CAD/CAM/CAE (Computer
Aided Design, Computer
Aided Manufacturing, and
Computer Aided
Engineering), 78

CAID (Computer Aided
Industrial Design), 78

CalComp Technology Inc., 196

calibration, 9
    color calibration, 11

Caligari Corporation, 104
    trueSpace 4.0, 128

Cambridge Animation
Systems, 105
    Animo, 39, 102

camera action,
compositing, 173

cameras, 105, 143
    angle of view, 101
    banking, 103
    digital cameras, 370
    nodal point, 119
    nodal point offset, 120
    zoom, 167

Canoma v1.0, 79

canvas, 41

CAPS (Computer Animation
Product System), 144,

CAPS (Computer Animation
Paint System), 426

Captain Power, Omnibus
Computer Graphics Inc., 294

*Captain Power and the Soldiers
of the Future*, 424-425

Caricature "Cari" software, 433

Carlson, Wayne, 292

Carpenter, Loren, 415

Cartesian coordinate system, 9

Casino, 432

Casper, 432

cast shadow, 144

cathode ray tube (CRT), 369

CATIA (Computer Aided
Three-dimensional Interactive
Application), 79

Catmull, Dr. Ed, 247, 282,
350-351, 405
    TWEEN, 407

CAVE, Z-A Production,
346-347

CBB ("could be better"), 176

CCP (Cranston/Csuri
Productions), 229-232
    CGRG, 291
    Kristoff, Jim, 229-231

Celco (Constantine
Engineering Laboratories
Co.), 197
    eXtreme fx, 200

center matte, 177

central processing unit
(CPU), 368

centroids, 79

CFC (Computer Film
Company), 224-226
    Fruit Machine, 225
    Memphis Belle, 226

CG, 134
    history of. *See* history of CG
    realism, 134-136
    shadows, 135
    smooth surfaces, 135

CG images, straight lines, 134

CG renderings, 136-138

CG Supe, 455

CG: West World, 404

CGA (Color Graphics
Adapter), 367

CGATS (Committee for
Graphics Arts Technologies
Standards), 16, 42

D

E

N

X-Z